The Pris<

Alice Brown

Alpha Editions

This edition published in 2024

ISBN 9789362518392

Design and Setting By
Alpha Editions
www.alphaedis.com
Email - info@alphaedis.com

As per information held with us this book is in Public Domain.
This book is a reproduction of an important historical work.
Alpha Editions uses the best technology to reproduce historical work
in the same manner it was first published to preserve its original nature.
Any marks or number seen are left intentionally to preserve.

Contents

I	- 1 -
II	- 9 -
III	- 17 -
IV	- 26 -
V	- 31 -
VI	- 42 -
VII	- 52 -
VIII	- 62 -
IX	- 70 -
X	- 81 -
XI	- 86 -
XII	- 96 -
XIII	- 98 -
XIV	- 107 -
XV	- 114 -
XVI	- 124 -
XVII	- 135 -
XVIII	- 146 -
XIX	- 151 -
XX	- 160 -
XXI	- 165 -
XXII	- 172 -
XXIII	- 182 -
XXIV	- 194 -

XXV	- 204 -
XXVI	- 214 -
XXVII	- 223 -
XXVIII	- 228 -
XXIX	- 237 -
XXX	- 247 -
XXXI	- 257 -
XXXII	- 263 -
XXXIII	- 272 -
XXXIV	- 278 -
XXXV	- 284 -
XXXVI	- 292 -
XXXVII	- 298 -
XXXVIII	- 307 -
XXXIX	- 314 -
XL	- 324 -

I

There could not have been a more sympathetic moment for coming into the country town—or, more accurately, the inconsiderable city—of Addington than this clear twilight of a spring day. Anne and Lydia French with their stepfather, known in domestic pleasantry as the colonel, had hit upon a perfect combination of time and weather, and now they stood in a dazed silence, dense to the proffers of two hackmen with the urgency of twenty, and looked about them. That inquiring pause was as if they had expected to find, even at the bare, sand-encircled station, the imagined characteristics of the place they had so long visualised. The handsome elderly man, clean-shaven, close-clipped, and, at intervals when he recalled himself to a stand against discouragement, almost military in his bearing, was tired, but entrenched in a patient calm. The girls were profoundly moved in a way that looked like gratitude: perhaps, too, exalted as if, after reverses, they had reached a passionately desired goal. Anne was the elder sister, slender and sweet, grave with the protective fostering instinct of mothers in a maidenly hiding, ready to come at need. She wore her plain blue clothes as if unconscious of them and their incomplete response to the note of time. A woman would have detected that she trimmed her own hat, a flat, wide-brimmed straw with a formless bow and a feather worthy only in long service. A man would have cherished the memory of her thin rose-flushed face with the crisp touches of sedate inquiry about the eyes. "Do you want anything?" Anne's eyes were always asking clearly. "Let me get it for you." But even a man thus tenderly alive to her charm would have thought her older than she was, a sweet sisterly creature to be reverentially regarded.

Lydia was the product of a different mould. She was the woman, though a girl in years and look, not removed by chill timidities from woman's normal hopes, the clean animal in her curved mouth, the trick of parting her lips for a long breath because, for the gusto of life, the ordinary breath wouldn't always do, and showing most excellent teeth, the little square chin, dauntless in strength, the eyes dauntless, too, and hair all a brown gloss with high lights on it, very free about her forehead. She was not so tall as Anne, but graciously formed and plumper. Curiously, they did not seem racially unlike the colonel who, to their passionate loyalties, was "father" not a line removed. In the delicacy of his patrician type he might even have been "grandfather", for he looked older than he was, the worsted prey of circumstance. He had met trouble that would not be evaded, and if he might be said to have conquered, it was only from regarding it with a perplexed immobility, so puzzling was it in a world where honour, he thought, was absolutely defined and a social crime as inexplicable as it was rending.

And while the three wait to have their outlines thus inadequately sketched, the hackman waits, too, he of a more persistent hope than his fellows who have gone heavily rolling away to the stable, it being now six o'clock and this the last train.

Lydia was a young woman of fervid recognitions. She liked to take a day and stamp it for her own, to say of this, perhaps: "It was the ninth of April when we went to Addington, and it was a heavenly day. There was a clear sky and I could see Farvie's beautiful nose and chin against it and Anne's feather all out of curl. Dear Anne! dear Farvie! Everything smelled of dirt, good, honest dirt, not city sculch, and I heard a robin. Anne heard him, too. I saw her smile." But really what Anne plucked out of the moment was a blurred feeling of peace. The day was like a cool, soft cheek, the cheek one kisses with calm affection, knowing it will not be turned away. It was she who first became aware of Denny, the hackman, and said to him in her liquid voice that laid bonds of kind responsiveness:

"Do you know the old Blake house?"

Denny nodded. He was a soft, loosely made man with a stubby moustache picked out in red and a cheerfully dishevelled air of having been up all night.

"The folks moved out last week," said he. "You movin' in?"

"Yes," Lydia supplied, knowing her superior capacity over the other two, for meeting the average man. "We're moving in. Farvie, got the checks?"

Denny accepted the checks and, in a neighbourly fashion, helped the station master in selecting the trunks, no large task when there was but a drummer's case besides. He went about this meditatively, inwardly searching out the way of putting the question that should elicit the identity of his fares. There was a way, he knew. But they had seated themselves in the hack, and now explained that if he would take two trunks along the rest could come with the freight due at least by to-morrow; and he had driven them through the wide street bordered with elms and behind them what Addington knew as "house and grounds" before he thought of a way. It was when he had bumped the trunks into the empty hall and Lydia was paying him from a smart purse of silver given her by her dancing pupils that he got hold of his inquisitorial outfit.

"I don't know," said Denny, "as I know you folks. Do you come from round here?"

Lydia smiled at him pleasantly.

"Good night," said she. "Get the freight round in the morning, won't you? and be sure you bring somebody to help open the crates."

Then Denny climbed sorrowfully up on his box, and when he looked round he found them staring there as they had stared at the station: only now he saw they were in a row and "holding hands".

"I think," said Lydia, in rather a hushed voice, as if she told the others a pretty secret, "it's a very beautiful place."

"You girls haven't been here, have you?" asked the colonel.

"No," said Anne, "you'd just let it when we came to live with you."

Both girls used that delicate shading of their adoptive tie with him. They and their mother, now these three years dead, had "come to live with" him when they were little girls and their mother married him. They never suggested that mother married him any time within their remembrance. In their determined state of mind he belonged not only to the never-ending end when he and they and mother were to meet in a gardened heaven with running streams and bowery trees, but as well to the vague past when they were little girls. Their own father they had memory of only as a disturbing large person in rough tweed smelling of office smoke, who was always trying to get somewhere before the domestic exigencies of breakfast and carriage would let him, and who dropped dead one day trying to do it. Anne saw him fall right in the middle of the gravel walk, and ran to tell mother father had stubbed his toe. And when she heard mother scream, and noted father's really humorous obstinacy about getting up, and saw the cook even and the coachman together trying to persuade him, she got a strong distaste for father; and when about two years afterward she was asked if she would accept this other older father, she agreed to him with cordial expectation. He was gentle and had a smooth, still voice. His clothes smelled of Russia leather and lead pencils and at first of very nice smoke: not as if he had sat in a tight room all day and got cured in the smoke of other rank pipes like a helpless ham, but as if a pleasant acrid perfume were his special atmosphere.

"They haven't done much to the garden, have they?" he asked now, poking with his stick in the beds under the windows. "I suppose you girls know what these things are, coming up. There's a peony. I do know that. I remember this one. It's the old dark kind, not pink. I don't much care for a pink piny."

The big front yard sloping up to the house was almost full of shrubbery in a state of overgrown prosperity. There were lilacs, dark with buds, and what

Anne, who was devotedly curious in matters of growing life, thought althea, snowball and a small-leaved yellow rose. All this runaway shrubbery looked, in a way of speaking, inpenetrable. It would have taken so much trouble to get through that you would have felt indiscreet in trying it. The driveway only seemed to have been brave enough to pass it without getting choked up, a road that came in at the big gateway, its posts marked by haughty granite balls, accomplished a leisurely curve and went out at another similar gateway as proudly decorated. The house held dignified seclusion there behind the shrubbery, waiting, Lydia thought, to be found. You could not really see it from the street: only above the first story and blurred, at that, by rowan trees. But the two girls facing it there at near range and the colonel with the charm of old affection playing upon him like airs of paradise, thought the house beautiful. It was of mellow old brick with white trimmings and a white door, and at the left, where the eastern sun would beat, a white veranda. It came up into a kindly gambrel roof and there were dormers. Lydia saw already how fascinating those chambers must be. There was a trellis over the door and jessamine swinging from it. The birds in the shrubbery were eloquent. A robin mourned on one complaining note and Anne, wise also in the troubles of birds, looked low for the reason and found, sitting with tail wickedly twitching at the tip, a brindled cat. Being gentle in her ways and considering that all things have rights, she approached him with crafty steps and a murmured hypnotic, "kitty! kitty!" got her hands on him, and carried him off down the drive, to drop him in the street and suggest, with a warning pat and conciliating stroke, the desirability of home.

The colonel, following Lydia's excited interest, poked with his stick for a minute or more at a bed under the front window, where something lush seemed to be coming up, and Lydia, losing interest when she found it was only pudding-bags, picked three sprays of flowering almond for decorating purposes and drew him toward a gate at the east side of the house where, down three rotting steps, lay level land. The end of it next the road was an apple orchard coming into an amazingly early bloom, a small secluded paradise. A high brick wall shut it from the road and ran down for fifty feet or so between it and the adjoining place. There a grey board fence took up the boundary and ran on, with a less definite markedness to the eye, until it skirted a rise far down the field and went on over the rise to lands unknown, at least to Lydia.

"Farvie, come!" she cried.

She pulled him down the crumbling steps to the soft sward and looked about her with a little murmured note of happy expectation. She loved the place at once, and gave up to the ecstasy of loving it "good and hard," she would have said. These impulsive passions of her nature had always made her greatest joys. They were like robust bewildering playmates. She took them to her heart, and into her bed at night to help her dream. There was nothing ever more warm and grateful than Lydia's acceptances and her trust in the bright promise of the new. Anne didn't do that kind of thing. She hesitated at thresholds and looked forward, not distrustfully but gravely, into dim interiors.

"Farvie, dear," said Lydia, "I love it just as much now as I could in a hundred years. It's our house. I feel as if I'd been born in it."

Farvie looked about over the orchard, under its foam of white and pink; his eyes suffused and he put his delicate lips firmly together. But all he said was:

"They haven't kept the trees very well pruned."

"There's Anne," said Lydia, loosing her hold of his sleeve. She ran light-footedly back to Anne, and patted her with warm receptiveness. "Anne, look: apple trees, pear trees, peach in that corner. See that big bush down there."

"Quince," said Anne dreamily. She had her hat off now, and her fine soft brown hair, in silky disorder, attracted her absent-minded care. But Lydia had pulled out the pin of her own tight little hat with its backward pointing quill and rumpled her hair in the doing and never knew it; now she transfixed the hat with a joyous stab.

"Never mind your hair," said she. "What idiots we were to write to the Inn. Why couldn't we stay here to-night? How can we leave it? We can't. Did you ever see such a darling place? Did you ever imagine a brick wall like that? Who built it, Farvie? Who built the brick wall?"

Farvie was standing with his hands behind him, thinking back, the girls knew well, over the years. A mournful quiet was in his face. They could follow for a little way the cause of his sad thoughts, and were willing, each in her own degree of impulse, to block him in it, make running incursions into the road, twitch him by the coat and cry, "Listen to us. Talk to us. You can't go there where you were going. That's the road to hateful memories. Listen to that bird and tell us about the brick wall."

Farvie was used to their invasions of his mind. He never went so far as clearly to see them as salutary invasions to keep him from the melancholy accidents of the road, an ambulance dashing up to lift his bruised hopes tenderly and take them off somewhere for sanitary treatment, or even some childish sympathy of theirs commissioned to run up and offer him a nosegay to distract him in his walk toward old disappointments and old cares. He only knew they were welcome visitors in his mind. Sometimes the mind seemed to him a clean-swept place, the shades down and no fire lighted, and these young creatures, in their heavenly implication of doing everything for their own pleasure and not for his, would come in, pull up the shades with a rush, light the fire and sit down with their sewing and their quite as necessary laughter by the hearth.

"It's a nice brick wall," said Anne, in her cool clear voice. "It doesn't seem so much to shut other people out as to shut us in."

She slipped her hand through the colonel's arm, and they both stood there at his elbow like rosy champions, bound to stick to him to the last, and the bird sang and something eased up in his mind. He seemed to be let off, in this spring twilight, from an exigent task that had shown no signs of easing. Yet he knew he was not really let off. Only the girls were throwing their glamour of youth and hope and bravado over the apprehensive landscape of his fortune as to-morrow's sun would snatch a rosier light from the apple blooms.

"My great-grandfather built the wall," said he. He was content to go back to an older reminiscent time when there were, for him, no roads of gloom. "He was a minister, you know: very old-fashioned even then, very direct, knew what he wanted, saw no reason why he shouldn't have it. He wanted a place to meditate in, walk up and down, think out his sermons. So he built the wall. The townspeople didn't take to it much at first, father used to say. But they got accustomed to it. He wouldn't care."

"There's a grape-vine over a trellis," said Anne softly. She spoke in a rapt way, as if she had said, "There are angels choiring under the trees. We can hum their songs."

"It makes an arbour. Farvie'll sit there and read his Greek," said Lydia. "We can't leave this place to-night. It would be ridiculous, now we've found it. It wouldn't be safe either. Places like this bust up and blow away."

"We can get up the beds to-morrow," said Anne. "Then we never'll leave it for a single minute as long as we live. I want to go over the house. Farvie, can't we go over the house?"

They went up the rotten steps, Lydia with a last proprietary look at the orchard, as if she sealed it safe from all the spells of night, and entered at the front door, trying, at her suggestion, to squeeze in together three abreast, so they could own it equally. It was a still, kind house. The last light lay sweetly in the room at the right of the hall, a large square room with a generous fireplace well blackened and large surfaces of old ivory paint. There was a landscape paper here, of trees in a smoky mist and dull blue skies behind a waft of cloud. Out of this lay the dining-room, all in green, and the windows of both rooms looked on a gigantic lilac hedge, and beyond it the glimmer of a white colonial house set back in its own grounds. The kitchen was in a lean-to, a good little kitchen brown with smoke, and behind that was the shed with dark cobwebbed rafters and corners that cried out for hoes and garden tools. Lydia went through the rooms in a rush of happiness, Anne in a still rapt imagining. Things always seemed to her the symbols of dearer things. She saw shadowy shapes sitting at the table and breaking bread together, saw moving figures in the service of the house, and generations upon generations weaving their webs of hope and pain and disillusionment and hope again. In the shed they stood looking out at the back door through the rolling field, where at last a fringe of feathery yellow made the horizon line.

"What's at the end of the field, Farvie?" Lydia asked.

"The river," said he. "Nothing but the river."

"I feel," said she, "as if we were on an island surrounded by jumping-off places: the bushes in front, the lilac hedge on the west, the brick wall on the east, the river at the end. Come, let's go back. We haven't seen the other two rooms."

These were the northeast room, a library in the former time, in a dim, pink paper with garlands, and the southeast sitting-room, in a modern yet conforming paper of dull blue and grey.

"The hall is grey," said Lydia. "Do you notice? How well they've kept the papers. There isn't a stain."

"Maiden ladies," said the colonel, with a sigh. "Nothing but two maiden ladies for so long."

"Don't draw long breaths, Farvie," said Lydia. "Anne and I are maiden ladies. You wouldn't breathe over us. We should feel terribly if you did."

"I was thinking how still the house had been," said he. "It used to be—ah, well! well!"

"They grew old here, didn't they?" said Anne, her mind taking the maiden ladies into its hospitable shelter.

"They were old when they came." He was trying to put on a brisker air to match these two runners with hope for their torch. "Old as I am now. If their poor little property had lasted we should have had hard work to pry them out. We should have had to let 'em potter along here. But they seem to like their nephew, and certainly he's got money enough."

"They adore him," said Lydia, who had never seen them or the nephew. "And they're lying in gold beds at this minute eating silver cheese off an emerald plate and hearing the nightingales singing and saying to each other,

'Oh, my! I *wish* it was morning so we could get up and put on our pan-velvet dresses and new gold shoes.'"

This effective picture Anne and the colonel received with a perfect gravity, not really seeing it with the mind's eye. Lydia's habit of speech demanded these isolating calms.

"I think," said Anne, "we'd better be getting to the Inn. We sha'n't find any supper. Lydia, which bag did you pack our nighties in?"

Lydia picked out the bag, carolling, as she did so, in high bright notes, and then remembered that she had to put on her hat. Anne had already adjusted hers with a careful nicety.

"You know where the Inn is, don't you, Farvie?" Lydia was asking, as they stood on the stone step, after Anne had locked the door, and gazed about them in another of their according trances.

He smiled at them, and his eyes lighted for the first time. The smile showed possibilities the girls had proven through their growing up years, of humour and childish fooling.

"Why, yes," said he, "it was here when I was born."

They went down the curving driveway into the street which the two girls presently found to be the state street of the town. The houses, each with abundant grounds, had all a formal opulence due chiefly to the white-pillared fronts. Anne grew dreamy. It seemed to her as if she were walking by a line of Greek temples in an afternoon hush. The colonel was naming the houses as they passed, with good old names. Here were the Jarvises, here the Russells, and here the Lockes.

"But I don't know," said he, "what's become of them all."

At a corner by a mammoth elm he turned down into another street, elm-shaded, almost as wide, and led them to the Inn, a long, low-browed structure built in the eighteenth century and never without guests.

II

The next morning brought a confusion of arriving freight, and Denny was supplicated to provide workmen, clever artificers in the opening of boxes and the setting up of beds. He was fired by a zeal not all curiosity, a true interest assuaged by certainty more enlivening yet.

"I know who ye be," he announced to the colonel. This was on his arrival with the first load. "I ain't lived in town very long, or I should known it afore. It's in the paper."

Mr. Blake frowned slightly and seemed to freeze all over the surface he presented to the world. He walked away without a reply, but Lydia, who had not heard, came up at this point to ask Denny if he knew where she could find a maid.

"Sure I do," said Denny, who was not Irish but consorted with common speech. "My wife's two sisters, Mary Nellen, Prince Edward girls."

"We don't want two," said Lydia. "My sister and I do a lot of the work."

"The two of them," said Denny, "come for the price of one. They're studyin' together to set up a school in Canada, and they can't be separated. They'd admire to be with nice folks."

"Mary? did you say?" asked Lydia.

"Mary Nellen."

"Mary and Ellen?"

"Yes, Mary Nellen. I'll send 'em up."

That afternoon they came, pleasant-faced square little trudges with shiny black hair and round myopic eyes. This near-sightedness when they approached the unclassified, resulted in their simultaneously making up the most horrible faces, the mere effort of focusing. Mary Nellen—for family affection, recognising their complete twin-ship, always blended them—were aware of this disfiguring habit, but relegated the curing of it to the day of their future prosperity. They couldn't afford glasses now, they said. They'd rather put their money into books. This according and instantaneous grimace Lydia found engaging. She could not possibly help hiring them, and they appeared again that night with two battered tin boxes and took up residence in the shed chamber.

There had been some consultation about the disposition of chambers. It resolved itself into the perfectly reasonable conclusion that the colonel must have the one he had always slept in, the southeastern corner.

"But there's one," said Lydia, "that's sweeter than the whole house put together. Have you fallen in love with it, Anne? It's that low, big room back of the stairs. You go down two steps into it. There's a grape-vine over the window. Whose chamber is that, Farvie?"

He stood perfectly still by the mantel, and the old look of introspective pain, almost of a surprised terror, crossed his face. Then they knew. But he delayed only a minute or so in answering.

"Why," said he, "that was Jeff's room when he lived at home."

"Then," said Anne, in her assuaging voice, "he must have it again."

"Yes," said the colonel. "I think you'd better plan it that way."

They said no more about the room, but Anne hunted out a set of Dickens and a dog picture she had known as belonging to Jeff, who was the own son of the colonel, and took them in there. Once she caught Lydia in the doorway looking in, a strangled passion in her face, as if she were going back to the page of an old grief.

"Queer, isn't it?" she asked, and Anne, knowing all that lay in the elision, nodded silently.

Once that afternoon the great brass knocker on the front door fell, and Mary Nellen answered and came to Lydia to say a gentleman was there. Should he be asked in? Mary Nellen seemed to have an impression that he was mysteriously not the sort to be admitted. Lydia went at once to the door whence there came to Anne, listening with a worried intensity, a subdued runnel of talk. The colonel, who had sat down by the library window with a book he was not reading, as if he needed to soothe some inner turmoil of his own by the touch of leathern covers, apparently did not hear this low-toned interchange. He glanced into the orchard from time to time, and once drummed on the window when a dog dashed across and ran distractedly back and forth along the brick wall. When Anne heard the front door close she met Lydia in the hall.

"Was it?" she asked.

Lydia nodded. Her face had a flush; the pupils of her eyes were large.

"Yes," said she. "His paper wanted to know whether Jeff was coming here and who was to meet him. I said I didn't know."

"Did he ask who you were?"

"Yes. I told him I'd nothing to say. He said he understood Jeff's father was here, and asked if he might see him. I said, No, he couldn't see anybody."

"Was he put out?" Anne had just heard Mary Nellen use the phrase. Anne thought it covered a good deal.

"No," said Lydia. She lifted her plump hands and threaded the hair back from her forehead, a gesture she had when she was tired. It seemed to spur her brain. "No," she repeated, in a slow thoughtfulness, "he was a kind of gentleman. I had an idea he was sorry for me, for us all, I suppose. I was sorry for him, too. He was trying to earn his living and I wouldn't let him."

"You couldn't."

"No," said Lydia, rather drearily, "I couldn't. Do you think Farvie heard?"

"I think not. He didn't seem to."

But it was with redoubled solicitude that they threw their joint energies into making supper inviting, so that the colonel might at least get a shred of easement out of a pleasant meal. Mary Nellen, who amicably divided themselves between the task of cooking and serving, forwarded their desires, making faces all the time at unfamiliar sauce-pans, and quite plainly agreed with them that men were to be comforted by such recognised device. Anne and Lydia were deft little housewives. They had a sober recognition of the pains that go to a well-ordered life, and were patient in service. Their father had no habit of complaint if the machinery creaked and even caused the walls to shudder with faulty action. Yet they knew their gentle ways contributed to his peace.

After supper, having seen that he was seated and ready for the little talk they usually had in the edge of the evening, Lydia wondered whether she ought to tell him a reporter had run them down; but while she balanced the question there came another clanging knock and Mary Nellen beckoned her. This one was of another stamp. He had to get his story, and he had overborne Mary Nellen and penetrated to the hall. Lydia could hear the young inexorable voice curtly talking down Mary Nellen and she closed the library door behind her. But when the front door had shut after the invader and Lydia came back, again with reddened cheeks and distended eyes, the colonel went to it and shot the bolt.

"That's enough for to-night," said he. "The next I'll see, but not till morning."

"You know we all thought it best you shouldn't," Anne said, always faintly interrogative. "So long as we needn't say who we are. They'd know who you were."

"His father," said Lydia, from an indignation disproportioned to the mild sadness she saw in the colonel's face. "That's what they'd say: his father. I don't believe Anne and I could bear that, the way they'd say it. I don't believe Jeff could either."

The colonel had, even in his familiar talk with them, a manner of old-fashioned courtesy.

"I didn't think it mattered much myself who saw them," he said, "when you proposed it. But now it has actually happened I see it's very unfitting for you to do it, very unfitting. However, I don't believe we shall be troubled again to-night."

But their peace had been broken. They felt irrationally like ill-defended creatures in a state of siege. The pretty wall-paper didn't help them out, nor any consciousness of the blossoming orchard in the chill spring air. The colonel noted the depression in his two defenders and, by a spurious cheerfulness, tried to bring them back to the warmer intimacies of retrospect.

"It was in this very room," he said, "that I saw your dear mother first."

Lydia looked up, brightly ready for diversion. Anne sat, her head bent a little, responsive to the intention of his speech.

"I was sitting here," said he, "alone. I had, I am pretty sure, this very book in my hand. I wasn't reading it. I couldn't read. The maid came in and told me a lady wanted to see me."

"What time of the day was it, Farvie?" Lydia asked, with her eager sympathy.

"It was the late afternoon," said he. "In the early spring. Perhaps it was a day like this. I don't remember. Well, I had her come in. Before I knew where I was, there she stood, about there, in the middle of the floor. You know how she looked."

"She looked like Lydia," said Anne. It was not jealousy in her voice, only yearning. It seemed very desirable to look like Lydia or their mother.

"She was much older," said the colonel. "She looked very worried indeed. I remember what she said, remember every word of it. She said, 'Mr. Blake, I'm a widow, you know. And I've got two little girls. What am I going to do with them?'"

"She did the best thing anybody could," said Lydia. "She gave us to you."

"I have an idea I cried," said the colonel. "Really I know I did. And it broke her all up. She'd come somehow expecting Jeff's father to account for the whole business and assure her there might be a few cents left. But when she saw me dribbling like a seal, she just ran forward and put her arms round me. And she said, 'My dear! my dear!' I hear her now."

"So do I," said Anne, in her low tone. "So do I."

"And you never'd seen each other before," said Lydia, in an ecstasy of youthful love for love. "I call that great."

"We were married in a week," said the colonel. "She'd come to ask me to help her, do you see? but she found I was the one that needed help. And I had an idea I might do something for her by taking the responsibility of her two little girls. But it was no use pretending. I didn't marry her for anything except, once I'd seen her, I couldn't live without her."

"Wasn't mother darling!" Lydia threw at him, in a passionate sympathy.

"You're like her, Lydia," said Anne again.

But Lydia shook her head.

"I couldn't hold a candle to mother," said she. "My eyes may be like hers. So is my forehead. So's my mouth. But I'm no more like mother———"

"It was her sympathy," said their father quietly, seeming to have settled it all a long time before. "She was the most absolutely loving person. You girls may be like her in that, too. I'm sure you're inconceivably good to me."

"I'd like to love people to death," said Lydia, with the fierceness of passion not yet named and recognised, but putting up its beautiful head now and then to look her remindingly in the eyes. "I'd like to love everybody. You first, Farvie, you and Anne. And Jeff. I'm going to love Jeff like a house-a-fire. He doesn't know what it is to have a sister. When he comes in I'm going to run up to him as if I couldn't wait to get him into the room, and kiss him and say, 'Here we are, Jeff. I'm Lyddy. Here's Anne.' You kiss him, too, Anne."

"Why," said Anne softly, "I wonder."

"You needn't stop to wonder," said Lydia. "You do it. He's going to realise he's got sisters anyway—and a father."

The same thought sprang at once into their three minds. It was not uncommon. They lived so close together, in such a unison of interests, that their minds often beat accordingly. Anne hesitatingly voiced the question.

"Do you think Esther'll meet him?"

"Impossible to say," the colonel returned, and Lydia's nipped lips and warlike glance indicated that she found it hideously impossible to say.

"I intend to find out," said she.

"I have an idea," said her father, as if he were in the kindest manner heading her off from a useless project, "that I'd better make a call on her myself, perhaps at once."

"She wouldn't see you when you came before," Lydia reminded him, in a hot rebellion against Jeff's wife who had not stood by him in his downfall. In the space of time that he had been outside the line of civilised life, an ideal of Jeff had been growing up in her own mind as in Anne's. They saw him as the wronged young chevalier without reproach whom a woman had forsaken in his need. Only a transcript of their girlish dreams could have told them what they thought of Jeff. His father's desolation without him, the crumbling of his father's life from hale middle age to fragile eld, this whirling of the leaves of time had seemed to bring them to a blazoned page where Jeff's rehabilitation should be wrought out in a magnificent sequence. The finish to that volume only: Jeff's life would begin again in the second volume, to be annotated with the approbation of his fellows. He would be lifted on the hands of men, their plaudits would upbear his soul, and he would at last triumph, sealed by the sanction of his kind. They grew intoxicated over it sometimes, in warm talks when their father was not there. He talked very little: a few words now and then to show what he thought of Jeff, a phrase or two where he unconsciously turned for them the page of the past and explained obscurities in the text they couldn't possibly elucidate alone—these they treasured and made much of, as the antiquary interprets his stone language. He never knew what importance they laid on every shred of evidence about Jeff. Perhaps if he had known he would have given them clearer expositions. To him Jeff was the dearest of sons that ever man begot, strangely pursued by a malign destiny accomplished only through the very chivalry and softness of the boy's nature. No hero, though; he would never have allowed his girls to build on that. And in all this rehabilitation of Jeff, as the girls saw it, there was one dark figure like the black-clad mourner at the grave who seems to deny the tenet of immortality: his wife, who had not stood by him and who was living here in Addington with her grandmother, had insisted on living with grandmother, in fact, as a cloak for her hardness. Sometimes they felt if they could sweep the black-clad figure away from the grave of Jeff's hopes, Jeff, in glorious apotheosis, would rise again.

"What a name for her—Esther!" Lydia ejaculated, with an intensity of hatred Anne tried to waft away by a little qualifying murmur. "Esther! Esthers are all gentle and humble and beautiful."

"She is a very pretty woman," said her father, with a wise gentleness of his own. Lydia often saw him holding the balance for her intemperate judgments, his grain of gold forever equalising her dross. "I think she'd be called a beautiful woman. Jeff thought she was."

"Do you actually believe, Farvie," said Lydia, "that she hasn't been to see him once in all these hideous years?"

"I know it," said he. "However, we mustn't blame her. She may be a timid woman. We must stand by her and encourage her and make it easier for her to meet him now. Jeff was very much in love with her. He'll understand her better than we do."

"I don't understand her at all," said Lydia, "unless you're going to let us say she's selfish and a traitor and———"

"No, no," said Anne. "We don't know her. We haven't even seen her. We must do what Farvie says, and then what Jeff says. I feel as if Jeff had thought things out a lot."

"Yes," said Lydia, and bit her lip on the implied reason that he'd had plenty of time.

"Yes," said the colonel gravely, in his own way. "I'd better go over there early to-morrow afternoon. Before the reporters get at her."

"Maybe they've done it already," Lydia suggested, and the gravity of his face accorded in the fear that it might be so.

Lydia felt no fear: a fiery exultation, rather. She saw no reason why Esther should be spared her share of invasion, except, indeed, as it might add to the publicity of the thing.

"You'll tell her, Farvie," Anne hesitated, "just what we'd decided to do about his coming—about meeting him?"

"Yes," said he. "In fact, I should consult her. She must have thought out things for herself, just as he must. I should tell her he particularly asked us not to meet him. But I don't think that would apply to her. I think it would be a beautiful thing for her to do. If reporters are there———"

"They will be," Lydia interjected savagely.

"Well, if they are, it wouldn't be a bad thing for them to report that his wife was waiting for him. It would be right and simple and beautiful. But if she doesn't meet him, certainly we can't. That would give rise to all kinds of publicity and pain. I think she'll see that."

"I don't think she'll see anything," said Lydia. "She's got a heart like a stone."

"Oh, don't say that," Anne besought her, "in advance."

"It isn't in advance," said Lydia. "It's after all these years."

III

The next day, after an early dinner—nobody in Addington dined at night—the colonel, though not sitting down to a definite conclave, went over with Anne and Lydia every step of his proposed call on Esther, as if they were planning a difficult route and a diplomatic mission at the end, and later, in a state of even more exquisite personal fitness than usual, the call being virtually one of state, he set off to find his daughter-in-law. Anne and Lydia walked with him down the drive. They had the air of upholding him to the last.

The way to Esther's house, which was really her grandmother's, he had trodden through all his earlier life. His own family and Esther's had been neighbours intimately at one, and, turning the familiar corner, he felt, with a poignancy cruel in its force, youth recalled and age confirmed. Here were associations almost living, they were so vivid, yet wraithlike in sheer removedness. It was all very subtle, in its equal-sided force, this resurrection of the forms of youth, to be met by the cold welcome of a change in him. The heart did quicken over its recognition of the stability of things, but with no robust urge such as it knew in other years; indeed it fluttered rather pathetically, as if it begged him to put no unwonted strain upon it now, as in that time foregone, when every beat cried out, "Heave the weight! charge up the hill! We're equal to it. If we're not, we'll die submerged in our own red fount." He was not taking age with any sense of egotistical rebellion; but it irked him like an unfamiliar weight patiently borne and for no reward. The sense of the morning of life was upon him; yet here he was fettered to his traitorous body which was surely going to betray him in the end. No miracle could save him from atomic downfall. However exultantly he might live again, here he should live no more, and though there was in him no fervency either of rebellion or belief, he did look gravely now at the pack of mortality he carried. It was carefully poised and handled. His life was precious to him, for he wanted this present coil of circumstance made plain before he should go hence and be seen no more.

The streets just now were empty. It was an hour of mid-afternoon when ladies had not dawned, in calling raiment, upon a world of other expectant ladies, and when the business man is under bonds to keep sequestered with at least the pretext of arduous tasks. The colonel had ample opportunity to linger by yards where shrubbery was coming out in shining buds, and draw into his grave consciousness the sense of spring. Every house had associations for him, as every foot of the road. Now he was passing the great yellow mansion where James Reardon lived. Reardon, of Irish blood and American public school training, had been Jeffrey's intimate, the sophisticated elder who had shown him, with a cool practicality that challenged emulation, the world and how it was to be bought. When there were magnates in Addington, James had been a poor boy. There were still magnates, and now he was one of them, so far as club life went and monetary transactions. He had never tried to marry an Addington girl, and therefore could not be said to have put his social merit absolutely to the touch. But luck had always served him. Perhaps it would even have done it there. He had gone into a broker's office, had made a strike with his savings and then another with no warning reversal, and got the gay habit of rolling up money like a snowball on a damp day. When the ball got too heavy for him to handle deftly, Jim dropped the game, only starting the ball down hill—if one may find symbolism for sedate investments—gathering weight as it went and, it was thought, at obstructive points persuading other little boys to push. The colonel had often wondered if Jeffrey had been one of those little boys. Now, at forty-five, Reardon lived a quiet, pottering life, a bachelor with a housekeeper and servants enough to keep the big yellow house in form. He read in a methodical way, really the same books over and over, collected prints with a conviction that a print is a print, exercised his big frame in the club gymnasium, took a walk of sanitary length morning and afternoon and went abroad once in two years.

"I've got money enough," he was accustomed to say, when the adventurous petitioned him to bolster new projects for swift returns, "all in gilt-edged securities. That's why I don't propose to lay awake an hour in my life, muddling over stocks. Why, it's destruction, man! it's death. It eats up your tissues faster than old age." The eccentricity of his verb indicated only the perfection of his tact. He had a perfect command of the English language, but a wilful lapse into colloquialisms endeared him, he knew, to his rougher kind. There was no more popular man. He was blond and open-featured. He spoke in a loud yet always sympathetic voice, and in skilfully different fashions he called every man brother.

Yet the colonel, his fancy entering the seclusion of the yellow house, rich in books that would have been sealed to even Jim's immediate forebears, rich in all possible mechanical appliances for the ease of life, speculated whether Reardon had, in the old days, been good for Jeff. Could he, with his infernal luck, have been good for any youth of Jeff's impetuous credulity? Mightn't Jeff have got the idea that life is an easy job? The colonel felt now that he had always distrusted Reardon's bluff bonhomie, his sympathetic voice, his booming implication that he was letting you into his absolutely habitable heart. He knew, too, that without word of his own his distrust had filtered out to Anne and Lydia, and that they were prepared, while they stood by Jeff to unformulated issues, to trip up Reardon, somehow bring him low and set Jeff up impeccable. Of this he was thinking gravely now, the different points of it starting up in his mind like sparks of light while he regarded Reardon's neat shrubs healthily growing, as if the last drop of fertilising had been poured into them at this spring awakening, and all pruned to a wholesome symmetry. Then, hearing the sound of a door and painfully averse to meeting Reardon, he went on and mounted the steps of the great brick house where his daughter-in-law lived. And here the adventure came to an abrupt stop. The maid, perfectly courteous and yet with an air of readiness even he, the most unsuspecting of men, could not fail to recognise, told him, almost before he had finished his inquiry, that Mrs. Blake was not at home. She would not be at home that afternoon. No, sir, not the next day. Madam Bell, Esther's grandmother, he asked for then. No, sir, she was not at home. Looking in the smooth sanguine face of the girl, noting mechanically her light eyelashes and the spaces between her teeth, he knew she lied. Yet he was a courteous gentleman, and did not report that to his inner mind. He bestowed his card upon Sapphira, and walked away at his sedate pace, more than anything puzzled. Esther was not proposing to take part in their coming drama. He couldn't count on her. He was doubly sorry because this defection was going to make Anne and Lydia hate her more than ever, and he was averse to the intensification of hatred. He was no mollycoddle, but he had an intuition that hatred is of no use. It hindered things, all sorts of things: kindliness, even justice.

The girls were waiting for him at the door, but reading his face, they seemed, while not withdrawing themselves bodily, really to slip away, in order not even tacitly to question him. They had a marvellous unwillingness to bring a man to the bar. There was no over-tactful display of absence, but their minds simply would not set upon and interrogate his, nor skulk round corners to spy upon it. But he had to tell them, and he was anxious to get it over. Just as they seemed now about to melt away to urgent tasks, he called them back.

"She's not at home," said he.

Anne looked a species of defeated interest. Lydia's eyes said unmistakably, "I don't believe it." The colonel was tired enough to want to say, "I don't either," but he never felt at liberty to encourage Lydia's too exuberant candour.

"She's not to be at home to-morrow," he said. "It looks as if she'd gone for—for the present," he ended lamely, put down his hat and went into the east room and took up his brown book.

"Oh!" said Lydia.

That was all he was to hear from her, and he was glad. He hadn't any assurance within him of the force to assuage an indignation he understood though he couldn't feel it. That was another of the levelling powers of age. You couldn't key your emotions up to the point where they might shatter something or perhaps really do some good. It wasn't only that you hadn't the blood and breath. It also didn't seem worth while. He was angry, in a measure, with the hidden woman he couldn't get at to bid her come and help him fight the battle that was hers even more indubitably than his; yet he was conscious that behind her defences was another world of passion and emotion and terribly strong desires, as valid as his own. She had her side. He didn't know what it was. He wanted really to avoid knowing, lest it weaken him through its appeal for a new sympathy; but he knew the side was there. This, he said to himself, with a half smile, was probably known as tolerance. It seemed to him old age.

So, from their benign choice, he had really nothing to say to Lydia or Anne. In the late afternoon Anne asked him to go to walk and show her the town, and he put her off. He was conscious of having drowsed away in his chair, into one of those intervals he found so inevitable, and that were, at the same time, so irritatingly foreign to his previous habits of life. He did not drop his pursuits definitely to take a nap. The nap seemed to take him, even when he was on the margin of some lake or river where he thought himself well occupied in seeing the moving to and fro of boats, for business and pleasure, just as his own boat had gallantly cut invisible paths on the air and water in those earlier years. The nap would steal upon him like an amiable yet inexorable joker, and throw a cloudy veil over his brain and eyes, and he would sink into a gulf he had not perceived. It lay at his feet, and something was always ready to push him into it. He thought sometimes, wondering at the inevitableness of it, that one day the veil would prove a pall.

But after their twilight supper, he felt more in key with the tangible world, and announced himself as ready to set forth. Lydia refused to go. She had something to do, she said; but she walked down the driveway with them, and waited until they had gone a rod or two along the street. The colonel turned away from Esther's house, as Lydia knew he would. She had not watched him for years without seeing how resolutely he put the memory of pain or loss behind him whenever manly honour would allow. The colonel's thin skin was his curse. Yet he wore it with a proud indifference it took a good deal of warm affection to penetrate. Lydia stood there and looked up and down the street. It had been a day almost hot, surprising for the season, and she was dressed in conformity in some kind of thin stuff with little dots of black. Her round young arms were bare to the elbow, and there was a narrow lacy frill about her neck. It was too warm really to need a hat or jacket, and this place was informal enough, she thought, to do away with gloves. Having rapidly decided that it was also a pity to cool resolution by returning to the house for any conventional trappings, she stepped to the pavement and went, with a light rapidity, along the road to Esther's.

She knew the way. When she reached the house she regarded it for a moment from the opposite side of the street, and Jim Reardon, coming out of his own gate for his evening's stroll to the Colonial Club, saw her and crossed, instead of continuing on his own side as he ordinarily did. She was a nymph-like vision of the twilight, and there was nothing of the Addington girl about her unconsidered ease. Jim looked at her deferentially, as he passed, a hand ready for his hat. But though Lydia saw him she dismissed him as quickly, perhaps as no matter for wonderment, and again because her mind was full of Esther. Now in the haste that dares not linger, she crossed the street and ascended the steps of the brick house. As she did so she was conscious of the stillness within. It might have been a house embodied out of her own dreams. But she did not ring, nor did she touch the circlet the brass lion of a knocker held obligingly in his mouth. She lifted the heavy latch, stepped in and shut the door behind her.

This was not the front entrance. The house stood on a corner, and this door led into a little square hall with a colonial staircase of charming right-angled turns going compactly up. Lydia looked into the room at her right and the one at her left. They were large and nobly proportioned, furnished in a faded harmony of antique forms. The arrangement of the house, she fancied, might be much like the colonel's. But though she thought like lightning in the excitement of her invasion, there was not much clearness about it; her heart was beating too urgently, and the blood in her ears had tightened them. No one was in the left-hand room, no one was in the right; only there was a sign of occupancy: a peach-coloured silk bag hung on the back of a chair and the lacy corner of a handkerchief stood up in its ruffly throat. The bag, the handkerchief, brought her courage back. They looked like a substantial Esther of useless graces she had to fight. And so passionately alive was she to everything concerning Jeffrey that it seemed base of a woman once belonging to him to parade lacy trifles in ruffly bags when he was condemned to coarse, hard usages. But having Esther to fight, she stepped into that room, and immediately a warm, yet, she had time to think, rather a discontented voice called from the room behind it:

"Is that you, Sophy?"

Lydia answered in an intemperate haste, and like many another rebel to the English tongue, she found a proper pronoun would not serve her for sufficient emphasis.

"No," she said, "it's me."

And she followed on the heels of her words, with a determined soft pace, to the room of the voice, and came upon a brown-eyed, brown-haired, rather plump creature in a white dress, who was lying in a long chair and eating candied fruit from a silver dish. This, Lydia knew, was Esther Blake. She had expected to feel for her the distaste of righteousness in the face of the wrong-doer: for Esther, she knew, was proven, by long-continued hardness of heart and behaviour, indubitably wrong. Here was Esther, Jeff's wife, not showing more than two-thirds of her thirty-three years, her brow unlined, her expression of a general sweetness indicating not only that she wished to please but that she had, in the main, been pleased. The beauty of her face was in its long eyelashes, absurdly long, as if nature had said, "Here's a by-product we don't know what to do with. Put it into lashes." Her hands were white and exquisitely cared for, and she wore no wedding ring. Lydia noted that, with an involuntary glance, but strangely it did not move her to any access of indignation. Anger she did feel, but it was, childishly, anger over the candied fruit. "How can you lie there and eat," she wanted to cry, "when Jeff is where he is?"

A little flicker ran over Esther's face: it might at first have been the ripple of an alarmed surprise, but she immediately got herself in hand. She put her exquisite feet over the side of the chair, got up and, in one deft motion, set the fruit on a little table and ran a hand lightly over her soft disorder of hair.

"Do excuse me," said she. "I didn't hear you."

"My name is French," said Lydia, in an incisive haste, "Lydia French. I came to talk with you about Jeff."

The shadow that went over Esther's face was momentary, no more than a bird's wing over a flowery plot; but it was a shadow only. There was no eagerness or uplift or even trouble at the name of Jeff.

"Father came this afternoon," said Lydia. "He wanted to talk things over. He couldn't get in."

"Oh," said Esther, "I'm sorry for that. So you are one of the step-children. Sit down, won't you. Oh, do take this chair."

Lydia was only too glad to take any chair and get the strain off her trembling knees. It was no trivial task, she saw, to face Jeff's wife and drag her back to wifehood. But she ignored the proffer of the softer chair. It was easier to take a straight one and sit upright, her brown little hands clenched tremblingly. Esther, too, took a chair the twin of hers, as if to accept no advantage; she sat with dignity and waited gravely. She seemed to be watchful, intent, yet bounded by reserves. It was the attitude of waiting for attack.

"This very next week, you know, Jeff will be discharged." Lydia spoke with the brutality born of her desperation. Still Esther watched her. "You know, don't you?" Lydia hurled at her. She had a momentary thought, "The woman is a fool." "From jail," she continued. "From the Federal Prison. You know, don't you? You heard he had been pardoned?"

Esther looked at her a full minute, her face slowly suffusing. Lydia saw the colour even flooding into her neck. Her eyes did not fill, but they deepened in some unusual way. They seemed to be saying, defiantly perhaps, that they could cry if they would, but they had other modes of empery.

"You know, don't you?" Lydia repeated, but more gently. She began to wonder now whether trouble had weakened the wife's brain, her power at least of receptivity.

"Yes," said Esther. "I know it, of course. To-day's paper had quite a long synopsis of the case."

Now Lydia flushed and looked defiant.

"I am glad to know that," she said. "I must burn the paper. Farvie sha'n't see it."

"There were two reporters here yesterday," said Esther. She spoke angrily now. Her voice hinted that this was an indignity which need not have been put upon her.

"Did you see them?" asked Lydia, in a flash, ready to blame her whatever she did.

But the answer was eloquent with reproach.

"Certainly I didn't see them. I have never seen any of them. When that horrible newspaper started trying to get him pardoned, reporters came here in shoals. I never saw them. I'd have died sooner."

"Did Jeff write you he didn't want to be pardoned? He did us."

"No. He hasn't written me for years."

She looked a baffling number of things now, voluntarily pathetic, a little scornful, as if she washed her hands gladly of the whole affair.

"Farvie thinks," said Lydia recklessly, "that you haven't written to him."

"How could I?" asked Esther, in a quick rebuttal which actually had a convincing sound, "when he didn't write to me?"

"But he was in prison."

"He hasn't had everything to bear," said Esther, rising and putting some figurines right on the mantel where they seemed to be right enough before. "Do you know any woman whose life has been ruined as mine has? Have you ever met one? Now have you?"

"Farvie's life is ruined," said Lydia incisively. "Jeff's life is ruined, too. I don't know whether it's any worse for a woman than for a man."

"Jeffrey," said Esther, "is taking the consequences of his own act."

"You don't mean to tell me you think he was to blame?" Lydia said, in a low tone charged with her own complexity of sentiment. She was horror-stricken chiefly. Esther saw that, and looked at her in a large amaze.

"You don't mean to tell me you think he wasn't?" she countered.

"Why, of course he wasn't!" Lydia's cheeks were flaming. She was impatiently conscious of this heat and her excited breath. But she had entered the fray, and there was no returning.

"Then who was guilty?" Esther asked it almost triumphantly, as if the point of proving herself right were more to her than the innocence of Jeff.

"That's for us to find out," said Lydia. She looked like the apostle of a holy war.

"But if you could find out, why haven't you done it before? Why have you waited all these years?"

"Partly because we weren't grown up, Anne and I. And even when we were, when we'd begun to think about it, we were giving dancing lessons, to help out. You know Farvie put almost every cent he had into paying the creditors, and then it was only a drop in the bucket. And besides Jeff pleaded guilty, and he kept writing Farvie to let it all stand as it was, and somehow, we were so sorry for Jeff we couldn't help feeling he'd got to have his way. Even if he wanted to sacrifice himself he ought to be allowed to, because he couldn't have his way about anything else. At least, that was what Anne and I felt. We've talked it over a lot. We've hardly talked of anything else. And we think Farvie feels so, too."

"You speak as if it were a sum of money he'd stolen out of a drawer," said Esther. Her cheeks were red, like exquisite roses. "It wasn't a sum of money. I read it all over in the paper the other day. He had stockholders' money, and he plunged, it said, just before the panic. He invested other people's money in the wrong things, and then, it said, he tried to realise."

"I can't help it," said Lydia doggedly. "He wasn't guilty."

"Why should he have said he was guilty?" Esther put this to her with her unchanged air of triumphant cruelty.

"He might, to save somebody else."

Esther was staring now and Lydia stared back, caught by the almost terrified surprise in Esther's face. Did she know about Jim Reardon? But Esther broke the silence, not in confession, if she did know: with violence rather.

"You never will prove any such thing. Never in the world. The money was in Jeff's hands. He hadn't even a partner."

"He had friends," said Lydia. But now she felt she had implied more than was discreet, and she put a sign up mentally not to go that way. Whatever Esther said, she would keep her own eyes on the sign.

IV

Still she returned to the assault. Her next question even made her raise her brows a little, it seemed so crude and horrible; she could have laughed outright at herself for having the nerve to put it. She couldn't imagine what the colonel would have thought of her. Anne, she knew, would have crumpled up into silken disaster like a flower under too sharp a wind.

"Aren't you going to ask Jeff here to live with you?"

Esther was looking at her in a fiery amaze Lydia knew she well deserved. "Who is this child," Esther seemed to be saying, "rising up out of nowhere and pursuing me into my most intimate retreats?" She answered in a careful hedging way that was not less pretty than her unconsidered speech:

"Jeffrey and I haven't been in communication for years."

Then Lydia lost her temper and put herself in the wrong.

"Why," said she, "you said that before. Besides, it's no answer anyway. You could have written to him, and as soon as you heard he was going to be pardoned, you could have made your plans. Don't you mean to ask him here?"

Esther made what sounded like an irrelevant answer, but it meant apparently something even solemn to her.

"My grandmother," said she, "is an old lady. She's bedridden. She's upstairs, and I keep the house very quiet on her account."

Lydia had a hot desire to speak out what she really felt: to say, "Your grandmother's being bedridden has no more to do with it than the cat." Lydia was prone to seek the cat for exquisite comparison. Persons, with her, could no more sing—or dance—than the cat. She found the cat, in the way of metaphor, a mysteriously useful animal. But the very embroidery of Esther's mode of speech forbade her invoking that eccentric aid. Lydia was not eager to quarrel. She would have been horrified if circumstance had ever provoked her into a rash word to her father, and with Anne she was a dove of peace. But Esther by a word, it seemed, by a look, had the power of waking her to unholy revolt. She thought it was because Esther was so manifestly not playing fair. Why couldn't she say she wouldn't have Jeff in the house, instead of sitting here and talking like a nurse in a sanitarium, about bedridden grandmothers?

"It isn't because we don't want him to come to us," said Lydia. "Farvie's been living for it all these years, and Anne and I don't talk of anything else."

"Isn't that interesting!" said Esther, though not as if she put a question. "And you're no relation at all." She made it, for the moment, seem rather a breach of taste to talk of nothing else but a man to whom Lydia wasn't a sister, and Lydia's face burned in answer. A wave of childish misery came over her. She wished she had not come. She wished she knew how to get away. And while she took in Esther's harmony of dress, her own little odds and ends of finery grew painfully cheap to her. But the telephone bell rang in the next room, and Esther rose and excused herself. While she was gone, Lydia sat there with her little hands gripped tightly. Now she wished she knew how to get out of the house another way, before Esther should come back. If it were not for the credit of the family, she would find the other way. Meantime Esther's voice, very liquid now that she was not talking to a sister woman, flowed in to her and filled her with a new distrust and hatred.

"Please come," said Esther. "I depend upon it. Do you mean you weren't ever coming any more?"

When she appeared again, Lydia was quivering with a childish anger. She had risen, and stood with her hands clasped before her. So she was in the habit of standing before her dancing class until the music should begin and lead her through the measures. She was delightful so and, from long training, entirely self-possessed.

"Good-bye," said she.

"Don't go," said Esther, in a conventional prettiness, but no such beguilement as she had wafted through the telephone. "It's been so pleasant meeting you."

Again Lydia had her ungodly impulse to contradict, to say: "No, it hasn't either. You know it hasn't." But she turned away and, head a little bent, walked out of the house, saying again, "Good-bye."

When she got out into the dusk, she went slowly, to cool down and think it over. It wouldn't do for the colonel and Anne to see her on the swell of such excitement, especially as she had only defeat to bring them. She had meant to go home in a triumphant carelessness and say: "Oh, yes, I saw her. I just walked right in. That's what you ought to have done, Farvie. But we had it out, and I think she's ready to do the decent thing by Jeff." No such act of virtuous triumph: she had simply been a silly girl, and Anne would find it out. Near the corner she met the man she had seen on her way in coming, and he looked at her again with that solicitous air of being ready to take off his hat. She went on with a consciousness of perhaps having achieved an indiscretion in coming out bareheaded, and the man proceeded to Esther's door. He was expected. Esther herself let him in.

Reardon had not planned to go to see her at that hour. He had meant to spend it at the club, feet up, trotting over the path of custom, knowing to a dot what men he would find there and what each would say. Old Dan Wheeler would talk about the advisability of eating sufficient vegetables to keep your stomach well distended. Young Wheeler would refer owlishly to the Maries and Jennies of an opera troupe recently in Addington, and Ollie Hastings, the oldest bore, would tell long stories, and wheeze. But Reardon was no sooner in his seat, with his glass beside him, than he realised he was disturbed, in some unexpected way. It might have been the pretty girl he met going into Esther's; it might have been the thought of Esther herself, the unheard call from her. So he left his glass untasted and telephoned her: "You all right?" To which Esther replied in a doubtful purr. "Want me to come up?" he asked, as he thought, against his will. And he swallowed a third of his firewater at a gulp and went to find her. He knew what he should find,—an Esther who bade him remember, by all the pliancy of her attractive body and every tone of her voice, how irreconcilably hard it was that she should have a husband pardoned out of prison, a husband of whom she was afraid.

Lydia found Anne waiting at the gate.

"Why, where've you been?" asked Anne, with all the air of a prim mother.

"Walking," said Lydia meekly.

"You'd better have come with us," said Anne. "It was very nice. Farvie told me things."

"Yes," said Lydia, "I wish I had."

"Without your hat, too," pursued Anne anxiously. "I don't know whether they do that here." Lydia remembered Reardon, and thought she knew.

They went to bed early, in a low state of mind. The colonel was tired, and Anne, watching him from above as he toiled up the stairs, wondered if he needed a little strychnia. She would remember, she thought, to give it to him in the morning. After they had said good-night, and the colonel, indeed, was in his bed, she heard the knocker clang and slipped down the stairs to answer. Halfway she stopped, for Mary Nellen, candle in hand, had arrived from the back regions, and was, with admirable caution, opening the door a crack. But immediately she threw it wide, and tossed her own reassurance over her shoulder, back to Anne.

"Mr. Alston Choate. To see your father."

So Anne came down the stairs, and Mr. Choate, hat in hand, apologised for calling so late. He was extremely busy. He had to be at the office over time, but he didn't want to-day's sun to go down and he not have welcomed Mr.

Blake. Anne had a chance, in the space of his delivering this preamble, to think what a beautiful person he was. He had a young face lighted by a twisted whimsical smile, and a capacious forehead, built out a little into knobs of a noble sort, as if there were ample chambers behind for the storing away of precedent. Altogether he would have satisfied every æsthetic requirement: but he had a broken nose. The portrait painter lusted for him, and then retired sorrowfully. But the nose made him very human. Anne didn't know its eccentricity was the result of breakage, but she saw it was quite unlike other noses and found it superior to them.

Alston Choate spent every waking minute of his life in the practice of law and the reading of novels; he was either digging into precedent, expounding it, raging over its futilities, or guiltily losing himself in the life of books. What he really loved was music and the arts, and he dearly liked to read about the people who had leisure to follow such lures, time to be emotional even, and indulge in pretty talk. Yet law was the giant he had undertaken to wrestle with, and he kept his grip. Sometime, he thought, the cases would be all tried or the feet of litigants would seek other doors. The wave of middle age would toss him to an island of leisure, and there he would sit down and hear music and read long books.

As he saw Anne coming down the stairs, he thought of music personified. A crowd of adjectives rose in his mind and, like attendant graces, grouped themselves about her. He could imagine her sitting at archaic instruments, calling out of them, with slim fingers, diaphanous melodies. Yet the beauty that surrounded her like a light mantle she had snatched up from nature to wear about her always, did not displace the other vision of beauty in his heart. It did not even jostle it. Esther Blake was, he knew, the sum of the ineffable feminine.

While he made that little explanation of his haste in coming and his fear that it was an untoward time, Anne heard him with a faint smile, all her listening in her upturned face. She was grateful to him. Her father, she knew, would be the stronger for men's hands to hold him up. She returned a little explanation. Father was so tired. He had gone to bed. Then it seemed to her that Choate did a thing unsurpassed in splendour.

"You are one of the daughters, aren't you?" he said.

"Yes," she answered. "I'm Anne."

Mary Nellen had delivered the candle to her hand, and she stood there holding it in a serious manner, as if it lighted some ceremonial. Then it was that Choate made the speech that clinched his hold upon her heart.

"When do you expect your brother?"

Anne's face flooded. He was not acting as if Jeff, coming from an unspeakable place, mustn't be mentioned. He was asking exactly as if Jeff had been abroad and the ship was almost in. It was like a pilot boat going out to see that he got in safely. And feeling the circumstance greatly, she found herself answering with a slow seriousness which did, indeed, carry much dignity.

"We are not sure. We think he may come directly through; but, on the other hand, he may be tired and not feel up to it."

Choate smiled his irregular, queer smile. He was turning away now.

"Tell him I shall be in soon," he said. "I fancy he'll remember me. Goodnight."

Lydia was hanging over the balustrade.

"Who was it?" she asked, as Anne went up.

Anne told her and because she looked dreamy and not displeased, Lydia asked:

"Nice?"

"Oh, yes," said Anne. "You've heard Farvie speak of him. Exactly what Farvie said."

Lydia had gone some paces in undressing. She stood there in a white wrapper, with her hair in its long braid, and stared at Anne for a considering interval.

"I think I'd better tell you," said she. "I've been to see her."

There was but one person who could have been meant, and yet that was so impossible that Anne stared and asked:

"Who?"

They had always spoken of Esther as Esther, among themselves, quite familiarly, but now Lydia felt she would die rather than mention her name.

"She is a hateful woman," said Lydia, "perfectly hateful."

"But what did you go for?" Anne asked, in a gentle perplexity.

"To find out," said Lydia, in a savage tearfulness, "what she means to do."

"And what does she?"

"Nothing."

V

The house, almost of its own will, slid into order. Mary Nellen was a wonderful person. She arranged and dusted and put questions to Anne as to Cicero and Virgil, and then, when Anne convoyed her further, to the colonel, and he found a worn lexicon in the attic and began to dig out translations and chant melodious periods. The daughters could have hugged Mary Nellen, bright-eyed and intent on advancement up the hill of learning, for they gave him something to do to mitigate suspense until his son should come. And one day at twilight, when they did not know it was going to be that day at all, but when things were in a complete state of readiness and everybody disposed to start at a sound, the front door opened and Jeffrey, as if he must not actually enter until he was bidden, stood there and knocked on the casing. Mary Nellen, having more than mortal wit, seemed to guess who he was, and that the colonel must not be startled. She appeared before Lydia in the dining-room and gave her a signalling grimace. Lydia followed her, and met the man, now a step inside the hall. Lydia, too, knew who it was. She felt the blood run painfully into her face, and hoped he didn't see how confused she was with her task of receiving him exactly right after all this time of preparation. There was no question of kissing or in any way sealing her sisterly devotion. She gave him a cold little hand, and he took it with the same bewildered acquiescence. She looked at him, it seemed to her, a long time, perhaps a full minute, and found him wholly alien to her dreams of the wronged creature who was to be her brother. He was of a good height, broad in the shoulders and standing well. His face held nothing of the look she had always wrought into it from the picture of his college year. It was rather square. The outline at least couldn't be changed. The chin, she thought, was lovable. The eyes were large and blue; stern, it seemed, but really from the habit of the forehead that had been scarred with deepest lines. The high cheekbones gave him an odd look as if she saw him in bronze. They stared at each other and Jeffrey thought he ought to assure her he wasn't a tramp, when Lydia found her voice.

"I'll tell Farvie," said she. She turned away from him, and immediately whirled back again. "I've got to do it carefully. You stay here."

But in the library where the colonel sat over Mary Nellen's last classic riddle, she couldn't break it at all.

"He's come," she said.

The colonel got up and Virgil slid to the floor.

"Where is he?" he called, in a sharp voice. It was a voice touched with age and apprehension. The girls hadn't known how old a man he was until they heard him calling for his son. Jeffrey heard it and came in with a few long steps, and his father met him at the door. To the two girls Jeff seemed astonished at the emotion he was awakening. How could he be, they wondered, when this instant of his release had been so terrible and so beautiful for a long time? The tears came rushing to their eyes, as they saw Farvie. He had laid aside all his gentle restraint, and put his shaking hands on Jeffrey's shoulders. And then he called him by the name he had been saying over in his heart for these last lean years:

"My son! my son!"

If they had kissed, Lydia would not have been surprised. But the two men looked at each other, the colonel took down his hands, and Jeffrey drew forward a chair for him.

"Sit down a minute," he said, quite gently, and then the girls knew that he really had been moved, though he hadn't shown it, and, ready to seize upon anything to love in him, they decided they loved his voice. When they had got away out of the room and stood close together in the dining-room, as if he were a calamity to be fled from, that was the only thing they could think of to break their silence.

"He's got a lovely voice," said Anne, and Lydia answered chokingly:

"Yes."

"Do you think he sings?" Anne pursued, more, Lydia knew, to loosen the tension than anything. "Farvie never told us that."

But Lydia couldn't answer any more, and then they both became aware that Mary Nellen had hurried out some supper from the pantry and put quite an array of candles on the table. She had then disappeared. Mary Nellen had great delicacy of feeling. Anne began to light the candles, and Lydia went back to the library. The colonel and Jeffrey were sitting there like two men with nothing in particular to say, but, because they happened to be in the same room, exchanging commonplaces.

"Supper's in the dining-room," said Lydia, in a weak little voice.

The colonel was about to rise, but Jeffrey said:

"Not for me."

"Have you had something?" his father asked, and Jeffrey answered:

"None for me—thank you."

The last two words seemed to be an afterthought. Lydia wondered if he hadn't felt like thanking anybody in years. There seemed to be nothing for her to do in this rigid sort of reunion, and she went back to Anne in the dining-room.

"He doesn't want anything," she said. "We can clear away."

They did it in their deft fashion of working together, and then sat down in the candlelight, making no pretence of reading or talk. All the time they could hear the two voices from the library, going on at regular intervals. At ten o'clock they were still going on, at eleven. Lydia felt a deadly sleepiness, but she roused then and said, in the midst of a yawn:

"I'm afraid Farvie'll be tired."

"Yes," said Anne. "I'll go and speak to them."

She went out of the room, and crossed the hall in her delicate, soft-stepping way. She seemed to Lydia astonishingly brave. Lydia could hear her voice from the other room, such a kind voice but steadied with a little clear authority.

"You mustn't get tired, Farvie."

The strange voice jumped in on the heels of hers, as if it felt it ought to be reproved.

"Of course not. I'd no idea how late it was."

Anne turned to Jeffrey. Lydia, listening, could tell from the different direction of the voice.

"Your room is all ready. It's your old room."

There was a pin-prick of silence and then the strange voice said quickly: "Thank you," as if it wanted to get everything, even civilities, quickly over.

Lydia sat still in the dining-room. The candles had guttered and gone down, but she didn't feel it possible to move out of her lethargy. She was not only sleepy but very tired. Yet the whole matter, she knew, was that this undramatic homecoming had deadened all her expectations. She had reckoned upon a brother ready to be called brother; she had meant to devote herself to him and see Anne devote herself, with an equal mind. And here was a gaunt creature with a sodden skin who didn't want anything they could do. She heard him say "Good-night." There was only one good-night, which must have been to the colonel, though Anne was standing by, and then she heard Anne, in a little kind voice, asking her father if he wouldn't have something hot before he went to bed. No, he said. He should sleep. His voice sounded exhilarated, with a thrill in it of some even gay relief, not at all like the voice that had said good-night. And Anne lighted his candle for him and watched him up the stairs, and Lydia felt curiously outside it all, as if they were playing the play without her. Anne came in then and looked solicitously at the guttered candles of which one was left with a winding-sheet, like a tipsy host that had drunk the rest under the table, and appeared to be comforting the others for having made such a spectacle of themselves to no purpose. Lydia was so sleepy now that there seemed to be several Annes and she heard herself saying fractiously:

"Oh, let's go to bed."

Through the short night she dreamed confusedly, always a dream about offering Farvie a supper tray, and his saying: "No, I never mean to eat again." And then the tray itself seemed to be the trouble, and it had to be filled all over. But nobody wanted the food.

In the early morning she awoke with the sun full upon her, for she had been too tired the night before to close a blind. She got out of bed and ran to the window. The night had been so confusing that she felt in very much of a hurry to see the day. Her room overlooked the orchard, outlined by its high red wall. For the first time, the wall seemed to have a purpose. A man in shirt and trousers was walking fast inside it, and while she looked he began to run. It was Jeffrey, the real Jeffrey, she felt sure; not the Jeffrey of last night who had been so far from her old conception of him that she had to mould him all over now to fit him into the orchard scene. He was running in a foolish, half-hearted way; but suddenly he seemed to call upon his will and set his elbows and ran hard. Lydia felt herself panting in sympathy. She had a distaste for him, too, even with this ache of pity sharper than any she had felt while she dreamed about him before he came. What did he want to do it for? she thought, as she watched him run. Why need he stir up in her a deeper sorrow than any she had felt? She stepped back from her stand behind the curtain, and began to brush her hair. She wasn't very happy. It was impossible to feel triumphant because he was out of prison. She had lost a cherished dream, that was all. After this she wouldn't wake in the morning thinking: "Some day he'll be free." She would think: "He's come. What shall we do with him?"

When she went down she found everybody had got up early, and Mary Nellen, with some prescience of it, had breakfast ready. Jeff, now in his coat, stood by the dining-room door with his father, talking in a commonplace way about the house as it used to be, and the colonel was professing himself glad no newer fashions had made him change it in essentials.

"Here they are," said he. "Here are the girls."

Anne, while Lydia entered from the hall, was coming the other way, from the kitchen where she had been to match conclusions with Mary Nellen about bacon and toast. Anne was flushed from the kitchen heat, and she had the spirit to smile and call, "Good morning." But Lydia felt halting and speechless. She had thought proudly of the tact she should show when this moment came, but she met it like a child. They sat down, and Anne poured coffee and asked how Farvie had slept. But before anybody had begun to eat, there was a knock at the front door, and Mary Nellen, answering it, came back to Anne, in a distinct puzzle over what was to be done now:

"It's a newspaper man."

Lydia, in her distress, gave Jeffrey a quick look, to see if he had heard. He put his napkin down. His jaw seemed suddenly to set.

"Reporters?" he asked his father.

The fulness had gone out of Farvie's face.

"I think you'd better let me see them," he began, but Jeffrey got up and pushed back his chair.

"No," said he. "Go on with your breakfast."

They heard him in the hall, giving a curt greeting. "What do you want?" it seemed to say. "Get it over."

There was a deep-toned query then, and Jeffrey answered, without lowering his voice, in what seemed to Lydia and Anne, watching the effect on their father, a reckless, if not a brutal, disregard of decencies:

"Nothing to say. Yes, I understand. You fellows have got to get a story. But you can't. I've been pardoned out, that's all. I'm here. That ends it."

It didn't end it for them. They kept on proffering persuasive little notes of interrogative sound, and possibly they advanced their claim to be heard because they had their day's work to do.

"Sorry," said Jeff, yet not too curtly. "Yes, I did write for the prison paper. Yes, it was in my hands. No, I hadn't the slightest intention of over-turning any system. Reason for doing it? Why, because that's the way the thing looked to me. Not on your life. I sha'n't write a word for any paper. Sorry. Good-bye."

The front door closed. It had been standing wide, for it was a warm morning, but Lydia could imagine he shut it now in a way to make more certain his tormentors had gone. While he was out there her old sweet sympathy came flooding back, but when he strode into the room and took up his napkin again, she stole one glance at him and met his scowl and didn't like him any more. The scowl wasn't for her. It was an introspective scowl, born out of things he intimately knew and couldn't communicate if he tried.

The colonel had looked quite radiantly happy that morning. Now his colour had died down, leaving in his cheeks the clear pallor of age, and his hands were trembling. It seemed that somebody had to speak, and he did it, faintly.

"I hope you are not going to be pursued by that kind of thing."

"It's all in the day's work," said Jeffrey.

He was eating his breakfast with a careful attention to detail. Anne thought he seemed like a painstaking child not altogether sure of his manners. She thought, too, with her swift insight into the needs of man, that he was horribly hungry. She was not, like Lydia, on the verge of impulse all the time, but she broke out here, and then bit her lip:

"I don't believe you did have anything to eat last night."

Lydia gave a little jump in her chair. She didn't see how Anne dared bait the scowling martyr. He looked at Anne. His scowl continued. They began to see he perhaps couldn't smooth it out. But he smiled a little.

"Because I'm so hungry?" he asked. His voice sounded kind. "Well, I didn't."

Lydia, now conversation had begun, wanted to be in it.

"Why not?" asked she, and Anne gave a little protesting note.

"I don't know," said Jeffrey, considering. "I didn't feel like it."

This he said awkwardly, but they all, with a rush of pity for him, thought they knew what he meant. He had eaten his food within restraining walls, probably in silence, and to take up the kind ceremonial of common life was too much for him. Anne poured him another cup of coffee.

"Seen Jim Reardon?" Jeffrey asked his father.

Anne and Lydia could scarcely forbear another glance at him. Here was Reardon, the evil influence behind him, too soon upon the scene. They would not have had his name mentioned until it should be brought out in Jeffrey's vindication.

"No," said the colonel. "Alston Choate called."

"I wonder what Reardon's doing now?" Jeffrey asked.

But his father did not know.

Jeffrey finished rapidly, and then leaned back in his chair, looked out of the window and forgot them all. Lydia felt one of her disproportioned indignations. She was afraid the colonel was not going to have the beautiful time with him their hopes had builded. The colonel looked older still than he had an hour ago.

"What shall we do, my son?" he asked. "Go for a walk—in the orchard?"

A walk in the street suddenly occurred to him as the wrong thing to offer a man returned to the battery of curious eyes.

"If you like," said Jeffrey indifferently. "Do you take one after breakfast?"

He spoke as if it were entirely for his father, and Anne and Lydia wondered, Anne in her kind way and the other hotly, how he could forget that all their passionate interests were for him alone.

"Not necessarily," said the colonel. They were rising. "I was thinking of you—my son."

"What makes you call me that?" Jeffrey asked curiously.

They were in the hall now, looking out beyond the great sun patch on the floor, to the lilac trees.

"What did I call you?"

"Son. You never used to."

Lydia felt she couldn't be quick enough in teaching him how dull he was.

"He calls you so because he's done it in his mind," she said, "for years and years. Your name wasn't enough. Farvie felt so—affectionate."

The last word sounded silly to her, and her cheeks were so hot they seemed to scald her eyes and melt out tears in them. Jeffrey gave her a little quizzical look, and slipped his arm through his father's. Anne, at the look, was suddenly relieved. He must have some soft emotions, she thought, behind the scowl.

"Don't you like it?" the colonel asked him. He straightened consciously under the touch of his son's arm.

"Oh, yes," said Jeffrey. "I like it. Only you never had. Except in letters. Come in here and I'll tell you what I'm going to do."

He had piloted the colonel into the library, and Anne and Lydia were disappearing into the dining-room where Mary Nellen was now supreme. The colonel called them, imperatively. There was such a note of necessity in his voice that they felt sure he didn't know how to deal, quite by himself, with this unknown quantity of a son.

"Girls, come here. I have to have my girls," he said to Jeffrey, "when anything's going to be talked over. They're the head of the house and my head, too."

The girls came proudly, if unwillingly. They knew the scowling young man didn't need them, might not want them indeed. But they were a part of Farvie, and he'd got to accept them until they found out, at least, how safe Farvie was going to be in his hands. Jeffrey wasn't thinking of them at all. He was accepting them, but they hadn't any share in his perspective. Lydia felt they were the merest little dots there. She giggled, one brief note to herself, and then sobered. She was as likely to laugh as to fume, and it began to seem very funny to her that in this drama of The Prisoner's Return she and Anne were barely to have speaking parts. The colonel sat in his armchair at the orchard window, and Jeffrey stood by the mantel and fingered a vase. Lydia, for the first time seeing his hands with a recognising eye, was shocked by them. They were not gentleman's hands, she thought. They were worn, and had calloused stains and ill-kept nails.

"I thought you'd like to know as soon as possible what I mean to do," he said, addressing his father.

"I'm glad you've got your plans," his father said. "I've tried to make some, but I couldn't—couldn't."

"I want first to find out just how things are here," said Jeffrey. "I want to know how much you've got to live on, and whether these girls have anything, and whether they want to stay on with you or whether they're doing it because—" Jeffrey now had a choking sense of emotions too big for him—"because there's no other way out."

"Do you mean," said Lydia, in a burst, before Anne's warning hand could stop her, "you want us to leave Farvie?"

The colonel looked up with a beseeching air.

"Good God, no!" said Jeffrey irritably. "I only want to know the state of things here. So I can tell what to do."

The colonel had got hold of himself, and straightened in his chair. The girls knew that motion. It meant, "Come, come, you derelict old body. Get into form."

"I've tried to write you fully," he said. "I hoped I gave you—a picture of the way we lived."

"You did. You have," said Jeffrey, still with that air of getting nowhere and being greatly irritated by it. "But how could I know how much these girls are sacrificing?"

"Sacrificing?" repeated the colonel helplessly, and Lydia was on the point of another explosion when Jeffrey himself held up his hand to her.

"Wait," he said. "Let me think. I don't know how to get on with people. They only make me mad."

That put a different face on it. Anne knew what he meant. Here he was, he for whom they had meant to erect arches of welcome, floored in a moment by the perplexities of family life.

"Of course," said Anne. She often said "of course" to show her sympathy. "You tell it your own way."

"Ah!" said Jeffrey, with a breath of gratitude. "Now you're talking. Don't you see———" he faced Anne as the only person present whose emotions weren't likely to get the upper hand———"don't you see I've got to know how father's fixed before I make any plans for myself?"

Anne nodded.

"We live pretty simply," she said, "but we can live. I keep the accounts. I can tell you how much we spend."

The colonel had got hold of himself now.

"I have twelve hundred a year," he said. "We do very well on that. I don't actually know how, except that Anne is such a good manager. She and Lydia have earned quite a little, dancing, but I always insisted on their keeping that for their own use."

Here Jeffrey looked at Anne and found her pinker than she had been. Anne was thinking she rather wished she had not been so free with her offer of accounts.

"Dancing," said he. "Yes. You wrote me. Do you like to dance?"

He had turned upon Lydia.

"Oh, yes," said she. "It's heavenly. Anne doesn't. Except when she's teaching children."

"What made you learn dancing?" he asked Anne.

"We wanted to do something," she said guiltily. She was afraid her tongue was going to betray her and tell the story of the lean year after their mother died when they found out that mother had lived a life of magnificent deception as to the ease of housekeeping on twelve hundred a year.

"Yes," said Jeffrey, "but dancing? Why'd you pick out that?"

"We couldn't do anything else," said Lydia impatiently. "Anne and I don't know anything in particular." She thought he might have been clever enough to see that, while too tactful to betray it. "But we look nice—together—and anybody can dance."

"Oh!" said Jeffrey. His eyes had a shade less of gravity, but he kept an unmoved seriousness of tone.

"About our living with Farvie," said Anne. "I can see you'd want to know."

"Yes," said he, "I do."

"We love to," said Anne. "We don't know what we should do if Farvie turned us out."

"My dear!" from the colonel.

"Why, he's our father," said Lydia, in a burst. "He's just as much our father as he is yours."

"Good!" said Jeffrey. His voice had warmed perceptibly. "Good for you. That's what I thought."

"If you'd rather not settle down here," said his father, in a tone of hoping Jeff would like it very much, "we shall be glad to let the house again and go anywhere you say. We've often talked of it, the girls and I."

Jeffrey did not thank them for that, or seem to hear it even.

"I want," said he, "to go West."

"Well," said Farvie, with a determined cheerfulness, "I guess the girls'll agree to that. Middle West?"

"No," said Jeffrey, "the West—if there is any West left. Somewhere where there's space." His voice fell, on that last word. It held wonder even. Was there such a thing, this man of four walls seemed to ask, as space?

"You'd want to go alone," said Anne softly. She felt as if she were breaking something to Farvie and adjuring him to bear it.

"Yes," said Jeffrey, in relief. "I've got to go alone."

"My son—" said the colonel and couldn't go on. Then he did manage. "Aren't we going to live together?"

"Not yet," said Jeffrey. "Not yet."

The colonel had thought so much about his old age that now he was near saying: "You know I haven't so very many years," but he held on to himself.

"He's got to go alone," said Anne. "But he'll come back."

"Yes," said Lydia, from the habit they had learned of heartening Farvie, "he'll come back."

But she was hotly resolving that he should learn his duty and stay here. Let her get a word with him alone.

"What I'm going to do out there I don't know," said Jeffrey. "But I am going to work, and I'm going to turn in enough to keep you as you ought to be. I want to stay here a little while first."

The colonel was rejuvenated by delight. Lydia wondered how anybody could see that look on his face and not try to keep it there.

"I've got," said Jeffrey, "to write a book."

"Oh, my son," said the colonel, "that's better than I hoped. The newspapers have had it all, how you've changed the prison paper, and how you built up a scheme of prison government, and I said to myself, 'When he comes out, he'll write a book, and good will come of it, and then we shall see that, under Providence, my son went to prison that he might do that.'"

He was uplifted with the wonder of it. The girls felt themselves carried along at an equal pace. This was it, they thought. It was a part of the providences that make life splendid. Jeffrey had been martyred that he might do a special work.

"Oh, no," said he, plainly bored by the inference. "That's not it. I'm going to write the life of a fellow I know."

"Who was he?" Anne asked, with a serious uplift of her brows.

"A defaulter."

"In the Federal Prison?"

"Yes."

VI

He looked at them, quite unconscious of the turmoil he had wakened in them. Lydia was ready to sound the top note of revolt. Her thoughts were running a definite remonstrance: "Write the life of another man when you should be getting your evidence together and proving your own innocence and the injustice of the law?" Anne was quite ready to believe there must be a cogent reason for writing the life of his fellow criminal, but she wished it were not so. She, too, from long habit of thought, wanted Jeffrey to attend to his own life now he had a chance. The colonel, she knew, through waiting and hoping, had fallen into an attitude of mind as wistful and expectant as hers and Lydia's. The fighting qualities, it seemed, had been ground out of him. The fostering ones had grown disproportionately, and sometimes, she was sure, they made him ache, in a dull way, with ruth for everybody.

"Did the man ask you to write his life?" he inquired.

"No," said Jeffrey. "I asked him if I could. He agreed to it. Said I might use his name. He's no family to squirm under it."

"You feel he was unjustly sentenced," the colonel concluded.

"Oh, no. He doesn't either. He mighty well deserved what he got. Been better perhaps if he'd got more. What I had in mind was to tell how a man came to be a robber."

Lydia winced at the word. Jeffrey had been commonly called a defaulter, and she was imperfectly reconciled to that: certainly not to a branding more ruthless still.

"I've watched him a good deal," said Jeffrey. "We've had some talk together. I can see how he did what he did, and how he'd do it again. It'll be a study in criminology."

"When does he—come out?" Anne hesitated over this. She hardly knew a term without offence.

"Next year."

"But," said she, "you wouldn't want to publish a book about him and have him live it down?"

"Why shouldn't I?" asked Jeffrey, turning on her. "He's willing."

"He can't be willing," Lydia broke in. "It's frightful."

"Well, he is," said Jeffrey. "There's nothing you could do to him he'd mind, if it gave him good advertising."

"What does he want to do," asked the colonel, "when he comes out?"

"Get into the game again. Make big money. And if it's necessary, steal it. Not that he wants to bunco. He's had his dose. He's learned it isn't safe. But he'd make some dashing *coup*; he couldn't help it. Maybe he'd get nabbed."

"What a horrid person!" said Lydia. "How can you have anything to do with him?"

"Why, he's interesting," said Jeffrey, in a way she found brutal. "He's a criminal. He's got outside."

"Outside what?" she persisted.

"Law. And he wouldn't particularly want to get back, except that it pays. But I'm not concerned with what he does when he gets back. I want to show how it seemed to him outside and how he got there. He's more picturesque than I am, or I'd take myself."

Blessed Anne, who had no grasp, she thought, of abstract values, but knew how to make a man able for his work, met the situation quietly.

"You could have the blue chamber, couldn't he, Farvie? and do your writing there."

Lydia flashed her a reproachful glance. She would have scattered his papers and spilled the ink, rather than have him do a deed like that. If he did it, it was not with her good-will. Jeff had drawn his frown the tighter.

"I don't know whether I can do it," he said. "A man has got to know how to write."

"You wrote some remarkable things for the *Nestor*," said the colonel, now hesitating. It had been one of the rules he and the girls had concocted for the treatment of a returning prisoner, never to refer to stone walls and iron bars. But surely, he felt, Jeff needed encouragement.

Jeff was ruthless.

"That was all rot," he said.

"What was?" Lydia darted at him. "Didn't you mean what you said?"

"It was idiotic for the papers to take it up," said Jeff. "They got it all wrong. 'There's a man,' they said, 'in the Federal Prison, Jeffrey Blake, the defaulter. Very talented. Has revolutionised the *Nestor*, the prison organ. Let him out, pardon him, simply because he can write.'"

"As I understand," said his father, "you did get the name of the paper changed."

"Well, now," said Jeff, appealingly, in a candid way, "what kind of name was that for a prison paper? *Nestor!* 'Who was Nestor?' says the man that's been held up in the midst of his wine-swilling and money-getting. Wise old man, he remembers. First-class preacher. Turn on the tap and he'll give you a maxim. 'Gee!' says he, 'I don't want advice. I know how I got here, and if I ever get out, I'll see to it I don't get in again.'"

Lydia found this talk exceedingly diverting. She disapproved of it. She had wanted Jeff to appear a dashing, large-eyed, entirely innocent young man, his mouth, full of axioms, prepared to be the stay of Farvie's gentle years. But this rude torrent of perverse philosophy bore her along and she liked it, particularly because she felt she should presently contradict and show how much better she knew herself. Anne, too, evidently had an unlawful interest in it, and wanted him to keep on talking. She took that transparent way of furthering the flow by asking a question she could answer herself.

"You called it *Prison Talk*, didn't you?"

"Yes," said Jeff. "They called it *Prison Talk.*"

"And all our newspapers copied your articles," said Anne, artfully guiding him forward, "the ones you called 'The New Republic.'"

"What d'they want to copy them for?" asked Jeff. "It was a fool thing to do. I'd simply written the letters to the men, to ask 'em if they didn't think the very devil of prison life was that we were outside. Not because we were inside, shut up in a jug. You could bear to be in a jug, if that was all. But you've got to have ties. You've got to have laws and the whole framework that's been built up from the cave man. Or you're desperate, don't you see? You're all alone. And a man will do a great deal not to be alone. If there's nothing for you to do but learn a trade, and be preached at by *Nestor*, and say to yourself, 'I'm outside'—why there's the devil in it."

He was trying to convince them as he had previously convinced others, those others who had lived with him under the penal law. He looked at Anne much as if she were a State or Federal Board and incidentally at Lydia, as if he would say:

"Here's a very young and insignificant criminal. We'll return to her presently. But she, too, is going to be convinced."

"And I don't say a man hasn't got to be infernally miserable when he's working out his sentence. He has. I don't want you to let up on him. Only I don't want him to get punky, so he isn't fit to come back when his term is over. I don't believe it's going to do much for him merely to keep the laws he's been chucked under, against his will, though he's got to keep 'em, or they'll know the reason why."

Lydia wondered who They were. She thought They might be brutal wardens and assembled before her, in a terrifying battalion, the straitjackets and tortures she'd found in some of the older English novels.

"So I said to the men: 'We've got to govern ourselves. We haven't got a damned word'"—really abashed he looked at Anne—"I beg your pardon. 'We haven't got a word to say in this government we're under; but say we have. Say the only thing we can do is to give no trouble, fine ourselves, punish ourselves if we do. The worst thing that can happen to us,' I said, 'is to hate law. Well, the best law we've got is prison law. It's the only law that's going to touch us now. Let's love it as if it were our mother. And if it isn't tough enough, let's make it tougher. Let's vote on it, and publish our votes in this paper.'"

"I was surprised," said his father, "that so much plain speaking was allowed."

"Advertising! Of course they allowed us," said Jeff. "It advertised us outside. Advertised the place. Officials got popular. Inside conduct went up a hundred per cent, just as it would in school. Men are only boys. As soon as the fellows got it into their heads we were trying to work out a republic in a jail, they were possessed by it. I wish you could see the letters that were sent in to the paper. You couldn't publish 'em, some of 'em. Too illiterate. But they showed you what was inside the fellows. Sometimes they were as smug as a prayer-meeting."

"Did this man write?" Lydia asked scornfully, with a distaste she didn't propose to lessen. "The one you're going to do the book about?"

"Oh, he's a crook," said Jeff indifferently. "Crook all through. If we'd been trying to build up a monarchy instead of a republic he'd have hatched up a scheme for looting the crown jewels. Or if we'd been founding a true and only church, he'd have suggested a trick for melting the communion plate."

"And you want to write his life!" said Lydia's look.

But Jeff cared nothing about her look. He was, with a retrospective eye, regarding the work he had been doing, work that had perhaps saved his reason as well as bought his freedom. Now he was spreading it out and letting them consider it, not for praise, but because he trusted them. He felt a few rivets giving in the case he had hardened about himself for so long a time. He thought he had got very hard indeed, and was even willing to invite a knock or two, to test his induration. But there was something curiously softening in this little group sitting in the shade of the pleasant room while the sunshine outside played upon growing leaves. He was conscious, wonderingly, that they all loved him very much. His father's letters had told him that. It seemed simple and natural, too, that these young women, who were not his sisters and who gave him, in his rough habit of life, a curious pain with their delicacy and softness—it seemed natural enough that they should, in a way not understood, belong to him. He had got gradually accustomed to it, from their growing up in his father's house from little girls to girls dancing themselves into public favour, and then, again, he had been living "outside" where ordinary conventions did not obtain. He had got used to many things in his solitary thoughts that were never tested by other minds in familiar intercourse. The two girls belonged there among accepted things. He looked up suddenly at his father, and asked the question they had least of all expected to hear:

"Where's Esther?"

The two girls made a movement to go, but he glanced at them frowningly, as if they mustn't break up the talk at this moment, and they hesitated, hand in hand.

"She's living here," said the colonel, "with her grandmother."

"Has that old harpy been over lately?"

"Madame Beattie?"

"Yes."

"Not to my knowledge."

Anne and Lydia exchanged looks. Madame Beattie was a familiar name to them, but they had never heard she was a harpy.

"Was she Esther's aunt?" Lydia inquired, really to give the talk a jog. She was accustomed to shake up her watch when it hesitated.

"Great-aunt," said Jeffrey. "Step-sister to Esther's grandmother. She must be sixty-five where grandmother's a good ten years older."

"She sang," said the colonel, forgetting, as he often did, they seemed so young, that everybody in America must at least have heard tradition of Madame Beattie's voice. "She lived abroad."

"She had a ripping voice," said Jeff. "When she was young, of course. That wasn't all. There was something about her that took them. But she lost her voice, and she married Beattie, and he died. Then she came back here and hunted up Esther."

His face settled into lines of sombre thought, puzzled thought, it seemed to Anne. But to Lydia it looked as if this kidnapping of Madame Beattie from the past and thrusting her into the present discussion was only a pretext for talking about Esther. Of course, she knew, he was wildly anxious to enter upon the subject, and there might be pain enough in it to keep him from approaching it suddenly. Esther might be a burning coal. Madame Beattie was the safe holder he caught up to keep his fingers from it. But he sounded now as if he were either much absorbed in Madame Beattie or very wily in his hiding behind her.

"I've often wondered if she came back. I've thought she might easily have settled on Esther and sucked her dry. No news of her?"

"No news," said the colonel. "It's years since she's been here. Not since—then."

"No," said Jeff. There was a new line of bitter amusement near his mouth. "I know the date of her going, to a dot. The day I was arrested she put for New York. Next week she sailed for Italy." But if Lydia was going to feel more of her hot reversals in the face of his calling plain names, she found him cutting them short with another question: "Seen Esther?"

"No," said the colonel.

A red spot had sprung into his cheek. He looked harassed. Lydia sprang into the arena, to save him, and because she was the one who had the latest news.

"I have," she said. "I've seen her."

She knew what grave surprise was in the colonel's face. But no such thing appeared in Jeff's. He only turned to her as if she were the next to be interrogated.

"How does she look?" he asked.

The complete vision of her stretched at ease eating fruit out of a silver dish, as if she had arranged herself to rouse the most violent emotions in a little seething sister, stirred Lydia to the centre. But not for a million dollars, she reflected, in a comparison clung to faithfully, would she tell how beautiful Esther appeared to even the hostile eye.

"She looked," said she coldly, "perfectly well."

"Where d'you see her?" Jeff asked.

"I went over," said Lydia. Her colour was now high. She looked as if you might select some rare martyrdom for her—quartering or gridironing according to the oldest recipes—and you couldn't make her tell less than the truth, because only the truth would contribute to the downfall of

Esther. "I went in without ringing, because Farvie'd been before and they wouldn't let him in."

"Lydia!" the colonel called remindingly.

"I found her reading—and eating." Lydia hadn't known she could be so hateful. Still she was telling the exact truth. "We talked a few minutes and I came away."

"Did she—" at last suddenly and painfully thrown out of his nonchalant run of talk, he stopped.

"She's a horrid woman," said Lydia, crimson with her own daring, and got up and ran out of the room.

Anne looked appealingly at Jeff, in a way of begging him to remember how young Lydia was, and perhaps how spoiled. But he wasn't disturbed. He only said to his father in a perfectly practical way:

"Women never did like her, you know."

So Anne got up and went out, thinking it was the moment for him and his father to pace along together on this road of masculine understanding. She found Lydia by the dining-room window, savagely drying her cheeks. Lydia looked as if she had cried hard and scrubbed the tears off and cried again, there was such wilful havoc in the pink smoothness of her face.

"Isn't he hateful?" she asked Anne, with an incredulous spite in her voice. "How could anybody that belonged to Farvie be so rough? I can't endure him, can you?"

Anne looked distressed. When there were disagreements and cross-purposes they made her almost ill. She would go about with a physical nausea upon her, wishing the world could be kind.

"But he's only just—free," she said.

They were still making a great deal of that word, she and Lydia. It seemed the top of earthly fortune to be free, and abysmal misery to have missed it.

"I can't help it," said Lydia. "What does he want to act so for? Why does he talk about such places, as if anybody could be in them?"

"Prisons?"

"Yes. And talking about going West as if Farvie hadn't just lived to get him back. And about her as if she wasn't any different from what he expected and you couldn't ask her to be anything else."

"But she's his wife," said Anne gently. "I suppose he loves her. Let's hope he does."

"You can, if you want to," said Lydia, with a wet handkerchief making another renovating attack on her face. "I sha'n't. She's a horrid woman."

They parted then, for their household deeds, but all through the morning Lydia had a fire of curiosity burning in her to know what Jeff was doing. He ought, she knew, to be sitting by Farvie, keeping him company, in a passionate way, to make up for the years. The years seemed sometimes like a colossal mistake in nature that everybody had got to make up for—make up to everybody else. Certainly she and Anne and Farvie had got to make up to the innocent Jeff. And equally they had all got to make up to Farvie. But going once noiselessly through the hall, she glanced in and saw the colonel sitting alone by the window, Mary Nellen's Virgil in his hand. He was well back from the glass, and Lydia guessed that it was because he wanted to command the orchard and not himself be seen. She ran up to her own room and also looked. There he was, Jeff, striding round in the shadow of the brick wall, walking like a man with so many laps to do before night. Sometimes he squared his shoulders and walked hard, but as if he knew he was going to get there—the mysterious place for which he was bound. Sometimes his shoulders sagged, and he had to drive himself. Lydia felt, in her throat, the aching misery of youth and wondered if she had got to cry again, and if this hateful, wholly unsatisfactory creature was going to keep her crying. As she watched, he stopped, and then crossed the orchard green directly toward her. She stood still, looking down on him fascinated, her breath trembling, as if he might glance up and ask her what business she had staring down there, spying on him while he did those mysterious laps he was condemned to, to make up perhaps for the steps he had not taken on free ground in all the years.

"Got a spade?" she heard him call.

"Yes." It was Anne's voice. "Here it is."

"Why, it's new," Lydia heard him say.

He was under her window now, and she could not see him without putting her head over the sill.

"Yes," said Anne. "I went down town and bought it."

Anne's voice sounded particularly satisfied. Lydia knew that tone. It said Anne had been able to accomplish some fit and clever deed, to please. It was as if a fountain, bubbling over, had said, "Have I given you a drink, you dog, you horse, you woman with the bundle and the child? Marvellous lucky I must be. I'll bubble some more."

Jeff himself might have understood that in Anne, for he said:

"I bet you brought it home in your hand."

"No takers," said Anne. "I bet I did."

"That heavy spade?"

"It wasn't heavy."

"You thought I'd be spading to keep from growing dotty. Good girl. Give it here."

"But, Jeff!" Anne's voice flew after him as he went. Lydia felt herself grow hot, knowing Anne had taken the big first step that had looked so impossible when they saw him. She had called him Jeff. "Jeff, where are you going to spade?"

"Up," said Jeff. "I don't care where. You always spade up, don't you?"

In a minute Lydia saw Anne, with the sun on her brown hair, the colonel, and Jeff with the shining spade like a new sort of war weapon, going forth to spade "up". Evidently Anne intended to have no spading at random in a fair green orchard. She was one of the conservers of the earth, a thrifty housewife who would have all things well done. They looked happily intent, the three, going out to their breaking ground. Lydia felt the tempest in her going down, and she wished she were with them. But her temper shut her out. She felt like a little cloud driven by some capricious wind to darken the face of earth, and not by her own willingness.

She went down to the noon dinner quite chastened, with the expression Anne knew, of having had a temper and got over it. The three looked as if they had had a beautiful time, Lydia thought humbly. The colour was in their faces. Farvie talked of seed catalogues, and it became evident that Jeff was spading up the old vegetable garden on the orchard's edge. Anne had a soft pink in her cheeks. They had all, it appeared, begun a pleasant game.

Lydia kept a good deal to herself that day. She accepted a task from Anne of looking over table linen and lining drawers with white paper. Mary Nellen was excused from work, and sat at upper windows making a hum of study like good little translating bees. Anne went back and forth from china closet to piles of dishes left ready washed by Mary Nellen, and the colonel, in the library, drowsed off the morning's work. Lydia had a sense of peaceful tasks and tranquil pauses. Her own pulses had quieted with the declining sun, and it seemed as if they might all be settling into a slow-moving ease of life at last.

"Where is he?" suddenly she said to Anne, in the midst of their weaving the household rhythm.

"Jeff?" asked Anne, not stopping. "He's spading in the garden."

"Don't you want to go out?" asked Lydia. She felt as if they had on their hands, not a liberated prisoner, but a prisoner still bound by their fond expectations of him. He must be beguiled, distracted from the memory of his broken fetters.

"No," said Anne. "He'll be tired enough to sleep to-night."

"Didn't he sleep last night?" Lydia asked, that old ache beginning again in her.

"I shouldn't think so," said Anne. "But he's well tired now".

And it was Lydia that night at ten who heard long breaths from the little room when she went softly up the back stairs to speak to Mary Nellen. There was a light on his table. The door was open. He sat, his back to her, his arms on the table, his head on his arms. She heard the long labouring breaths of a creature who could have sobbed if he had not kept a heavy hand on himself. They were, Lydia thought, like the breaths of a dear dog she had known who used to put his nose to the crack of the shut door and sigh into it, "Please let me in." It seemed to her acutely sensitive mind, prepared like a chemical film to take every impression Jeff could cast, as if he were lying prone at the door of the cruel beauty and breathing, "Please let me in." She wanted to put her hands on the bowed head and comfort him. Now she knew how Anne felt, Anne, the little mother heart, who dragged up compassion from the earth and brought it down from the sky for unfriended creatures. And yet all the solace Lydia had to offer was a bitter one. She would only have said:

"Don't cry for her. She isn't worth it. She's a hateful woman."

VII

Madame Beattie was near, and had that morning telegraphed Esther. The message was explicit, and, in the point of affection, diffuse. Old-fashioned, too: she longed to hold her niece in her arms. A more terrified young woman could not easily have been come on that day than Esther Blake, as she opened the envelope, afraid of detectives, of reporters, of anything connected with a husband lately returned from jail. But this was worse than she could have guessed. In face of an ordinary incursion she might shut herself up in her room and send Sophy to tell smooth fictions at the door. Reporters could hardly get at her, and her husband himself, if he should try, could presumably be routed. Aunt Patricia Beattie was another matter. Esther was so panicky that she ran upstairs with the telegram and tapped at grandmother's door. Rhoda Knox came in answer. She was a large woman of a fine presence, red cheekbones with high lights, and smooth black hair brushed glossy and carefully coiled. She was grandmother's attendant, helplessly hated by grandmother but professionally unmoved by it, a general who carried on intricate calculations to avoid what she called "steps." In the matter of steps, she laid bonds on high and low. A deed that would have taken her five minutes to do she passed on to the next available creature, even if it required twenty minutes' planning to hocus him into accepting it. She had the intent look of the schemer: yet she was one who meant well and simply preferred by nature to be stationary. Grandmother feared her besides hating her, though loving the order she brought to pass.

Esther slipped by her, and went to the bed where grandmother was lying propped on pillows, an exceedingly small old woman who was even to lifelong friends an enigma presumably without an answer. She had the remote air of hating her state of age, which did not seem a natural necessity but a unique calamity, a trap sprung on her and, after the nature of traps, most unexpectedly. When she was young she had believed the old walked into the trap deliberately because it was provided on a path they were tired of. But she wasn't tired, and yet the trap had clutched her. She had a small face beautifully wrought upon by lines, as if she had given a cunning artificer the preparation of a mask she was paying dearly for and yet didn't prize at all. An old-fashioned nightcap with a frill covered her head, and she had tied herself so tightly into it that he must be a bold adventurer who would get at the thoughts inside. Her little hands were shaded by fine frills. She looked, on the whole, like a disenchanted lingerer in the living world, a useless creature for whom fostering had done so much that you might ask: "What is this illustration of a clean old woman? What is it for? What does it teach?"

Esther, with her telegram, stood beside the bed.

"Grandmother," said she, in the perfect tone she used toward her, clear and not too loud, "Aunt Patricia Beattie is coming."

Grandmother lifted large black eyes dulled by the broken surface of age, to Esther's face. There was no envy in the gaze but wonder chiefly.

"Is that youth?" the eyes inquired. "Useless, not especially admirable—but curious."

Esther, waiting there for recognition, felt the discomfort grandmother always seemed to stir into her mood. Her rose-touched skin was a little more suffused, though not beyond a furtherance of beauty.

"Aunt Patricia is coming," she repeated. "When I heard from her last she was in Poland."

"Her name is Martha," said grandmother. "Don't let her come in here." She had a surprising voice, of a barbaric quality, the ring of metal. Hearing it you were mentally translated for an instant, and thought of far-off, palm-girt islands and savages beating strange instruments and chanting to them uncouth syllables. "Rhoda Knox, don't let her get up here."

"How can I keep her out?" asked Esther. "You'll have to see her. I can't live down there alone with her. I couldn't make her happy."

A satirical light shivered across grandmother's eyes.

"Where is your husband?" she inquired. "Here?"

"Here?" repeated Esther. "In this house?"

"Yes."

"He isn't coming here. It would be very painful for him."

The time had been when grandmother, newer to life, would have asked, "Why?" But she knew Esther minutely now; all her turns of speech and habits of thought were as a tale long told. Once it had been a mildly fascinating game to see through what Esther said to what she really meant. It was easy, once you had the clue, too easy, all certainties, with none of the hazards of a game. Esther, she knew, lived with a lovely ideal of herself. The imaginary Esther was all sympathy; she was even self-sacrificing. No shining quality lay in the shop window of the world's praise but the real Esther snatched it and adorned herself with it. The Esther that was talked in the language of the Esther that ought to be. If she didn't want to see you, she told you it would be inconvenient for you to come. If she wanted to tell you somebody had praised the rose of her cheek, she told you she was so touched by everybody's goodness in loving to give pleasure; then she proved her point by naive repetition of the pretty speech. Sometimes she even, in the humility of the other Esther, deprecated the flattery as insincere; but not before she had told you what it was.

"I haven't seen her since—I haven't seen her for years," she said. "She wasn't happy with me then. She'll be much less likely to be now."

"Older," said grandmother. "More difficult. Keep her out of here."

It seemed to Esther there was no sympathy for her in the world, even if she got drum and fife and went out to beat it up. One empty victory she had achieved: grandmother had at least spoken to her. Sometimes she turned her face to the wall and lay there, not even a ruffle quivering. Esther moved away, but Rhoda Knox was beforehand with her. Rhoda held a letter.

"Mrs. Blake, could you take this down?" she asked, in a faultless manner, and yet implacably. "And let it go out when somebody is going?"

Esther accepted the letter helplessly. She knew how Rhoda sat planning to get her errands done. Yet there was never any reason why you should not do them. She ran downstairs carrying the letter, hating it because it had got itself carried against her will, and went at once to the telephone. And there her voice had more than its natural appeal, because she was so baffled and angry and pitied herself so much.

"Could you come in? I'm bothered. Yes," in answer to his question, "in trouble, I'm afraid."

Alston Choate came at once; her voice must have told him moving things, for he was full of warm concern. Esther met him with a dash of agitation admirably controlled. She was not the woman to alarm a man at the start. Let him get into a run, let him forget the spectators by the way, and even the terrifying goal where he might be crowned victor even before he chose. Only whip up his blood until the guidance of them both was hers, not his. So he felt at once her need of him and at the same time her distance from him. It was a wonderfully vivifying call: nothing to fear from her, but exhilarating feats to be undertaken for her sake.

"I'm frightened at last," she told him. That she was a brave woman the woman she had created for her double had persuaded her. "I had to speak to somebody."

Choate looked really splendid in the panoply of his simplicity and restraints and courtesy. A man can be imposing in spite of a broken nose.

"What's gone wrong?" he asked.

"Aunt Patricia is coming."

Choate had quite forgotten Aunt Patricia. She had been too far in the depths of Poland for Esther to summon up her shade. Possibly it was a dangerous shade to summon, lest the substance follow. But now she sketched Aunt Patricia with hesitating candour, but so that he lost none of her undesirability, and he listened with a painstaking courtesy.

"You say you're afraid of her?" he said, at the end. "Let her come. She may not want to stay."

"She is so—different," faltered Esther. She looked at him with humid eyes. It was apparent that Aunt Patricia was different in a way not to be commended.

Now Choate thought he saw how it was.

"You mean she's been banging about Europe," he said, "living in *pensions*, trailing round with second-rate professionals. I get that idea, at least. Am I right?"

"She's frightfully bohemian, of course," said Esther. "Yes, that's what I did mean."

"But she's not young, you know," said Choate, in an indulgent kindliness Esther was quite sure he kept for her alone. "She won't be very rackety. People don't want the same things after they're sixty."

"She smokes," said Esther, in a burst of confidence. "She did years ago when nice women weren't doing it."

He smiled at this, but tenderly. He didn't leave Addington very often, but he did know what a blaze the vestals of the time keep up.

"No matter," said he, "so long as you don't."

"She drinks brandy," said Esther, "and tells things. I can't repeat what she tells. She's different from anybody I ever met—and I don't see how I can make her happy."

By this time Choate saw there was nothing he could do about Aunt Patricia, and dismissed her from his orderly mind. She was not absolutely pertinent to Esther's happiness. But he looked grave. There was somebody, he knew, who was pertinent.

"I haven't succeeded in seeing Jeff yet," he began, with a slight hesitation. It seemed to him it might be easier for her to hear that name than the formal words, "your husband". She winced. Choate saw it and pitied her, as she knew he would. "Is he coming—here?"

She looked at him with large, imploring eyes.

"Must I?" he heard her whispering, it seemed really to herself.

"I don't see how you can help it, dear," he answered. The last word surprised him mightily. He had never called her "dear". She hadn't even been "Esther" to him. But the warmth of his compassion and an irritation that had been working in him with Jeff's return—something like jealousy, it might even be—drove the little word out of doors and bade it lodge with her and so betray him. Esther heard the word quite clearly and knew what volumes of commentary it carried; but Choate, relieved, thought it had passed her by. She was still beseeching him, even caressing him, with the liquid eyes.

"You see," she said, "he and I are strangers—almost. He's been away so long."

"You haven't seen him," said Choate, like an accusation. He had often had to bruise that snake. He hoped she'd step on it for good.

"No," said Esther. "He didn't wish it."

Choate's sane sense told him that no man could fail to wish it. If Jeff had forbidden her to come at the intervals when he could see his kin, she should have battered down his denials and gone to him. She should have left on his face the warm touch of hers and the cleansing of her tears. Choate had a tremendous idea of the obligations of what he called love. He hid what he thought of it in the fastnesses of a shy heart, but he took delight and found strength, too, in the certainty that there is unconquerable love, and that it laughs at even the locksmiths that fasten prison doors. He knew what a pang it would have been to him if he had seen Esther Blake going year after year to carry her hoarded sweetness to another man. But he wished she had done it. Some hardy, righteous fibre in him would have been appeased.

"He's happier away from me," said Esther, shaking her head. "His father understands him. I don't. Why, before he went away we weren't so very happy. Didn't you know that?"

Choate was glad and sorry.

"Weren't you?" he responded. "Poor child!"

"No. We'd begun to be strangers, in a way. And it's gone on and on, and of course we're really strangers now."

The Esther she meant to be gave her a sharp little prick here—that Esther seemed to carry a needle for the purpose of these occasional pricks, though she used it less and less as time went on—and said to her, "Strangers before he went away? Oh, no! I'd like to think that. It makes the web we're spinning stronger. But I can't. No. That isn't true."

"So you see," said the real Esther to Choate, "I can't do anything. I sit here alone with my hands tied, and grandma upstairs—of course I can't leave grandma—and I can't do anything. Do you think—" she looked very challenging and pure—"do you think it would be wicked of me to dream of a divorce?"

Choate got up and walked to the fireplace. He put both hands on the mantel and gripped it, and Esther, with that sense of implacable mastery women feel at moments of sexual triumph, saw the knuckles whiten.

"Wouldn't it be better," she said, "for him? I don't care for myself, though I'm very lonely, very much at sea; but it does seem to me it would be better for him if he could be free and build his life up again from the beginning."

Choate answered in a choked voice that made him shake his head impatiently:

"It isn't better for any man to be free."

"Not if he doesn't care for his wife?" the master torturer proceeded, more and more at ease now she saw how tight she had him.

Choate turned upon her. His pale face was scarred with an emotion as deep as the source of tears, though she exulted to see he had no tears to show her. Men should, she felt, be strong.

"Don't you know you mustn't say that kind of thing to me?" he asked her. "Don't you see it's a temptation? I can't listen to it. I can't consider it for a minute."

"Is it a temptation?" she asked, in a whisper, born, it seemed, of unacknowledged intimacies between them. The whisper said, "If it is a temptation, it is not a temptation to you alone."

Choate was not looking at her, but he saw her, with the eyes of the mind: the brown limpid look, the uplift of her quivering face, the curve of her throat and the long ripple to her feet. He walked out of the room; it was the only thing for a decent man to do, in the face of incarnate appeal, challenge, a vitality so intense, and yet so unconscious of itself, he knew, that it was, in its purity, almost irresistible. In the street he was deaf to the call of a friend and passed another without seeing him. They chaffed him about it afterward. He was, they told him, thinking of a case.

Esther went about the house in an exhilarated lightness. She sang a little, in a formless way. She could not manage a tune, but she had a rhythmic style of humming that was not unpleasant to hear and gave her occasional outlet. It was the animal in the desert droning and purring to itself in excess of ease. She felt equal to meeting Aunt Patricia even.

About dusk Aunt Patricia came in the mediæval cab with Denny driving. There was no luggage. Esther hoped a great deal from that. But it proved there was too much to come by cab, and Denny brought it afterward, shabby trunks of a sophisticated look, spattered with labels. Madame Beattie alighted from the cab, a large woman in worn black velvet, with a stale perfume about her. Esther was at the door to meet her, and even in this outer air she could hardly help putting up her nose a little at the exotic smell. Madame Beattie was swarthy and strong-featured with a soft wrinkled skin unnatural from over-cherishing. She had bright, humorously satirical eyes; and her mouth was large. Therefore you were surprised at her slight lisp, a curious childishness which Esther had always considered pure affectation. She had forgotten it in these later years, but now the sound of it awakened all the distaste and curiosity she had felt of old. She had always believed if Aunt Patricia spoke out, the lisp would go. The voice underneath the lisp was a sad thing when you remembered it had once been "golden ". It was raucous yet husky, a gin voice, Jeffrey had called it, adding that she had a gin cough. All this Esther remembered as she went forward prettily and submitted to Aunt Patricia's perfumed kiss. The ostrich feathers in the worn velvet travelling hat cascaded over them both, and bangles clinked in a thin discord with curious trinkets hanging from her chatelaine. Evidently the desire to hold her niece in her arms had been for telegraphic purposes only.

When they had gone in and Aunt Patricia was removing her gloves and accepting tea—she said she would not take her hat off until she went upstairs—she asked, with a cheerful boldness:

"Where's your husband?"

Esther shrank perceptibly. No one but Lydia had felt at liberty to pelt her with the incarcerated husband, and she was not only sensitive in fact but from an intuition of the prettiest thing to do.

"Oh, I knew he was out," said Madame Beattie. "I keep track of your American papers. Isn't he here?"

"He's in town," said Esther, in a low voice. Her cheeks burned with hatred of the insolence of kin which could force you into the open and strip you naked.

"Where?"

"With his father."

"Does his father live alone?"

"No. He has step-daughters."

"Children of that woman that married him out of hand when he was over sixty? Ridiculous business! Well, what's Jeff there for? Why isn't he with you?"

Madame Beattie had a direct habit of address, and, although she spoke many other languages fluently, in the best of English. There were times when she used English with an extreme of her lisping accent, but that was when it seemed good business so to do. This she modified if she found herself cruising where New England standards called for plain New England speech.

"Why isn't he with you?" she asked again.

The tea had come and Madame Beattie lifted her cup in a manner elegantly calculated to display, though ingenuously, a hand loaded with rings.

"Dear auntie," said Esther, widening eyes that had been potent with Alston Choate but would do slight execution among a feminine contingent, "Jeffrey wouldn't be happy with me."

"Nonsense," said Aunt Patricia, herself taking the teapot and strengthening her cup. "What do you mean by happy?"

"He is completely estranged," said Esther. "He is a different man from what he used to be."

"Of course he's different. You're different. So am I. He can't take up things where he left them, but he's got to take them up somewhere. What's he going to do?"

"I don't know," said Esther. She drank her tea nervously. It seemed to her she needed a vivifying draught. "Auntie, you don't quite understand. We are divorced in every sense."

That sounded complete, and she hoped for some slight change of position on the part of the inquisitor.

"Of course you went to see him while he was in prison?" auntie pursued inexorably.

"No," said Esther, in a voice thrillingly sweet. "He didn't wish it."

Auntie helped herself to tea. Esther made a mental note that an extra quantity must be brewed next time.

"You see," said Madame Beattie, putting her cup down and settling back into her chair with an undue prominence of frontal velvet, "you have to take these things like a woman of the world. What's all this talk about feelings, and Jeff's being unhappy and happy? He's married you, and it's a good thing for you both you've got each other to turn to. This kind of sentimental talk does very well before marriage. It has its place. You'd never marry without it. But after the first you might as well take things as they come. There was my husband. I bore everything from him. Then I kicked over the traces and he bore everything from me. But when we found everybody was doing us and we should be a great deal stronger together than apart, we came together again. And he died very happily."

Esther thought, in her physical aversion to auntie, that he must indeed have been happy in the only escape left open to him.

"Where is Susan?" auntie inquired, after a brief interlude of coughing. It could never be known whether her coughs were real. She had little dry coughs of doubt, of derision, of good-natured tolerance; but perhaps she herself couldn't have said now whether they had their origin in any disability.

"Grandma is in her room," said Esther faintly. She felt a savage distaste for facing the prospect of them together, auntie who would be sure to see grandmother, and grandmother who would not be seen. "She lies in bed."

"All the time?"

"Yes."

"Not all the time!"

"Why, yes, auntie, she lies in bed all the time."

"What for? Is she crippled, or paralysed or what?"

"She says she is old."

"Old? Susan is seventy-six. She's a fool. Doesn't she know you don't have to give up your faculties at all unless you stop using them?"

"She says she is old," repeated Esther obstinately. It seemed to her a sensible thing for grandmother to say. Being old kept her happily in retirement. She wished auntie had a similar recognition of decencies.

"I'll go to my room now," said Madame Beattie. "What a nice house! This is Susan's house, isn't it?"

"Yes." Esther had now retired to the last defences. She saw auntie settling upon them in a jovial ease. It might have been different, she thought, if Alston Choate had got her a divorce years ago and then married her.

"Come," she said, with an undiminished sweetness, "I'll take you to your room."

VIII

Addington, so Jeffrey Blake remembered when he came home to it, was a survival. Naïve constancies to custom, habits sprung out of old conditions and logical no more, and even the cruder loyalties to the past, lived in it unchanged. This was as his mind conceived it. His roots had gone deeper here than he knew while he was still a part of it, a free citizen. The first months of his married life had been spent here, but as his prosperity burned the more brilliantly, he and Esther had taken up city life in winter, and for the summer had bought a large and perfectly equipped house in a colony at the shore. That, in the crash of his fortunes, had gone with other wreckage, and now he never thought of it with even a momentary regret. It belonged to that fevered time when he was always going fast and faster, as if life were a perpetual speeding in a lightning car. But of Addington he did think, in the years that were so much drear space for reflection, and though he felt no desire to go back, the memory of it was cool and still. The town had distinct social strata, the happier, he felt, in that. There were the descendants of old shipbuilders and merchants who drew their sufficient dividends and lived on the traditions of times long past. All these families knew and accepted one another. Their peculiarities were no more to be questioned than the eccentric shapes of clouds. The Daytons, who were phenomenally ugly in a bony way, were the Daytons. Their long noses with the bulb at the base were Dayton noses. The Madisons, in the line of male descent from distinguished blood, drank to an appalling extent; but they were Madisons, and you didn't interdict your daughters' marrying them. The Mastertons ate no meat, and didn't believe in banks. They kept their money in queer corners, and there was so much of it that they couldn't always remember where, and the laundress had orders to turn all stockings before wetting, and did indeed often find bills in the toe. But the laundress, being also of Addington, though of another stratum, recognised this as a Masterton habit, and faithfully sought their hoarded treasure for them, and delivered it over with the accuracy of an accountant. She wouldn't have seen how the Mastertons could help having money in their clothes unless they should cease being Mastertons. Nor was it amazing to their peers, meeting them in casual talk, to realise that they were walking depositories of coin and bills. A bandit on a lonely road would, if he were born in Addington, have forborne to rob them. These and other personal eccentricities Jeffrey Blake remembered and knew he should find them ticking on like faithful clocks. It was all restful to recall, but horrible to meet. He knew perfectly what the attitude of Addington would be to him. Because he was Addington born, it would stand by him, and with a double loyalty for his father's sake. That loyalty, beautiful or stupid as you might find it, he could not bear. He hoped, however, to escape it by making his father the briefest visit possible and then getting off to the West. Anne had reminded him that Alston Choate had called, and he had commented briefly:

"Oh! he's a good old boy."

But she saw, with her keen eyes gifted to read the heart, that he was glad he had not seen him. The first really embarrassing caller came the forenoon after Madame Beattie had arrived at Esther's, Madame Beattie herself in the village hack with Denny, uncontrollably curious, on the box. Madame Beattie paid twenty-five cents extracted from the tinkling chatelaine, and dismissed Denny, but he looked over his shoulder regretfully until he had rounded the curve of the drive. Meantime she, in her plumes and black velvet, was climbing the steps, and Jeffrey, who was on the side veranda, heard her and took down his feet from the rail, preparatory to flight. But she was aware of him, and stepped briskly round the corner. Before he reached the door she was on him.

"Here, Jeff, here!" said she peremptorily and yet kindly, as you might detain a dog, and Jeff, pausing, gazed at her in frank disconcertment and remarked as frankly:

"The devil!"

Madame Beattie threw back her head on its stout muscular neck and laughed, a husky laugh much like an old man's wheeze.

"No! no!" said she, approaching him and extending an ungloved hand, "not so bad as that. How are you? Tell its auntie."

Jeffrey laughed. He took the hand for a brief grasp, and returned to the group of chairs, where he found a comfortable rocker for her.

"How in the deuce," said he, "did you get here so quick?"

Madame Beattie rejected the rocker and took a straight chair that kept her affluence of curves in better poise.

"Quick after what?" she inquired, with a perfect good-nature.

Jeffrey had seated himself on the rail, his hands, too, resting on it, and he regarded her with a queer terrified amusement, as if, in research, he had dug up a strange object he had no use for and might find it difficult to place. Not to name: he could name her very accurately.

"So quick after I got here," he replied, with candour. "I tell you plainly, Madame Beattie, there isn't a cent to be got out of me. I'm done, broke, down and out."

Madame Beattie regarded him with an unimpaired good-humour.

"Bless you, Jeff," said she, "I know that. What are you going to do, now you're out?"

The question came as hard as a stroke after the cushioned assurance preceding it. Jeff met it as he might have met such a query from a man to whom he owed no veilings of hard facts.

"I don't know," said he. "If I did know I shouldn't tell you."

Madame Beattie seemed not to suspect the possibility of rebuff.

"Esther hasn't changed a particle," said she.

Jeff scowled, not at her, but absently at the side of the house, and made no answer.

"Aren't you coming down there?" asked Madame Beattie peremptorily, with the air of drumming him up to some task that would have to be reckoned with in the end. "Come, Jeff, why don't you answer? Aren't you coming down?"

Jeffrey had ceased scowling. He had smoothed his brows out with his hand, indeed, as if their tenseness hurt him.

"Look here," said he, "you ask a lot of questions."

She laughed again, a different sort of old laugh, a fat and throaty one.

"Did I ever tell you," said she, "what the Russian grand duke said when I asked him why he didn't marry?"

"No," said Jeff, quite peaceably now. She was safer in the company of remembered royalties.

Madame Beattie sought among the jingling decorations of her person for a cigarette, found it and offered him another.

"Quite good," she told him. "An Italian count keeps me supplied. I don't know where the creature gets them."

Then, after they had lighted up, she returned to her grand duke, and Jeff found the story sufficiently funny and laughed at it, and she pulled another out of her well-stored memory, and he laughed at that. Madame Beattie told her stories excellently. She knew how little weight they carry smothered in feminine graces and coy obliquities from the point. Graces had long ceased to interest her as among the assets of a life where man and woman have to work to feed themselves. Now she sat down with her brother man and emulated him in ready give and take. Jeffrey forsook the rail which had subtly marked his distance from her; he took a chair, and put his feet up on the rail. Madame Beattie's neatly shod and very small feet went up on a chair, and she tipped the one she was sitting in at a dangerous angle while she exhaled luxuriously, and so Lydia, coming round the corner in a simple curiosity to know who was there, found them, laughing uproariously and dim with smoke. Lydia had her opinions about smoking. She had seen women indulge in it at some of the functions where she and Anne danced, but she had never found a woman of this stamp doing it with precisely this air. Indeed, Lydia had never seen a woman of Madame Beattie's stamp in her whole life. She stopped short, and the two could not at once get hold of themselves in their peal of accordant mirth. But Lydia had time to see one thing for a certainty. Jeff's face had cleared of its brooding and its intermittent scowl. He was enjoying himself. This, she thought, in a sudden rage of scorn, was the kind of thing he enjoyed: not Farvie, not Anne's gentle ministrations, but the hooting of a horrible old woman. Madame Beattie saw her and straightened some of the laughing wrinkles round her eyes.

"Well, well!" said she. "Who's this?"

Then Jeffrey, becoming suddenly grave, as if, Lydia thought, he ought to be ashamed of laughing in such company, sprang to his feet, and threw away his cigarette.

"Madame Beattie," said he, "this is Miss Lydia French."

Madame Beattie did not rise, as who, indeed, so plumed and black-velveted should for a slip of a creature trembling with futile rage over a brother proved wanting in ideals? She extended one hand, while the other removed the cigarette from her lips and held it at a becoming distance.

"And who's Miss Lydia French?" said she. Then, as Lydia, pink with embarrassment and disapproval, made no sign, she added peremptorily, "Come here, my dear."

Lydia came. It was true that Madame Beattie had attained to privilege through courts and high estate. When she herself had ruled by the prerogative of a perfect throat and a mind attuned to it, she had imbibed a sense of power which was still dividend-paying even now, though the throat was dead to melody. When she really asked you to do anything, you did it, that was all. She seldom asked now, because her attitude was all careless tolerance, keen to the main chance but lax in exacting smaller tribute, as one having had such greater toll. But Lydia's wilful hesitation awakened her to some slight curiosity, and she bade her the more commandingly. Lydia was standing before her, red, unwillingly civil, and Madame Beattie reached forward and took one of her little plump work-roughened hands, held it for a moment, as if in guarantee of kindliness, and then dropped it.

"Now," said she, "who are you?"

Jeffrey, seeing Lydia so put about, answered for her again, but this time in terms of a warmth which astonished him as it did Lydia.

"She is my sister Lydia."

Madame Beattie looked at him in a frank perplexity.

"Now," said she, "what do you mean by that? No, no, my dear, don't go." Lydia had turned by the slightest movement. "You haven't any sisters, Jeff. Oh, I remember. It was that romantic marriage." Lydia turned back now and looked straight at her, as if to imply if there were any qualifying of the marriage she had a word to say. "Wasn't there another child?" Madame Beattie continued, still to Jeff.

"Anne is in the house," said he.

He had placed a chair for Lydia, with a kindly solicitude, seeing how uncomfortable she was; but Lydia took no notice. Now she straightened slightly, and put her pretty head up. She looked again as she did when the music was about to begin, and her little feet, though they kept their decorous calm, were really beating time.

"Well, you're a pretty girl," said Madame Beattie, dropping her lorgnon. She had lifted it for a stare and taken in the whole rebellious figure. "Esther didn't tell me you were pretty. You know Esther, don't you?"

"No," said Lydia, in a wilful stubbornness; "I don't know her."

"You've seen her, haven't you?"

"Yes, I've seen her."

"You don't like her then?" said Madame astutely. "What's the matter with her?"

Something gave way in Lydia. The pressure of feeling was too great and candour seethed over the top.

"She's a horrid woman."

Or was it because some inner watchman on the tower told her Jeff himself had better hear again what one person thought of Esther? Madame Beattie threw back her plumed head and laughed, the same laugh she had used to annotate the stories. Lydia immediately hated herself for having challenged it. Jeffrey, she knew, was faintly smiling, though she could not guess his inner commentary:

"What a little devil!"

Madame Beattie now turned to him.

"Same old story, isn't it?" she stated. "Every woman of woman born is bound to hate her."

"Yes," said Jeff.

Lydia walked away, expecting, as she went, to be called back and resolving that no inherent power in the voice of aged hatefulness should force her. But Madame Beattie, having placed her, had forgotten all about her. She rose, and brushed the ashes from her velvet curves.

"Come," she was saying to Jeffrey, "walk along with me."

He obediently picked up his hat.

"I sha'n't go home with you," said he, "if that's what you mean."

She took his arm and convoyed him down the steps, leaning wearily. She had long ago ceased to exercise happy control over useful muscles. They even creaked in her ears and did strange things when she made requests of them.

"You understand," said Jeffrey, when they were pursuing a slow way along the street, he with a chafed sense of ridiculous captivity. "I sha'n't go into the house. I won't even go to the door."

"Stuff!" said the lady. "You needn't tell me you don't want to see Esther."

Jeff didn't tell her that. He didn't tell her anything. He stolidly guided her along.

"There isn't a man born that wouldn't want to see Esther if he'd seen her once," said Madame Beattie.

But this he neither combated nor confirmed, and at the corner nearest Esther's house he stopped, lifted the hand from his arm and placed it in a stiff rigour at her waist. He then took off his hat, prepared to stand while she went on. And Madame Beattie laughed.

"You're a brute," said she pleasantly, "a dear, sweet brute. Well, you'll come to it. I shall tell Esther you love her so much you hate her, and she'll send out spies after you. Good-bye. If you don't come, I'll come again."

Jeffrey made no answer. He watched her retreating figure until it turned in at the gate, and then he wheeled abruptly and went back. An instinct of flight was on him. Here in the open street he longed for walls, only perhaps because he knew how well everybody wished him and their kindness he could not meet.

Madame Beattie found Esther at the door, waiting. She was an excited Esther, bright-eyed, short of breath.

"Where have you been?" she demanded.

Madame Beattie took off her hat and stabbed the pin through it. Her toupée, deranged by the act, perceptibly slid, but though she knew it by the feel, that eccentricity did not, in the company of a mere niece, trouble her at all. She sank into a chair and laid her hat on the neighbouring stand.

"Where have you been?" repeated Esther, a pulse of something like anger beating through the words.

Madame Beattie answered idly: "Up to see Jeff."

"I knew it!" Esther breathed.

"Of course," said Madame Beattie carelessly. "Jeff and I were quite friends in old times. I was glad I went. It cheered him up."

"Did he—" Esther paused.

"Ask for you?" supplied Madame Beattie pleasantly. "Not a word."

Here Esther's curiosity did whip her on. She had to ask:

"How does he look?"

"Oh, youngish," said Madame. "Rather flabby. Obstinate. Ugly, too."

"Ugly? Plain, do you mean?"

"No. American for ugly—obstinate, sore-headed. He's hardened. He was rather a silly boy, I remember. Had enthusiasms. Much in love. He isn't now. He's no use for women."

Esther looked at her in an arrested thoughtfulness. Madame Beattie could have laughed. She had delivered the challenge Jeff had not sent, and Esther was accepting it, wherever it might lead, to whatever duelling ground. Esther couldn't help that. A challenge was a challenge. She had to answer. It was a necessity of type. Madame Beattie saw the least little flickering thought run into her eyes, and knew she was involuntarily charting the means of summons, setting up the loom, as it were, to weave the magic web. She got up, took her hat, gave her toupée a little smack with the hand, and unhinged it worse than ever.

"You'll have to give him up," she said.

"Give him up!" flamed Esther. "Do you think I want—"

There she paused and Madame Beattie supplied temperately:

"No matter what you want. You couldn't have him."

Then she went toiling upstairs, her chained ornaments clinking, and only when she had shut the door upon herself did she relax and smile over the simplicity of even a feminine creature so versed in obliquity as Esther. For Esther might want to escape the man who had brought disgrace upon her, but her flying feet would do her no good, so long as the mainspring of her life set her heart beating irrationally for conquest. Esther had to conquer even when the event would bring disaster: like a chieftain who would enlarge his boundaries at the risk of taking in savages bound to sow the dragon's teeth.

IX

That evening the Blake house had the sound and look of social life, voices in conversational interchange and lights where Mary Nellen excitedly arrayed them. Alston Choate had come to call, and following him appeared an elderly lady whom Jeffrey greeted with more outward warmth than he had even shown his father. Alston Choate had walked in with a simple directness as though he were there daily, and Anne impulsively went forward to him. She felt she knew him very well. They were quite friends. Alston, smiling at her and taking her hand on the way to the colonel and Jeff, seemed to recognise that, and greeted her less formally than the others. The colonel was moved at seeing him. The Choates were among the best of local lineage, men and women distinguished by clear rigidities of conduct. Their friendship was a promissory note, bound to be honoured to the full. Lydia was for some reason abashed, and Jeff, both she and Anne thought, not adequately welcoming. But how could he be, Anne considered. He was in a position of unique loneliness. He lacked fellowship. Nobody but Alston, in their stratum at least, had come in person. No wonder he looked warily, lest he assume too much.

Before they settled down, the elderly lady, with a thud of feet softly shod, walked through the hall and stood at the library door regarding them benignantly. And then Jeff, with an outspoken sound of pleasure and surprise, got up and drew her in, and Choate smiled upon her as if she were delightfully unlike anybody else. The colonel, with a quick, moved look, just said her name:

"Amabel!"

She gave warm, quick grasps from a firm hand, gave them all round, not seeming to know she hadn't met Anne and Lydia, and at once took off her bonnet. It had strings and altogether belonged to an epoch at least twenty years away. The bonnet she "laid aside" on a table with a certain absent care, as ladies were accustomed to treat bonnets before they got into the way of jabbing them with pins. Then she sat down, earnestly solicitous and attentive as at a consultation. Anne thought she was the most beautiful person she had ever seen. It was a pity Miss Amabel Bracebridge could not have known that impetuous verdict. It would have brought her a surprised, spontaneous laugh: nothing could have convinced her it was not delicious foolery. She was tall and broad and heavy. When she stood in the doorway, she seemed to fill it. Now that she sat in the chair, she filled that, a soft, stout woman with great shoulders and a benign face, a troubled face, as if she were used to soothing ills, yet found for them no adequate recompense. Her dark grey dress was buttoned in front, after the fashion of a time long past. It was so archaic in cut, with a little ruffle at neck and sleeves, that it did more than adequate service toward maturing her. Indeed, there was no youth about Miss Amabel, except the youth of her eyes and smile. There were childlike wistfulness and hope, but experience chiefly, of life, of the unaccounted for, the unaccountable. She had, above all, an expression of well-wishing. Now she sat and looked about her.

"Dear me!" she said, "how pleasant it is to see this house open again."

"But it's been open," Lydia impulsively reminded her.

"Yes," said Miss Amabel. "But not this way." She turned to Jeff and regarded him anxiously. "Don't you smoke?" she asked.

He laughed again. He was exceedingly pleased, Anne saw, merely at seeing her. Miss Amabel was exactly as he remembered her.

"Yes," said he. "Want us to?"

She put up her long eyebrows and smiled as if in some amusement at herself.

"I've learned lately," she said, "that gentlemen are so devoted to it they feel lost without it."

"Light up, Choate," said Jeffrey. "My sisters won't mind. Will you?" He interrogated Anne. "They get along with me."

No, Anne didn't mind, and she rose and brought matches and little trays. Lydia often wondered how Anne knew the exact pattern of man's convenience. But though Choate accepted a cigar, he did not light it.

"Not now," he said, when Jeffrey offered him a light; he laid the cigar down, tapping it once or twice with his fine hand, and Anne thought he refrained in courtesy toward her and Lydia.

"This is very pleasant," said the colonel suddenly. "It's good to see you, Amabel. Now I feel myself at home."

But what, after the first settling was over, had they to say? The same thought was in all their minds. What was Jeffrey going to do? He knew that, and moved unhappily. Whatever he was going to do, he wouldn't talk about it. But Miss Amabel was approaching him with the clearest simplicity.

"Jeff, my dear," she said, "I can't wait to hear about your ideal republic."

And then, all his satisfaction gone and his scowl come back, Jeff shook his head as if a persistent fly had lighted on him, and again he disclaimed achievement.

"Amabel," said he, "I'm awfully sick of that, you know."

"But, dear boy, you revolutionised—" she was about to add, "the prison," but stumbled lamely—"the place."

"The papers told us that," said Choate. It was apparent he was helping somebody out, but whether Jeff or Miss Amabel even he couldn't have said.

"It isn't revolutionised," said Jeff. He turned upon Choate brusquely. "It's exactly the same."

"They say it's revolutionised," Miss Amabel offered anxiously.

"Who says so?" he countered, now turning on her.

"The papers," she told him. "You didn't write me about it. I asked you all sorts of questions and you wouldn't say a word."

"But you wrote me," said Jeff affectionately, "every week. I got so used to your letters I sha'n't be able to do without them; I shall have to see you every day."

"Of course we're going to see each other," she said. "And there's such a lot you can do."

She looked so earnestly entreating that Choate, who sat not far from her, gave a murmured: "Ah, Miss Amabel!" In his mind the half-despairing, wholly loving thought had been: "Good old girl! You're spending yourself and all your money, but it's no use—no use."

She was going on with a perfect clarity of purpose.

"Oh, you know, Jeff can do more for us than anybody else."

"What do you want done for you?" he inquired.

His habit of direct attack gave Lydia a shiver. She was sure people couldn't like it, and she was exceedingly anxious for him to be liked. Miss Amabel turned to Farvie.

"You see," she said, "Addington is waking up. I didn't dwell very much on it," she added, now to Jeff, "when I wrote you, because I thought you'd like best to think of it as it was. But now—"

"Now I'm out," said Jeff brutally, "you find me equal to it."

"I think," said Miss Amabel, "you can do so much for us." Nothing troubled her governed calm. It might almost be that, having looked from high places into deep ones, no abyss could dizzy her. "Weedon Moore feels as I do."

"Weedon Moore?" Jeffrey repeated, in a surprised and most uncordial tone. He looked at Choate.

"Yes," said Choate, as if he confirmed not only the question but Jeff's inner feeling, "he's here. He's practising law, and besides that he edits the *Argosy*."

"Owns it, too, I think," said Farvie. "They told me so at the news-stand."

"Well," said Choate pointedly, "it's said Miss Amabel owns it."

"Then," said Jeff, including her abruptly, "you've the whip-hand. You can get Moore out of it. What's he in it for anyway? Did you have to take him over with the business?"

Miss Amabel was plainly grieved.

"Now why should you want to turn him out of it?" she asked, really of Choate who had started the attack. "Mr. Moore is a very able young man, of the highest ideals."

Jeff laughed. It was a kindly laugh. Anne was again sure he loved Miss Amabel.

"I can't see Moore changing much after twenty-five," he said to Choate, who confirmed him briefly:

"Same old Weedie."

"Mr. Moore is not popular," said Miss Amabel, with dignity, turning now to Farvie. "He never has been, here in Addington. He comes of plain people."

"That's not it, Miss Amabel," said Choate gently. "He might have been spawned out of the back meadows or he might have been—a Bracebridge." He bowed to her with a charming conciliation and Miss Amabel sat a little straighter. "If we don't accept him, it's because he's Weedon Moore."

"We were in school with him, you know: in college, too," said Jeff, with that gentleness men always accorded her, men of perception who saw in her the motherhood destined to diffuse itself, often to no end: she was so noble and at the same time so helpless in the crystal prison of her hopes. "We knew Weedie like a book."

Miss Amabel took on an added dignity, proportioned to the discomfort of her task. Here she was defending Weedon Moore whom her outer sensibilities rejected the while his labelled virtues moved her soul.

Sometimes when she found herself with people like these to-night, manifestly her own kind, she was tired of being good.

"I don't know any one," said she, "who feels the prevailing unrest more keenly than Weedon Moore."

At that instant, Mary Nellen, her eyes brightening as these social activities increased, appeared in the doorway, announcing doubtfully:

"Mr. Moore."

Jeffrey, as if actually startled, looked round at Choate who was unaffectedly annoyed. Anne, rising to receive the problematic Moore, thought they had an air of wondering how they could repel unwarranted invasion. Miss Amabel, in a sort of protesting, delicate distress, was loyally striving to make the invader's path plain.

"I told him I was coming," she said. "It seems he had thought of dropping in." Then Anne went out on the heels of Mary Nellen, hearing Miss Amabel conclude, as she left, with an apologetic note unfamiliar to her soft voice, "He wants you to write something, Jeff, for the *Argosy*."

Anne, even before seeing him, became conscious that Mary Nellen regarded the newcomer as undesirable; and when she came on him standing, hat in hand, she agreed that Weedon Moore was, in his outward integument, exceedingly unpleasant: a short, swarthy, tubby man, always, she was to note, dressed in smooth black, and invariably wearing or carrying, with the gravity of a funeral mourner, what Addington knew as a "tall hat". When the weather gave him countenance, he wore a black coat with a cape. One flashing ring adorned his left hand, and he indulged a barbaric taste in flowing ties. Seeing Anne, he spoke at once, and if she had not been prepared for him she must have guessed him to be a man come on a message of importance. There was conscious emphasis in his voice, and there needed to be if it was to accomplish anything: a high voice, strident, and, like the rest of him, somehow suggesting insect life. He held out his hand and Anne most unwillingly took it.

"Miss French," said he, with no hesitation before her name, "how is Jeff?"

The mere inquiry set Anne vainly to hoping that he need not come in. But he gave no quarter.

"I said I'd run over to-night, paper or no paper. I'm frightfully busy, you know, cruelly, abominably busy. But I just wanted to see Jeff."

"Won't you come in?" said Anne.

Even then he did not abandon his hat. He kept his hold on it, bearing it before him in a way that made Anne think absurdly of shields and bucklers.

When, in the library, she turned to present him, as if he were an unpleasant find she had got to vouch for somehow, the men were already on their feet and Jeff was setting forward a chair. She could not help thinking it was a clever stage business to release him from the necessity of shaking hands. But Moore did not abet him in that informality. His small hand was out, and he was saying in a sharp, strained voice, exactly as if he were making a point of some kind, an oratorical point:

"Jeff, my dear fellow! I'm tremendously glad to see you."

Anne thought Jeff might not shake hands with him at all. But she saw him steal a shamefaced look at Miss Amabel and immediately, as if something radical had to be done when it came to the friend of a beloved old girl like her, strike his hand into Moore's, with an emphasis the more pronounced for his haste to get it over. Moore seemed enraptured at the handshake and breathless over the occasion. Having begun shaking hands he kept on with enthusiasm: the colonel, Miss Amabel and Lydia had to respond to an almost fervid greeting.

Only Choate proved immune. He had vouchsafed a cool: "How are you, Weedie?" when Moore began, and that seemed all Moore was likely to expect. Then they all sat down and there was, Lydia decided, as she glanced from one to another, no more pleasure in it. There was talk. Moore chatted so exuberantly, his little hands upon his fattish knees, that he seemed to squeeze sociability out of himself in a rapture of generous willingness to share all he had. He asked the colonel how he liked Addington, and was not abashed at being reminded that the colonel had known Addington for a good many years.

"Still it's changed," said Moore, regarding him almost archly. "Addington isn't the place it was even a year ago."

"I hope we've learned something," said Miss Amabel earnestly and yet prettily too.

"My theory of Addington," said Choate easily, "is that we all wish we were back in the Addington of a hundred years ago."

"You'd want to be in the dominant class," said Moore. There was something like the trammels of an unwilling respect over his manner to Choate; yet still he managed to be rallying. "When the old merchants were coming home with china and bales of silk and Paris shoes for madam. And think of it," said he, raising his sparse eyebrows and looking like a marionette moulded to express something and saying it with painful clumsiness, almost grotesquerie, "the ships are bringing human products now. They're bringing us citizens, bone and sinew of the republic, and we cry back to china and bales of silk."

"I didn't answer you, Moore," said Choate, turning to him and speaking, Lydia thought, with the slightest arrogance. "I should have wanted to belong to the governing class—of course."

"Now!" said Miss Amabel. She spoke gently, and she was, they saw, pained at the turn the talk had taken. "Alston, why should you say that?"

"Because I mean it," said Alston. His quietude seemed to carry a private message to Moore, but he turned to her, as he spoke and smiled as if to ask her not to interpret him harshly. "Of course I should have wanted to be in the dominant class. So does everybody, really."

"No, my dear," said Miss Amabel.

"No," agreed Choate, "you don't. The others like you didn't. I won't embarrass you by naming them. You want to sit submerged, you others, and be choked by slime, if you must be, and have the holy city built up on your shoulders. But the rest of us don't. Moore here doesn't, do you, Weedie?"

Weedon gave a quick embarrassed laugh.

"You're so droll," said he.

"No," said Choate quietly, "I'm not being droll. Of course I want to belong to the dominant class. So does the man that never dominated in his life. He wants to overthrow the over-lords so he can rule himself. He wants to crowd me so he can push into a place beside me."

Moore laughed with an overdone enjoyment.

"Excellent," he said, squeezing the words out of his knees. "You're such a humourist."

If he wanted to be offensive, that was the keenest cut he could have delivered.

"I have often thought," said the colonel, beginning in a hesitating, deferent way that made his utterance rather notable, "that we saddle what we call the lower orders with motives different from our own."

"Precisely," Choate clipped in. "We used to think, when they committed a perfectly logical crime, like stealing a sheep or a loaf of bread, that it was absolutely different from anything we could have done. Whereas in their places we should have tried precisely the same thing. Just as cleanliness is a matter of bathtubs and temperature. We shouldn't bathe if we had to break the ice over a quart of water and then go out and run a trolley car all day."

Lydia's face, its large eyes fixed upon him, said so plainly "I don't believe it" that he laughed, with a sudden enjoyment of her, and, after an instant of wider-eyed surprise, she laughed too.

"And here's Miss Amabel," Choate went on, in the voice it seemed he kept for her, "going to the outer extreme and believing, because the labouring man has been bled, that he's incapable of bleeding you. Don't you think it, Miss Amabel. He's precisely like the rest of us. Like me. Like Weedon here. He'll sit up on his platform and judge me like forty thousand prophets out of Israel; but put him where I am and he'll cling with his eyelids and stick there. Just as I shall."

Miss Amabel looked deeply troubled and also at a loss.

"I only think, Alston," she said, "that so much insight, so much of the deepest knowledge comes of pain. And the poor have suffered pain so many centuries. They've learned things we don't know. Look how they help one another. Look at their self-sacrifice."

"Look at your own self-sacrifice," said Choate.

"Oh, but they know," said she. The flame of a great desire was in her face. "I don't know what it is to be hungry. If I starved myself I shouldn't know, because in somebody's pantry would be the bread-box I could put my hand into. They know, Alston. It gives them insight. When they remember the road they've travelled, they're not going to make the mistakes we've made."

"Oh, yes, they are," said Choate. "Pardon me. There are going to be robbers and pirates and Napoleons and get-rich-quicks born for quite a while yet. And they're not going to be born in my class alone—nor Weedon's."

Weedon squirmed at this, and even Jeff thought it rather a nasty cut. But Jeff did not know yet how well Choate knew Weedon in the ways of men. And Weedon accepted no rebuff. He turned to Jeff, distinctly leaving Choate as one who would have his little pleasantries.

"Jeff," he said, "I want you to do something for the *Argosy*."

Jeff at once knew what.

"Queer," he said, "how you all think I've got copy out of jail."

Anne resented the word. It was not jail, she thought, a federal prison where gentlemen, when they have done wrong or been, like Jeff, falsely accused, may go with dignity.

"My dear," said Miss Amabel, in a manner at once all compassion and inexorable demand, "you've got so much to tell us. You men in that—

place," she stumbled over the word and then accepted it—"discussed the ideal republic. You made it, by discussing it."

"Yes," said Choate, in voice of curious circumspection as if he hardly knew what form even of eulogy might hurt, "it was an astonishing piece of business. You can't expect people not to notice a thing like that."

"I can't help it," said Jeff. "I don't want such a row made over it."

Whether the thing was too intimate, too near his heart still beating sluggishly it might be, from prison air, could not be seen. But Miss Amabel, exquisitely compassionate, was yet inexorable, because he had something to give and must not withhold.

"The wonderful part of it is," she said, "that when you have built up your ideal government, prison ceases to be prison. There won't be punishment any more."

"Oh, don't you make that mistake," said Jeff, instantly, moved now too vitally to keep out of it. "There are going to be punishments all along the line. The big punishment of all, when you've broken a law, is that you're outside. If it's a small break, you're not much over the sill. If it's a big break, you're absolutely out. Outside, Amabel, outside!" He never used the civil prefix before her name, and Anne wondered again whether the intimacy of the letters accounted for this sweet informality. "You're banished. What's worse than that?"

"Oh, but," said she, her plain, beautiful face beaming divinity on him as one of the children of men, "I don't want them to be banished. If anybody has sinned—has broken the law—I want him to be educated. That's all."

"Look here," said Jeff, He bent forward to her and laid the finger of one trade-stained hand in the other palm. "You're emasculating the whole nation. Let us be educated, but let us take our good hard whacks."

"Hear! hear!" said Choate, speaking mildly but yet as a lawyer, who spent his life in presenting liabilities for or against punishment. "That's hot stuff."

"I believe in law," said Jeff rapidly. "Sometimes I think that's all I believe in now."

Anne and Lydia looked at him in a breathless waiting upon his words. He had begun to justify himself to their crescent belief in him, the product of the years. His father also waited, but tremulously. Here was the boy he had wanted back, but he had not so very much strength to accord even a fulfilled delight. Jeff, forgetful of everybody but the old sybil he was looking at, sure of her comprehension if not her agreement, went on.

"I'd rather have bad laws than no laws. I believe in Sparta. I believe in the Catholic Church, if only because it has fasts and penances. We've got to toe the mark. If we don't, something's got to give it to us good and hard, the harder the better, too. Are we children to be let off from the consequences of what we've done? No, by God! We're men and we've got to learn."

Suddenly his eyes left Miss Amabel's quickened face and he glanced about him, aware of the startled tensity of gaze among the others. Moore, with a little book on his knee, was writing rapidly.

"Notes?" Jeff asked him shortly. "No, you don't."

He got up and extended his hand for the book, and Moore helplessly, after a look at Miss Amabel, as if to ask whether she meant to see him bullied, delivered it. Jeff whirled back two leaves, tore them out, crumpled them in his hand and tossed them into the fireplace.

"You can't do that, Moore," he said indifferently, and Choate murmured a monosyllabic assent.

Moore never questioned the bullying he so prodigally got. He never had at college even; he was as ready to fawn the next day. It seemed as if the inner man were small, too small for sound resentment. Jeff sat down again. He looked depressed, his countenance without inward light. But Lydia and Anne had rediscovered him. Again he was their hero, reclothed indeed in finer mail. Miss Amabel rose at once. She shook hands with the colonel, and asked Anne and Lydia to come to see her.

"Don't you do something, you two girls?" she asked, with her inviting smile. "I'm sure Jeff wrote me so."

"We dance," said Lydia, in a bubbling bright voice, as if she had run forward to be sure to get the chance of answering. "Let us come and dance for you. We can dance all sorts of things."

And Lydia was so purely childlike and dear, after this talk of punishments and duties, that involuntarily they all laughed and she looked abashed.

"Perhaps you know folk-dances," said Miss Amabel.

"Oh, yes," said Lydia, getting back her spirit. "There isn't one we don't know."

And they laughed again and Miss Amabel tied on her bonnet and went away attended by Choate, with Weedon Moore a pace behind, holding his hat, until he got out of the house, as it might be at a grotesque funeral.

Miss Amabel had called back to Lydia:

"You must come and train my classes in their national dancing."

Lydia, behind the colonel and Jeff as they stood at the front door, seized Anne's hand and did a few ecstatic little steps.

The colonel was bright-eyed and satisfied with his evening. "Jeff," said he, before they turned to separate, "I always thought you were meant for a writer."

Jeff looked at him in a dull denial, as if he wondered how any man, life being what it is, could seek to bound the lot of another man. His face, flushed darkly, was seamed with feeling.

"Father," said he, in a voice of mysterious reproach, "I don't know what I was meant to be."

X

It was Lydia who found out what Jeff meant himself to be, for the next day, in course of helping Mary Nellen, she went to his door with towels. Mr. Jeffrey had gone out, Mary Nellen said. She had seen him spading in the orchard, and if Miss Lydia wanted to carry up the towels! there was the dusting, too. Lydia, at the open door, stopped, for Jeff was sitting at his writing table, paper before him. He flicked a look at her, absently, as at an intruder as insignificant as undesired, and because the sacredness of his task was plain to her she took it humbly. But Jeff, then actually seeing her, rose and put down his pen.

"I'll take those," he said.

It troubled him vaguely to find her and Anne doing tasks. He had a worried sense that he and the colonel were living on their kind offices, and he felt like assuring Lydia she shouldn't carry towels about for either of them long. Then, as she did not yield them but looked, housekeeper-wise, at the rack still loaded with its tumbled reserves, he added:

"Give them here."

"You mustn't leave your writing," said Lydia primly if shyly, and delivered up her charge.

Jeff stepped out after her into the hall. He had left dull issues at his table, and Lydia seemed very sweet, her faith in him chiefly, though he didn't want any more of it.

"Don't worry about my writing," said he.

"Oh, no," she answered, turning on him the clarity of her glance. "I shouldn't. Authors never want it talked about."

"That's not it," said he. She found him tremendously in earnest. "I'm not an author."

"But you will be when this is written."

"I don't know," he said, "how I can make you see. The whole thing is so foreign to your ideas about books and life. It only happened that I met a man—in there—" he hesitated over it, not as regarding delicacies but only as they might affect her—"a man like a million others, some of 'em in prison, more that ought to be. Well, he talked to me. I saw what brought him where he was. It was picturesque."

"You want other people to understand," said Lydia, bright-eyed, now she was following him. "For—a warning."

His frown was heavy. Now he was trying to follow her.

"No," he said, "you're off there. I don't take things that way. But I did see it so plain I wanted everybody to see it, too. Maybe that was why I did want to write it down. Maybe I wanted to write it for myself, so I should see it plainer. It fascinated me."

Lydia felt a helpless yearning, because things were being so hard for him. She wished for Anne who always knew, and with a word could help you out when your elucidation failed.

"You see," Jeff was going on, "there's this kind of a brute born into the world now, the kind that knows how to make money, and as soon as he's discovered his knack, he's got the mania to make more. It's an obligation, an obsession. Maybe it's only the game. He's in it, just as much as if he'd got a thousand men behind him, all looting territory. It might be for a woman. But it's the game. And it's a queer game. It cuts him off. He's outside."

And here Lydia had a simple and very childlike thought, so inevitable to her that she spoke without consideration.

"You were outside, too."

Jeff gave a little shake of the head, as if that didn't matter now he was here and explaining to her.

"And the devil of it is, after they're once outside they don't know they are."

"Do you mean, when they've done something and been found guilty and—"

"I mean all along the line. When they've begun to think they'll make good, when they've begun to play the game."

"For money?"

"Yes, for money, for pretty gold and dirty bills and silver. That's what it amounts to, when you get down to it, behind all the bank balances and equities. There's a film that grows over your eyes, you look at nothing else. You don't think about—" his voice dropped and he glanced out at the walled orchard as if it were even a sacred place—"you don't think about grass, and dirt, and things. You're thinking about the game."

"Well," said Lydia joyously, seeing a green pathway out, "now you've found it's so, you don't need to think about it any more."

"That's precisely it," said he heavily. "I've got to think about it all the time. I've got to make good."

"In the same way?" said Lydia, looking up at him childishly. "With money?"

"Yes," said he, "with money. It's all I know. And without capital, too. And I'm going to keep my head, and do it within the law. Yes, by God! within the law. But I hate to do it. I hate it like the devil."

He looked so hard with resolution that she took the resolution for pride, though she could not know whether it was a fine pride or a heaven-defying one.

"You won't do just what you did before?" asserted Lydia, out of her faith in him.

"Oh, yes, I shall."

She opened terrified eyes upon him.

"Be a promoter?"

"I don't know what I shall be. But I know the money game, and I shall have to play it and make good."

She ventured a question touching on the fancies that were in her mind, part of the bewildering drama that might attend on his return. She faltered it out. It seemed too splendid really to assault fortune like that. And yet perhaps not too splendid for him. This was the question.

"And pay back—" There she hesitated, and he finished for her.

"The money I lost in a hole? Well, we'll see." This last sounded indulgent, as if he might add, "little sister ".

Lydia plucked up spirit.

"There's something else I hoped you'd do first."

"What is it?"

"I want you to prove you're innocent."

She found herself breathless over the words. They brought her very near him, and after all she was not sure what kind of brother he was, save that he had to be supremely loved. He looked pale to her now, of a yellowed, unhappy hue, and he was staring at her fixedly.

"Innocent!" he repeated. "What do you mean by innocent?"

Lydia took heart again, since he really did invite her on.

"Why, of course," she said, "we all know—Farvie and Anne and I—we know you never did it."

"Did what?"

"Lost all that money. Took it away from people."

The softness of her voice was moving to him. He saw she meant him very well indeed.

"Lydia," said he, "I lost the money. Don't make any mistake about that."

"Yes, you were a promoter," she reminded him. "You were trying to get something on the market." She seemed to be assuring him, in an agonised way, of his own good faith. "And people bought shares. And you took their money. And—" her voice broke here in a sob of irrepressible sympathy— "and you lost it."

"Yes," said he patiently. "I found myself in a tight place and the unexpected happened—the inconceivable. The market went to pieces. And of course it was at the minute I was asked to account for the funds I had. I couldn't. So I was a swindler. I was tried. I was sentenced, and I went to prison. That's all."

"Oh," said Lydia passionately, "but do you suppose we don't know you're not the only person concerned? Don't you suppose we know there's somebody else to blame?"

Jeff turned on her a sudden look so like passion of a sort that she trembled back from him. Why should he be angry with her? Did he stand by Reardon to that extent?

"What do you mean?" he asked her. "Who's been talking to you?"

"We've all been talking," said Lydia, with a frank simplicity, "Farvie and Anne and I. Of course we've talked. Especially Anne and I. We knew you weren't to blame."

Jeff turned away from her and went back into his room. He shut the door, and yet so quietly that she could not feel reproved. Only she was sad. The way of being a sister was a harder one than she had looked for. But she felt bound to him, even by stronger and stronger cords. He was hers, Farvie's and Anne's and hers, however unlikely he was to take hold of his innocence with firm hands and shake it in the public face.

Jeff, in his room, stood for a minute or more, hands in his pockets, staring at the wall and absently thinking he remembered the paper on it from his college days. But he recalled himself from the obvious. He looked into his inner chamber of mind where he had forbidden himself to glance since he had come home, lest he see there a confusion of idea and desire that should make him the weaker in carrying out the inevitabilities of his return. There was one thing in decency to be expected of him at this point: to give his father a period of satisfaction before he left him to do what he had not yet clearly determined on. It was sufficiently convincing to tell Lydia he intended to make good, but he had not much idea what he meant by it. He was conscious chiefly that he felt marred somehow, jaded, harassed by life, smeared by his experience of living in a gentlemanly jail. The fact that he had left it did not restore to him his old feeling of owning the earth. He had, from the moment of his conviction and sentence, been outside, and his present liberty could not at once convey him inside.

He was, he knew, for one thing, profoundly tired. Nothing, he felt sure, could give him back the old sense of air in his lungs. Confinement had not deprived him of air. He had smiled grimly to himself once or twice, as he thought what the sisters' idea of his prison was likely to be. They probably had conjured up fetid dungeons. There were chains of a surety, certainly a clank or two. As he remembered it, there was a clanking in his mind, quite sufficient to fulfil the prison ideal. And then he thought, with a sudden desire for man's company, the expectation that would take you for granted, that he'd go down and see old Reardon. Reardon had not been to call, but Jeff was too sick of solitariness to mind that.

He went out without seeing anybody, the colonel, he knew, being at his gentle task of cramming for Mary Nellen's evening lesson. Jeff had not been in the street since the walk he had cut short with Madame Beattie. He felt strange out in the world now, as if the light blinded him or the sun burned him, or there were an air too chill—all, he reflected, in a grim discovery, the consequence of being outside and not wanting houses to see you or persons to bow and offer friendly hands. Reardon would blow such vapours away with a breath of his bluff voice. But as he reached the vestibule of the yellow house, Reardon himself was coming out and Jeff, with a sick surprise, understood that Reardon was not prepared to see him.

XI

Reardon stood there in his middle-aged ease, the picture of a man who has nothing to do more hazardous than to take care of himself. His hands were exceedingly well-kept. His cravat, of a dull blue, was suited to his fresh-coloured face, and, though this is too far a quest for the casual eye, his socks also were blue, an admirable match. Jeff was not accustomed, certainly in these later years, to noting clothes; but he did feel actually unkempt before this mirror of the time. Yet why? For in the old days also Reardon had been rather vain of outward conformity. He had striven then to make up by every last nicety of dress and manner for the something his origin had lacked. It was not indeed the perfection of his dress that disconcerted; it was the kind of man Reardon had grown to be: for of him the clothes did, in their degree, testify. Jeffrey was conscious that every muscle in Reardon's body had its just measure of attention. Reardon had organised the care of that being who was himself. He had provided richly for his future, wiped out his past where it threatened to gall him, and was giving due consideration to his present. He meant supremely to be safe, and to that end he had entrenched himself on every side. Jeff felt a very disorganised, haphazard sort of being indeed before so complete a creature. And Reardon, so far from breaking into the old intimacy that Jeff had seen still living behind them in a sunny calm, only waiting for the gate to be opened on it again, stood there distinctly embarrassed and nothing more.

"Jeff!" said he. "How are you?" That was not enough. He found it lacking, and added, with a deepened shade of warmth, "How are you, old man?"

Now he put out his hand, but it had been so long in coming that Jeff gave no sign of seeing it.

"I'll walk along with you," he said.

"No, no." Reardon was calling upon reserves of decency and good feeling. "You'll do nothing of the sort. Come in."

"No," said Jeff. "I was walking. I'll go along with you."

Now Reardon came down the steps and put an insistent hand on his shoulder.

"Jeff," said he, "come on in. You surprised me. That's the truth. I wasn't prepared. I hadn't looked for you."

Jeff went up the steps; it seemed, indeed, emotional to do less. But at the door he halted and his eyes sought the chairs at hand.

"Can't we," said he, "sit down here?"

Reardon, with a courteous acquiescence, went past one of the chairs, leaving it for him, and dropped into another. Jeff took his, and found nothing to say. One of them had got to make a civil effort. Jeff, certain he had no business there, took his hand at it.

"This was the old Pelham house?"

Reardon assented, in evident relief, at so remote a topic.

"I bought it six years ago. Had it put in perfect repair. The plumbing cost me—well! you know what old houses are."

Jeff turned upon him.

"Jim," said he quietly, "what's the matter?"

"Nothing's the matter," said Reardon, blustering. "My dear boy! I'm no end glad to see you."

"Oh, no," said Jeff. "No, you're not. You've kicked me out. What's the reason? My late residence? Oh, come on, man! Didn't expect to see me? Didn't want to? That it?"

Suddenly the telephone rang, and the English man-servant came out and said, with a perfect decorum:

"Mrs. Blake at the telephone, sir."

Jeff was looking at Reardon when he got the message and saw his small blue eyes suffused and the colour hot in his cheeks. The blond well-kept man seemed to be swelling with embarrassment.

"Excuse me," he said, got up and went inside, and Blake heard his voice in brief replies.

When he came back, he looked harassed, fatigued even. His colour had gone down and left him middle-aged. Jeff had not only been awaiting him, but his glance had, as well. His eyes were fixed upon the spot where Reardon's face, when he again occupied his chair, would be ready to be interrogated.

"What Mrs. Blake?" Jeff asked.

Reardon sat down and fussed with the answer.

"What Mrs. Blake?" he repeated, and flicked a spot of dust from his trousered ankle lifted to inspection.

"Yes," said Jeff, with an outward quiet. "Was that my wife?"

Again the colour rose in Reardon's face. It was the signal of an emotion that gave him courage.

"Why, yes," he said, "it was."

"What did she want?"

"Jeff," said Reardon, "it's no possible business of yours what Esther wants."

"You call her Esther?"

"I did then."

An outraged instinct of possession was rising in Reardon. Esther suddenly meant more to him than she had in all this time when she had been meaning a great deal. Alston Choate had power to rouse this primitive rage in him, but he could always conquer it by reasoning that Alston wouldn't take her if he could get her. There were too many inherited reserves in Alston. Actually, Reardon thought, Alston wouldn't really want a woman he had to take unguardedly. But here was the man who, by every rigour of conventional life, had a right to her. It could hardly be borne. Reardon wasn't used to finding himself dominated by primal impulses. They weren't, his middle-aged conclusions told him, safe. But now he got away from himself slightly and the freedom of it, while it was exciting, made him ill at ease. The impulse to speak really got the better of him.

"Look here, Blake," he said—and both of them realised that it was the first time he had used that surname; Jeff had always been a boy to him—"it's very unwise of you to come back here at all."

"Very unwise?" Jeff repeated, in an unmixed amazement, "to come back to Addington? My father's here."

"Your father needn't have been here," pursued Reardon doggedly. Entered upon what seemed a remonstrance somebody ought to make, he was committed, he thought, to going on. "It was an exceedingly ill-judged move for you all, very ill-judged indeed."

Jeff sat looking at him from a sternness that made a definite setting for the picture of his wonder. Yet he seemed bent only upon understanding.

"I don't say you came back to make trouble," Reardon went on, pursued now by the irritated certainty that he had adopted a course and had got to justify it. "But you're making it."

"How am I making it?"

"Why, you're making her damned uncomfortable."

"Who?"

Reardon had boggled over the name. He hardly liked to say Esther again, since it had been ill-received, and he certainly wouldn't say "your wife". But he had to choose and did it at a jump.

"Esther," he said, fixing upon that as the least offensive to himself.

"How am I making my wife uncomfortable?" Jeff inquired.

"Why, here you are," Reardon blundered, "almost within a stone's throw. She can't even go into the street without running a chance of meeting you."

Jeff threw back his head and laughed.

"No," he said, "she can't, that's a fact. She can't go into the street without running the risk of meeting me. But if you hadn't told me, Reardon, I give you my word I shouldn't have thought of the risk she runs. No, I shouldn't have thought of it."

Reardon drew a long breath. He had, it seemed to him, after all done wisely. The note of human brotherhood came back into his voice, even an implication that presently it might be actually soothing.

"Well, now you do see, you'll agree with me. You can't annoy a woman. You can't keep her in a state of apprehension."

Jeff had risen, and Reardon, too, got on his feet. Jeff seemed to be considering, and very gravely, and Reardon, frowning, watched him.

"No," said Jeff. "No. Certainly you can't annoy a woman." He turned upon Reardon, but with no suggestion of resentment. "What makes you think I should annoy her?"

"Why, it isn't what you'd wilfully do." Now that the danger of violence was over, Reardon felt that he could meet his man with a perfect reasonableness, and tell him what nobody else was likely to. "It's your being here. She can't help going back. She remembers how things used to be. And then she gets apprehensive."

"How they used to be," Jeff repeated thoughtfully. He sounded stupid standing there and able, apparently, to do nothing better than repeat. "How was that? How do you understand they used to be?"

Reardon lost patience. You could afford to, evidently, with so numb an antagonist.

"Why, you know," he said. "You remember how things used to be."

Jeff looked full at him now, and there was a curious brightness in his eyes.

"I don't," he said. "I should have said I did, but now I hear you talk I give you my word I don't. You'll have to tell me."

"She never blamed you," said Reardon expansively. He was beginning to pity Jeff, the incredible density of him, and he spoke incautiously. "She understood the reasons for it. You were having your business worries and you were harassed and nervous. Of course she understood. But that didn't prevent her from being afraid of you."

"Afraid of me!" Jeff took a step forward and put one hand on a pillar of the porch. The action looked almost as if he feared to trust himself, finding some weakness in his legs to match this assault upon the heart. "Esther afraid of me?"

Reardon, feeling more and more benevolent, dilated visibly.

"Most natural thing in the world. You can see how it would be. I suppose her mind keeps harking back, going over things, you know; and here you are on the same street, as you might say."

"No," said Jeff, stupidly, as if that were the case in point, "it isn't the same street."

He withdrew his hand from the pillar now with a decisiveness that indicated he had got to depend on his muscles at once, and started down the steps. Reardon made an indeterminate movement after him and called out something; but Jeff did not halt. He went along the driveway, past the proudly correct shrubs and brilliant turf and into the street. He had but the one purpose of getting to Esther as soon as possible. As he strode along, he compassed in memory all the seasons of passion from full bloom to withering since he saw her last. When he went away from her to fulfil his sentence, he had felt that identity with her a man must recognise for a wife passionately beloved. He had left her in a state of nervous collapse, an ignoble, querulous breakdown, due, he had to explain to himself, to her nature, delicately strung. There was nothing heroic about the way she had taken his downfall. But the exquisite music of her, he further tutored himself, was not set to martial strains. She was the loveliness of the twilight, of the evening star. And then, when his days had fallen into a pallid sequence, she had kept silence. It was as if there had been no wife, no Esther. At first he made wild appeals to her, to his father for the assurance that she was living even. Then one day in the autumn when he was watching a pale ray of sunshine that looked as if it had been strained through sorrow before it got to him, the verdict, so far as his understanding went, was inwardly pronounced. His mind had been working on the cruel problem and gave him, unsought, the answer. That was what she meant to do: to separate her lot from his. There never would be an Esther any more. There never had been the Esther that made the music of his strong belief in her.

At first he could have dashed himself against the walls in the impotence of having such bereavement to bear with none of the natural outlets to assuage it. Then beneficent healing passions came to his aid, though not, he knew, the spiritual ones. He descended upon scorn, and finally a cold acceptance of what she was. And then she seemed to have died, and in the inexorable sameness of the days and nights he dismissed her memory, and he meditated upon life and what might be made of it by men who had still the power to make. But now hurrying to her along the quiet street, one clarifying word explained her, and, unreasoningly, brought back his love. She had been afraid—afraid of him who would, in the old phrase, have, in any sense, laid down his life for her: not less willingly, the honourable name he bore among honourable men. A sense of renewal and bourgeoning was upon him, that feeling of waking from a dream and finding the beloved is, after all, alive. The old simple words came back to him that used to come in prison when they dropped molten anguish upon his heart:

—"After long grief and pain,To find the arms of my true loveRound me once again."

At least, if he was never to feel the soft rapture of his love's acceptance, he might find she still lived in her beauty, and any possible life would be too short to teach her not to be afraid. He reached the house quickly and, with the haste of his courage, went up the steps and tried the latch. In Addington nearly every house was open to the neighbourly hand. But of late Esther had taken to keeping her bolt slipped. It had dated from the day Lydia made hostile entrance. Finding he could not walk in unannounced, he stood for a moment, his intention blank. It did not seem to him he could be named conventionally to Esther, who was afraid of him. And then, by a hazard, Esther, who had not been out for days, and yet had heard of nobody's meeting him abroad, longed for the air and threw wide the door. There she was, by a God-given chance. It was like predestined welcome, a confirming of his hardihood. In spite of the sudden blight and shadow on her face, instinctive recoil that meant, he knew, the closing of the door, he grasped her hands, both her soft white hands, and seemed, to his anguished mind, to be dragging himself in by them, and even in the face of that look of hers was over the threshold and had closed the door.

"Esther," he said. "Esther, dear!"

The last word he had never expected to use to her, to any woman again. Still she regarded him with that horrified aversion, not amazement, he saw. It was as if she had perhaps expected him, had anticipated this very moment, and yet was not ready, because, such was her hard case, no ingenuity could possibly prepare her for it. This he saw, and it ran on in a confirming horrible sequence from Reardon's speech.

"Esther!" he repeated. He was still holding her hands and feeling they had no possibility of escape from each other, she in the weakness of her fear and he in passionate ruth. "Are you afraid of me?"

That was her cue.

"Yes," she whispered.

"Were you always, dear?" he went on, carried by the tide of his despairing love. (Or was it love? It seemed to him like love, for he had not felt emotion such as this through the dry pangs of his isolation.) "Years ago, when we were together—why, you weren't afraid then?"

"Oh, yes, I was," she said. Now that she could translate his emotion in any degree, she felt the humility of his mind toward her, and began to taste her own ascendancy. He was suing to her in some form, and the instinct which, having something to give may yet withhold it, fed her sense of power.

"Why, we were happy," said Jeffrey, in an agony of wonder. "That's been my only comfort when I knew we couldn't be happy now. I made you happy, dear."

And since he hung, in a fevered anticipation, upon her answer, she could reply, still from that sense of being the arbitress of his peace:

"I never was happy, at the last. I was afraid."

He dropped her hands.

"What of?" he said to himself stupidly. "In God's name, what of?"

The breaking of his grasp had released also some daring in her. They were still by the door, but he was between her and the stairs. He caught the glance of calculation, and instinct told him if he lost her now he should never get speech of her again.

"Don't," he said. "Don't go."

Again he laid a hand upon her wrist, and anger came into her face instead of that first candid horror. She had heard something, a step upstairs, and to that she cried: "Aunt Patricia!" three times, in a piercing entreaty.

It was not Madame Beattie who came to the stair-head and looked down; it was Rhoda Knox. After the glance she went away, though in no haste, and summoned Madame Beattie, who appeared in a silk negligee of black and white swirls like witch's fires and, after one indifferent look, called jovially:

"Hullo, Jeff!"

But she came down the stairs and Esther, seeing his marauding entry turned into something like a visit under social sanction, beat upon his wrist with her other hand and cried two hot tears of angry impotence.

"For heaven's sake, Esther," Madame Beattie remarked, at the foot of the stairs, "what are you acting like this for? You look like a child in a tantrum."

Esther ceased to be in a tantrum. She had a sense of the beautiful, and not even before these two invaders would she make herself unfitting. She addressed Madame Beattie in a tone indicating her determination not to speak to Jeff again.

"Tell him to let me go."

Jeff answered. Passion now had turned him cold, but he was relentless, a man embarked on a design to which he cannot see the purpose or the end, but who means to sail straight on.

"Esther," he said, "I'm going to see you now, for ten minutes, for half an hour. You may keep your aunt here if you like, but if you run away from me I shall follow you. But you won't run away. You'll stay right here."

He dropped her wrist.

"Oh, come into the library," said Madame Beattie. "I can't stand. My knees are creaking. Come, Esther, ask your husband in."

Madame Beattie, billowing along in the witch-patterned silk and clicking on prodigiously high heels and Esther with her head haughtily up, led the way, and Jeff, following them, sat down as soon as they had given him leave by doing it, and looked about the room with a faint foolish curiosity to note whether it, too, had changed. Madame Beattie thrust out a pretty foot, and Esther, perched on the piano stool, looked rigidly down at her trembling hands. She was very pale. Suddenly she recovered herself, and turned to Madame Beattie.

"He had just come," she said. "He came in. I didn't ask him to. He had not—" a little note like fright or triumph beat into her voice—"he had not—kissed me."

She turned to him as if for a confirmation he could not in honesty refuse her, and Madame Beattie burst into a laugh, one of perfect acceptance of things as they are, human frailties among the first.

"Esther," she said, "you're a little fool. If you want a divorce what do you give yourself away for? Your counsel wouldn't let you."

The whole implication was astounding to Jeff; but the only thing he could fix definitely was the concrete possibility that she had counsel.

"Who is your counsel, Esther?" he asked her.

But Esther had gone farther than discretion bade.

"I am not obliged to say," she answered, with a stubbornness equal to his own, whatever that might prove. "I am not obliged to say anything. But I do think I have a right to ask you to tell Aunt Patricia that I have not taken you back, in any sense whatever. Not—not condoned."

She slipped on the word and he guessed that it had been used to her and that although she considered it of some value, she had not technically taken it in.

"What had you to condone in me, Esther?" he asked her gently. Suddenly she seemed to him most pathetic in her wilful folly. She had always been, she would always be, he knew, a creature who ruled through her weakness, found it an asset, traded on it perhaps, and whereas once this had seemed to him enchanting, now, in the face of ill-fortune it looked pitifully inadequate and base.

"I was afraid of you," she insisted. "I am now."

"Well!" said Jeff. He found himself smiling at Madame Beattie, and she was answering his smile. Perhaps it was rather the conventional tribute on his part, to conceal that he might easily have thrown himself back in his chair behind the shelter of his hands, or gone down in any upheaval of primal emotions; and perhaps he saw in her answer, if not sympathy, for she was too impersonal for that, a candid understanding of the little scene and an appreciation of its dramatic quality. "Then," said he, after his monosyllable, "there is nothing left me but to go." When he had risen, he stood looking down at his wife's beautiful dusky head. Incredible to think it had ever lain on his breast, or that the fact of its cherishing there made no difference to her embryo heart! A tinge of irony came into his voice. "And I am willing to assure Madame Beattie," he proceeded, "in the way of evidence, that you have not in any sense taken me back, nor have you condoned anything I may have done."

As he was opening the outer door, in a confusion of mind that communicated itself disturbingly to his eyes and ears, he seemed to hear Madame Beattie adjuring Esther ruthlessly not to be a fool.

"Why, he's a man, you little fool," he heard her say, not with passion but a negligent scorn ample enough to cover all the failings of their common sex. "He's more of a man than he was when he went into that hideous place. And after all, who sent him there?"

Jeff walked out and closed the door behind him with an exaggerated care. It hardly seemed as if he had the right, except in a salutary humbleness, even to touch a door which shut in Esther to the gods of home. He went back to his father's house, and there was Lydia singing as she dusted the library. He walked in blindly not knowing whether she was alone; but here was a face and a voice, and his heart was sore. Lydia, at sight of him, laid down her cloth and came to meet him. Neither did she think whether they were alone, though she did remember afterward that Farvie had gone into the orchard for his walk. Seeing Jeff's face, she knew some mortal hurt was at work within him, and like a child, she went to him, and Jeff put his face down on her cheek, and his cheek, she felt, was wet. And so they stood, their arms about each other, and Lydia's heart beat in such a sick tumult of rage and sorrow that it seemed to her she could not stand so and uphold the heavy weight of his grief. In a minute she whispered to him:

"Have you seen her?"

"Yes."

"Was she—cruel?"

"Don't! don't!" Jeff said, in a broken voice.

"Do you love her?" she went on, in an inexorable fierceness.

"No! no! no!" And then a voice that did not seem to be his and yet was his, came from him and overthrew all his old traditions of what he had been and what he must therefore be: "I only love you."

Then, Lydia knew, when she thought of it afterward, in a burning wonder, they kissed, and their tears and the kiss seemed as one, a bond against the woman who had been cruel to him and an eternal pact between themselves. And on the severing of the kiss, terrible to her in her innocence, she flung herself away from him and ran upstairs. Her flight was noiseless, as if now no one must know, but he heard the shutting of a door and the sound of a turning key.

XII

That night Anne was wakened from her sleep by a wisp of a figure that came slipping to her bedside, announced only by the cautious breathing of her name:

"Anne! Anne!" her sister was whispering close to her cheek.

"Why, Lyd," said Anne, "what is it?"

The figure was kneeling now, and Anne tried to rise on her elbow to invite Lydia in beside her. But Lydia put a hand on her shoulder and held her still.

"Whisper," she said, and then was silent so long that Anne, waiting and hearing her breathe, stared at her in the dark and wondered at her.

"What is it, lovey?" she asked at length, and Lydia's breathing hurried into sobs, and she said Anne's name again, and then, getting a little control of herself, asked the question that had brought her.

"Anne, when people kiss you, is it different if they are men?"

Now Anne did rise and turned the clothes back, but Lydia still knelt and shivered.

"You've been having bad dreams," said Anne. "Come in here, lovey, and Anne'll sing 'Lord Rendal.'"

"I mean," said Lydia, from her knees, "could anybody kiss me, except Farvie, and not have it like Farvie—I mean have it terrible—and I kiss him back—and—Anne, what would it mean?"

"That's a nightmare," said Anne. "Now you've got all cool and waked up, you run back to bed, unless you'll get in here."

Lydia put a fevered little hand upon her.

"Anne, you must tell me," she said, catching her breath. "Not a nightmare, a real kiss, and neither of us wanting to kiss anybody, and still doing it and not being sorry. Being glad."

She sounded so like herself in one of her fiercenesses that Anne at last believed she was wholly awake and felt a terror of her own.

"Who was it, Lydia?" she asked sternly. "Who is it you are thinking about?"

"Nobody," said Lydia, in a sudden curt withdrawal. She rose to her feet. "Yes, it was a nightmare."

She padded out of the room and softly closed the door, and Anne, left sitting there, felt unreasoning alarm. She had a moment's determination to follow her, and then she lay down again and thought achingly of Lydia who was grown up and was yet a child. And still, Anne knew, she had to come to woman's destiny. Lydia was so compact of sweetnesses that she would be courted and married, and who was Anne, to know how to marry her rightly? So she slept, after a troubled interval; but Lydia lay awake and stared the darkness through as if it held new paths to her desire. What was her desire? She did not know, save that it had all to do with Jeff. He had been cruelly used. He must not be so dealt with any more. Her passion for his well-being, germinating and growing through the years she had not seen him, had come to flower in a hot resolve that he should be happy now. And in some way, some headlong, resistless way, she knew she was to make his happiness, and yet in her allegiance to him there was trouble and pain. He had made her into a new creature. The kiss had done it.

He would not, Lydia thought, have kissed her if it were wrong, and yet the kiss was different from all others and she must never tell. Nor must it come again. She was plighted to him, not as to a man free to love her, but to his well-being; and it was all most sacred and not to be undone. She was exalted and she was shuddering with a formless sense of the earth sway upon her. She had ever been healthy-minded as a child; even the pure imaginings of love had not beguiled her. But now something had come out of the earth or the air and called to her, and she had answered; and because it was so inevitable it was right—yet right for only him to know. Who else could understand?

XIII

Lydia did not think she dreaded seeing him next morning. The fabric they had begun to weave together looked too splendid for covering trivial little fears like that. Or was it strong enough to cover anything? Yet when he came into the room where they were at breakfast she could not look at him with the same unwavering eyes. She had, strangely, and sadly too, the knowledge of life. But if she had looked at him she would have seen how he was changed. He had pulled himself together. Whether what happened or what might happen had tutored him, he was on guard, ready—for himself most of all. And after breakfast where Anne and the colonel had contributed the mild commonplaces useful at least in breaking such constraints, he followed the colonel into the library and sat down with him. The colonel, from his chair by the window, regarded his son in a fond approval. Even to his eyes where Jeff was always a grateful visitant, the more so now after he had been so poignantly desired, he was this morning the more manly and altogether fit. But Jeff was not going to ingratiate himself.

"Father," said he, "I've got to get out."

Trouble of a wistful sort sprang into the colonel's face. But he spoke with a reasonable mildness, desirous chiefly of meeting his boy half way.

"You said so. But not yet, I hope."

"At once," said Jeffrey. "I am going at once. To-day perhaps. To-morrow anyway. I've simply got to get away."

The colonel, rather impatiently, because his voice would tremble, asked as Lydia had done:

"Have you seen Esther?"

This Jeff found unreasonably irritating. Bitter as the sight of her had been and unspeakable her repudiation, he felt to-day as if they did not pertain. The thing that did pertain with a biting force was to remove himself before innocent young sisterly girls idealised him to their harm. But he answered, and not too ungraciously:

"Yes, I've seen Esther. But that's nothing to do with it. Esther is—what she's always been. Only I've got to get away."

The colonel, from long brooding over him, had a patience comparable only to a mother's. He was bitterly hurt. He could not understand. But he could at least attain the only grace possible and pretend to understand. So he answered with a perfect gentleness:

"I see, Jeff, I see. But I wish you could find it possible to put it off—till the end of the week, say."

"Very well," said Jeff, in a curt concession, "the end of this week."

He got up and went out of the room and the house, and the colonel, turning to look, saw him striding down the slope to the river. Then the elder man's hands began to tremble, and he sat pathetically subject to the seizure. Anne, if she had found him, would have known the name of the thing that had settled upon him. She would have called it a nervous chill. But to him it was one of the little ways of his predestined mate, old age. And presently, sitting there ignominiously shuddering, he began to be amused at himself, for he had a pretty sense of humour, and to understand himself better than he had before. Face to face with this ironic weakness, he saw beyond the physiologic aspect of it, the more deeply into his soul. The colonel had been perfectly sure that he had taken exquisite care of himself, these last years, because he desired to see his son again, and also because Jeff, while suffering penalty, must be spared the pain of bereavement. So he had formed a habit, and now it was his master. He had learned self-preservation, but at what a cost! Where were the sharp sweet pangs of life that had been used to assail him before he anchored in this calm? Daring was a lost word to him. Was it true he was to have no more stormy risings of hot life, no more passions of just rage or even righteous hate, because he had taught himself to rule his blood? Now when his heart ached in anticipatory warning over his son's going, why must he think of ways to be calm, as if being calm were the aim of man? Laboriously he had learned how not to waste himself, and the negation of life which is old age and then death had fallen upon him. He laughed a little, bitterly, and Anne, coming to find him as she did from time to time, to make sure he was comfortable, smiled, hearing it, and asked:

"What is it, Farvie?"

He looked up into her kind face as if it were strange to him. At that moment he and life were having it out together. Even womanly sweetness could not come between.

"Anne," said he, "I'm an old man."

"Oh, no, Farvie!" She was smoothing his shoulder with her slender hand. "No!"

But even she could not deny it. To her youth, he knew, he must seem old. Yet her service, her fostering love, had only made him older. She had copied his own attitude. She had helped him not to die, and yet to sink into the ambling pace of these defended years.

"Damn it, Anne!" he said, with suddenly frowning brow, and now she started. She had never heard an outbreak from courtly Farvie. "I wish I'd been more of a man."

She did not understand him, and her eyes questioned whether he was ill. He read the query. That was it, he thought impotently. They had all three of them been possessed by that, the fear that he was going to be ill.

"Yes," he said, "I wish I'd been more of a man. I should be more of a man now."

She slipped away out of the room. He thought he had frightened her. But in a moment she was back with some whiskey, hot, in a glass. The colonel wanted to order her off and swear his nerves would be as taut without it. But how could he? There was the same traitorous trembling in his legs, and he put out his hand and took the glass, and thanked her. The thanks sounded like the courteous, kind father she knew; but when she had carried the glass into the kitchen she stood a moment, her hand on the table, and thought, the lines of trouble on her forehead: what had been the matter with him?

Jeff, when he got out of the house, walked in a savage hurry down to the end of the lot, and there, feeling no more at ease with himself, skirted along the bank bordered by inlets filled with weedy loveliness, and came to the lower end of the town where the cotton mills were. He glanced up at them as he struck into the street past their office entrance, and wondered what the stock was quoted at now, and whether an influx of foreigners had displaced the old workmen. It had looked likely before he went away. But he had no interest in it. He had no interest in Addington, he thought: only in the sad case of Lydia thrown up against the tumultuous horde of his released emotions and hurt by them and charmed by them and, his remorseful judgment told him, insulted by them. He could not, even that morning, have told how he felt about Lydia, or whether he had any feeling at all, save a proper gratitude for her tenderness to his father. But he had found her in his path, when his hurt soul was crying out to all fostering womanhood to save him from the ravening claw of woman's cruelty. She had felt his need, and they had looked at each other with eyes that pierced defences. And then, incarnate sympathy, tender youth, she had rested in his arms, and in the generosity of her giving and the exquisiteness of the gift, he had been swept into that current where there is no staying except by an anguish of denial. It was chaos within him. He did not think of his allegiance to Esther, nor was he passionately desirous, with his whole mind, of love for this new Lydia. He was in a whirl of emotion, and hated life where you could never really right yourself, once you were wrong.

He kept on outside the town, and presently walked with exhilaration because nobody knew him and he was free, and the day was of an exquisite beauty, the topmost flower of the waxing spring. The road was marked by elms, aisled and vaulted, and birds called enchantingly. He was able to lay aside cool knowledge of the fight whereby all things live and, such was the desire of his mind, to partake of pleasure, to regard them as poets do and children and pitiful women: the birds as lumps of free delight, winged particles of joy. The song-birds were keen participants of sport, killing to eat, and bigger birds were killing them. But because they sang and their feathers were newly painted, he let himself ignore that open scandal and loved them for an angel choir.

Coming to another village, though he knew it perfectly he assumed it was undiscovered land, and beyond it lay in a field and dozed, his hat over his eyes, and learned how blessed it is to be alone in freedom, even afar from Lydias and Esthers. Healing had not begun in him until that day. Here were none to sympathise, none to summon him to new relations or recall the old. The earth had taken him back to her bosom, to cherish gravely, if with no actual tenderness, that he might be of the more use to her. If he did not that afternoon hear the grass growing, at least something rose from the mould that nourished it, into his eyes and ears and mouth and the pores of his skin, and helped him on to health. At five he remembered his father, who had begged him not to go away, got up and turned back on his steps. Now he was hungry and bought rolls and cheese at a little shop, and walked on eating them. The dusk came, and only the robin seemed of unabated spirit, flying to topmost twigs, and giving the evening call, the cry that was, he thought, "grief! grief!" and the following notes like a sob.

Jeffrey came into Addington by another road, one that would take him into town along the upland, and now he lingered purposely and chose indirect ways because, although it was unlikely that any one would know him, he shrank from the prospect of demanding eyes. At nine o'clock even he was no farther than the old circus ground, and, nearing it, he heard, through the evening stillness, a voice, loud, sharp, forensic. It was hauntingly familiar to him, a voice he might not know at the moment, yet one that had at least belonged to some part of his Addington life. The response it brought from him, in assaulted nerves and repugnant ears, was entirely distasteful. Whatever the voice was, he had at some time hated it. Why it was continuing on that lifted note he could not guess. With a little twitch of the lips, the sign of a grim amusement, he thought this might even be an orator, some wardroom Demosthenes, practising against the lonely curtain of the night.

"You have no country," the voice was bastinadoing the air. "And you don't need one. Your country is the whole earth and it belongs to you."

Jeff halted a rod before the nearer entrance to the field. He had suddenly the sense of presences. The nerves on his skin told him humanity was near. He went on, with an uncalculated noiselessness, for the moment loomed important, and since what humanity was there was silent—all but that one hateful voice—he, approaching in ignorance, must be still. The voice, in its strident passion, rose again.

"The country for a man to serve is the country that serves him. The country that serves him is the one without a king. Has this country a king? It has a thousand kings and a million more that want to be. How many kings do you want to reign over you? How many are you going to accept? It is in your hands."

It ceased, and another voice, lower but full of a suppressed passion, took up the tale, though in a foreign tongue. Jeff knew the first one now: Weedon Moore's. He read at once the difference between Moore's voice and this that followed. Moore's had been imploring in its assertiveness, the desire to convince. The other, in the strange language, carried belief and sorrow even. It also longed to convince, but out of an inner passion hot as the flame of love or grief. The moon, riding superbly, and coming that minute out of her cloud, unveiled the scene. An automobile had halted on a slight elevation and in it stood Moore and a taller man gesticulating as he spoke. And about them, like a pulsing carpet lifted and stirred by a breeze of feeling, were the men Jeff's instinct had smelled out. They were packed into a mass. And they were silent. Weedon Moore began again.

"Kill out this superstition of a country. Kill it out, I say. Kill out this idea of going back to dead men for rules to live by. The dead are dead. Their Bibles and their laws are dead. There's more life in one of you men that has tasted it through living and suffering and being oppressed than there is in any ten of their kings and prophets. They are dead, I tell you. We are alive. It was their earth while they lived on it. It's our earth to-day."

Jeff was edging nearer, skirting the high fence, and while he did it, the warm voice of the other man took up the exposition, and now Jeff understood that he was Moore's interpreter. By the time he had finished, Jeff was at the thin edge of the crowd behind the car, and though one or two men turned as he moved and glanced at him, he seemed to rouse no uneasiness. Here, nearer them in the moonlight, he saw what they were: workmen, foreign evidently, with bared throats and loosely worn hair, some, their caps pushed back, others without hats at all, seeking, it seemed, coolness in this too warm adjuration.

"Their symbol," said Moore, "is the flag. They carry it into foreign lands. Why? For what they call religion? No. For money—money—money. When the flag waves in a new country, blood begins to flow, the blood of the industrial slave. Down with the flag. Our symbol is the sword."

The voice of the interpreter, in an added passion, throbbed upon the climbing period. Moore had moved him and, forgetful of himself, he was dramatically ready to pass his ardour on. Jeff also forgot himself. He clove like a wedge through the thin line before him, and leaped on the running-board.

"You fool," he heard himself yelling at Moore, who in the insecurity of his tubbiness was jarred and almost overturned, "you're robbing them of their country. You're taking away the thing that keeps them from falling down on all-fours and going back to brute beasts. My God, Moore, you're a traitor! You ought to be shot."

He had surprised them. They did not even hustle him, but there were interrogatory syllables directed to the interpreter. Moore recovered himself. He gave a sharp sound of distaste, and then, assuming his civilised habit, said to Jeff in a voice of specious courtesy, yet, Jeff knew, a voice of hate:

"These are mill operatives, Blake, labourers. They know what labour is. They know what capitalists are. Do you want me to tell 'em who you are?"

Who you are? Jeff knew what it meant. Did he want Moore to tell them that he was a capitalist found out and punished?

"Tell and be damned," he said. "See here!" He was addressing the interpreter. "You understand English. Fair play. Do you take me? Fair play is what English men and American men work for and fight for. It's fair play to give me a chance to speak, and for you to tell these poor devils what I say. Will you?"

The man nodded. His white teeth gleamed in the moonlight. Jeff fancied his eyes gleamed, too. He was a swarthy creature and round his neck was knotted a handkerchief, vivid red. Jeff, with a movement of the arm, crowded Moore aside. Moore submitted. Used, as he was, to being swept out of the way, all the energies that might have been remonstrant in him had combined in a controlling calm to serve him until the day when he should be no longer ousted. Jeff spoke, and threw his voice, he hoped, to the outskirts of the crowd, ingenuously forgetting it was not lungs he wanted but a bare knowledge of foreign tongues.

"This man," said he, "tells you you've no country. Don't you let him lie to you. Here's your country under your feet. If you can't love it enough to die for it, go back to your own country, the one you were born in, and love that, for God's sake." He judged he had said enough to be carried in the interpreter's memory, and turned upon him. "Go on," said he imperatively. "Say it."

But even then he had no idea what the man would do. The atmosphere about them was not thrilling in responsive sympathy. Silence had waited upon Moore, and this, Jeff could not help feeling, was silence of a different species. But the interpreter did, slowly and cautiously, it seemed, convey his words. At least Jeff hoped he was conveying them. When his voice ceased, Jeff took up the thread.

"He tells you you've no country. He says your country is the world. You're not big enough to need the whole world for your country. I'm not big enough. Only a few of them are, the prophets and the great dead men he thinks so little of. Dig up a tract of ground and call it your country and make it grow and bloom and have good laws—why, you fools!" His patience broke. "You fools, you're being done. You're being led away and played upon. A man's country isn't the spot where he can get the best money to put into his belly. His country is his country, just as his mother is his mother. He can worship the Virgin Mary, but he loves his mother best."

Whether the name hit them like blasphemy, whether the interpreter caught fire from it or Moore gave a signal, he could not tell. But suddenly he was being hustled. He was pulled down from the car with a gentle yet relentless force, was conscious that he was being removed and must submit. There were sounds now, the quick syllables of the southern races, half articulate to the uninstructed ear but full of idiom and passion, and through his own silent struggle he was aware that the interpreter was soothing, directing, and inexorably guiding the assault. They took him, a resistless posse of them, beyond the gap, and the automobile followed slowly and passed him just outside. It halted, and Moore addressed him hesitatingly:

"I could take you back to town."

Moore didn't want to say this, but he remembered Miss Amabel and the two charming girls, all adoring Jeff, and his ever-present control bade him be civilised. Jeff did not answer. He was full of a choking rage and blind desire for them to get their hands off him. Not in his imprisonment even had he felt such debasement under control as when these lithe creatures hurried him along. Yet he knew then that his rage was not against them, innocent servitors of a higher power. It was against the mean dominance of Weedon Moore.

The car passed swiftly on and down the road to town.

Then the men left him as suddenly as trained dogs whistled from their prey. He felt as if he had been merely detained, gently on the whole, at the point the master had designated, and looked about for the interpreter. It seemed to him if he could have speech with that man he could tell him in a sentence what Weedon Moore was, and charge him not to deliver these ignorant creatures of another race into his mucky hands. But if the interpreter was there he could not be distinguished. Jeff called, a word or two, not knowing what to say, and no one answered. The crowd that had been eagerly intent on a common purpose, to get him out of the debating place, split into groups. Individuals detached themselves, silently and swiftly, and melted away. Jeff heard their footsteps on the road, and now the voices began, quietly but with an eager emphasis. He was left alone by the darkened field, for even the moon, as if she joined the general verdict, slipped under a cloud.

Jeff stood a moment nursing, not his anger, but a clearheaded certainty that something must be done. Something always had to be done to block Weedon Moore. It had been so in the old days when Moore was not dangerous: only dirty. Now he was debasing the ignorant mind. He was a demagogue. The old never-formulated love for Addington came back to Jeff in a rush, not recognised as love an hour ago, only the careless affection of usage, but ready, he knew, to spring into something warmer when her dear old bulwarks were assailed. You don't usually feel a romantic passion for your mother. You allow her to feed you and be patronised by you and stand aside to let victorious youth pass on. But see unworthy hands touching her worn dress—the hands of Weedon Moore!—and you snatch it from their grasp.

Jeff still stood there thinking. This, the circus-ground was where he and the other boys had trysted in a delirious ownership of every possible "show", where they had met the East and gloated on nature's poor eccentricities. Now here he was, a man suddenly set in his purpose to deliver the old town from Weedon Moore. They couldn't suffer it, he and the rest of the street of solid mansions dating back to ancient dignities. These foreign children who had come to work for them should not be bred in disbelief in Addington traditions which were as good as anything America had to offer. Jeff was an aristocrat from skin to heart, because he was sensitive, because he loved beauty and he didn't want the other man to come too close; he didn't like tawdry ways to press upon him. But while he had been shut into the seclusion of his own thoughts, these past years, he had learned something. He had strengthened passions that hardly knew they were alive until now events awoke them. One was the worship of law, and one was that savage desire of getting to the place where we love law so much that we welcome punishment. He recalled himself from this dark journey back into his cell, and threw up his head to the heavens and breathed in air. It was the air of freedom. Yet it was only the freedom of the body. If he forgot now the beauty of that austere goddess, the law, then was he more a prisoner than when he had learned her face in loneliness and pain. He walked out of the grounds and along the silent road, advised through keen memory, by sounds and scents, of spots he had always known, and went into the town and home. There were lights, but for all the sight of people Addington might have been abed.

He opened the front door softly and out of the library Anne came at once as if she had been awaiting him.

"Oh," she said, in a quick trouble breaking bounds, though gently, now there was another to share it, "I'm afraid Farvie's sick."

XIV

"What is it?" said he. "What's the matter?"

But Anne, after a second glance at his tired face, was all concern for him.

"Have you had something to eat?" she asked.

He put that aside, and said remindingly:

"What is it about father?"

Anne stood at the foot of the stairs. She had the air of defending the way, lest he rush up before he was intelligently prepared.

"We don't know what it is. He went all to pieces. It was just after you had gone. I found him there, shaking. He just said to me: 'I'll go to bed.' So I helped him. That's all I know."

Jeff felt an instant and annoyed compunction. He had dashed off, to the tune of his own wild mood, and left his father to the assaults of emotions perhaps as overwhelming and with no young strength to meet them.

"I'll go up," said he. "Did you call a doctor?"

"No. He wouldn't let me."

Jeff ran up the stairs and found Lydia in a chair outside the colonel's door. She looked pathetically tired and anxious. And so young: if she had arranged herself artfully to touch the sympathies she couldn't have done it to more effect. Her round arms were bare to the elbow, her hands were loosely clasped, and she was sitting, like a child, with her feet drawn up under her on the rung of the chair. She looked at him in a solemn relief but, he saw with a relief of his own, no sensitiveness to his presence apart from the effect it might have on her father.

"He's asleep," she said, in a whisper. "I'm sitting here to listen."

Jeffrey nodded at her in a bluff way designed to express his certainty that everything was going to be on its legs again now he had come home. For the first time he felt like the man in the house, and the thin tonic braced him. He opened the door of his father's room and went in. The colonel's voice came at once:

"That you, Jeff?"

"Yes," said Jeff. He sat down by the bedside in the straight-backed chair that had evidently been comfortable enough for the sisters' anxious watch. "What's the matter, father?"

The colonel moved slightly nearer the edge of the bed. His eyes brightened, Jeff noted by the light of the shaded lamp. He was glad to get his son home again.

"Jeff," said he, "I've been lying here making up my mind I'd tell you."

Jeffrey rose and closed the door he had left open a crack out of courtesy to the little watcher there. He came back to the bed, not with a creaking caution, but like a man bringing a man's rude solace. He could not believe his father was seriously undone. But, whatever was the matter, the colonel was glad to talk. Perhaps, loyal as he was, even he could scarcely estimate his own desire to turn from soft indulgences to the hard contact of a man's intelligence.

"Jeff," said he, "I'm in a bad place. I've met the last enemy."

"Oh, no, you haven't," said Jeff, at random. "The last enemy is Death. That's what they say, don't they? Well, you're years and years to the good. Don't you worry."

"Ah, but the last enemy isn't Death," said the colonel wisely. "Don't you think it. The last enemy is Fear. Death's only the executioner. Fear delivers you over, and then Death has to take you, whether or no. But Fear is the arch enemy."

Sane as he looked and spoke, this was rather impalpable, and Jeffrey began to doubt his own fitness to deal with psychologic quibbles. But his father gave short shrift for questioning.

"I'm afraid," he said quite simply.

"What are you afraid of?" Jeff felt he had to meet him with an equal candour.

"Everything."

They looked at each other a moment and then Jeff essayed a mild, "Oh, come!" because there was nothing more to the point.

"I've taken care of myself," said the colonel, with more vigour, "till I'm punk. I can't stand a knockdown blow. I couldn't stand your going away. I went to bed."

"Is my going a knockdown blow?"

There was something pathetic in hearing that, but pleasurable, too, in a warm, strange way.

"Why, yes, of course it is."

"Well, then," said Jeff, "don't worry. I won't go."

"Oh, yes, you will," said the colonel instantly, "or you'll be punk. I'd rather go with you. I told you that. But it wouldn't do. I should begin to pull on you. And you'd mother me as they do, these dear girls."

"Yes," said Jeffrey thoughtfully. "Yes. They're dear girls."

"There's nothing like them," said the colonel. "There never was anything like their mother." Then he stopped, remembering she was not Jeff's mother, too. But Jeff knew all about his own mother, the speed and shine and bewildering impulse of her, and how she was adored. But nobody could have been soothed and brooded over by her, that gallant fiery creature. Whatever she might have become if she had lived, love of her then was a fight and a devotion, flowers and stars and dreams. "And it isn't a thing for me to take, this sort of attachment, Jeff. I ought to give it. They ought to be having the kind of time girls like. They ought not to be coddling an old man badly hypped."

Jeff nodded here, comprehendingly. Yes, they did need the things girls like: money, clothes, fun. But he vaulted away from that disquieting prospect, and faced the present need.

"Have you had anything to eat?"

"Oh, yes," the colonel said. "Egg-nog. Anne makes it. Very good."

"See here," said Jeff, "don't you want to get up and slip your clothes on, and I'll forage round and fish out cold hash or something, and we'll have a kind of a mild spree?"

A slow smile lighted the colonel's face, rather grimly.

He admired the ease with which Jeff grasped the situation.

"Don't you start them out cooking," he advised.

"No, I'll find a ham-bone or something. Only slip into your trousers. Get your shoes on your feet. We'll smoke a pipe together."

"You're right," said the colonel, with vigour. "We'll put on our shoes."

Jeff, on his way to the door, heard him throwing off the bedclothes. His own was the harder part. He had to meet the tired, sweet servitors without and announce a man's fiat. There they were, Lydia still in her patient attitude, and Anne on the landing, her head thrown back and the pure outline of her chin and throat like beauty carved in the air. At the opening of the door they were awake with an instant alertness. Lydia's feet came noiselessly to the floor, and Jeff understood, with a pang of pity for her, that she had perched uncomfortably to keep herself awake. This soft creature would never understand. He addressed himself to Anne, who believed in the impeccable rights of man and could take uncomprehended ways for granted.

"He's going to get up."

Anne made a movement toward the door.

"No," said Jeffrey. He was there before her, and, though he smiled at her, she knew she was not to pass. "I'll see to him. You two run off to bed."

They were both regarding him with a pale, anxious questioning. But Anne's look cleared.

"Come, Lydia," said she, and as Lydia, cramped with sleep, trudged after her, she added wisely, "It'll be better for them both."

When they were gone, Jeffrey did go down to the kitchen, rigid in the order Mary Nellen always left. He entered boldly on a campaign of ruthless ravaging, found bread and cheese and set them out, and a roast most attractive to the eye. He lighted candles, and then a lamp with a gay piece of red flannel in its glass body, put there by Mary Nellen, who, though on Homeric knowledge bent, kept religiously all the ritual of home. The colonel's slippered step was coming down the stairs. Jeffrey went out into the hall and beckoned. He looked stealth and mischief, and the colonel grimaced wisely at him. They went into the kitchen and sat down to their meal like criminals. The colonel had to eat, in vying admiration of Jeff, ravenous from his day's walk. When they drew back, Jeff pulled out his pipe. He was not an incessant smoker, but in this first interval of his homecoming all small indulgences were sweet. He paused in filling, finger on the weed.

"Where's yours?" he asked.

The colonel shook his head.

"Don't smoke?" Jeff inquired.

"I haven't for a year or so." He was shamefaced over it. "The fact is—Jeff, I'm nothing but a malingerer. I thought—my heart—"

"Very wise," said Jeffrey, his eyes half-closed in a luxurious lighting up. "Very wise indeed. But just to-night—don't you think you'd better have a whiff to-night?" The colonel shook his head, but Jeff sent out an advance signal of blue smoke. "Where is it?" said he.

"Oh, I suppose it's in my bureau drawer," said the colonel, with impatience. "Left hand. I kept it; I don't know why."

"Yes," said Jeffrey. "Of course you kept your pipe."

He ran softly upstairs, opening and shutting doors with an admirable quiet, and put his hand on the old briarwood. From Anne's room he heard a low crooning. She was awake then, but with mind at ease or she wouldn't sing like that. He could imagine how Lydia had dropped off to sleep, like a burden of sweet fragrances cast on the bosom of the night, an unfinished prayer babbled on her lips. But to think of Lydia now was to look trouble in the face, and he returned to his father not so thoroughly in the spirit of a specious gaiety. It did him good, though, to see the colonel's fingers close on the old pipe, with a motion of the thumb, indicating a resumed habit, caressing a smooth, warm boss. The colonel soberly but luxuriously lighted up, and they sat and puffed a while in silence. Jeffrey drew up a chair for his father's feet and another for his own.

"What's your idea," he said,' at length, "of Weedon Moore?"

The colonel took his pipe out and replaced it.

"Rather a dirty fellow, wasn't he?"

"Yes. That is, in college."

"What d' he do?"

The colonel had never been told at the time. He knew Moore was an outcast from the gang.

"Everything," said Jeffrey briefly. "And told of it," he added.

The colonel nodded. Jeffrey put Moore aside for later consideration, and made up his mind pretty generously to talk things over. The habit of his later years had been all for silence, and the remembered confidences of the time before had involved Esther. Of that sweet sorcery he would not think. As he stood now, the immediate result of his disaster had been to callous surfaces accessible to human intercourse and at the same time cause him, in the sensitive inner case of him, to thank the ruling powers that he need never again, seeing how ravaging it is, give himself away. But now because his father had got to have new wine poured into him, he was giving himself away, just as, on passionate impulse, he had given himself away to Lydia. He put his question desperately, knowing how inexorably it committed him.

"Do you suppose there's anything in this town for me to do?"

The colonel produced at once the possibility he had been privately cherishing.

"Alston Choate—"

"I know," said Jeffrey. "I sha'n't go to Choate. You know what Addington is. Before I knew it, I should be a cause. Can't you and I hatch up something?"

The colonel hesitated.

"It would be simple enough," he said, "if I had any capital."

"You haven't," said Jeff, rather curtly, "for me to fool away. What you've got you must save for the girls."

The same doubt was in both their minds. Would Addington let him earn his living in the bald give and take of everyday commerce? Would it half patronise and half distrust him? He thought, from old knowledge of it, that Addington would behave perfectly but exasperatingly. It was passionate in its integrity, but because he was born out of the best traditions in it, a temporary disgrace would be condoned. If he opened a shop, Addington would give him a tithe of its trade, from duty and, as it would assuredly tell itself, for the sake of his father. But he didn't want that kind of nursing. He was sick enough at the accepted ways of life to long for wildernesses, ocean voyages on rough liners, where every man is worked hard enough to let his messmate alone. He was hurt, irremediably hurt, he knew, in what stands in us for the affections. But here were affections still, inflexibly waiting. They had to be reckoned with. They had to be nurtured and upheld, no matter how the contacts of life hit his own skin. He tried vaguely, and still with angry difficulty, to explain himself.

"I want to stand by you, father. But you won't get much satisfaction out of me."

The colonel thought he should get all kinds of satisfaction. His glance told that. How much of the contentment of it, Jeffrey wondered, with a cynical indulgence for life as it is, came from tobacco and how much from him?

"You see I'm not the chap I was," he blundered, trying to open his father's eyes to the abysmal depth of his futility.

"You're older," said the colonel. "And—you'll let me say it, won't you, Jeff?" He felt very timid before his rough-tongued, perhaps coarsened son. "You seem to me to have got a lot out of it."

Out of his imprisonment! The red mounted to Jeffrey's forehead. He took out his pipe, emptied it carefully and laid it down.

"Father," he said slowly, "I'm going to tell you the truth. When we're young we're full of yeast. We know it all. We think we're going to do it all. But we're only seething and working inside. It's a dream, I suppose. We live in it and we think we've got it all. But it's a horribly uncomfortable dream."

The colonel gave his little acquiescing nod.

"I wouldn't have it again," he said. "No, I wouldn't go back."

"And I give you my word," said Jeffrey, slowly thinking out his way, though it looked to him as if there were really no way, "I'm as much at sea as I was then. It's not the same turmoil, but it's a turmoil. I was pulled up short. I was given plenty of time to think. Well, I thought—when I hadn't the nerve to keep myself from doing it."

"You said some astonishing things in the prison paper," his father ventured. The whole thing seemed so gravely admirable to him—Jeff and the prison as the public knew them—that he wished Jeff himself could get comfort out of it.

"Some few things I believe I settled, so far as I understand them." Jeff was frowning at the table where his hand beat an impatient measure. "I saw things in the large. I saw how the nations—all of 'em, in living under present conditions—could go to hell quickest. That's what they're bent on doing. And I saw how they could call a halt if they would. But how to start in on my own life, I don't know. You'd think I'd had time enough to face the thing and lick it into shape. I haven't. I don't know any more what to do than if I'd been born yesterday—on a new planet—and not such an easy one."

While the colonel had bewailed his own limitations a querulous discontent had ivoried his face. Now it had cleared and left the face sedate and firm in a gravity fitted to its nobility of line.

"Jeff," he said. He leaned over the table and touched Jeffrey's hand.

Jeff looked up.

"What is it?" he asked.

"The reason you're not prepared to go on is because you don't care. You don't care a hang about yourself."

Jeffrey debated a moment. It was true. His troublesome self did not seem to him of any least account.

"Well," said he, "let's go to bed."

But they shook hands before they parted, and the colonel did not put his pipe away in the drawer. He left it on the mantel, conveniently at hand.

XV

Next morning Anne, after listening at the colonel's door and hearing nothing, decided not to tap. She went on downstairs to be saluted by a sound she delighted in: a low humming. It came from the library where her father was happily and most villainously attacking the only song he knew: "Lord Lovell." Anne's heart cleared up like a smiling sky. She went in to him, and he, at the window, his continued humming like the spinning of a particularly eccentric top, turned and greeted her, and he seemed to be very well and almost gay. He showed no sign of even remembering yesterday, and when presently Jeffrey came in and then Lydia, they all behaved, Anne thought, like an ordinary family with no queer problems round the corner.

After breakfast Jeffrey turned to Lydia and said quite simply: "Come into the orchard and walk a little."

But to Lydia, Anne saw, with a mild surprise, his asking must have meant something not so simple. Her face flushed all over, and a misty sweetness, like humility and gratitude, came into her eyes. Jeffrey, too, caught that morning glow, only to find his task the sadder. How to say things to her! and after all, what was it possible to say? They went down into the orchard, and Lydia, by his side, paced demurely. He saw she was trying to fit her steps to his impatient stride, and shortened up on it. He felt very tender toward Lydia. At last, when it seemed as if they might be out of range of the windows, and, he unreasonably felt, more free, he broke out abruptly:

"I've got a lot of things to say to you." Lydia glanced up at him with that wonderful, exasperating look, half humility, and waited. It seemed to her he must have a great deal to say. "I don't believe it's possible for you—for a girl—to understand what it would be for a man in my place to come home and find everybody so sweet and kind. I mean you—and Anne."

Now he felt nothing short of shame. But she took him quickly enough. He didn't have to go far along the shameful road. She glanced round at him again, and, knowing what the look must be, he did not meet it. He could fancy well the hurt inquiry leaping into those innocent eyes.

"What have I done," she asked, and his mind supplied the accusatory inference, "that you don't love me any more?"

He hastened to answer.

"You've been everything that's sweet and kind." He added, whether wisely or not he could not tell, what seemed to him the truth: "I haven't got hold of myself. I thought it would be an easy stunt to come back and stay a while and then go away and get into something permanent. But it's no such thing. Lydia, I don't understand people very well. I don't understand myself. I'm afraid I'm a kind of blackguard."

"Oh, no," said Lydia gravely. "You're not that."

She did not understand him, but she was, in her beautiful confidence, sure he was right. She was hurt. There was the wound in her heart, and that new sensation of its actually bleeding; but she had a fine courge of her own, and she knew grief over that inexplicable pang must be put away until the sight of it could not trouble him.

"I'm going to ask you a question," said Jeffrey shortly, in his distaste for asking it at all. "Do you want me to take father away with me, you and Anne?"

"Are you going away?" she asked, in an irrepressible tremor.

"Answer me," said Jeffrey.

She was not merely the beautiful child he had thought her. There was something dauntless in her, something that could endure. He felt for her a quick passion of comradeship and the worship men have for women who seem to them entirely beautiful and precious enough to be saved from disillusion.

"If I took him away with me—and of course it would be made possible," he was blundering over this in decency—"possible for you to live in comfort—wouldn't you and Anne like to have some life of your own? You haven't had any. Like other girls, I mean."

She threw her own question back to him with a cool and clear decision he hadn't known the soft, childish creature had it in her to frame.

"Does he want us to go?"

"Good God, no!" said Jeffrey, faced, in the instant, by the hideous image of ingratitude she conjured up, his own as well as his father's.

"Do you?"

"Lydia," said he, "you don't understand. I told you you couldn't. It's only that my sentence wasn't over when I left prison. It's got to last, because I was in prison."

"Oh, no! no!" she cried.

"I've muddled my life from the beginning. I was always told I could do things other fellows couldn't. Because I was brilliant. Because I knew when to strike. Because I wasn't afraid. Well, it wasn't so. I muddled the whole thing. And the consequence is, I've got to keep on being muddled. It's as if you began a chemical experiment wrong. You might go on messing with it to infinity. You wouldn't come out anywhere."

"You think it's going to be too hard for us," she said, with a directness he thought splendid.

"Yes. It would be infernally hard. And what are you going to get out of it? Go away, Lydia. Live your life, you and Anne, and marry decent men and let me fight it out."

"I sha'n't marry," said Lydia. "You know that."

He could have groaned at her beautiful wild loyalty. The power of the universe had thrown them together, and she was letting that one minute seal her unending devotion. But her staunchness made it easier to talk to her. She could stand a good deal, the wind and rain of cruel fact. She wouldn't break.

"Lydia," said he, "you are beautiful to me. But I can't let you go on seeming beautiful, if—if you're so divinely kind to me and believing, and everything that's foolish—and dear."

"You mean," said Lydia, "you're afraid I should think wrong thoughts about you—because there's Esther. Oh, I know there's Esther. But I didn't mean to be wicked. And you didn't. It was so—so above things. So above everything."

Her voice trembled too much for her to manage it. He glanced at her and saw her lip was twitching violently, and savagely thought a man sometime would have a right to kiss it. And yet what did he care? To kiss a woman's lips was a madness or a splendour that passed. He knew there might be, almost incredibly, another undying passion that did last, made up of endurance and loyalty and the free rough fellowship between men. This girl, this soft yet unyielding thing, was capable of that. But she must not squander it on him who was bankrupt. Yet here she was, in her house of dreams, tended by divine ministrants of the ideal: the old lying servitors that let us believe life is what we make it and deaf to the creatures raging there outside who swear it is made irrevocably for us. He was sure they lied, these servitors in the house of maiden dreams. Yet how to tell her so! And would he do it if he could?

"You see," he said irrelevantly, "I want you to have your life."

"It will be my life," she said. "To take care of Farvie, as we always have. To make things nice for you in the house. I don't believe you and Farvie'd like it at all without Anne and me."

She was announcing, he saw, quite plainly, that she didn't want a romantic pact with him. They had met, just once, for an instant, in the meeting of their lips, and Lydia had simply taken that shred of triumphant life up to the mountain-top to weave her nest of it: a nest where she was to warm all sorts of brooding wonders for him and for her father. There was nothing to be done with her in her innocence, her ignorance, her beauty of devotion.

"It doesn't make any difference about me," he said. "I'm out of the running in every possible way. But it makes a lot of difference about you and Anne."

"It doesn't make any difference to Anne," said Lydia astutely, "because she's going to heaven, and so she doesn't care about what she has here."

He was most amusedly anxious to know whether Lydia also was going to heaven.

"Do you care what happens to you here?" he asked.

"Yes," she answered instantly. "I care about staying with my folks."

The homely touch almost conquered him. He thought perhaps such a fierce little barbarian might even find it better to eat bitter bread with her own than to wander out into strange flowery paths.

"Are you going to heaven, too, Lydia?" he ventured. "With Anne?"

"I'm going everywhere my folks go," she said, with composure. "Now I can't talk any more. I told Mary Nellen I'd dust while they do the silver."

The atmosphere of a perfectly conventional living was about them. Jeffrey had to adjure himself to keep awake to the difficulties he alone had made. He had come out to confess to her the lawlessness of his mind toward her, and she was deciding merely to go on living with him and her father, which meant, in the first place, dusting for Mary Nellen. They walked along the orchard in silence, and Jeffrey, with relief, also took a side track to the obvious. Absently his eyes travelled along the orchard's level length, and his great thought came to him. The ground did it. The earth called to him. The dust rose up impalpably and spoke to him.

"Lydia," said he, "I see what to do."

"What?"

The startled brightness in her eyes told him she feared his thought, and, not knowing, as he did, how great it was, suspected him of tragic plans for going away.

"I'll go to work on this place. I'll plough it up. I'll raise things, and father and I'll dig."

As he watched her interrogatively the colour faded from her face. The relief of hearing that homespun plan had chilled her blood, and she was faint for an instant with the sickness of hearty youth that only knows it feels odd to itself and concludes the strangeness is of the soul. But she did not answer, for Anne was at the window, signalling.

"Come in," said Lydia. "She wants us."

Miss Amabel, in a morning elegance of black muslin and silk gloves, was in the library. Anne looked excited and the colonel, there also, quite pleasurably stirred. Lydia was hardly within the door when Anne threw the news at her.

"Dancing classes!"

"At my house," said Miss Amabel. She put a warm hand on Lydia's shoulder and looked down at her admiringly: wistfully as well. "Can anything," the look said, "be so young, so unthinkingly beautiful and have a right to its own richness? How could we turn this dower into the treasury of the poor and yet not impoverish the child herself?" "We'll have an Italian class and a Greek. And there are others, you know, Poles, Armenians, Syrians. We'll manage as many as we can."

They sat down to planning classes and hours, and Jeffrey, looking on, noted how keen the two girls were, how intent and direct. They balked at money. If the classes were for the poor, they proposed giving their time as Miss Amabel gave her house. But she disposed of that with a conclusive gravity, and a touch, Jeffrey was amused to see, of the Addington manner. Miss Amabel was pure Addington in all her unconsidered impulses. She wanted to give, not to receive. Yet if you reminded her that giving was the prouder part, she would vacate her ground of privilege with a perfect simplicity sweet to see. When she got up Jeffrey rose with her, and though he took the hand she offered him, he said:

"I'm going along with you."

And they were presently out in Addington streets, walking together almost as it might have been when they walked from Sunday school and she was "teacher". He began on her at once.

"Amabel, dear, what are you running with Weedon Moore for?"

She was using her parasol for a cane, and now, in instinctive remonstrance, she struck it the more forcibly on the sidewalk and had to stop and pull it out from a worn space between the bricks.

"I'm glad you spoke of Weedon," she said. "It's giving me a chance to say some things myself. You know, Jeffrey, you're very unjust to Weedon."

"No, I'm not," said Jeff.

"Alston Choate is, too."

"Choate and I know him, better than you or any other woman can in a thousand years."

"You think he's the same man he was in college."

"Fellows like Moore don't change. There's something inherently rotten in 'em you can't sweeten out."

"Jeffrey, I assure you he has changed. He's a power for good. And when he gets his nomination, he'll be more of a power yet."

"Nomination. For what?"

"Mayor."

"Weedon Moore mayor of this town? Why, the cub! We'll duck him, Choate and I." They were climbing the rise to her red brick house, large and beautiful and kindly. It really looked much like Miss Amabel herself, a little unkempt, but generous and belonging to an older time. They went in and Jeffrey, while she took off her bonnet and gloves, stood looking about him in the landscape-papered hall.

"Go into the east room, dear," said she. "Why, Jeff, what is it?"

He was standing still, looking now up the stairs.

"Oh," said he, "I believe I'm going to cry. It hasn't changed—any more than you have. You darling!"

Miss Amabel put her hand on his shoulder, and he drew it to his lips; and then she slipped it through his arm and they went into the east room together, which also had not changed, and Jeff took his accustomed place on the sofa under the portrait of the old judge, Miss Amabel's grandfather. Jeff shook off sentiment, the softness he could not afford.

"I tell you I won't have it," he said. "Weedon Moore isn't going to be mayor of this town. Besides he can't. He hasn't been in politics—"

"More or less," said she.

"Run for office?"

"Yes."

"Ever get any?"

"No."

"There! what d'I tell you?"

"But he has a following of his own now," said she, in a quiet triumph, he thought. "Since he has done so much for labour."

"What's he done?"

"He has organised—"

"Strikes?"

"Yes. He's been all over the state, working."

"And talking?"

"Why, yes, Jeff! Don't be unjust. He has to talk."

"Amabel," said Jeffrey, with a sudden seriousness that drew her renewed attention, "have you the slightest idea what kind of things Moore is pouring into the ears of these poor devils that listen to him?"

She hesitated.

"Have you, now?" he insisted.

"Well, no, Jeffrey. I haven't heard him. There's rather a strong prejudice here against labour meetings. So Weedon very wisely talks to the men when he can get them alone."

"Why wisely? Why do you say that?"

"Because we want to spread knowledge without rousing prejudice. Then there isn't so much to fight."

"What kind of knowledge is Weedon Moore spreading? Tell me that."

Her plain face glowed with the beauty of her aspiration.

"He is spreading the good tidings," she said softly, "good tidings of great joy."

"Don't get on horseback, dear," he said, inexorably, but fondly. "I'm a plain chap, you know. I have to have plain talk. What are the tidings?"

She looked at him in a touched solemnity.

"Don't you know, Jeff," she said, "the working-man has been going on in misery all these centuries because he hasn't known his own power? It's like a man's dying of thirst and not guessing the water is just inside the rock and the rock is ready to break. He's only to look and there are the lines of cleavage." She sought in the soft silk bag that was ever at her hand, took out paper and pen and jotted down a line.

"What are you writing there?" Jeffrey asked, with a certainty that it had something to do with Moore.

"What I just said," she answered, with a perfect simplicity. "About lines of cleavage. It's a good figure of speech, and it's something the men can understand."

"For Moore? You're writing it for Moore?"

"Yes." She slipped the pad into her bag.

"Amabel," said he, helpless between inevitable irritation and tenderest love of her, "you are a perfectly unspoiled piece of work from the hand of God Almighty. But if you're running with Weedon Moore, you're going to do an awful lot of harm."

"I hope not, dear," she said gravely, but with no understanding, he saw, that her pure intentions could lead her wrong.

"I've heard Weedon Moore talking to the men."

She gave him a look of acute interest.

"Really, Jeff? Now, where?"

"The old circus-ground. I heard him. And he's pulling down, Amabel. He's destroying. He's giving those fellows an idea of this country that's going to make them hate it, trample it—" He paused as if the emotion that choked him made him the more impatient of what caused it.

"That's it," said she, her own face settling into a mournful acquiescence. "We've earned hate. We must accept it. Till we can turn it into love."

"But he's preaching discontent."

"Ah, Jeffrey," said she, "there's a noble discontent. Where should we be without it?"

He got up, and shook his head at her, smilingly, tenderly. She had made him feel old, and alien to this strange new day.

"You're impossible, dear," said he, "because you're so good. You've only to see right things to follow them and you believe everybody's the same."

"But why not?" she asked him quickly. "Am I to think myself better than they are?"

"Not better. Only more prepared. By generations of integrity. Think of that old boy up there." He glanced affectionately at the judge, a friend since his childhood, when the painted eyes had followed him about the room and it had been a kind of game to try vainly to escape them. "Take a mellow soil like your inheritance and the inheritance of a lot of 'em here in Addington. Plant kindness in it and decency and—"

"And love of man," said Miss Amabel quietly.

"Yes. Put it that way, if you like it better. I mean the determination to play a square game. Not to gorge, but make the pile go round. Plant in that kind of a soil and, George! what a growth you get!"

"I don't find fewer virtues among my plainer friends."

"No, no, dear! But you do find less—less background."

"That's our fault, Jeff. We've made their background. It's a factory wall. It's the darkness of a mine."

"Exactly. Knock a window in here and there, but don't chuck the reins of government into the poor chaps' hands and tell 'em to drive to the devil."

Her face flamed at him, the bonfire's light when prejudice is burned.

"I know," she said, "but you're too slow. You want them educated first. Then you'll give them something—if they deserve it."

"I won't give them my country—or Weedon Moore's country—to manhandle till they're grown up, and fit to have a plaything and not smash it."

"I would, Jeffrey."

"You would?"

"Yes. Give them power. They'll learn by using it. But don't waste time. Think of it! All the winters and summers while they work and work and the rest of us eat the bread they make for us."

"But, good God, Amabel! there isn't any curse on work. If your Bible tells you so, it's a liar. You go slow, dear old girl; go slow."

"Go slow?" said Amabel, smiling at him. "How can I? Night and day I see those people. I hear them crying out to me."

"Well, it's uncomfortable. But it's no reason for your delivering them over to demagogues like Weedon Moore."

"He's not a demagogue."

There was a sad bravado in her smile, and he answered with an obstinacy he was willing she should feel.

"All the same, dear, don't you try to make him tetrarch over this town. The old judge couldn't stand for that. If he were here to-day he wouldn't sit down at the same table with Weedie, and he wouldn't let you."

She followed him to the door; her comfortable hand was on his arm.

"Weedon will begin his campaign this fall," she said. Evidently she felt bound to define her standpoint clearly.

"Where's his money?" They were at the door and Jeffrey turned upon her. "Amabel, you're not going to stake that whelp?"

She flushed, from guilt, he knew.

"I am not doing anything unwise," she said, with the Addington dignity.

Thereupon Jeffrey went away sadly.

XVI

Jeffrey began to dig, and his father, without definite intention, followed him about and quite eagerly accepted lighter tasks. They consulted Denny as to recognised ways of persuading the earth, and summoned a ploughman and his team, and all day Jeffrey walked behind the plough, not holding it, for of that art he was ignorant, but in pure admiration. He asked questions about planting, and the ploughman, being deaf, answered in a forensic bellow, so that Addington, passing the brick wall in its goings to and fro, heard, and communicated to those at home that Jeffrey Blake, dear fellow, was going back to the land. Jeffrey did, as he had cynically foreseen, become a cause. All persons of social significance came to call, and were, without qualification, kind. Sometimes he would not see them, but Anne one day told him how wrong he was. If he hid himself he put a burden on his father, who stood in the breach, and talked even animatedly, renewing old acquaintance with a dignified assumption of having nothing to ignore. But when the visitors were gone the red in his cheek paled something too much, and Anne thought he was being unduly strained.

After that Jeffrey doggedly stayed by. He proved rather a silent host, but he stood up to the occasion, and even answered the general query whether he was going into business by the facer that he and his father had gone into it. They were market-gardening. The visitors regretted that, so far as Addington manners would permit, because they had noticed the old orchard was being ploughed, and that of course meant beans at least. Some of the older ladies recalled stories of dear Doctor Blake's pacing up and down beside the wall. They believed you could even find traces of the sacred path; but one day Jeffrey put an end to that credulous ideal by saying you couldn't now anyway, since it had been ploughed. Then, he saw, he hurt Addington and was himself disquieted. Years ago he had been amused when he hit hard against it and they flew apart equally banged; now he was grown up, whether to his advantage or not, and it looked to him as if Addington ought by this time to be grown up too.

It was another Addington altogether from the one he had left, though a surface of old tradition and habit still remained to clothe it in a semblance of past dignity and calm. Not a public cause existed in the known world but Addington now had a taste of it, though no one but Miss Amabel did much more than talk with fervour. The ladies who had once gone delicately out to teas and church, as sufficient intercourse with this world and preparation for the next, now had clubs and classes where they pounced on subjects not even mentionable fifty years ago, and shook them to shreds in their well-kept teeth. There was sprightly talk about class-consciousness, and young women who, if their incomes had been dissipated by inadequate trusteeship, would once have taught school according to a gentle ideal, now went away and learned to be social workers, and came back to make self-possessed speeches at the Woman's Club and present it with new theories to worry. This all went on under the sanction of Addington manners, and kept concert pitch rather high.

On all topics but one Addington agreed to such an extent that discussion really became more like axioms chanted in unison; but when it came to woman suffrage society silently but exactly split. There were those who would stick at nothing, even casting a vote. There were those who said casting a vote was unwomanly, and you couldn't possibly leave the baby long enough to do it. Others among the antis were reconciled to its coming, if it came slowly enough not to agitate us. "Of course," said one of these, a Melvin who managed her ample fortune with the acumen of a financier, "it will come sometime. But we are none of us ready. We must delay it as long as we can." So she and the like-minded drove into the country round and talked about preventing the extension of the suffrage to women until hard-working, meagre-living people who had not begun to think much about votes, save as a natural prerogative of man, thought about them a great deal, and incidentally learned to organise and lobby, and got a very good training for suffrage when it should come. It did no harm, nor did the fervour of the other side do good. The two parties got healthfully tired with the exercise and "go" of it all, and at least they stirred the pot. But whatever they said or did, suffragists and antis never, so to speak, "met". The subject, from some occult sense of decorum, was tabu. If an anti were setting forth her views when a suffragist entered the room she instantly ceased and began to talk about humidity or the Balkans. A suffragist would no more have marshalled her arguments for the overthrow of an equal than she would have corrected a point of etiquette. But each went out with zeal into New England villages for the conversion of social underlings.

When they elected Jeffrey into a cause they did it with a rush, and they also elected his wife. Through her unwelcoming door poured a stream of visitors, ostensibly to call on Madame Beattie, but really, as Esther saw with bitterness, to recommend this froward wife to live with her husband. Feeling ran very high there. Addington, to a woman, knew exactly the ideal thing for Esther to have done. She should have "received" him—that was the phrase—and helped him build up his life—another phrase. This they delicately conveyed to her in accepted innuendos Addington knew how to handle. Esther once told Aunt Patricia there were women selected by the other women to "do their dirty work ". But what she really meant was that Addington had a middle-aged few of the old stock who, with an arrogant induration in their own position, out of which no attacking humour could deliver them, held, as they judged, the contract to put questions. These it was who would ask Esther over a cup of tea: "Are you going on living in this house, my dear?" or: "Shall you join your husband at his father's? And will his father and the step-children stay on there?" And the other women, of a more circuitous method or a more sensitive touch, would listen and, Esther felt sure, discuss afterward what the inquisitors had found out: with an amused horror of the inquisitors and a grateful relish of the result. Esther sometimes thought she must cry aloud in answer; but though a flush came into her face and gave her an added pathos, she managed, in a way of gentle obstinacy, to say nothing, and still not to offend. And Madame Beattie sat by, never saving her, as Esther knew she might, out of her infernal cleverness, but imperturbably and lightly amused and smoking cigarettes all over the tea things. As a matter of fact, the tea things and their exquisite cloth were unpolluted, but Esther saw figuratively the trail of smoke and ashes, like a nicotian Vesuvius, over the home. She still hated cigarettes, which Addington had not yet accepted as a feminine diversion, though she had the slight comfort of knowing it forgave in Madame Beattie what it would not have tolerated in an Addingtonian. "Foreign ways," the ladies would remark to one another. "And she really is a very distinguished woman. They say she visits everywhere abroad."

Anne and Lydia were generally approved as modest and pretty girls; and Miss Amabel's classes in national dances became an exceedingly interesting feature of the town life. Anne and Lydia were in this dancing scheme all over. They were enchanted with it, the strangeness and charm of these odd citizens of another world, and made friends with little workwomen out of the shops, and went home with them to see old pieces of silver and embroidery, and plan pageants—this in the limited English common to them. Miss Amabel, too, was pleased, in her wistful way that always seemed to be thanking you for making things come out decently well. She had one big scheme: the building up of homespun interests between old Addington and these new little aliens who didn't know the Addington history or its mind and heart.

One night after a dancing class in her dining-room the girls went, with pretty good-nights, and Anne with them. She was hurrying down town on some forgotten errand, and refused Lydia's company. For Lydia was tired, and left alone with Miss Amabel, she settled to an hour's laziness. She knew Miss Amabel liked having her there, liked her perhaps better than Anne, who was of the beautiful old Addington type and not so piquing. Lydia had, across her good breeding, a bizarre other strain, not bohemian, not gipsy, but of a creature who is and always will be, even beyond youth, new to life.

There were few conventions for Lydia. She did not instinctively follow beaten paths. If the way looked feasible and pleasant, she cut across.

"You're a little tired," said Miss Amabel, hesitating. She knew this was violating the etiquette of dancing. To be tired, Anne said, and Lydia, too, was because you hadn't the "method".

"It isn't the dancing," said Lydia at once, as Miss Amabel knew she would.

"No. But you've seemed tired a good deal of the time lately. Does anything worry you?"

"No," said Lydia soberly. She looked absent-minded, as if she sought about for what did worry her.

"You don't think your father's working too hard, planting?"

"Oh, no! It's good for him. He gets frightfully tired. They both do. But Farvie sleeps and eats and smokes. And laughs! That's Jeffrey. He can always make Farvie laugh." She said the last rather wonderingly, because she knew Jeffrey hadn't, so far as she had seen him, much light give and take and certainly no hilarity of his own. "But I suppose," she added wisely, as she had many times to herself, "Farvie's so pleased even to look at him and think he's got him back."

Miss Amabel disposed a pillow more invitingly on the old sofa that had spacious hollows in it, and Lydia obeyed the motion and lay down. It was not, she thought, because she was tired. Only it would please Miss Amabel. But the heart had gone out of her. If she looked as she felt, she realised she must be wan. But it takes more than the sorrows of youth to wash the colour out of it. She felt an impulse now to give herself away.

"It's only," she said, "we're not getting anywhere. That worries me."

"With your work?" Miss Amabel was waving a palm-leaf fan, from no necessity but the tranquillity induced by its rhythmic sway.

"Oh, no. About Jeffrey. Didn't you know we meant to clear him, Anne and I?"

"Clear him, dear? What of?"

"Why, what he was accused of," said Lydia.

"But he had his trial, you know. He was found guilty. He pleaded guilty, dear. That was why he was sentenced."

"Oh, but we all know why he pleaded guilty," said Lydia. "It was to save somebody else."

"Not exactly to save her," said Miss Amabel. "She wouldn't have been tried, you know. She wasn't guilty in that sense. Of course she was, before the fact. But that's not being legally guilty. It's only morally so."

Lydia was staring at her with wide eyes.

"Do you mean Esther?" she asked.

"Why, yes, of course I mean Esther."

"But I don't. I mean that dreadful man."

She put her feet to the floor and sat upright, smoothing her hair with hurried fingers. At least if she could talk about it with some one who wasn't Anne with whom she had talked for years knowing exactly what Anne would say at every point, it seemed as if she were getting, even at a snail's pace, upon her road. But Miss Amabel was very dense.

"My dear," said she, "I don't know what you mean."

"I mean the man that was in the scheme with him, in a way, and got out and sold his shares while they were up, and let the crash come on Jeffrey when he was alone."

"James Reardon?"

Lydia hated him too much to accept even a knowledge of his name.

"He was a promoter, just as Jeffrey was," she insisted, with her pretty sulkiness. "He was the one that went West and looked after the mines. And if there was nothing in them, he knew it. But he let Jeffrey go on trying to—to place the shares—and when Jeffrey went under he was safely out of the way. And he's guilty."

Miss Amabel looked at her thoughtfully and patiently.

"I'm afraid he isn't guilty in any sense the law would recognise," she said. "You see, dear, there are things the law doesn't take into account. It can't. You believe in Jeffrey. So do I. But I think you'll have to realise Jeffrey lost his head. And he did do wrong."

"Oh, how can you say a thing like that?" cried Lydia, in high passion. "And you've known him all your life."

Miss Amabel was not astute. Her nobility made it a condition of her mind to be unsuspecting. She knew the hidden causes of Jeffrey's downfall. She was sure his father knew, and it never seemed to her that these two sisters were less than sisters to him. What she herself knew, they too must have learned; out of this believing candour she spoke.

"You mustn't forget there was the necklace, and Madame Beattie expecting to be paid."

Lydia was breathless in her extremity of surprise.

"What necklace?" asked she.

"Don't you know?"

Miss Amabel's voice rose upon the horror of her own betrayal.

"What do you mean?" Lydia was insisting, with an iteration that sounded like repeated onslaughts, a mental pounce, to shake it out of her. "What do you mean?"

Miss Amabel wore the dignified Addington aloofness.

"I am very sorry," said she. "I have been indiscreet."

"But you'll tell me, now you've begun," panted Lydia. "You'll have to tell me or I shall go crazy."

"We must both control ourselves," said Miss Amabel, with a further retreat to the decorum of another generation. "You are not going crazy, Lydia. We are both tired and we feel the heat. And I shall not tell you."

Lydia ran out of the room. There was no other word for the quickness of her going. She fled like running water, and having worn no hat, she found herself bareheaded in the street, hurrying on to Esther's. An instinct told her she could only do her errand, make her assault, it seemed, on those who knew what she did not, if she never paused to weigh the difficulties: her hatreds, too, for they had to be weighed. Lydia was sure she hated Madame Beattie and Esther. She would not willingly speak to them, she had thought, after her last encounters. But now she was letting the knocker fall on Esther's door, and had asked the discreet maid with the light eyelashes, who always somehow had an air of secret knowledge and amusement, if Madame Beattie were at home, and gave her name. The maid, with what seemed to Lydia's raw consciousness an ironical courtesy, invited her into the library and left her there in its twilight tranquillity. Lydia stood still, holding one of her pathetically small, hard-worked hands over her heart, and shortly, to her gratitude, Sophy was back and asked her to go up to Madame Beattie's room.

The maid accompanying her, Lydia went, with her light step, afraid of itself lest it turn coward, and in the big dark room at the back of the house, its gloom defined by the point of light from a shaded reading candle, she was left, and stood still, almost wishing for Sophy whose footfalls lessened on the stairs. There were two bits of light in the room, the candle and Madame Beattie's face. Madame Beattie had taken off her toupée, and for Lydia she had not troubled to put it on. She lay on the bed against pillows, a down quilt drawn over her feet, regardless of the seasonable warmth, and a disorder of paper-covered books about her. One she held in her ringed hand, and now she put it down, her eyeglasses with it, and turned the candle so that the light from the reflector fell on Lydia's face.

"I wasn't sure which girl it was," she said, in a tone of mild good-nature. "It's not the good one. It's you, mischief. Come and sit down."

Madame Beattie did not apologise for giving audience in her bedchamber. In the old royal days before the downfall of her kingdom she had accorded it to greater than Lydia French. Lydia's breath came so fast now that it hurt her. She stepped forward, but she did not take the low chair which really had quite a comfortable area left beyond Madame Beattie's corset and stockings. She stood there in the circle of light and said desperately:

"What was it about your necklace?"

She had created an effect. Madame Beattie herself gasped.

"For God's sake, child," said she, "what do you know about my necklace?"

"I don't know anything," said Lydia. "And I want to know everything that will help Jeff."

She broke down here, and cried bitterly. Madame Beattie lay there looking at her, at first with sharp eyes narrowed, as if she rather doubted whose emissary Lydia might be. Then her face settled into an astonished yet astute calm and wariness.

"You'll have to sit down," said she. "It's a long story." So Lydia sank upon the zone left by the corset and stockings. "Who's been talking to you?" asked Madame Beattie: but Lydia looked at her and dumbly shook her head. "Jeff?"

"No. Oh, no!"

"His father?"

"Farvie? Not a word."

Madame Beattie considered.

"What business is it of yours?" she asked.

Lydia winced. She was used to softness from Anne and the colonel. But she controlled herself. If she meant to enter on the task of exonerating Jeffrey, she must, she knew, make herself impervious to snubs.

"Anne and I are doing all we can to help Jeffrey," she said. "He doesn't know it. Farvie doesn't know it. But there's something about a necklace.

And it had ever so much to do with Jeffrey and his case. And I want to know."

Madame Beattie chuckled. Her worn yellowed face broke into satirical lines, hateful ones, Lydia thought. She was like a jeering unpleasant person carved for a cathedral and set up among the saints.

"I'll tell you about my necklace," said she. "I'm perfectly willing to. Perhaps you can do something about it. Something for me, too."

It was a strange, vivid picture: that small arc of light augmenting the dusk about them, and Lydia sitting rapt in expectation while Madame Beattie's yellowed face lay upon the obscurity, an amazing portraiture against the dark. It was a picture of a perfect consistency, of youth and innocence and need coming to the sybil for a reading of the leaves of life.

"You see, my dear," said Madame Beattie, "years ago I had a necklace given me—diamonds." She said it with emotion even. No one ever heard her rehearse her triumphs on the lyric stage. They were the foundation of such dignity as her life had known; but the gewgaws time had flung at her she did like, in these lean years, to finger over. "It was given me by a Royal Personage. He had to do a great many clever things to get ahead of his government and his exchequer to give me such a necklace. But he did."

"Why did he?" Lydia asked.

It was an innocent question designed to keep the sybil going. Madame Beattie's eyes narrowed slightly. You could see what she had been in the day of her power.

"He had to," said she, with an admiringly dramatic simplicity. "I wanted it."

"But—" began Lydia, and Madame Beattie put up a small hand with a gesture of rebuttal.

"Well, time went on, and he needed the necklace back. However, that doesn't belong to the story. Some years ago, just before your Jeff got into trouble, I came over here to the States. I was singing then more or less." A concentrated power, of even a noble sort, came into her face. There was bitterness too, for she had to remember how disastrous a venture it had been. "I needed money, you understand. I couldn't have got an audience over there. I thought here they might come to hear me—to say they'd heard me—the younger generation—and see my jewels. I hadn't many left. I'd sold most of them. Well, I was mistaken. I couldn't get a house. The fools!" Scorn ate up her face alive and opened it out, a sneering mask. They were fools indeed, she knew, who would not stir the ashes of such embers in search of one spark left. "I'm a very strong woman. But I rather broke down then. I came here to Esther. She was the only relation I had, except my stepsister, and she was off travelling. Susan was always ashamed of me. She went to Europe on purpose. Well, I came here. And Esther wished I was at the bottom of the sea. But she liked my necklace, and she stole it."

Esther, as Lydia had seen her sitting in a long chair and eating candied fruit, had been a figure of such civilised worth, however odious, that Lydia said involuntarily, in a loud voice:

"She couldn't. I don't believe it."

"Oh, but she did," said Madame Beattie, looking at her with the coolness of one who holds the cards. "She owned she did."

"To you?"

"To Jeff. He was madly in love with her then. Married, you understand, but frightfully in love. Yes, she owned it. I always thought that was why he wasn't sorry to go to jail. If he'd stayed out there was the question of the necklace. And Esther. He didn't know what to do with her."

"But he made her give it back," said Lydia, out of agonised certainty that she must above all believe in him.

"He couldn't. She said she'd lost it."

Lydia stared at her, and her own face went white. Now the picture of youth and age confronting each other was of the sybil dealing inexorable hurts and youth anguished in the face of them.

"She said she'd lost it," Madame Beattie went on, in almost chuckling enjoyment of her tale. "She said it had bewitched her. That was true enough. She'd gone to New York. She came back by boat. Crazy thing for a woman to do. And she said she stayed on deck late, and stood by the rail and took the necklace out of her bag to hold it up in the moonlight. And it slipped out of her hands."

"Into the water?"

"She said so."

"You don't believe it." Lydia read that clearly in the contemptuous old face.

"Well, now, I ask you," said Madame Beattie, "was there ever such a silly tale? A young woman of New England traditions—yes, they're ridiculous, but you've got to reckon with them—she comes home on a Fall River boat and doesn't even stay in her cabin, but hangs round on decks and plays with priceless diamonds in the moonlight. Why, it's enough to make the cat laugh."

Madame Beattie, in spite of her cosmopolitan reign, was at least local enough to remember the feline similes Lydia put such dependence on, and she used this one with relish. Lydia felt the more at home.

"But what did she do with it?" she insisted.

"I don't know," said Madame Beattie idly. "Put it in a safety deposit in New York perhaps. Don't ask me."

"But don't you care?" cried Lydia, all of a heat of wonder—terror also at melodramatic thieving here in simple Addington.

"I can care about things without screaming and sobbing," said Madame Beattie briefly. "Though I sobbed a little at the time. I was a good deal unstrung from other causes. But of course I laid it before Jeff, as her husband—"

"He must have been heartbroken."

"Well, he was her husband. He was responsible for her, wasn't he? I told him I wouldn't expose the creature. Only he'd have to pay me for the necklace."

The yellow-white face wavered before Lydia. She was trying to make her brain accept the raw material Madame Beattie was pouring into it and evolve some product she could use.

"But he couldn't pay you. He'd just got into difficulties. You said so."

"Bless you, he hadn't got into any difficulty until Esther pushed him in by helping herself to my necklace. He turned crazy over it. He hadn't enough to pay for it. So he went into the market and tried a big *coup* with all his own money and the money he was holding—people subscribed for his mines, you know, or whatever they were—and that minute there was a panic. And the courts, or whatever it was, got hold of him for using the mails for fraudulent purposes or whatever, and he lost his head. And that's all there was about it."

Lydia's thoughts were racing so fast it seemed to her that she—some inner determined frightened self in her—was flying to overtake them.

"Then you did it," she said. "You! you forced him, you pushed him—"

"To pay me for my necklace," Madame Beattie supplied. "Of course I did. It was a very bad move, as it proved. I was a fool; but then I might have known. Old Lepidus told me the conjunction was bad for me."

"Who was Lepidus?"

"The astrologer. He died last month, the fool, and never knew he was going to. But he'd encouraged me to come on my concert tour, and when that went wrong I lost confidence. It was a bad year, a bad year."

A troop of conclusions were rushing at Lydia, all demanding to be fitted in.

"But you've come back here," she said, incredulous that things as they actually were could supplement the foolish tale Madame Beattie might have stolen out of a silly book. "You think Esther did such a thing as that, and yet you're here with her in this house."

"That's why I'm here," said Madame Beattie patiently. "Jeff's back again, and the necklace hasn't been fully paid for. I've kept my word to him. I haven't exposed his wife, and yet he hasn't recognised my not doing it."

The vision of Jeffrey fleeing before the lash of this implacable taskmaster was appalling to Lydia.

"But he can't pay you," said she. "He's no money. Not even to settle with his creditors."

"That's it," said Madame Beattie. "He's got to make it. And I'm his first creditor. I must be paid first."

"You haven't told him so?" said Lydia, in a manner of fending her off.

"It isn't time. He hasn't recovered his nerve. But he will, digging in that absurd garden."

"And when you think he has, you'll tell him?"

"Why, of course." Madame Beattie reached for her book and smoothed the pages open with a beautiful hand. "It'll do him good, too. Bring him out of thinking he's a man of destiny, or whatever it is he thinks. You tell him. I daresay you've got some influence with him. That's why I've gone into it with you."

"But you said you promised him not to tell all this about Esther. And you've told me."

"That's why. Get him to work. Spur him up. Talk about his creditors. Now run away. I want to read."

XVII

Lydia did run away and really ran, home, to see if the dear surroundings of her life were intact after all she had heard. Since this temporary seclusion in a melodramatic tale, she almost felt as if she should never again see the vision of Mary Nellen making cake or Anne brushing her long hair and looking like a placid saint. The library was dim, but she heard interchanging voices there, and knew Jeffrey and his father were in tranquil talk. So she sped upstairs to Anne's room, and there Anne was actually brushing her hair and wearing precisely that look of evening peace Lydia had seen so many times.

"I thought I'd go to bed early," she said, laying down the brush and gathering round her hair to braid it. "Why, Lyd!"

It was a hot young messenger invading her calm. Anne looked like one who, the day done, was placidly awaiting night; but Lydia was the day itself, her activities still unfinished.

"I've found it out," she announced. "All of it. She made him do it."

Then, while Anne stared at her, she sat down and told her story, vehemently, with breaks of breathless inquiry as to what Anne might think of a thing like this, finally with dragging utterance, for her vitality was gone; and at the end, challenging Anne with a glance, she turned cold: for it came over her that Anne did not believe her.

Anne began braiding her hair again. During Lydia's incredible story she had let it slip from her hand. And Lydia could see the fingers that braided were trembling, as Anne's voice did, too.

"What a dreadful old woman!" said Anne.

"Madame Beattie?" Lydia asked quickly. "Oh, no, she's not, Anne. I like her."

"Like her? A woman like that? She doesn't even look clean."

Lydia answered quite eagerly.

"Oh, yes, Anne, I really like her. I thought I didn't when I heard her talk. Sometimes I hated her. But I understand her somehow. And she's clean. Really she is. It's the kind of clothes she wears." Lydia, to her own surprise at this tragic moment, giggled a little here. Madame Beattie, when in full fig, as she had first seen her, looked to her like pictures of ancient hearses with plumes. "She's all right," said Lydia. "She's just going to have what belongs to her, that's all. And if I were in her place and felt as she does, I would, too."

Anne, with an air of now being ready for bed, threw the finished braid over her back. She was looking at Lydia with her kind look, but, Lydia could also see, compassionately.

"But, Lyd," she said, "the reason I call her a dreadful old woman is that she's told you all this rigmarole. It makes me quite hot. She sha'n't amuse herself by taking you in like that. I won't have it."

"Anne," said Lydia, "it's true. Don't you see it's true?"

"It's a silly story," said Anne. She could imagine certain things, chiefly what men and women would like, in order to make them comfortable, but she had no appetite for the incredible. "Do you suppose Esther would have stolen her aunt's diamonds? Or was it pearls?"

"Yes, I do," said Lydia stoutly. "It's just like her."

"She might do other things, different kinds of things that are just as bad. But stealing, Lyd! Why, think! Esther's a lady."

"Ladies are just like anybody else," said Lydia sulkily. She thought she might have to consider that when she was alone, but at this moment the world was against her and she had to catch up the first generality she could find.

"And for a necklace to be so valuable," said Anne, "valuable enough for Jeff to risk everything he had to try to pay for it—"

Lydia felt firmer ground. She read the newspapers and Anne did not.

"Now, Anne," said she, "you're 'way off. Diamonds cost thousands and thousands of dollars, and so do pearls."

"Why, yes," said Anne, "royal jewels or something of that sort. But a diamond necklace brought here to Addington in Madame Beattie's bag—"

Lydia got up and went over to her. Her charming face was hot with anger, and she looked, too, so much a child that she might in a minute stamp her foot or scream.

"Why, you simpleton!" said she.

"Lydia!" Anne threw in, the only stop-gap she could catch at in her amaze. This was her "little sister", but of a complexion she had never seen.

"Don't you know what kind of a person Madame Beattie is? Why, she's a princess. She's more than a princess. She's had kings and emperors wallowing round the floor after her, begging to kiss her hand."

Anne looked at her. Lydia afterward, in her own room, thought, with a gale of hysterical laughter, "She just looked at me." And Anne couldn't find a word to crush the little termagant. Everything that seemed to pertain was either satirical, as to ask, "Did she tell you so?" or compassionate, implying cerebral decay. But she did venture the compassion.

"Lydia, don't you think you'd better go to bed?"

"Yes," said Lydia promptly, and went out and shut the door.

And on the way to her room, Anne noted, she was singing, or in a fashion she had in moments of triumph, tooting through closed lips, like a trumpet, the measures of a march. In half an hour Anne followed her, to listen at her door. Lydia was silent. Anne hoped she was asleep.

In the morning there was the little termagant again with that same triumph on her face, talking more than usual at the breakfast table, and foolishly, as she hadn't since Jeffrey came. It had always been understood that Lydia had times of foolishness; but it had seemed, after Jeffrey appeared among them clothed in tragedy, that everything would be henceforth on a dignified, even an austere basis. But here she was, chaffing the colonel and chattering childish jargon to Anne. Jeffrey looked at her, first with a tolerant surprise. Then he smiled. Seeing her so light-hearted he was pleased. This was a Lydia he approved of. He need neither run clear of her poetic emotions nor curse himself for calling on them. He went out to his hoeing with an unformulated idea that the tension of social life had let up a little.

Lydia did no dusting of tables or arranging of flowers in a vase. By a hand upon Anne's arm she convoyed her into the hall, and said to her:

"Get your hat. We're going to see Mr. Alston Choate."

"What for?" asked Anne.

"I'm going to tell him what Madame Beattie told me." Lydia's colour was high. She looked prodigiously excited, and as if something was so splendid it could hardly be true. And then, as Anne continued to stare at her with last night's stare, she added, not as if she launched a thunderbolt, but as giving Anne something precious that would please her very much: "I'm going to engage him for Jeffrey's case. Get your hat, Anne. Or your parasol. My nose doesn't burn as yours does. Come, come."

She stood there impatiently tapping her foot as she used to, years ago, when mother was slow about taking her out in the p'ram. Anne turned away.

"You're a Silly Billy," said she. "You're not going to see Mr. Choate."

"Won't you go with me?" Lydia inquired.

"No, of course I sha'n't. And you won't go, either."

"Yes, I shall," said Lydia. "I'm gone."

And she was, out of the door and down the walk. Anne, following helplessly a step, thought she must be running, she was so quickly lost. But Lydia was not running. With due respect, taught her by Anne, for the customs of Addington, she had put on her head the little white-rose-budded hat she had snatched from the hall and fiercely pinned it, and she was walking, though swiftly, in great decorum to Madison Street where the bank was and the post-office and the best stores, and upstairs in the great Choate building, the office of Alston Choate. Lydia tapped at the office door, but no one answered. Then she began to dislike her errand, and if it had not been for the confounding of Anne, perhaps she would have gone home. She tapped again and hurt her knuckles, and that brought her courage back.

"Come in," called a voice, much out of patience, it seemed. She opened the door and there saw Alston Choate, his feet on the table, reading "Trilby." Alston thought he had a right to at least one chapter; he had opened his mail and dictated half a dozen letters, and the stenographer, in another room, was writing them out. He looked up under a frowning brow, and seeing her there, a Phillis come to town, shy, rosy, incredible, threw his book to the table and put down his feet.

"I beg your pardon," said he, getting up, and then Lydia, seeing him in the attitude of conventional deference, began to feel proper supremacy. She spoke with a demure dignity of which the picturesque value was well known to her.

"I've come to engage you for our case."

He stared at her an instant as Anne had, and she sinkingly felt he had no confidence in her. But he recovered himself. That was not like Anne. She had not recovered at all.

"Will you sit down?" he said.

He drew forward a chair. It faced the light, and Lydia noted, when he had taken the opposite one, that they were in the technical position for inquisitor and victim. He waited scrupulously, and when she had seated herself, also sat down.

"Now," said he.

It was gravely said, and reconciled Lydia somewhat to the hardness of her task. At least he would not really make light of her, like Anne. Only your family could do that. She sat there charming, childlike even, all soft surfaces and liquid gleam of eyes, so very young that she was wistful in it. She hesitated in her beginning.

"I understand," she said, "that everything I say to you will be in confidence. O Mr. Choate!" she implored him, with a sudden breaking of her self-possession, "you wouldn't tell, would you?"

Alston Choate did not allow a glint to lighten the grave kindliness of his glance. Perhaps he felt no amusement; she was his client and very sweet.

"Never," said he, in the manner of an uncle to a child. "Tell me anything you like. I shall respect your confidence."

"I saw Madame Beattie last night," said Lydia; and she went on to tell what Madame Beattie had said. She warmed to it, and being of a dramatic type, she coloured the story as Madame Beattie might have done. There was a shade of cynicism here, a tang of worldliness there; and it sounded like the hardest fact. But when she came to Esther, she saw his glance quicken and fasten on hers the more keenly, and when she told him Madame Beattie believed the necklace had not been lost at all, he was looking at her with astonishment even.

"You say—" he began, and made her rehearse it all again in snatches. He cross-examined her, not, it seemed, as if he wished to prove she lied, but to take in her monstrous truth. And after they had been over it two or three times and she felt excited and breathless and greatly fagged by the strain of saying the same thing in different ways, she saw in his face the look she had seen in Anne's.

"Why," she cried out, in actual pain, "you don't believe me."

Choate didn't answer that. He sat for a minute, considering gravely, and then threw down the paper knife he had been bending while she talked. It was ivory, and it gave a little shallow click on the table and that, slight as it was, made her nerves jump. She felt suddenly that she was in deeper than she had expected to be.

"Do you realise," he began gravely, "what you accuse Mrs. Blake of?"

Lydia had not been used to think of her by that name and she asked, with lifted glance:

"Esther?"

"Yes. Mrs. Jeffrey Blake."

"She took the necklace," said Lydia. She spoke with the dull obstinacy that made Anne shake her sometimes and then kiss her into kindness, she was so pretty.

But Alston Choate, she saw, was not going to find it a road to prettiness. He was after the truth like a dog on a scent, and he didn't think he had it yet.

"Madame Beattie," he said, "tells you she believes that Esther—" his voice slipped caressingly on the word with the lovingness of usage, and Lydia saw he called her Esther in his thoughts—"Madame Beattie tells you she believes that Esther did this—this incredible thing."

The judicial aspect fell away from him, and the last words carried only the man's natural distaste. Lydia saw now that whether she was believed or not, she was bound to be most unpopular. But she stood to her guns.

"Madame Beattie knows it. Esther owned it, I told you."

"Owned it to Madame Beattie?"

"To Jeff, anyway. Madame Beattie says so."

"Do you think for a moment she was telling you the truth?"

"But that's just the kind of women they are," said Lydia, at once reckless and astute. "Esther's just the woman to take a necklace, and Madame Beattie's just the woman to tell you she's taken it."

"Miss Lydia," said Choate gravely, "I'm bound to warn you in advance that you mustn't draw that kind of inference."

Lydia lost her temper. It seemed to her she had been talking plain fact.

"I shall draw all the inferences I please," said she, "especially if they're true. And you needn't try to mix me up by your law terms, for I don't understand them."

"I have been particularly careful not to," said Choate rather stiffly; but still, she saw, with an irritating proffer of compassion for her because she didn't know any better. "I am being very unprofessional indeed. And I still advise you, in plain language, not to draw that sort of inference about a lady—" There he hesitated.

"About Esther?" she inquired viciously.

"Yes," said he steadily, "about Mrs. Jeffrey Blake. She is a gentlewoman."

So Anne had said: "Esther is a lady." For the moment Lydia felt more imbued with the impartiality of the law than both of them. Esther's being a lady had, she thought, nothing whatever to do with her stealing a necklace, if she happened to like necklaces. She considered herself a lady, but she could also see herself, under temptation, doing a desperado's deeds. Not stealing a necklace: that was tawdry larceny. But she could see herself trapping Esther in a still place and cutting her dusky hair off so that she'd betray no more men. For she began to suspect that Alston Choate, too, was caught in the lure of Esther's inexplicable charm. Lydia was at the moment of girlhood nearly done where her accumulated experience, half of it not understood, was prepared to spring to life and crystallise into clearest knowledge. She was a child still, but she was ready to be a woman. Alston Choate now was gazing at her with his charming smile, and Lydia hardened under it, certain the smile was meant for mere persuasiveness.

"Besides," he said, "the necklace wasn't yours. You don't want to bring Mrs. Blake to book for stealing a necklace which isn't your own?"

"But I'm not doing it for myself," said Lydia instantly. "It's for Jeffrey."

"But, Jeffrey—" Alston paused. He wanted to put it with as little offence as might be. "Jeffrey has been tried for a certain offence and found guilty."

"He wasn't really guilty," said Lydia. "Can't you see he wasn't? Esther stole the necklace, and Madame Beattie wanted it paid for, and Jeffrey tried to do it and everything went to pieces. Can't you really see?"

She asked it anxiously, and Alston answered her with the more gentleness because her solicitude made her so kind and fair.

"Now," said he, "this is the way it is. Jeffrey pleaded guilty and was sentenced. If everything you say is true—we'll assume it is—he would have been tried just the same, and he would have been sentenced just the same. I don't say his counsel mightn't have whipped up a lot of sympathy from the jury, but he wouldn't have got off altogether. And besides, you wouldn't have had him escape in any such conceivable way. You wouldn't have had him shield himself behind his wife."

Lydia was looking at him with brows drawn tight in her effort to get quite clearly what she thought might prove at any instant a befogged technicality. But it all sounded reasonable enough, and she gratefully understood he was laying aside the jurist's phraseology for her sake.

"But," said she, "mightn't Esther have been tried for stealing the necklace?"

He couldn't help laughing, she seemed so ingenuously anxious to lay Esther by the heels. Then he sobered, for her inhumanity to Esther seemed to him incredible.

"Why, yes," said he, "if she had been suspected, if there'd been evidence—"

"Then I call it a wicked shame she wasn't," said Lydia. "And she's got to be now. If it isn't my business, it's Madame Beattie's, and I'll ask her to do it. I'll beg it of her."

With that she seemed still more dangerous to him, like an explosive put up in so seemly a package that at first you trust it until you see how impossible it is to handle. He spoke with a real and also a calculated impressiveness.

"Miss Lydia, will you let me tell you something?"

She nodded, her eyes fixed on his.

"One thing my profession has taught me. It's so absolutely true a thing that it never fails. And it's this: it is very easy to begin a course of proceeding, but, once begun, it's another thing to stop it. Now before you start this ball rolling—or before you egg on Madame Beattie—let's see what you're going to get out of it."

"I don't expect to get anything," said Lydia, on fire. "I'm not doing it for myself."

"Let's take the other people then. Your father is a man of reputation. He's going to be horrified. Jeff is going to be broken-hearted under an attack upon his wife."

"He doesn't love her," said Lydia eagerly. "Not one bit."

Choate himself believed that, but he stared briefly at having it thrown at him with so deft a touch. Then he went on.

"Mrs. Blake is going to be found not guilty."

"Why is she?" asked Lydia calmly. It seemed to her the cross-questioning was rightly on her side.

"Why, good God! because she isn't guilty!" said Alston with violence, and did not even remember to be glad no legal brother was present to hear so irrational an explosion. He hurried on lest she should call satiric attention to its thinness. "And as for Madame Beattie, she'll get nothing out of it. For the necklace being lost, she won't get that."

"Oh," said Lydia, the more coolly, as she noted she had nettled him on the human side until the legal one was fairly hidden, "but we don't think the necklace is lost."

"Who don't?" he asked, frowning.

"Madame Beattie and I."

"Where do you think it is then?"

"We think Esther's got it somewhere."

"But you say she lost it."

"I say she said she lost it," returned Lydia, feeling the delight of sounding more accurate every minute. "We don't think she did lose it. We think she lied."

Alston Choate remembered Esther as he had lately seen her, sitting in her harmonious surroundings, all fragility of body and sweetness of feeling, begging him to undertake the case that would deliver her from Jeffrey because she was afraid—afraid. And here was this horribly self-possessed little devil—he called her a little devil quite plainly in his mind—accusing that flower of gentleness and beauty of a vulgar crime.

"My God!" said he, under his breath.

And at that instant Anne, flushed and most sweet, hatted and gloved, opened the door and walked in. She bowed to Alston Choate, though she did not take his outstretched hand. He was receiving such professional insult, Anne felt, from one of her kin that she could scarcely expect from him the further grace of shaking hands with her. Lydia, looking at her, saw with an impish glee that Anne, the irreproachable, was angry. There was the spark in her eye, decision in the gesture with which she made at once for Lydia.

"Why, Anne," said Lydia, "I never saw you mad before."

Tears came into Anne's eyes. She bit her lip. All the proprieties of life seemed to her at stake when she must stand here before this most dignified of men and hear Lydia turn Addington courtesies into farce.

"I came to get you," she said, to Lydia. "You must come home with me."

"I can't," said Lydia. "I am having a business talk with Mr. Choate. I've asked him to undertake our case."

"Our case," Anne repeated, in a perfect despair. "Why, we haven't any case."

She turned to Choate and he gave her a confirming glance.

"I've been telling your sister that, virtually," said he. "I tell her she doesn't need my services. You may persuade her."

"Well," said Lydia cheerfully, rising, for they seemed to her much older than she and, though not to be obeyed on that account, to be placated by outward civilities, "I'm sorry. But if you don't take the case I shall have to go to some one else."

"Lydia!" said Anne. Was this the soft creature who crept to her arms of a cold night and who prettily had danced her way into public favour?

Alston Choate was looking thoughtful. It was not a story to be spread broadcast over Addington. He temporised.

"You see," he ventured, turning again to Lydia with his delightful smile which was, with no forethought of his own, tremendously persuasive, "you haven't told me yet what anybody is to get out of it."

"I thought I had," said Lydia, taking heart once more. If he talked reasonably with her, perhaps she could persuade him after all. "Why, don't you see? it's just as easy! I do, and I've only thought of it one night. Don't you see, Madame Beattie's here to hound Jeffrey into paying her for the necklace. That's going to kill him, just kill him. Anne, I should think you could see that."

Anne could see it if it were so. But Lydia, she thought, was building on a dream. The hideous old woman with the ostrich feathers had played a satiric joke on her, and here was Lydia in good faith assuming the joke was real.

"And if we can get this cleared up," said Lydia calmly, feeling very mature as she scanned their troubled faces, "Madame Beattie can just have her necklace back, and Jeff, instead of thinking he's got to start out with that tied round his neck, can set to work and pay his creditors."

Alston Choate was looking at her, frowning.

"Do you realise, Miss Lydia, what amount it is Jeffrey would have to pay his creditors? Unless he went into the market again and had a run of unbroken luck—and he's no capital to begin on—it's a thing he simply couldn't do. And as to the market, God forbid that he should ever think of it."

"Yes," said Anne fervently, "God forbid that. Farvie can't say enough against it."

Lydia's perfectly concrete faith was not impaired in the least.

"It isn't to be expected he should pay it all," said she. "He's got to pay what he can. If he should die to-morrow with ten dollars saved toward paying back his debts—"

"Do you happen to know what sum of money represents his debts?" Alston threw in, as you would clutch at the bit of a runaway horse.

"I know all about it," said Lydia. She suddenly looked hot and fierce. "I've done sums with it over and over, to see if he could afford to pay the interest too. And it's so much it doesn't mean anything at all to me one minute, and another time I wake up at night and feel it sitting on me, jamming me flat. But you needn't think I'm going to stop for that. And if you won't be my lawyer I can find somebody that will. That Mr. Moore is a lawyer. I'll go to him."

Anne, who had been staring at Lydia with the air of never having truly seen her, turned upon Choate, her beautiful eyes distended in a tragical appeal.

"Oh," said she, "you'll have to help us somehow."

So Alston Choate thought. He was regarding Lydia, and he spoke with a deference she was glad to welcome, a prospective client's due.

"I think," said he, "you had better leave the case with me."

"Yes," said Lydia. She hoped to get out of the room before Anne saw how undone she really was. "That's nice. You think it over, and we'll have another talk. Come along, Anne. Mary Nellen wants some lemons."

XVIII

What Alston Choate did, after ten minutes' frowning thought, was to sit down and write a note to Madame Beattie. But as he dipped his pen he said aloud, half admiring and inconceivably irritated: "The little devil!" He sent the note to Madame Beattie by a boy charged to give it, if possible, into her hand, and in an hour she was there in his office, ostrich plumes and all. She was in high feather, not adequately to be expressed by the plumes, and at once she told him why.

"I believe that little wild-fire's been here to see you already. Has she? and talking about necklaces?"

Madame Beattie was sitting upright in the office chair, fanning herself and regarding him with a smile as sympathetic as if she had been the cause of no disturbing issue.

"You'll pardon me for asking you to come here," said Alston. "But I didn't know how to get at you without Mrs. Blake's knowledge."

"Of course," said Madame Beattie composedly. "She was there when the note came, and curious as a cat."

"I see," said Alston, tapping noiselessly with his helpful paper knife, "that you guess I've heard some rumours that—pardon me, Madame Beattie—started from you."

"Yes," said she, "that pretty imp has been here. Quite right. She's a clever child. Let her stir up something, and they may quiet it if they can."

"Do you mind telling me," said Alston, "what this story is—about a necklace?"

"I've no doubt she's told you just as well as I could," said Madame Beattie. "She sat and drank it all in. I bet ten pounds she remembered word for word."

"As I understand, you say—"

"Don't tell me I 'say.' I had a necklace worth more money than I dared tell that imp. She wouldn't have believed me. And my niece Esther is as fond of baubles as I am. She stole the thing. And she said she lost it. And it's my opinion—and it's the imp's opinion—she's got it somewhere now."

Alston tapped noiselessly, and regarded her from under brows judicially stern. He wished he knew recipes for frightening Madame Beattie. But, he suspected, there weren't any. She would tell the truth or she would not, as she preferred. He hadn't any delusions about Madame Beattie's cherishing truth as an abstract duty. She was after results. He made a thrust at random.

"I can't see your object in stirring up this matter. If you had any ground of evidence you'd have made your claim and had it settled long ago."

"Not fully," said Madame Beattie, fanning.

"Then you were paid something?"

"Something? How far do you think 'something' would go toward paying for the loss of a diamond necklace? Evidently you don't know the history of that necklace. If you were an older man you would. The papers were full of it for years. It nearly caused a royal separation—they were reconciled after—and I was nearly garroted once when the thieves thought I had it in a hand-bag. There are historic necklaces and this is one. Did you ever hear of Marie Antoinette's?"

"Yes," said Alston absently. He was thinking how to get at her in the house where she lived. How would some of his novelists have written out Madame Beattie and made her talk? "And Maupassant's." This he said ruminatingly, but the lawyer in him here put down a mark. "Note," said the mark, "Maupassant's necklace. She rose to that." There was no doubt of it. A quick cross-light, like a shiver, had run across her eyes. "You know Maupassant's story," he pursued.

"I know every word of Maupassant. Neat, very neat."

"You remember the wife lost the borrowed necklace, and she and her husband ruined themselves to pay for it, and then they found it wasn't diamonds at all, but paste."

"I remember," said Madame Beattie composedly. "But if it had been a necklace such as mine an imitation would have cost a pretty penny."

"So it wasn't the necklace itself," he hazarded. "You wouldn't have brought a priceless thing over here. It was the imitation."

Madame Beattie broke out, a shrill staccato, into something like anger. But it might not have been anger, he knew, only a means of hostile communication.

"You are a rude young man to put words into my mouth, a rude young man."

"I beg your pardon," said Alston. "But this is rather a serious matter. And I do want to know, as a friend of Mrs. Jeffrey Blake."

"And counsel confided in by that imp," she supplied shrewdly.

"Yes, counsel retained by Miss Lydia French. I want to know whether you had with you here in America the necklace given you by—" Here he hesitated. He wondered whether, according to her standards, he was unbearably insulting, or whether the names of royal givers could really be mentioned.

"A certain Royal Personage," said Madame Beattie calmly.

"Or," said Alston, beginning after a safe hiatus, "whether you had had an imitation made, and whether the necklace said to be lost was the imitation."

"Well, then I'll tell you plainly," said Madame Beattie, in a cheerful concession, "I didn't have an imitation made. And you're quite within the truth with your silly 'said to be's.' For it was said to be lost. Esther said it. And she no more lost it than she went to New York that time to climb the Matterhorn. Do you know Esther?"

"Yes," said Alston with a calculated dignity, "I know her very well."

"Oh, I mean really know her, not enough to take her in to dinner or snatch your hat off to her."

"Yes, I really know her."

"Then why should you assume she's not a liar?" Madame Beattie asked this with the utmost tranquillity. It almost robbed the insult of offence. But Alston's face arrested her, and she burst out laughing. "My dear boy," said she, "you deal with evidence and you don't know a liar when you see her. Esther isn't all kinds of a liar. She isn't an amusing one, for instance. She hasn't any imagination. Now if I thought it would make you jump, I should tell you there was a tiger sitting on the top of that bookcase. I should do it because it would amuse me. But Esther never'd think of such a thing." She was talking to him now with perfect good-humour because he actually had glanced up at the bookcase, and it was tribute to her dramatic art. "She tells only the lies she has to. Esther's the perfect female animal hiding under things when there's something she's afraid of in the open and then telling herself she hid because she felt like being alone. The little imp wouldn't do that," said Madame Beattie admiringly. "She wouldn't be afraid of anything, or if she was she'd fight the harder. I shouldn't want to see the blood she'd draw."

Alston was looking at her in a fixed distaste.

"Esther is your niece," he began.

"Grandniece," interrupted Madame Beattie.

"She's of your blood. And at present you are her guest—"

"Oh, no, I'm not. The house is Susan's. Susan and I are step-sisters. Half the house ought to have been left to me, only Grandfather Pike knew I was worshipped, simply worshipped in Paris, and he wrote me something scriptural about Babylon."

"At any rate," said Alston, "you are technically visiting your niece, and you come here and tell me she is a thief and a liar."

"You sent for me," said Madame Beattie equably. "And I actually walked over. I thought it would be good for me, but it wasn't. Isn't that a hack out there? If it's that Denny, I think I'll get him to take me for a little drive. Don't come down."

But Alston went in a silence he recognised as sulky, and put her into the carriage with a perfect solicitude.

"I must ask you," he said stiffly before he closed the carriage door, "not to mention this to Mrs. Blake."

"Bless you, no," said Madame Beattie. "I'm going to let you stir the pot, you and that imp. Tell him to drive out into the country somewhere for half an hour. I suppose I've got to get the air."

But he was not to escape that particular coil so soon. Back in his office again, giving himself another ten minutes of grave amused consideration, before he called the stenographer, he looked up, at the opening of the door, and saw Anne. She came forward at once and without closing the door, as if to assure him she would not keep him long. There was no misreading the grave trouble of her face. He met her, and now they shook hands, and after he had closed the door he set a chair for her. But Anne refused it.

"I came to tell you how sorry I am to have troubled you so," she began. "Of course Lydia won't go on with this. She won't be allowed to. I don't know what could stop her," Anne admitted truthfully. "But I shall do what I can. Farvie mustn't be told. He'd be horrified. Nor Jeff. I must see what I can do."

"You are very much troubled," said Alston, in a tone of grave concern. It seemed to him Anne was a perfect type of the gentlewoman of another time, not even of his mother's perhaps, but of his grandmother's when ladies were a mixture of fine courage and delicate reserve. That type had, in his earliest youth, seemed inevitable. If his mother had escaped from it, it was because she was the inexplicable wonder of womankind, unlike the rest and rarer than all together.

Anne looked at him, pleading in her eyes.

"Terribly," she said, "terribly troubled. Lydia has always been impulsive, but not unmanageable. And I don't in the least know what to do."

"Suppose you leave it with me," said Alston, his deference an exquisite balm to her hurt feeling. Then he smiled, remembering Lydia. "I don't know what to do either," he said. "Your sister's rather terrifying. But I think we're safe enough so long as she doesn't go to Weedon Moore."

Anne was wordlessly grateful, but he understood her and not only went to the door with her but down the stairs as well. And she walked home treasuring the memory of his smile.

XIX

The day Jeffrey began to spade up the ground he knew he had got hold of something bigger than the handle of the spade. It was something rudely beneficent, because it kept him thinking about his body and the best way to use it, and it sent him to bed so tired he lay there aching. Not aching for long though: now he could sleep. That seemed to him the only use he could put himself to: he could work hard enough to forget he had much of an identity except this physical one. He had not expected to escape that horrible waking time between three and four in the morning when he had seen his life as an ignorant waste of youth and power. It was indeed confusion, nothing but that: the confusion of overwhelming love for Esther, of a bravado of display when he made money for them both to spend, of the arrogant sense that there was always time enough, strength enough, sheer brilliant insight enough to dance with life and drink with it and then have abundance of everything left. And suddenly the clock had struck, the rout was over and there was nothing left. It had all been forfeit. He hardly knew how he had come out of prison so drained of courage when he had been so roistering with it before he went in. Sometimes he had thought, at three o'clock in the morning, that it was Esther who had drained him: she, sweet, helpless, delicate flower of life. She had not merely been swayed by the wind that worsted him. She had perhaps been broken by it. Or at least it had done something inexplicable which he, entirely out of communication with her, had not been able to understand. And he had come back to find her more lovely than ever, and wearing no mark of the inner cruelties he had suffered and had imagined she must share with him.

He believed that his stay in prison had given him an illuminating idea of what hell really is: the vision of heaven and a certainty of the closed door. Confronted with an existence pared down to the satisfying of its necessities, he had loathed the idea of luxury while he hated the daily meagreness. Life had stopped for him when he entered inexorable bounds. It could not, he knew, be set going. Some clocks have merely stopped. Others are smashed. It had been the only satisfaction of his craving instincts to build up a scheme of conduct for the prison paper: but it had been the vision of a man lost to the country of his dreams and destined to eternal exile. Now all these aches and agonies of the past were lulled by the surge of tired muscles. He worked like a fury and the colonel, according to his strength, worked with him. They talked little, and chiefly about the weather prospects and the ways of the earth. Sometimes Anne would appear, and gently draw the colonel in, to advise her about something, and being in, he was persuaded to an egg-nog or a nap. But he also was absorbed, she saw, though he went at a slower pace than Jeff. He who had been old seemed to be in physical revolt; he was not sitting down to wait for death. He was going to dig the ground, even if he dug his grave, and not look up to see what visitant was waiting for him. It might be the earthly angel of a renewed and sturdy life. It might be the last summoner. But death, he told himself stoutly, though in a timorous bravado, waited for all.

Jeffrey's manuscript was laid aside. On Sundays he was too tired to write, too sleepy at night. For Lydia and Anne, it was, so far as family life went, a time of arrested intercourse. Their men were planting and could not talk to them, or tired and could not talk then. The colonel had even given up pulling out classical snags for Mary Nellen. He would do it in the evening, he said; but every evening he was asleep. Lydia had developed an astounding intimacy with Madame Beattie, and Anne was troubled. She told Alston Choate, who came when he thought there was a chance of seeing her alone, because he was whole-heartedly sorry for her, at the mercy of the vagaries of the little devil, as he permitted himself to call Lydia in his own mind.

"Madame Beattie," Anne said, "isn't a fit companion for a young girl. She can't be."

Alston remembered the expression of satiric good-humour on Madame Beattie's face, and was not prepared wholly to condemn her. He thought she could be a good fellow by habit without much trying, and he was very sure that, with a girl, she would play fair. But if he had heard Madame Beattie this morning in June, as she took Lydia to drive, he might not have felt so assured. These drives had become a matter of custom now. At first, Madame Beattie had taken Denny and an ancient victoria, but she tired of that.

"The man's as curious as a cat," she said to Lydia. "He can move his ears. That's to hear better. Didn't you see him cock them round at us? Can you drive?"

"Yes, Madame Beattie," said Lydia. "I love to."

"Then we'll have a phaeton, and you shall drive."

Nobody knew there was a phaeton left in Addington. But nobody had known there was a victoria, and when Madame Beattie had set her mind upon each, it was in due course forthcoming, vehicles apparently of an equal age and the same extent of disrepair. So they set forth together, the strange couple, and jogged, as Madame Beattie said. She would send the unwilling Sophy, who had a theory that she was to serve Esther and nobody else, and that scantily, over with a note. The Blake house had no telephone. Jeff, for unformulated reasons, owned to a nervous distaste for being summoned. And the note would say:

"Do you want to jog?"

Lydia always wanted to, and she found it the more engaging because Madame Beattie told her it drove Esther to madness and despair.

"She's furious," said Madame Beattie, with her lisp. "It's very silly of her. She doesn't want to go with me herself. Not that I'd have her. But you are an imp, my dear, and I like you."

This warm morning, full of sun and birds, they were jogging up Haldon Hill, a way they took often because it only led down again and motorists avoided it. Madame Beattie, still thickly clad and nodded over by plumes, lounged and held her parasol with the air of ladies in the Bois. Lydia, sitting erect and hatless, looked straight ahead, though the reins were loose, anxiously piercing some obscurity if she might, but always a mental one. Her legal affairs were stock still. Alston Choate talked with her cordially, though gravely, about her case, dissuading her always, but she was perfectly aware he was doing nothing. When she taxed him with it, he reminded her that he had told her there was nothing to do. But he assured her everything would be attempted to save her father and Anne from anxiety, and incidentally herself. About this Madame Beattie was asking her now, as they jogged under the flicker of leaves.

"What has that young man done for you, my dear, young Choate?"

"Nothing," said Lydia.

She put her lips together and thought what she would do if she were Jeff.

"But isn't he agitating anything?"

"Agitating?"

"Yes. That's what he must do, you know. That's all he can do."

Lydia turned reproachful eyes upon her.

"You think so, too," she said.

"Why, yes, dear imp, I know it. Jeff's case is ancient history. We can't do anything practical about it, so what we want is to agitate—agitate—until he leaves his absurd plaything—carrots, is it, or summer squash?—and gets into business in a civilised way. The man's a genius, if only his mind wakes up. Let him think we're going to spread the necklace story far and wide, let him see Esther about to be hauled before public opinion—"

"He doesn't love Esther," said Lydia, and then savagely bit her lip.

"Don't you believe it," said Madame Beattie sagely. "She's only to crook her finger. Agitate. Why, I'll do it myself. There's that dirty little man that wants an interview for his paper. I'll give him one."

"Weedon Moore?" asked Lydia. "Anne won't let me know him."

"Well, you do know him, don't you?"

"I saw him once. But when I threaten to take Jeff's case to him, if Mr. Choate won't stir himself, Anne says I sha'n't even speak to him. He isn't nice, she thinks. I don't know who told her."

"Choate, my dear," said Madame Beattie. "He's afraid Moore will get hold of you. He's blocking your game, that's all."

Madame Beattie, the next day, did go to Weedon Moore's office. He was unprepared for her and so the more agonisingly impressed. Here was a rough-spoken lady who, he understood, was something like a princess in other countries, and she was offering him an interview.

Madame Beattie showed she had the formula, and could manage quite well alone.

"The point is the necklace," said she, sitting straight and fanning herself, regarding him with so direct a gaze that he pressed his knees in nervous spasms. "You don't need to ask me how old I am nor whether I like this country. The facts are that I was given a very valuable necklace—by a Royal Personage. Bless you, man! aren't you going to take it down?"

"Yes, yes," stammered Moore. "I beg your pardon."

He got block and pencil, and though the attitude of writing relieved him from the necessity of looking at her, he felt the sweat break out on his forehead and knew how it was dampening his flat hair.

"The necklace," said Madame Beattie, "became famous. I wore it just enough to give everybody a chance to wonder whether I was to wear it or not. The papers would say, 'Madame Beattie wore the famous necklace.'"

"Am I permitted to say—" Weedon began, and then wondered how he could proceed.

"You can say anything I do," said Madame Beattie promptly. "No more. Of course not anything else. What is it you want to say?"

Weedon dropped the pencil, and under the table began to squeeze inspiration from his knees.

"Am I permitted," he continued, aghast at the liberty he was taking, "to know the name of the giver?"

"Certainly not," said Madame Beattie, but without offence. "I told you a Royal Personage. Besides, everybody knows. If your people here don't, it's because the're provincial and it doesn't matter whether they know it or not. I will continue. The necklace, I told you, became almost as famous as I. Then there was trouble."

"When?" ventured Weedon.

"Oh, a long time after, a very long time. The Royal Personage was going to be married and her Royal Highness—"

"Her Royal Highness?"

"Of course. Do you suppose he would have been allowed to marry a commoner? That was always the point. She made a row, very properly. The necklace was famous and some of the gems in it are historic. She was a thrifty person. I don't blame her for it. She wasn't going to see historic jewels drift back to the rue de la Paix. So they made me a proposition."

Moore was forgetting to be shy. He licked his lips, the story promised so enticingly.

"As I say," Madame Beattie pursued, "they made me a proposition." She stopped and Moore, pencil poised, looked at her inquiringly. She closed her fan, with a decisive snap, and rose. "There," said she, "you can elaborate that. Make it as long as you please, and it'll do for one issue."

Weedon felt as if somehow he had been done.

"But you haven't told me anything," he implored. "Everybody knows as much as that."

"I reminded you of that," said Madame Beattie. "But I know several things everybody doesn't know. Now you do as I tell you. Head it: 'The True Story of Patricia Beattie's Necklace. First Instalment.' And you'll sell a paper to every man, woman and baby in this ridiculous town. And when the next day's paper doesn't have the second instalment, they'll buy the next and the next to see if it's there."

"But I must have the whole in hand," pleaded Weedon.

"Well, you can't. Because I sha'n't give it to you. Not till I'm ready. You can publish a paragraph from time to time: 'Madame Beattie under the strain of recollection unable to continue her reminiscences. Madame Beattie overcome by her return to the past.' I'm a better journalist than you are."

"I'm not a journalist," Weedon ventured. "I practise law."

"Well, you run the paper, don't you? I'm going now. Good-bye."

And so imbued was he with the unassailable character of her right to dictate, that he did publish the fragment, and Addington bought it breathlessly and looked its amused horror over the values of the foreign visitor.

"Of course, my dear," said the older ladies—they called each other "my dear" a great deal, not as a term of affection, but in moments of conviction and the desire to impress it—"of course her standards are not ours. Nobody would expect that. But this is certainly going too far. Esther must be very much mortified."

Esther was not only that: she was tearful with anger and even penetrated to her grandmother's room to rehearse the circumstance, and beg Madam Bell to send Aunt Patricia away. Madam Bell was lying with her face turned to the wall, but the bedclothes briefly shook, as if she chuckled.

"You must tell her to go," said Esther again. "It's your house, and it's a scandal to have such a woman living in it. I don't care for myself, but I do care for the dignity of the family." Esther, Madam Bell knew, never cared for herself. She did things from the highest motives and the most remote. "Will you," Esther insisted, "will you tell her to leave?"

"No," said grandmother, from under the bedclothes. "Go away and call Rhoda Knox."

Esther went, angry but not disconcerted. The result of her invasion was perhaps no more bitter than she had expected. She had sometimes talked to grandmother for ten minutes, meltingly, adjuringly, only to be asked, at a pause, to call Rhoda Knox. To-day Rhoda, with a letter in her hand, was just outside the door.

"Would you mind, Mrs. Blake," she said, "asking Sophy to mail this?"

Esther did mind, but she hardly ventured to say so. With bitterness in her heart, she took the letter and went downstairs. Everybody, this swelling heart told her, was against her. She still did not dare withstand Rhoda, for the woman took care of grandmother perfectly, and if she left it would be turmoil thrice confounded. She hated Rhoda the more, having once heard Madame Beattie's reception of a request to carry a message when she was going downstairs.

"Certainly not," said Madame Beattie. "That's what you are here for, my good woman. Run along and take down my cloak and put it in the carriage."

Rhoda went quite meekly, and Esther having seen, exulted and thought she also should dare revolt. But she never did.

And now, having gone to grandmother in her mortification and trouble, she knew she ought to go to Madame Beattie with her anger. But she had not the courage. She could hear the little satiric chuckle Madame Beattie would have ready for her. And yet, she knew, it had to be done. But first she sent for Weedon Moore. The interview had but just been published, and Weedon, coming at dusk, was admitted by Sophy to the dining-room, where Madame Beattie seldom went. Esther received him with a cool dignity. She was pale. Grandmother would no doubt have said she made herself pale in the interest of pathos; but Esther was truly suffering. Moore, fussy, flattered, ill at ease, stood before her, holding his hat. She did not ask him to sit down. There was an unspoken tradition in Addington, observed by everybody but Miss Amabel, that Moore was not, save in cases of unavoidable delay, to be asked to sit. He passed his life, socially, in an upright posture. But Esther began at once, fixing her mournful eyes on his.

"Mr. Moore, I am distressed about the interview in your paper."

Moore, standing, could not squeeze inspiration out of his knees, and missed it sorely.

"Mrs. Blake," said he, "I wouldn't have distressed you for the world."

"I can't speak to my aunt about it," said Esther. "I can't trust myself. I mustn't wound her as I should be forced to do. So I have sent for you. Mr. Moore, has she given you other material?"

"Not a word," said Weedon earnestly. "If you could prevail upon her—" There he stopped, remembering Esther was on the other side.

"I shall have to be very frank with you," said Esther. "But you will remember, won't you, that it is in confidence?"

"Yes, ma'am," said Moore. He had never fully risen above former conditions of servitude when he ran errands and shovelled paths for Addington gentry. "You can rely on me."

"My aunt," said Esther delicately, with an air of regret and several other picturesque emotions mingled carefully, "my aunt has one delusion. It is connected with this necklace, which she certainly did possess at one time. She imagines things about it, queer things, where it went and where it is now. But you mustn't let her tell you about it, and if she insists you mustn't allow it to get into print. It would be taking advantage, Mr. Moore. Truly it would." And as a magnificent concession she drew forward a chair, and Weedon, without waiting to see her placed, sank into it and put his hands on his knees. "You must promise me," Esther half implored, half insisted. "It isn't I alone. It's everybody that knows her. We can't, in justice to her, let such a thing get into print."

Weedon was much impressed, by her beauty, her accessibility and his own incredible position of having something to accord. But he had a system of mental bookkeeping. There were persons who asked favours of him, whom he put down as debtors. "Make 'em pay," was his mentally jotted note. If he did them an obliging turn, he kept his memory alert to require the equivalent at some other time. But he did not see how to make Esther pay. So he could only temporise.

"I'd give anything to oblige you, Mrs. Blake," he said, "anything, I assure you. But I have to consider the paper. I'm not alone there, you know. It's a question of other people."

Esther was familiar with that form of withdrawal. She herself was always escaping by it.

"But you own the paper," she combated him. "Everybody says so."

"I have met with a great deal of misrepresentation," he replied solemnly. "Justice is no more alive to-day than liberty." Then he remembered this was a sentence he intended to use in his speech to-night on the old circus-ground, and added, as more apposite, "I'd give anything to serve you, Mrs. Blake, I assure you I would. But I owe a certain allegiance—a certain allegiance—I do, really."

With that he made his exit, backing out and bowing ridiculously over his hat. And Esther had hardly time to weigh her defeat, for callers came. They began early and continued through the afternoon, and they all asked for Madame Beattie. It was a hot day and Madame Beattie, without her toupée and with iced *eau sucrée* beside her, was absorbedly reading. She looked up briefly, when Sophy conveyed to her the summons to meet lingering ladies below, and only bade her: "Excuse me to them. Say I'm very much engaged."

Then she went on reading. Esther, when the message was suavely but rather maliciously delivered by Sophy, who had a proper animosity for her social betters, hardly knew whether it was easier to meet the invaders alone or run the risk of further disclosure if Madame Beattie appeared. For though no word was spoken of diamonds or interviews or newspapers, she could follow, with a hot sensitiveness, the curiosity flaring all over the room, like a sky licked by harmless lightnings. When a lady equipped in all the panoply of feminine convention asked for grandmother's health, she knew the thought underneath, decently suppressed, was an interest, no less eager for being unspoken, in grandmother's attitude toward the interview. Sometimes she wanted to answer the silent question with a brutal candour, to say: "No, grandmother doesn't care. She was perfectly horrible about it. She only laughed." And when the stream of callers had slackened somewhat she telephoned Alston Choate, and asked if he would come to see her that evening at nine. She couldn't appoint an earlier hour because she wasn't free. And immediately after that, Reardon telephoned her and asked if he might come, rather late, he hesitated, to be sure of finding her alone. And when she had to put him off to the next night, he spoke of the interview as "unpardonable ". He was coming, no doubt, to bring his condolence.

XX

Jeffrey himself had not seen the interview. He had only a mild interest in Addington newspapers, and Anne had carefully secreted the family copy lest the colonel should come on it. But on the afternoon when Esther was receiving subtly sympathetic townswomen, Jeffrey, between the rows of springing corn, heard steps and looked up from his hoeing. It was Lydia, the *Argosy* in hand. She was flushed not only with triumph because something had begun at last, but before this difficulty of entering on the tale with Jeff. Pretty child! his heart quickened at sight of her in her blue dress, sweet arms and neck bare because Lydia so loved freedom. But, in that his heart did respond to her, he spoke the more brusquely, showing he had no right to find her fair.

"What is it?"

Lydia, in a hurry, the only way she knew of doing it, extended the paper, previously folded to expose the headline of Madame Beattie's name. Jeff, his hoe at rest in one hand, took the paper and looked at it frowningly, incredulously. Then he read. A word or two escaped him near the end. Lydia did not quite hear what the word was, but she thought he was appropriately swearing. Her eyes glistened. She had begun to agitate. Jeff had finished and crushed the paper violently together, with no regard to folds.

"Oh, don't," said Lydia. "You can't get any more. They couldn't print them fast enough."

Jeff passed it to her with a curt gesture of relinquishing any last interest in it.

"That's Moore," he said. "It's like him."

Lydia was at once relieved. She had been afraid he wasn't going to discuss it at all.

"You don't blame her, do you?" she prompted.

"Madame Beattie?" He was thinking hard and scowling. "No."

"Anne blames her. She says no lady would have done it."

"Oh, you can't call names. That's Madame Beattie," said Jeff absently. "She's neither principles nor morals nor the kind of shame other women feel. You can't judge Madame Beattie."

"So I say," returned Lydia, inwardly delighted and resolving to lose no time in telling Anne. "I like her. She's nice. She's clever. She knows how to manage people. O Jeff, I wish you'd talk with her."

"About this?" He was still speaking absently. "It wouldn't do any good. If it amuses her or satisfies her devilish feeling toward Esther to go on talking and that slob will get it into print—and he will—you can't stop her."

"What do you mean by her feeling toward Esther?" Lydia's heart beat so that she drew a long breath to get it into swing again.

"We can't go into that," said Jeff. "It runs back a long way. Only everything she can do to worry Esther or frighten her—why, she'd do it, that's all. That's Madame Beattie."

Lydia knew this was the path that led to the necklace. Why couldn't she tell him she knew the story and enlist him on Madame Beattie's side and hers, the side that was fighting for him and nothing else? But she did not dare. All she could do was to say, her hands cold against each other and her voice choked:

"O Jeff, I wish you'd give this up."

"What?"

He was recalled now from memories the printed paper had wakened in him, and looking at her kindly. At least Lydia was sure he was, because his voice sounded so dear. She could not know his eyes were full of an adoring gentleness over her who seemed to him half child, half maiden, and tumultuously compassionate. She made a little timid gesture of the hand over the small area about them.

"This," she said. "You mustn't stay here and hoe corn. You must get into business and show people—"

Her voice choked. It refused absurdly to go on.

"Why, Lydia," said he, "I thought you knew. This is the only way for a man to keep alive. When I've got a hoe in my hand—" He could not quite explain it. He had always had a flow of words on paper, but since he had believed his life was finished his tongue had been more and more lethargic. It would not obey his brain because, after all, what could the brain report of his distrustful heart? Lydia had a moment of bitter mortification because she had not seemed to understand. Anne understood, she knew, and had tried, with infinite patience, to help on this queer experiment, both for Jeff's sake and Farvie's. Tears rushed to her eyes.

"I can't help it," she said. "I want you to be doing something real."

"Lydia!" said Jeff. His kind, persuasive voice was recalling her to some ground of conviction where she could share his certainty that things were going as well as they could. "This is almost the only real thing in the world—the ground. About everything else is a game. This isn't a game. It's making something grow that won't hurt anybody when it's grown. I can't harm anybody by planting corn. And I can sell the corn," said Jeff, with a lighter shade of voice. Lydia knew he was smiling to please her. "Denny's going to peddle it out for me at backdoors. I'd do it myself, only I'm afraid they'd buy to help on 'poor Jeffrey Blake'."

When he spoke of the ground Lydia gave the loose dirt a little scornful kick and got the powdered dust into her neat stockings. She, too, loved the ground and all the sweet usages of homely life; but not if they kept him from a spectacular triumph. She was desperate enough to venture her one big plea.

"Jeff, you know you've got a lot of money to earn—to pay back—"

And there she stopped. He was regarding her gravely, but the moment he spoke she knew it was not in any offence.

"Lydia, I give you my word I couldn't do the kind of thing you want me to. I've found that out at last. You'd like me to cut into the market and make a lot of money and throw it back at the people I owe. I couldn't do it. My brain wouldn't let me. It's stopped—stopped short. A man knows when he's done for. I'm absolutely and entirely done. All I hope for is to keep father from finding it out. He seems to be getting his nerve back, and if he really does that I may be able to go away and do something besides dig. But it won't be anything spectacular, Lydia. It isn't in me."

Lydia turned away from him, and he could fancy the bright tears dropping as she walked. "Oh, dear!" he heard her say. "Oh, dear!"

"Lydia!" he called, in an impatience of tenderness and misery. "Come back here. Don't you know I'd do anything on earth I could for you? But there's nothing I can do. You wouldn't ask a lame man to dance. There! that shows you. When it comes to dancing you can understand. I'm a cripple, Lydia. Don't you see?"

She had turned obediently, and now she smeared the tears away with one small hand.

"You don't understand," she said. "You don't understand a thing. We've thought of it all this time, Anne and I, how you'd come out and be proved not guilty—"

"But, Lydia," he said gravely, "I was guilty. And besides being guilty of things the courts condemned me for, I was guilty of things I had to condemn myself for afterward. I wasn't a criminal merely. I was a waster and a fool."

"Yes," said Lydia, looking at him boldly, "and if you were guilty who made you so? Who pushed you on?"

She had never entirely abandoned her theory of Reardon. He and Esther, in her suspicion, stood side by side. Looking at him, she rejoiced in what she thought his confirmation. The red had run into his face and he looked at her with brightened eyes.

"You don't know anything about it," he said harshly. "I did what I did. And I got my medicine. And if there's a decent impulse left in me to-day, it was because I got it."

Lydia walked away through the soft dirt and felt as if she were dancing. He had looked guilty when she had asked him who pushed him on. He and she both knew it was Esther, and a little more likelihood of Madame Beattie's blackguarding Esther in print must rouse him to command the situation.

Jeffrey finished his row, and then hurried into the house. It was the late afternoon, and he went to his room and dressed, in time for supper. Lydia, glancing at him as he left the table, thought exultantly: "I've stirred him up, at least. Now what is he going to do?"

Jeffrey went strolling down the drive, and quickened his steps when the shrubbery had him well hidden from the windows. Something assured him it was likely Weedon Moore lived still in the little sharp-gabled house on a side street where he had years ago. His mother had been with him then, and Jeff remembered Miss Amabel had scrupulously asked for her when Moore came to call. The little house was unchanged, brightly painted, gay in diamond trellis-work and picked out with scarlet tubs of hydrangea in the yard. A car stood at the gate, and Weedon, buttoning his coat, was stepping in. The car ran past, and Jeff saw that the man beside Moore was the interpreter of that night at the old circus-ground.

"So," he thought, "more ginger for the labouring man."

He turned about and walking thoughtfully, balked of his design, reflected with distaste that grew into indignation on Moore's incredible leadership. It seemed monstrous. Here was ignorance fallen into the hands of the demagogue. It was an outrage on the decencies. And then Madame Beattie waved to him from Denny's hack, and he stepped into the road to speak to her.

"I was going to see you," she said. "Get in here."

Jeff got in and disposed his length as best he might in the cramped interior, redolent now of varied scents, all delicate but mingled to a suffocating potency.

"Tell him to drive along outside the town," she bade. "Were you going to see me?"

"No," said Jeffrey, after executing her order. "I've told you I can't go to see you."

"Because Esther made that row? absurd! It's Susan's house."

"I'm not likely to go into it," said Jeff drily, "unless I am summoned."

"She's a fool."

"But I don't mind telling you where I was going," said Jeff. "I was going to lick Weedon Moore—or the equivalent."

"Not on account of my interview?" said Madame Beattie, laughing very far down in her anatomy. Her deep laugh, Jeff always felt, could only have been attained by adequate support in the diaphragm. "Bless you, dear boy, you needn't blame him. I went to him. Went to his office. Blame me."

"Oh, I blame you all right," said Jeff, "but you're not a responsible person. A chap that owns a paper is."

"I wish you'd met him," she said, in great enjoyment. "Where'd he go, Jeffrey? Can't we find him now?"

"I suspect he went to the old circus-ground. I caught him there talking to Poles and Finns and Italians and Greeks, telling them the country was no good and they owned it."

"Why, the fellow can't speak to them." Madame Beattie, being a fluent linguist, had natural scorn of a tubby little New Englander who said "ma'am".

"Oh, he had an interpreter."

"We'll drive along there," said Madame Beattie. "You tell Denny. I should dearly like to see them. Poles, do you say? I didn't know there were such people in town."

Jeffrey, rather curious himself, told Denny, and they bowled cumbrously along. He felt in a way obliged to proffer a word or two about the interview.

"What the devil made you do it anyway?" he asked her; but Madame Beattie chuckled and would not answer.

XXI

All the way along, in the warm twilight, Madame Beattie was gay over the prospect of being fought for. With the utmost precision and unflagging spirit she arranged a plausible cause for combat, and Jeffrey, not in the least intending to play his allotted part, yet enjoyed the moment fully.

"You shall do it," Madame Beattie assured him, as if she permitted him to enter upon a task for which there was wide competition. "You shall thrash him, and he will put it in his paper, and the European papers will copy."

"I haven't much idea the *Argosy* is read in foreign capitals," Jeff felt bound to assure her.

"Oh, but we can cable it. The French journals—they used to be very good to me."

With that her face darkened, not in a softening melancholy, but old bitterness and defeat. She was not always able to ignore the contrast between the spring of youth and this meagre eld. Jeffrey saw the tremendous recognition she assuredly had had, grown through the illusive fructifying of memory into something overwhelming, and he was glad starved vanity might once more be fed. She seemed to him a most piteous spectacle, youth and power in ruins, and age too poor to nourish even a vine to drape the crumbling walls.

"Patricia Beattie," she continued, "again a *casus belli*. Combat between two men—" "There won't be any combat," Jeff reminded her. "If I kick Weedie, he'll take it lying down. That's Weedie."

"I shall stand by," said Madame Beattie. "If you go too far I shall interfere. So you can go as far as you like."

"I do rather want to know what Weedie's at," said Jeff. "But I sha'n't kick him. He doesn't deserve it at one time any more than another, though he has different degrees of making himself offensive."

She was ingenuously disappointed. She even reproached him:

"You said you were going to do it."

"That was in my haste," said Jeffrey. "I can't lick him with a woman standing by. I should feel like a fool."

Denny was drawing up at the circus-ground.

"Well," said Madame Beattie, "you've disappointed me tremendously. That's all I can say."

It was dark now, and though the season was more advanced, Jeffrey could imagine that this was the moment of his arrival that other night, save that he was not now footsore or dull in the mind. But the same dusk of crowding forms lay thickly on the field, and there, he knew, was the stationary car; there were the two figures standing in it, Moore and his interpreter. He could fill out the picture with a perfect accuracy, Moore gesticulating and throwing frenzy into his high-pitched voice, which now came stridently. Madame Beattie breathed out excitement. Nothing so spiced had ever befallen her in Addington.

"Is he actually speaking?" she asked, in a hoarse whisper. "They say insects make noises with their hind legs. It's more like that than a voice. Take me round there, Jeffrey."

He was quite willing. With a good old pal like this to egg you on, he thought, there actually was some fun left. So he handed her out, and told Denny to wait for them, and they skirted the high board fence to the gap in the back. Madame Beattie, holding up her long dress in one hand and tripping quite nimbly, was clinging to his arm. By the gap they halted for her to recover breath; she drew her hand from Jeff's arm, opened her little bag, took out a bit of powder paper and mechanically rubbed her face. Jeff looked on indulgently. He knew she did not expect to need an enhanced complexion in this obscurity. The act refreshed her, that was all.

Weedon, it was easy to note, was battering down tradition.

"They talk about their laws," he shrilled. "I am a lawyer, and I tell you it breaks my heart every time I go back to worm-eaten precedent. But I have to do it, because, if I didn't talk that language the judges wouldn't understand me. Do you know what precedent is? It is the opinion of some man a hundred years ago on a case tried a hundred years ago. Do we want that kind of an opinion? No. We want our own opinions on cases that are tried to-day."

The warm rapid voice of the interpreter came in here, and Madame Beattie, who was standing apart from Jeffrey, touched his arm. He bent to listen.

"The man's a fool," said she.

"No," said Jeffrey, "he's not a fool. He knows mighty well what he's saying and how it'll take."

"If I had all the lawbooks in the world," said Weedon, "I'd pile them up here on this ground we've made free ground because we have free speech on it, and I'd touch a match to them, and by the light they made we'd sit down here and frame our own laws. And they would be laws for the rich as well as the poor. Columbus did one good thing for us. He discovered a new world. The capitalists have done their best to spoil it, and turn it into a world as rotten as the old ones. But Columbus showed us you can find a new world if you try. And we're going to have a new world out of this one yet. New laws, new laws, I tell you, new laws!"

He screamed it at the end, this passion for new laws, and the interpreter, though he had too just an instinct to take so high a key, followed him with an able crescendo. Weedie thought he had his audience in hand, though it was the interpreter who really had it, and he ventured another stroke:

"I don't want them to tell me what some man taught in Bible days. I want to know what a man thinks right here in Addington. I don't want them to tell me what they thought in Greece and Rome. Greece and Rome are dead. The only part of them that's alive is the Greece and Rome of to-day."

When the interpreter passed this on, he stopped at a dissentient murmur. There were those who knew the bright history of their natal country and adored it.

"Oh, the man's a fool," said Madame Beattie again. "I'm going in there."

She took up the tail of her gown, put her feather-crowned head through the gap in the fence and drew her august person after, and Jeffrey followed her. He had a gay sense of irresponsibility, of seeking the event. He was grateful to Madame Beattie. They went on, and as it was that other night, some withdrew to leave a pathway and others stared, but, finding no specific reason, did not hinder them. Madame Beattie spoke once or twice, a brief mandate in a foreign tongue, and that, Jeff noted, was effective. She stepped up on the running-board of the car and laid her hand on the interpreter's arm.

"You may go, my friend," said she, quite affectionately. "I do not need you." Then she said something, possibly the same thing, Jeff thought, in another language, and the man laughed. Madame Beattie, without showing sign of recognising Moore, who was at her elbow, bent forward into the darkness and gave a shrill call. The crowd gathered nearer. Its breath was but one breath. The blackness of the assemblage was as if you poured ink into water and made it dense. Jeffrey felt at once how sympathetic they were with her. What was the cry she gave? Was it some international password or a gipsy note of universal import? Had she called them friend in a tongue they knew? Now she began speaking, huskily at first, with tumultuous syllables and wide open vowels, and at the first pause they cheered. The inky multitude that had kept silence, by preconcerted plan, while Weedon Moore talked to them, lost control of itself and yelled. She went on speaking and they crashed in on her pauses with more plaudits, and presently she laid her hand on Jeffrey's shoulder and said to him:

"Come up here beside me."

He shook his head. He was highly entertained, but the mysterious game was hers and Weedie's. She gave an order, it seemed, in a foreign tongue, and the thing was managed. The interpreter had stepped from the car, and now gentle yet forcible hands lifted down Weedon Moore, and set him beside it and other hands as gently set up Jeffrey in his place. There he stood with her in a dramatic isolation, but so great was the carrying power of her mystery that he did not feel himself a fool. It was quite natural to be there for some unknown purpose, at one with her and that warmly breathing mass: for no purpose, perhaps, save that they were all human and meant the same thing, a general good-will. She went on speaking, and Jeffrey knew there was fire in her words. He bent to the interpreter beside the car and asked, at the man's ear:

"What is she saying?"

The interpreter turned and looked him in the face. They were not more than three inches apart, and Jeffrey, gazing into the passionate black eyes, tasting, as it were, the odour of the handsome creature and feeling his breath, was not repelled, but had a sudden shyness before him, as if the man's opinion of him were an attack on his inmost self, an attack of adoring admiration.

"What is she saying?" he repeated, and for answer the interpreter snatched one of Jeff's hands and seemed about to kiss it.

"For God's sake, don't do that," Jeff heard himself saying, and withdrew his hand and straightened at a safe distance from the adoring face, and he heard Madame Beattie going on in her fiery periods. Whatever she was saying, they loved it, loved it to the point of madness. They cheered her, and the interpreter did not check them, but cheered too. To Jeffrey it was all a medley of strange thoughts. Here he was, in the crowd and not of it, greatly moved and yet not as the others were, because he did not understand. And though the voice and the answering enthusiasm went on for a long time, and still he did not understand, he was not tired but exhilarated only. The moon, the drifting clouds, the dramatic voice playing upon the hearts of the multitude, their hot responses, all this gave him a sense of augmented life and the feel of his own past youth. Suddenly he fancied Madame Beattie's voice failed a little; something ebbed in it, not so much force as quality.

"That's all," she said, in a quick aside to him. "Let's go." She gave an order, in English now, and a figure started out of the crowd and cranked the car.

"We can't go in this," Jeffrey said to her. "This is Moore's car."

But Madame Beattie had seated herself majestically. Her feathers even were portentous in the moonlight, like the plumage of some gigantic bird. She gave another order, whereupon the man who had cranked the machine took his place in it, and the crowd parted for them to pass. Jeffrey was amused and dashed. He couldn't leave her, nor could they sail away in Weedon's car. He put a hand on her arm.

"See here, Madame Beattie," said he, "we can't do this. We must get out at the gate, at least."

But Madame Beattie was bowing graciously to right and left. Once she rose for an instant and addressed a curt sentence to the crowd, and in answer they cheered, a full-mouthed chorus of one word in different tongues.

"What are they yelling?" Jeffrey asked.

"It's for you," Madame Beattie said composedly. "They're cheering you."

"Me? How do you know? That's not my name."

"No. It's The Prisoner. They're calling you The Prisoner."

They were at the gate now, and turned into the road and, with a free course before him, the man put on speed and they were away. Jeffrey bent forward to him, but Madame Beattie pulled him back.

"What are you doing?" she inquired. "We're going home."

"This is Moore's car," Jeffrey reminded her.

"No, it isn't. It's the proletariat's car." She rolled the *r* surprisingly. "Do you suppose he comes out here to corrupt those poor devils without making them pay for being corrupted? Jeffrey, take off your coat."

"What for?" He had resigned himself to his position. It was a fit part of the whole eccentric pastime, and after all it was only Weedie's car.

"I shall take cold. I got very warm speaking. My voice—"

To neither of them now was it absurd. Though it was years since she had had a voice the habit of a passionate care was still alive in her. Jeffrey had come on another rug, and wrapped it round her. He went back to his first wonder.

"But what is there in being a prisoner to start up such a row?"

Madame Beattie had retired into the rug. She sunk her chin in it and would talk no more. Without further interchange they drew up at her house.

Jeffrey got out and helped her, and she stood for a moment, pressing her hand on his arm, heavily, as an old woman leans.

"Ah, Jeffrey," said she rapidly, in a low but quite a naked tone with no lisping ornament, "this is a night. To think I should have to come back here to this God-forsaken spot for a minute of the old game. Hundreds hanging on my voice—" he fancied she had forgotten now whether she had not sung to them—"and feeling what I told them to feel. They're capital people. We'll talk to them again."

She had turned toward the door and now she came back and struck his arm violently with her hand.

"Jeff," said she passionately, "you're a fool. You've still got your youth and you won't use it. And the world looks like this—" she glanced up at the radiant sky. "Even in Addington, the moon is after us trying to seduce us to the old pleasures. You've got youth. Use it. For God's sake, use it."

Now she did go up the steps and having rung the bell for her, ignoring the grim knocker that looked as if it would take more than one summons to get past its guard, Jeff told the man to drive back for Mr. Moore. The car had gone, and still Madame Beattie rang. She knew and Jeffrey suspected suddenly that Esther was paying her out for illicit roaming. Suddenly Madame Beattie raised her voice and called twice:

"Esther! Esther!"

The sound echoed in the silent street, appallingly to one who knew what Addington streets were and what proprieties lined them. Then the door did open. Jeffrey fancied the smooth-faced maid had slipped the bolt. Esther, from what he knew of her, was not by to face the music. He heard the door shut cautiously and walked away, but not to go immediately home. What did Madame Beattie mean by telling him to use his youth? All he wanted was to hold commerce with the earth and dig hard enough to keep himself tired so that he might sleep. For since he had come out of prison he was every day more subject to this besetment of recalling the past. It was growing upon him that he had always made wrong choices. Youth, what seemed to him through the vista of vanished time a childhood even, when he was but little over twenty, had been a delirium of expectation in a world that was merely a gay-coloured spot where, if you were reasonably fit, as youth should be, you could always snatch the choicest fruit from the highest bough. Then he had met Esther, and the world stopped being a playground and became an ordered pageant, and he was the moving power, trying to make it move faster or more lightly, to please Esther who was sitting in front to see it move, and who was of a decided mind in pageants. It was always Esther who was to be pleased. These things he had not thought of willingly during his imprisonment, because it was necessary not to think, lest the discovery of the right causes that brought him there should turn his brain. But now he had leisure and freedom and a measure of solitude, and it began to strike him that heretofore, being in the pageant and seeing it move, he had not enjoyed it over much. There had been a good deal of laughter and light and colour—there had to be, since these were the fruits Esther lived on—but there had been no affectionate converse with the world. Strange old Madame Beattie! she had brought him the world to-night. She had taken strangers from its furthest quarters and welded them into a little community that laughed and shouted and thought according things. That they had hailed him, even as a prisoner, brought him a little warmth. It was mysterious, but it seemed they somehow liked him, and he went into the quiet house and to bed with the feeling of having touched a hand.

XXII

Within a week Jeffrey, going down town in his blue blouse to do an errand at the stores, twice met squads of workmen coming from the mill—warm-coloured, swarthy men, most of them young. He was looking at them in a sudden curiosity as to their making part of Weedon Moore's audience, when bright pleasure rippled over the dark faces. They knew him; they were mysteriously glad to see him. Caps were snatched off. Jeffrey snatched at his in return. There was a gleam of white teeth all through the squad; as he passed in the ample way they made for him, he felt foolishly as if they were going to stretch out kind detaining hands. They looked so tropically warm and moved, he hardly knew what greeting he might receive. "What have I done?" he thought. "Are they going to kiss me?" He wished he could see Madame Beattie and ask her what she had really caused to happen.

But on a later afternoon, at his work in the field, he saw Miss Amabel carefully treading among corn hills, very hot though in her summer silk and with a parasol. She always did feel the heat but patiently, as one under bonds of meekness to the God who sent it; but to-day her discomfort was within. Jeffrey threw down his hoe and wiped his face. There was a bench under the beech tree shade. He had put it there so that his father might be beguiled into resting after work. When she reached the edge of the corn, he advanced and took her parasol and held it over her.

"Ladies shouldn't come out here," he said. "They must send Mary Nellen to fetch me in."

Miss Amabel sat down on the bench and did a little extra breathing, while she looked at him affectionately.

"You are a good boy, Jeff," said she, at length, "whatever you've been doing."

"I've been hoeing," said Jeff. "Here, let me."

He took her large fine handkerchief, still in its crisp folds, and with an absurd and yet pretty care wiped her face with it. He wiped it all over, the moist forehead, the firm chin where beads stood glistening, and Miss Amabel let him, saying only as he finished:

"Father used to perspire on his chin."

"There," said Jeffrey. He folded the handkerchief and returned it to its bag. "Now you're a nice dry child. I suppose you've got your shoes full of dirt. Mine are when I've been out here."

"Never mind my shoes," said she. "Jeff, how nice you are. How much you are to-day like what you used to be when you were a boy."

"I feel rather like it nowadays," said Jeff, "I don't know why. Except that I come out here and play by myself and they all let me alone."

"But you mustn't play tricks," said Miss Amabel. "You must be good and not play tricks on other people."

Jeff drew up his knees and clasped his hands about them. His eyes were on the corn shimmering in the heat.

"What's in your bonnet, dear?" said he. "I hear a buzz."

"What happened the other night?" she asked. "It came to my ears, I won't say how."

"Weedie told you. Weedie always told."

"I don't say it was Mr. Weedon Moore."

She was speaking with dignity, and Jeffrey laughed and unclasped his hands to pat her on the arm.

"I wonder why it makes you so mad to have me call him Weedie."

She answered rather hotly, for her.

"You wouldn't do it, any of you, if you weren't disparaging him."

"Oh, we might. Out of affection. Weedie! good old Weedie! can't you hear us saying that?"

"No, I can't. You wouldn't say it that way. Don't chaff me, Jeff. What do they say now—'jolly' me? Don't do that."

Again Jeffrey gave her a light touch of affectionate intimacy.

"What is it?" said he. "What do you want me to do?"

"I want you to let Weedon Moore talk to people who are more ignorant than the rest of us, and tell them things they ought to know. About the country, about everything."

"You don't want me to spoil Weedie's game."

"It isn't a game, Jeff. That young man is giving up his time, and with the purest motives, to fitting our foreign population for the duties of citizenship. He doesn't disturb the public peace. He takes the men away after their day's work—"

"Under cover of the dark."

"He doesn't run any risk of annoying people by assembling in the streets."

"Weedie doesn't want any decent man to know his game, whatever his game is."

"I won't answer that, Jeffrey. But I feel bound to say you are ungenerous. You've an old grudge against Weedon Moore. You all have, all you boys who were brought up with him. So you break up the meeting."

"Now, see here, Amabel," said Jeff, "we haven't a grudge against him. Anyhow, leave me out. Take a fellow like Alston Choate. If he's got a grudge against Moore, doesn't it mean something?"

"You hated him when you were boys," said Amabel. "Those things last. Nothing is so hard to kill as prejudice."

"As to the other night," said Jeffrey, "I give you my word it was as great a surprise to me as it was to Moore. I hadn't the slightest intention of breaking up the meeting."

"Yet you went there and you took that impossible Martha Beattie with you—"

"Patricia, not Martha."

"I have nothing to do with names she assumed for the stage. She was Martha Shepherd when she lived in Addington. No doubt she is entitled to be called Beattie; but Martha is her Christian name."

"Now you're malicious yourself," said Jeff, enjoying the human warmth of her. "I never knew you to be so hateful. Why can't you live and let live? If I'm to let your Weedie alone, can't you keep your hands off poor old Madame Beattie?"

Miss Amabel turned upon him a look where just reproof struggled with wounded pride.

"Jeffrey, I didn't think you'd be insincere with me."

"Hang it, Amabel, I'm not. You're one of the few unbroken idols I've got. Sterling down to the toes. Didn't you know it?"

"And yet you did take Madame Beattie to Moore's rally."

"Rally? So that's what he calls it."

"And you did prompt her to talk to those men in their language—several languages, I understand, quick as lightning, one after the other—and to say things that counteracted at once all Mr. Moore's influence."

"Now," said Jeffrey, in a high degree of interest, "we're getting somewhere. What did I say to them? What did I say through Madame Beattie?"

"We don't know."

"Ask Moore."

"Mr. Moore doesn't know."

"He can ask his interpreter, can't he?"

"Andrea? He won't tell."

Jeffrey released his knees and lay back against the bench. He gave a hoot of delighted laughter, and Lydia, watching them from the window, thought of Miss Amabel with a wistful envy and wondered how she did it.

"Weedie's own henchman won't go back on her," he exclaimed, in an incredulous pleasure. "Now what spell has that extraordinary old woman over the south of Europe?"

"South of Europe?"

"Why, yes, the population you've got here. It's south of Europe chiefly, isn't it? eastern Europe?—the part Weedie hasn't turned into ward politicians yet. Who is Andrea? This is the first time I have heard his honourable name. Weedon's interpreter."

"He has the fruit store on Mill Street."

"Ah! Amabel, do you know what this interview has done for me? It's given me a perfectly overwhelming desire to speak the tongues."

"Foreign languages, Jeff?"

"Any language that will help me beat Weedie at his game, or give me a look at the cards old Madame Beattie holds. I feel a fool. Why can't I know what they're talking about when they can kick up row enough under my very nose to make you come and rag me like this?"

"Jeff," said Miss Amabel, "unless you are prepared to go into social work seriously and see things as Mr. Moore sees them—"

Jeff gave a little crow of derision and she coloured. "It wouldn't hurt you, Jeff, to see some things as he does. The necessity of getting into touch with our foreign population—"

"I'll do that all right," said Jeffrey. "That's precisely what I mean. I'm going to learn foreign tongues and talk to 'em."

"They say Madame Beattie speaks a dozen or so and I don't know how many dialects."

"Oh, I can't compete with Madame Beattie. She's got the devil on her side."

Miss Amabel rose to her feet and stood regarding him sorrowfully. He looked up at her with a glance full of affection, yet too merry for her heavy mood. Then he got on his feet and took her parasol.

"You haven't noticed the corn," said he. "Don't you know you must praise the work of a man's hands?"

"I don't know whether it's a good thing for you or not," said she. "Yes, it must have been, so far. You're tanned."

"I feel fit enough."

"You don't look over twenty."

"Oh, I'm over twenty, thank you," said Jeff. A shadow settled on his face; it even touched his eyes, mysteriously, and dulled them. "I'm not tanned all through."

"But you're only doing this for a time?"

"I don't know, Amabel. I give you my word I don't know the next step after to-day—or this hill of corn—or that."

"If you wanted capital, Jeff—"

He took up a fold of her little shoulder ruffle and put it to his lips, and Lydia saw and wondered.

"No, dear," said he. "I sha'n't need your money. Only don't you let Weedie have it, to muddle away in politics."

She was turning at the edge of the corn and looking at him perplexedly. Her mission hadn't succeeded, but she loved him and wanted to make that manifest.

"I can't bear to have you doing irresponsible things with Madame Beattie. She's not fit—"

"Not fit for me to play with? Madame Beattie won't hurt me."

"She may hurt Lydia."

"Lydia!"

The word leaped out of some deep responsiveness she did not understand.

"Don't you know how much they are together? They go driving."

"Well, what's that? Madame Beattie's a good old sport. She won't harm Lydia."

But instead of keeping up his work, he went on to the house with her. Miss Amabel would not go in and when he had said good-bye to her—affectionately, charmingly, as if to assure her that, after all, she needn't fear him even with Weedie who wasn't important enough to slay—he entered the house in definite search of Lydia. He went to the library, and there she was, in the window niche, where she sat to watch him. Day by day Lydia sat there when he was in the garden and she was not busy and he knew it was a favourite seat of hers for, glancing over his rows of corn, he could see the top of her head bent over a book. He did not know how long she pored over a page with eyes that saw him, a wraith of him hovering over the print, nor that when their passionate depths grew hungrier for the actual sight of him, how she threw one glance at his working figure and bent to her book again. As he came suddenly in upon her she sprang up and faced him, the book closed upon a trembling finger.

"Lydia," said he, "you're great chums with Madame Beattie, aren't you?"

Lydia gave a little sigh of a relief she hardly understood. What she expected him to ask her she did not know, but there were strange warm feelings in her heart she would not have shown to Jeff. She could have shown them before that minute—when he had said the thing that ought not even to be remembered: "I only love you." Before that, she thought, she had been quite simply his sister. Now she was a watchful servitor of a more fervid sort. Jeffrey thought she was afraid of being scolded about her queer old crony.

"Sit down," he said. "There's nothing to be ashamed of in liking Madame Beattie. You do like her, don't you?"

"Oh, yes," said Lydia. "I like her very much."

She had sunk back in her chair and closed the book though she kept it in her lap. Jeffrey sat astride a chair and folded his arms on the top. Some of the blinds had been closed to keep out the heat, and the dusk hid the deep, crisp lines of his face. Under his moist tossed hair it was a young face, as Miss Amabel had told him, and his attitude became a boy.

"Lydia," said he, "what do you two talk about?"

"Madame Beattie and I?"

"Yes. In those long drives, for instance, what do you say?"

Lydia looked at him, her eyes narrowed slightly, and Jeffrey knew she did not want to tell. When Esther didn't want to tell, a certain soft glaze came over her eyes. Jeffrey had seen the glaze for a number of years before he knew what it meant. And when he found out, though it had been a good deal of a shock, he hardly thought the worse of Esther. He generalised quite freely and concluded that you couldn't expect the same standards of women as from men; and after that he was a little nervous and rather careful about the questions he asked. But Lydia's eyes had no glaze. They were desperate rather, the eyes of a little wild thing that is going to be frightened and possibly caught. Jeffrey felt quite excited, he was so curious to know what form the lie would take.

"Politics," said Lydia.

Jeffrey broke out into a laugh.

"Oh, come off!" said he. "Politics. Not much you don't."

Lydia laughed, too, in a sudden relief and pleasure. She didn't like her lie, it seemed.

"No," said she, "we don't. But I tell Anne if people ask questions it's at their own risk. They must take what they get."

"Anne wouldn't tell a lie," said Jeffrey.

She flared up at him.

"I wouldn't either. I never do. You took me by surprise."

"Does Madame Beattie talk to you about her life abroad?"

He ventured this. But she was gazing at him in the clearest candour.

"Oh, no." "About what, Lydia? Tell me. It bothers me."

"Did Miss Amabel bother you?" The charming face was fiery.

"I don't need Amabel to tell me you're taking long drives with Madame Beattie. She's a battered old party, Lydia. She's seen lots of things you don't want even to hear about."

She was gazing at him now in quite a dignified surprise.

"If you mean things that are not nice," she said, "I shouldn't listen to them. But she wouldn't want me to. Madame Beattie is—" She saw no adequate way to put it.

But Jeffrey understood her. He, too, believed Madame Beattie had a decency of her own.

"Never mind," said he. "Only I want to keep you as you are. So would father. And Anne."

Lydia sat straight in her chair, her cheeks scarlet from excitement, her eyes speaking with the full power of their limpid beauty. What if she were to tell him how they talked of Esther and her cruelty, and of him and his misfortunes, and of the need of his at once setting out to reconstruct his life? But it would not do. This youth here astride the chair didn't seem like the Jeff who was woven into all she could imagine of tragedy and pain. He looked like the Jeff she had heard the colonel tell about, who had been reckless and impulsive and splendid, and had been believed in always and then had grown up into a man who made and lost money and was punished for it. He was speaking now in his new coaxing voice.

"There's one thing you could tell me. That wouldn't do any harm."

"What?" asked Lydia.

"Your old crony must have mentioned the night we ran away with Weedon Moore's automobile."

"Oh, yes," said Lydia. Her eyes were eloquent now. "She told me."

"Did she tell you what she said to Weedon's crowd, to turn them round like a flock of sheep and bring them over to us?"

"Oh, yes, she told me."

"What was it?"

But Lydia again looked obstinate, though she ventured a little plea of her own.

"Jeff, you must go into politics."

"Not on your life."

"The way is all prepared."

"Who prepared it? Madame Beattie?"

"You are going," said Lydia, this irrepressibly and against her judgment, "to be the most popular man in Addington."

"Gammon!" This he didn't think very much of. If this was how Lydia and Madame Beattie spent their hours of talk, let them, the innocents. It did nobody harm. But he was still conscious of a strong desire: to protect Lydia, in her child's innocence, from evil. He wondered if she were not busy enough, that she had time to take up Madame Beattie. Yet she and Anne seemed as industrious as little ants.

"Lydia," said he, "what if I should have an Italian fruit-seller come up here to the house and teach Italian to you and me—and maybe Anne?"

"Andrea?" she asked.

"Do you know him?"

"Madame Beattie does." She coloured slightly, as if all Madame Beattie's little secrets were to be guarded.

"We'll have him up here if he'll come, and we'll learn to pass the bread in Italian. Shall we?"

"I'd love to," said Lydia. "We're learning now, Anne and I."

"Of Andrea?"

"Oh, no. But we're picking up words as fast as we can, all kinds of dialects. From the classes, you know, Miss Amabel's classes. It's ridiculous to be seeing these foreigners twice a week and not understand them or not have them half understand us."

"It's ridiculous anyway," said Jeffrey absently. He was regarding the shine on Lydia's brown hair. "What's the use of Addington's being overrun with Italy and Greece and Poland and Russia? We could get men enough to work in the shops, good straight stock."

"Well," said Lydia conclusively, "we've got them now. They're here. So we might as well learn to understand them and make them understand us."

Jeff smiled at her, the little soft young thing who seemed so practical. Lydia looked like a child, but she spoke like the calm house mother who had had quartered on her a larger family than the house would hold and yet knew the invaders must be accommodated in decent comfort somewhere. He sat there and stared at her until she grew red and fidgety. He seemed to be questioning something in her inner mind.

"What is it?" she asked.

"Nothing," said Jeff, and got up and went away to his own room. He had been thinking of her clear beauties of simple youthful outline and pure restraints, and wondering why the world wasn't made so that he could take her little brown hand in his and walk off with her and sit all day on a piney bank and listen to birds and find out what she thought about the prettiness of things. She was not his sister, she was not his child, though the child in her so persuaded him; and in spite of the dewy memory of her kiss she could not be his love. Yet she was most dear to him.

He threw himself down on the sofa and clasped his hands under his head, and he laughed suddenly because he was taking refuge in the thought of Esther. That Esther had become sanctuary from his thoughts of Lydia was an ironic fact indeed, enough to make mirth crack its cheeks. But since he was bound to Esther, the more he thought of her the better. He was not consciously comparing them, the child Lydia and the equipped siren, to Esther's harm. Only he knew at last what Esther was. She was Circe on her island. Its lights hung high above the wave, the sound of its music beat across the foam. Reardon heard the music; so did Alston Choate. Jeffrey knew that, in the one time he had heard Choate speak of her, a time when he had been in a way compelled to; and though it was the simplest commonplace, something new was beating in his voice. Choate had heard Esther's music, he had seen the dancing lights, and Esther had been willing he and all men should. There was no mariner who sailed the seas so insignificant as not to be hailed by Esther. That was the trouble. Circe's isle was there, and she was glad they knew it. Jeffrey did not go so far as to think she wanted inevitably to turn them into beasts, but he knew she was virtually telling them she had the power. That had been one of the first horrors of his disenchantment, when she had placed herself far enough away from him by neither writing to him nor visiting him; then he had seen her outside the glamour of her presence. Once he had been proud when the eyes of all men followed her. That was in the day of his lust for power and life, when her empery seemed equal in degree to his. Something brutal used to come up in him when men looked boldly at her, and while he wanted to quench the assault of their hot eyes it was always with the equal brutality: "She's mine." That was while he thought she walked unconscious of the insult. But when he knew she called it tribute, a rage more just than jealousy came up in him, and he hated something in her as he hated the men desiring her.

Yet now the thought of her was his refuge. She was not his, but he was hers to the end of earthly time. There was no task for him to do but somehow to shield Lydia from the welling of her wonderful devotion to him. If Esther was Circe on her island, Lydia was the nymph in a clear mountain brook of some undiscovered wood where the birds came to bathe, but no hoof had ever muddied the streams. If she had, out of her hero-worship, conceived a passion for him, he had an equal passion for her, of protectingness and sad certainty that he could do no better than ensure her distance from him.

XXIII

Jeffrey, in his working clothes, went down to Mill Street and found Andrea presiding over a shop exhaling the odour of pineapple and entrancing to the eye, with its piled ovals and spheres of red and yellow, its diversities of hue and surface. It was a fruit shop, and God had made the fruit beautiful and Andrea had disposed it so. His wife, too, was there, a round, dark creature in a plaid skirt and a shirt waist with islands of lace over a full bosom, her black hair braided and put round and round her head, and a saving touch of long earrings to tell you she was still all peasant underneath. A soft round-faced boy was in charge, and ran out to tell Jeffrey prices. But they all knew him. Jeffrey felt the puzzle begin all over when Andrea came hurrying out, like a genial host at an inn, hands outstretched, and his wife followed him. They looked even adoring, and again Jeffrey wondered, so droll was their excess of welcome, if he were going to be embraced. The boy, too, was radiant, and, like an acolyte at some ritual, more humbly though exquisitely proffered his own fit portion of worship. Jeffrey, it being the least he could offer, shook hands all round. Then he asked Andrea:

"Who do you think I am? What did Madame Beattie tell you?"

Andrea spread his hands dramatically, palms outward, and implied brokenly that though he understood English he did not speak it to such an extent as would warrant him in trying to explain what was best left alone. He would only repeat a word over and over, always with an access of affection, and when Jeffrey asked:

"Does that mean 'prisoner'?" he owned it did. It seemed to hold for the three the sum of human perfectibility. Jeffrey was The Prisoner, and therefore they loved him. He gave up trying to find out more; it seemed to him he could guess the riddle better if he had a word or two of Andrea's language to help him, and he asked summarily if they couldn't have some lessons together. Wouldn't Andrea come up to the house and talk Italian? Andrea blossomed out in gleam of teeth and incredible shininess of eyes. He would come. That night? Yes, he would come that night. So Jeffrey shook hands again all round and went away, curiously ill at ease until he had turned the corner; the warmth of their adoration seemed burning into his back.

But that night Andrea did not come. The family had assembled, Anne a little timid before new learning, Lydia sitting on the edge of her chair determined to be phenomenal because Jeffrey must be pleased, and even Mary Nellen with writing pads and pencils at the table to scrape up such of the linguistic leavings as they might. At nine o'clock the general attention began to relax, and Lydia widely yawned. Jeffrey, looking at her, caught the soft redness of her mouth and thought, forgetful of Circe's island where he had taken refuge, how sweet the little barbarian was.

But nobody next day could tell him why Andrea had not come, not even Andrea himself. Jeffrey sought him out at the fruit-stand and Andrea again shone with welcome. But he implied, in painfully halting English, that he could not give lessons at all. Nor could any of his countrymen in Addington.

Jeffrey stood upon no ceremony with him.

"Why the devil," said he, "do you talk to me as if you'd begun English yesterday? You forget I've heard you translating bunkum up on the circus-ground."

Andrea's eyes shone the more enchantingly. He was shameless, though. He took nothing back, and even offered Jeffrey an enormous pineapple, with the air of wanting to show his good-will and expecting it to be received with an equal open-heartedness. Jeffrey walked away with the pineapple, beaten, and reflecting soberly, his brow tightened into a knot. Things were going on just outside his horizon, and he wasn't to know. Who did know? Madame Beattie, certainly. The old witch was at the bottom of it. She had, for purposes of her own, wound the foreign population round her finger, and she was going to unwind them when the time came to spin a web. A web of many colours, he knew it would be, doubtless strong in some spots and snarled in others. Madame Beattie was not the person to spin a web of ordinary life.

He went on in his blue working clothes, absently taking off his hat to the ladies he met who looked inquiringly at him and then quite eagerly bowed. Jeff was impatient of these recognitions. The ladies were even too gracious. They were anxious to stand by him in the old Addington way, and as for him, he wanted chiefly to hoe his corn and live unseen. But his feet did not take him home. They led him down the street and up the stairs into Alston Choate's office, and there, hugging his pineapple, he entered, and found Alston sitting by the window in the afternoon light, his feet on a chair and a novel in his hand. This back window of the office looked down over the river, and beyond a line of willows to peaceful flats, and now the low sun was touching up the scene with afternoon peace. Alston, at sight of him, took his legs down promptly. He, too, was more eager in welcome because Jeffrey was a marked figure, and went so seldom up other men's stairs. Alston threw his book on the table, and Jeffrey set his pineapple beside it.

"There's a breeze over here," said Alston, and they took chairs by the window.

For a minute Jeffrey looked out over the low-lying scene. He drew a quick breath. This was the first time he had overlooked the old playground since he had left Addington for his grown-up life.

"We used to sail the old scow down there," he said. "Remember?"

Choate nodded.

"She's down there now in one of the yards, filled with red geraniums."

They sat for a while in the silence of men who find it unexpectedly restful to be together and need not even say so. Yet they were not here at all. They were boys of Addington, trotting along side by side in the inherited games of Addington. Alston offered Jeffrey a smoke, and Jeff refused it.

"See here," said he, "what's Madame Beattie up to?"

Choate turned a startled glance on him. He did not see how Jeffrey, a stranger in his wife's house, should know anything at all was up.

"She's been making things rather lively," he owned. "Who told you?"

"Told me? I was in it, at the beginning. She and I drove out by chance, to hear Moore doing his stunt in the circus-ground. That began it. But now, it seems, she's got some devil's influence over Moore's gang. She's told 'em something queer about me."

"She's told 'em something that makes things infernally uncomfortable for other people," said Choate bluntly. "Did you know she had squads of them—Italians, Poles, Abyssinians, for all I know, playing on dulcimers—she's had them come up at night and visit her in her bedroom. They jabber and hoot and smoke, I believe. She's established an informal club—in that house."

Alston's irritation was extreme. It was true Addington to refer to foreign tongues as jabber, and "that house", Jeffrey saw, was a stiff paraphrase for Esther's dwelling-place. He perceived here the same angry partisanship Reardon had betrayed. This was the jealous fire kindled invariably in men at Esther's name.

"How do you know?" he asked.

Alston hesitated. He looked, not abashed, but worried, as if he did not see precisely the road of good manners in giving a man more news about his wife than the man was able to get by himself.

"Did Esther tell you?" Jeff inquired.

"Yes. She told me."

"When?"

"Several times. She has been very uncomfortable. She has needed counsel."

Choate had gone on piling up what might have been excuses for Esther, from an irritated sense that he was being too closely cross-examined. He had done a good deal of it himself in the way of his profession, and he was aware that it always led to conclusions the victim had not foreseen and was seldom willing to face. And he had in his mind not wholly recognised yet unwelcome feelings about Esther. They were not feelings such as he would have allowed himself if he had known her as a young woman living with her husband in the accepted way. He did not permit himself to state that Esther herself might not, in that case, have mingled for him the atmosphere she breathed about him now. But Jeffrey did not pursue the dangerous road of too great candour. He veered, and asked, as if that might settle a good many questions:

"What's the matter with this town, anyway?"

"Addington?" said Choate. "You find it changed?"

"Changed! I believe you. Addington used to be a perfect picture—like a summer landscape—you know the kind. You walked into the picture the minute you heard the name of Addington. It was full of nice trees and had a stream and cows with yellow light on them. When you got into Addington you could take a long breath."

For the first time in his talk with anybody since he came home Jeff was feeling lubricated. He couldn't express himself carelessly to his father, who took him with a pathetic seriousness, nor to the girls, to whom he was that horribly uncomfortable effigy, a hero. But here was another fellow who, he would have said, didn't care a hang, and Jeff could talk to him.

"There's no such picture now," Alston assured him. "The Addington we knew was Victorian."

"Yes. It hadn't changed in fifty years. What's it changing for now?"

"My dear boy," said Alston seriously, because he had got on one of his own hobbies that he couldn't ride in Addington for fear of knocking ladies off their legs, "don't you know what's changing the entire world? It's the birth of compassion."

"Compassion?"

"Yes. Sympathy, ruth, pity. I looked up the synonyms the other day. But we're at the crude, early stages of it, and it's devilish uncomfortable.

Everybody's so sorry for everybody that we can't tell the kitchen maid to scour the knives without explaining."

Jeff was rather bewildered.

"Are we so compassionate as all that?" he asked.

"Not really. It's my impression most of us aren't compassionate at all."

"Amabel is."

"Oh, yes, Amabel and Francis of Assisi and a few others. But the rest of us have caught the patter and it makes us 'feel good'. We wallow in it. We feel warm and self-righteous—comfy, mother says, when she wants to tuck me up at night same as she used to after I'd been in swimming and got licked. Yes, we're compassionate and we feel comfy."

"But what's Weedon Moore got to do with it? Is Weedie compassionate?"

"Oh, Weedie's working Amabel and telling the mill hands they're great fellows and very much abused and ought to own the earth. Weedie wants their votes."

"Then Weedie is up for office? Amabel told me so, but I didn't think Addington'd stand for it. Time was when, if a man like Weedie had put up his head, nobody'd have taken the trouble to bash it. We should have laughed."

"We don't laugh now," said Choate gravely. There was even warning in his voice. "Not since Weedie and his like have told the working class it owns the earth."

"And doesn't it?"

"Yes. In numbers. It can vote itself right into destruction—which is what it's doing."

"And Weedie wants to be mayor."

"God knows what he wants. Mayor, and then governor and—I wouldn't undertake to say where Weedie'd be willing to stop. Not short of an ambassadorship."

"Choate," said Jeffrey cheerfully, "you're an alarmist."

"Oh, no, I'm not. A man like Weedie can get anywhere, because he's no scruples and he can rake in mere numbers to back him. And it's all right. This is a democracy. If the majority of the people want a demagogue to rule over them, they've a perfect right to go to the devil their own way."

"But where's he get his infernal influence? Weedie Moore!"

"He gets it by telling every man what the man wants to hear. He gets hold of the ignorant alien, and tells him he is a king in his own right. He tells him Weedie'll get him shorter and shorter hours, and make him a present of the machinery he runs—or let him break it—and the poor devil believes him. Weedie has told him that's the kind of a country this is. And nobody else is taking the trouble to tell him anything else."

"Well, for God's sake, why don't they?"

"Because we're riddled with compassion, I tell you. If we see a man poorer than we are, we get so apologetic we send him bouquets—our women do."

"Is that what the women here are doing?"

"Oh, yes. If there's a strike over at Long Meadow they put on their furs and go over and call on a few operatives and find eight living in one room, in a happy thrift, and they come back and hold an indignation meeting and 'protest'."

"You're not precisely a sentimentalist, are you?" said Jeff. He was seeing Choate in the new Addington as Choate presented it.

"No, by George! I want to see things clarified and the good old-fashioned virtues come back into their place—justice and common-sense. Compassion is something to die for. But you can't build states out of it alone. It makes me sick—sick, when I see men getting dry-rot."

Jeff's face was a map of dark emotion. His mind went back over the past years. He had not been made soft by the nemesis that laid him by the heels. He had been terribly hardened in some ways, so calloused that it sometimes seemed to him he had not the actual nerve surface for feeling anything. The lambent glow of beauty might fall upon him unheeded; even its lightnings might not penetrate his shell. But that had been better than the dry-rot of an escape from righteous punishment.

"You know, Choate," said he, "I believe the first thing for a man to learn is that he can't dodge penalties."

"I believe you. Though if he dodges, he doesn't get off. That's the other penalty, rot inside the rind. All the palliatives in the world—the lying securities and false peace—all of them together aren't worth the muscle of one man going out to bang another man for just cause. And getting banged!"

Jeff was looking at him quizzically.

"Where do you live," said he, "in the new Addington or the old one?"

Choate answered rather wearily, as if he had asked himself that question and found the answer disheartening.

"Don't know. Guess I'm a non-resident everywhere. I curse about Addington by the hour—the new Addington. But it's come, and come to stay."

"You going to let Moore administer it?"

"If he's elected."

"He can't be elected. We won't have it. What you going to do?"

"Nothing, in politics," said Alston. "They're too vile for a decent man to touch."

Jeffrey thought he had heard the sound of that before. Even in the older days there had been some among the ultra-conservative who refused to pollute their ideals by dropping a ballot. But it hadn't mattered much then. Public government had been as dual in its nature as good and evil, sometimes swaying to the side of one party, sometimes the other; but always, such had been traditional influence, the best man of a party had been nominated. Then there was no talk of Weedon Moores.

"Do you suppose Weedie's going on with his circus-ground rallies?" he asked.

"They say not."

"Who?"

"Oh, I've kept a pretty close inquiry afoot. I'm told the men won't go."

"Why not?"

"Madame Beattie won't let them."

"The devil she won't! What's the old witch's spell?"

"I don't know. Esther—" he caught himself up—"Mrs. Blake doesn't know. She only knows, as I tell you, the men come to the house, and talk things over. And I hear from reliable sources, Weedie summons them and the men simply won't go. So I assume Madame Beattie forbids it."

"It's not possible." Jeff had withdrawn his gaze from the old playground and sat staring thoughtfully at his legs, stretched to their fullest length. "I rather wish I could talk with her," he said, "Madame Beattie. I don't see how I can though, unless I go there."

"Jeff," said Alston, earnestly, "you mustn't do that."

He spoke unguardedly, and now that the words were out, he would have recalled them. But he made the best of a rash matter, and when Jeff frowned up at him, met the look with one as steady.

"Why mustn't I?" asked Jeff.

It was very quietly said.

"I beg your pardon," Choate answered. "I spoke on impulse."

"Yes. But I think you'd better go on."

Alston kept silence. He was looking out of the window now, pale and immovably obstinate.

"Do you, by any chance," said Jeff, "think Esther is afraid of me?"

Choate faced round upon him, immediately grateful to him.

"That's it," he said. "You've said it. And since it's so, and you recognise it, why, you see, Jeff, you really mustn't, you know."

"Mustn't go there?" said Jeff almost foolishly, the thing seemed to him so queer. "Mustn't see my wife, because she says she is afraid of me?"

"Because she *is* afraid of you," corrected Choate impulsively, in what he might have told himself was his liking for the right word. But he had a savage satisfaction in saying it. For the instant it made it seem as if he were defending Esther.

"I'd give a good deal," said Jeff slowly, "to hear just how Esther told you she was afraid of me. When was it, for example?"

"It was at no one time," said Choate unwillingly. Yet it seemed to him Jeff did deserve candour at all their hands.

"You mean it's been a good many times?"

"I mean I've been, in a way, her adviser since—"

"Since I've been in jail. That's very good of you, Choate. But do you gather Esther has told other people she is afraid of me, or that she has told you only?"

"Why, man," said Choate impatiently, "I tell you I've been her adviser. Our relations are those of client and counsel. Of course she's said it to nobody but me."

"Not to Reardon," Jeff's inner voice was commenting satirically. "What would you think if you knew she had said it to Reardon, too? And how many more? She has spun her pretty web, and you're a prisoner. So is Reardon. You've each a special web. You are not allowed to meet."

He laughed out, and Alston looked at him in a sudden offence. It seemed to Alston that he had been sacrificing all sorts of delicacies that Jeff might be justly used, and the laugh belittled them both. But Jeff at that instant saw, not Alston, but a new vision of life. It might have been that a tide had rushed in and wiped away even the prints of Esther's little feet. It might have been that a wind blew in at the windows of his mind and beat its great wings in the corners of it and winnowed out the chaff. As he saw life then his judgments softened and his irritations cooled. Nothing was left but the vision of life itself, the uncomprehended beneficence, the consoler, the illimitable beauty we look in the face and do not see. For an instant perhaps he had caught the true proportions of things and knew at last what was worth weeping over and what was matter for a healthy mirth. It was all mirth perhaps, this show of things Lord God had set us in. He had not meant us to take it dumbly. He had hoped we should see at every turn how queer it is, and yet how orderly, and get our comfort out of that. He had put laughter behind every door we open, to welcome us. Grief was there, too, but if we fully understood Lord God and His world, there would be no grief: only patience and a gay waiting on His time. And all this came out of seeing Alston Choate, who thought he was a free man, hobbled by Esther's web.

Jeffrey got up and Alston looked at him in some concern, he was so queer, flushed, laughing a little, and with a wandering eye. At the door he stopped.

"About Weedie," he said. "We shall have to do something to Weedie. Something radical. He's not going to be mayor of Addington. And I rather think you'll have to get into politics. You'd be mayor yourself if you'd get busy."

Jeffrey had no impulse to-day to go and ask Esther if she were afraid of him as he had when Reardon told him the same tale. He wasn't thinking of Esther now. He was hugging his idea to his breast and hurrying with it, either to entrust it to somebody or to wrap it up in the safety of pen and ink while it was so warm. And when he got home he came on Lydia, sitting on the front steps, singing to herself and cuddling a kitten in the curve of her arm. Lydia with no cares, either of the house or her dancing class or Jeff's future, but given up to the idleness of a summer afternoon, was one of the most pleasing sights ever put into the hollow of a lovely world. Jeffrey saw her, as he was to see everything now, through the medium of his new knowledge. He saw to her heart and found how sweet it was, and how full of love for him. He saw Circe's island, and knew, since the international codes hold good, he must remember his allegiance to it. He still owned property there; he must pay his taxes. But this Eden's garden which was Lydia was his chosen home. He was glad to see it so. He must, he knew, hereafter see things as they are. And they would not be tragic to him. They would be curious and funny and dear: for they all wore the mantle of life. He sat down on a lower step, and Lydia looked at him gravely, yet with pleasure, too.

"Lydia," said he, "do you know what they're calling me, these foreigners Madame Beattie's training with?"

She nodded.

"The Prisoner," said Jeff. "That's what I am—The Prisoner."

She hastened to reassure him.

"They don't do it to be hateful. It's in love. That's what they mean it in—love."

Jeff made a little gesture of the hand, as if he tossed off something so lightly won.

"Never mind how they mean it. That's not what I'm coming to. It's that they call me The Prisoner. Well, ten minutes ago it just occurred to me that we're all prisoners. I saw it as it might be a picture of life and all of us moving in it. Alston Choate's a prisoner to Esther. So's Reardon. Only it's not to Esther they're prisoners. It's to the big force behind her, the sorcery of nature, don't you see? Blind nature."

She was looking at him with the terrified patience of one compelled to listen and yet afraid of hearing what threatens the safe crystal of her own bright dream: that apprehensive look of woman, patient in listening, but beseeching the speaker voicelessly not to kill warm personal certainties with the abstractions he thinks he has discovered. Jeffrey did not understand the look. He was enamoured of his abstraction.

"And all the mill hands have been slaves to Weedon Moore because he told them lies, and now they're prisoners to Madame Beattie because she's telling them another kind of lie, God knows what. And Addington is prisoner to catch-words."

"But what are we prisoner to?" Lydia asked sharply, as if these things were terrifying. "Is Farvie a prisoner?"

"Why, father, God bless him!" said Jeff, moved at once, remembering what his father had to fight, "he's prisoner to his fear of death."

"And Anne? and I?"

Jeff sat looking at her in an abstracted thoughtfulness.

"Anne?" he repeated. "You? I don't know. I shouldn't dare to say. I've no rights over Anne. She's so good I'm shy of her. But if I find you're a prisoner, Lydia, I mean you shall be liberated. If nature drives you on as it drives the rest of us to worship something—somebody—blindly, and he's not worth it, you bet your life I'll save you."

She leaned back against the step above, her face suddenly sick and miserable. What if she didn't want to be saved? the sick face asked him. Lydia was a truth-teller. She loved Jeff, and she plainly owned it to herself and felt surprisingly at ease over it. She was born to the dictates of nice tradition, but when that inner warmth told her she loved Jeff, even though he was bound to Esther, she didn't even hear tradition, if it spoke. All she could possibly do for Jeff, who unconsciously appealed to her every instant he looked at her with that deep frown between his brows, seemed little indeed. Should she say she loved him? That would be easy. But were his generalities about life strong enough to push her and her humilities aside? That was hard to bear.

"And," he was saying, "once we know we're prisoners, We can be free."

"How?" said Lydia hopefully. "Can we do the things we like?"

"No, by God! there's only one way of getting free, and that's by putting yourself under the law."

Lydia's heart fell beyond plummet's sounding. She did not want to put herself under any stricter law than that of heart's devotion. She had been listening to it a great deal, of late. They were sweet things it told her, and not wicked things, she thought, but all of humble service and unasked rewards.

Jeff was roaming on, beguiled by his new thoughts and the sound of his own voice.

"It's perfectly true what I used to write in that beggarly prison paper. The only way to be really free is to be bound—by law. It's the big paradox. Do you know what I'm going to do?"

She shook her head. He was probably, her apprehensive look said, going to do something that would take him out of the pretty paradise where she longed to set him galloping on the road to things men ought to have.

"I am going in to tear up the stuff I'm writing about that man I knew there in the prison. What does God Almighty care about him? I'm going to write a book and call it 'Prisoners,' and show how I was a prisoner myself, to money, and luxury, and the game and—" he would not mention Esther, but Lydia knew where his mind stumbled over the thought of her—"and how I got my medicine. And how other fellows will have to take theirs, these fellows Weedie's gulling and Addington, because it's a fool wrapped up in its own conceit and stroking the lion's cub till it's grown big enough to eat us."

He got up and Lydia called to him:

"What is the lion's cub?"

"Why, it's the people. And Weedon Moore is showing it how hungry it is by chucking the raw meat at it and the saucers of blood. And pretty soon it'll eat us and eat Weedie too."

He went in and up the stairs and Lydia fancied she heard the tearing of papers in his room.

XXIV

The dry branch has come alive. The young Jeff Lydia had known through Farvie was here, miraculously full of hope and laughter. Jeff was as different after that day as a man could be if he had been buried and revived and cast his grave-clothes off. He measured everything by his new idea and the answers came out pat. The creative impulse shot up in him and grew. He knew what it was to be a prisoner under penalty, every cruel phase of it; and now that he saw everybody else in bonds, one to an unbalanced law of life we call our destiny, one to cant, one to greed, one to untended impulse, he was afire to let the prisoners out. If they knew they were bound they could throw off these besetments of mortality and walk in beauty. Old Addington, the beloved, must free herself. Too long had she been held by the traditions she had erected into forms of worship. The traditions lasted still, though now nobody truly believed in them. She was beating her shawms and cymbals in the old way, but to a new tune, and the tune was not the song of liberty, he believed, but a child's lullaby. In that older time she had decently covered discomfiting facts, asserted that she believed revealed religion, and blessed God, in an ingenuous candour, for setting her feet in paths where she could walk decorously. But now that she was really considering new gods he wanted her to take herself in hand and find out what she really worshipped. What was God and what was Baal? Had she the nerve to burn her sacrifices and see? He began to understand her better every day he lived with her. Poor old Addington! she had been suddenly assaulted by the clamour of the times; it told her shameful things were happening, and she had, with her old duteous responsiveness, snatched at remedies. The rich, she found, had robbed the poor. Therefore let there be no more poverty, though not on that account less riches. And here the demagogue arose and bade her shirk no issue, even the red flag. God Himself, the demagogue informed her, gives in His march of time spectacular illustration of temporal vanity. The earthquake ruins us, the flood engulfs us, fire and water are His ministers to level the pomp of power. Therefore, said the demagogue, forget the sweet abidingness of home, the brooding peace of edifices, the symbolic uses of matter to show us, though we live but in tents of a night, that therein is a sign of the Eternal City. Down with property. Addington had learned to distrust one sort of individual, and she instantly believed she could trust the other individual who was as unlike him as possible. Because Dives had been numb to human needs, Lazarus was the new-discovered leader. And the pitiful part of it all was that though Addington used the alphabet and spoke the language of "social unrest", it did it merely with the relish of playing with a new thing. It didn't make a jot of difference in its daily living. It didn't exert itself over its local government, it didn't see the Weedon Moores were honeycombing the soil with sedition. It talked, and talked, and knew the earth would last its time.

When Jeffrey tore up the life of his fellow prisoner he did it as if he tore his own past with it. He sat down to write his new book which was, in a way, an autobiography. He had read the enduring ones. He used to think they were crudely honest, and he meant now to tell the truth as brutally as the older men: how, in his seething youth, when he scarcely knew the face of evil in his arrogant confidence that he was strong enough to ride it bareback without falling off, if it would bring him to his ends, he leaped into the money game. And at that point, he owned ingenuously, he would have to be briefly insincere. He could unroll his own past, but not Esther's. The minute the stage needed her he realised he could never summon her. He might betray himself, not her. It was she, the voice incarnate of greed and sensuous delight, that had whipped him along his breathless course, and now he had to conceal her behind a wilful lie and say they were his own delights that lured him.

He sat there in his room writing on fiery nights when the moths crowded outside the screen and small sounds urged the freedom and soft beguilement of the season, even in the bounds of streets. The colonel, downstairs, sat in a determined patience over Mary Nellen's linguistic knots, what time he was awake long enough to tackle them, and wished Jeff would bring down his work where he could be glanced at occasionally even if he were not to be spoken to. The colonel had thought he wanted nothing but to efface himself for his son, and yet the yearning of life within him made him desire to live a little longer even by sapping that young energy. Only Lydia knew what Jeff was doing, and she gloried in it. He was writing a book, mysterious work to her who could only compass notes of social import, and even then had some ado to spell. But she read his progress by the light in his eyes, his free bearing and his broken silence. For now Jeff talked. He talked a great deal. He chaffed his father and even Anne, and left Lydia out, to her own pain. Why should he have kissed her that long ago day if he didn't love her, and why shouldn't he have kept on loving her? Lydia was asking herself the oldest question in the woman's book of life, and nobody had told her that nature only had the answer. "If you didn't mean it why did you do it?" This was the question Lydia heard no answer to.

Jeff was perpetually dwelling upon Addington, torn between the factions of the new and old. He asked Lydia seriously what she should recommend doing, to make good citizens out of bamboozled aliens. Lydia had but one answer. She should, she said, teach them to dance. Then you could get acquainted with them. You couldn't get acquainted if you set them down to language lessons or religious teaching, or tried to make them read the Constitution. If people had some fun together, Lydia thought, they pretty soon got to understand one another because they were doing a thing they liked, and one couldn't do it so well alone. That was her recipe. Jeff didn't take much stock in it. He was not wise enough to remember how eloquent are the mouths of babes. He went to Miss Amabel as being an expert in sympathy, and found her shy of him. She was on the veranda, shelling peas, and in her checked muslin with father's portrait braided round with mother's hair pinning together her embroidered collar. To Jeff, clad in his blue working-clothes, she looked like motherhood and sainthood blended. He sat himself down on the lower step, clasped his knees and watched her, following the movements of her plump hands.

"We can't get too homesick for old Addington while we have you to look at," said he.

She stopped working for one pod's space and looked at him.

"Are you homesick for old Addington?" she asked. "Alston Choate says that. He says it's a homesick world."

"He's dead right," said Jeff.

"What do you want of old Addington?" said she. "What do we need we haven't got?"

Jeff thought of several words, but they wouldn't answer. Beauty? No, old Addington was oftener funny than not. There was no beauty in a pint-pot. Even the echoes there rang thin. Peace? But he was the last man to go to sleep over the task of the day.

"I just want old Addington," he said. "Anyway I want to drop in to it as you'd drop into the movies. I want to hesitate on the brink of doing things that shock people. Nobody's shocked at anything now. I want to see the blush of modesty. Amabel, it's all faded out."

She looked at him, distressed.

"Jeff," said she, "do you think our young people are not—what they were?"

He loved her beautiful indirection.

"I don't want 'em to be what they were," said he, "if they have to lie to do it. I don't know exactly what I do want. Only I'm homesick for old Addington. Amabel, what should you say to my going into kindergarten work?"

"You always did joke me," said she. "Get a rise out of me? Is that what you call it?"

"I'm as sober as an owl," said Jeff. "I want these pesky Poles and Syrians and all the rest of them to learn what they're up against when they come over here to run the government. I'm on the verge, Amabel, of hiring a hall and an interpreter, and teaching 'em something about American history, if there's anything to teach that isn't disgraceful."

"And yet," said she, "when Weedon Moore talks to those same men you go and break up the meeting."

"But bless you, dear old girl," said Jeff, "Weedon was teaching 'em the rules for wearing the red flag. And I'm going to give 'em a straight tip about Old Glory. When I've got through with 'em, you won't know 'em from New Englanders dyed in the wool."

She meditated.

"If only you and Weedon would talk it over," she ventured, "and combine your forces. You're both so clever, Jeff."

"Combine with Weedie? Not on your life. Why, I'm Weedie's antidote. He preaches riot and sedition, and I'm the dose taken as soon as you can get it down."

Then she looked at him, though affectionately, in sad doubt, and Jeff saw he had, in some way, been supplanted in her confidence though not in her affection. He wouldn't push it. Amabel was too precious to be lost for kindergarten work.

When they had talked a little more, but about topics less dangerous, the garden and the drought, he went away; but Amabel padded after him, bowl in hand.

"Jeff," said she, "you must let me say how glad I am you and Weedon are really seeing things from the same point of view."

"Don't make any mistake about that," said Jeff. "He's trying to bust Addington, and Tin trying to save it. And to do that I've got to bust Weedie himself."

He went home then and put his case to Lydia, and asked her why, if Miss Amabel was so willing to teach the alien boy to read and teach the alien girl to sew, she should be so cold to his pedagogical ambitions. Lydia was curiously irresponsive, but at dusk she slipped away to Madame Beattie's. To Lydia, what used to be Esther's house had now become simply Madame Beattie's. She had her own shy way of getting in, so that she need not come on Esther nor trouble the decorous maid. Perhaps Lydia was a little afraid of Sophy, who spoke so smoothly and looked such cool hostility. So she tapped at the kitchen door and a large cook of sound principles who loved neither Esther nor Sophy, let her in and passed her up the back stairs. Esther had strangely never noted this adventurous way of entering. She was rather unobservant about some things, and she would never have suspected a lady born of coming in by the kitchen for any reason whatever. Esther, too, had some of the Addington traditions ingrain.

Madame Beattie was in bed, where she usually was when not in mischief, the summer breeze touching her toupée as tenderly as it might a young girl's flossy crown. She always had a cool drink by her, and she was always reading. Sometimes she put out her little ringed hand and moved the glass to hear the clink of ice, and she did it now as Lydia came in. Lydia liked the clink. It sounded festive to her. That was the word she had for all the irresponsible exuberance Madame Beattie presented her with, of boundless areas where you could be gay. Madame Beattie shut her book and motioned to the door. But Lydia was already closing it. That was the first thing when they had their gossips. Lydia came then and perched on the foot of the bed. Her promotion from chair to bed marked the progress of their intimacy.

"Madame Beattie," said she, "I wish you and I could go abroad together."

Madame Beattie grinned at her, with a perfect appreciation.

"You wouldn't like it," said she.

"I should like it," said Lydia. Yet she knew she did not want to go abroad. This was only an expression of her pleasure in sitting on a bed and chatting with a game old lady. What she wanted was to mull along here in Addington with occasional side dashes into the realms of discontent, and plan for Jeff's well-being. "He wants to give lectures," said she. "To them."

The foreign contingent was always known to her and Madame Beattie as They.

"The fool!" said Madame Beattie cheerfully. "What for?"

"To teach them to be good."

"What does he want to muddle with that for?"

"Why, Madame Beattie, you know yourself you're talking to them and telling them things."

"But that isn't dressing 'em in Governor Winthrop's knee breeches," said Madame Beattie, "and making Puritans of 'em. I'm just filling 'em up with Jeff Blake, so they'll follow him and make a ringleader of him whether he wants it or not. They'll push and push and not see they're pushing, and before he knows it he'll be down stage, with all his war-paint on. You never saw Jeff catch fire."

"No," said Lydia, lying. The day he took her hands and told her what she still believed at moments—he had caught fire then.

"When he catches fire, he'll burn up whatever's at hand," said the old lady, with relish. "Get his blood started, throw him into politics, and in a minute we shall have him in business, and playing the old game."

"Do you want him to play the old game?" asked Lydia.

"I want him to make some money."

"To pay his creditors."

"Pay your grandmother! pay for my necklace. Lydia, I've scared her out of her boots."

"Esther?" Lydia whispered.

Madame Beattie whispered, too, now, and a cross-light played over her eyes.

"Yes. I've searched her room. And she knows it. She thinks I'm searching for the necklace."

"And aren't you?"

"Bless you, no. I shouldn't find it. She's got it safely hid. But when she finds her upper bureau drawer gone over—Esther's very methodical—and the next day her second drawer and the next day the shelves in her closet, why, then—"

"What then?" asked Lydia, breathless.

"Then, my dear, she'll get so nervous she'll put the necklace into a little bag and tell me she is called to New York. And she'll take the bag with her, if she's not prevented."

"What should prevent her? the police?"

"No, my dear, for after all I don't want the necklace so much as I want somebody to pay me solid money for it. But when the little bag appears, this is what I shall say to Esther, perhaps while she's on her way downstairs to the carriage. 'Esther,' I shall say, 'get back to your room and take that little bag with you. And make up to handsome Jeff and tell him he's got to stir himself and pay me something on account. And you can keep the diamonds, my dear, if you see Jeff pays me something.'"

"She'd rather give you the diamonds," said Lydia.

"My dear, she sets her life by them. Do you know what she's doing when she goes to her room early and locks the door? She's sitting before the glass with that necklace on, cursing God because there's no man to see her."

"You can't know that," said Lydia.

She was trembling all over.

"My dear, I know women. When you're as old as I am, you will, too: even the kind of woman Esther is. That type hasn't changed since the creation, as they call it."

"But I don't like it," said Lydia. "I don't think it's fair. She hates Jeff—"

"Nonsense. She doesn't hate any man. Jeff's poor, that's all."

"She does hate him, and yet you're going to make him pay money so she can keep diamond necklaces she never ought to have had."

"Make him pay money for anything," said the old witch astutely, "money he's got or money he hasn't got. Set his blood to moving, I tell you, and before he knows it he'll be tussling for dear life and stamping on the next man and getting to the top."

Lydia didn't want him to tussle, but she did want him at the top. She had not told Madame Beattie about the manuscript growing and growing on Jeff's table every night. It was his secret, his and hers, she reasoned; she hugged the knowledge to her heart.

"That's all," said Madame Beattie, in that royal way of terminating interviews when she wanted to get back to literature. "Only when he begins to address his workingmen you tell me."

Lydia, on her way downstairs, passed Esther's room and even stood a second breathlessly taking in its exquisite order. Here was the bower where the enchantress slept, and where she touched up her beauty by the secret processes Lydia, being very young and of a pollen-like freshness, despised. This was not just of Lydia. Esther took no more than a normal care of her complexion, and her personal habits were beyond praise. Lydia stood there staring, her breath coming quick. Was the necklace really there? If she saw it what could she do? If the little bag with the necklace inside it sat there waiting to be taken to New York, what could she do then? She fled softly down the stairs.

Addington was a good deal touched when Jeffrey Blake took the old town hall and put a notice in the paper saying he would give a talk there on American History in the administration of George Washington. He would speak in English and parts of the lecture would be translated, if necessary, by an able interpreter. Ladies considered seriously whether they ought not to go, to encourage him, and his father was sure it was his own right and privilege. But Jeff choked that off. He settled the matter at the supper table.

"Look here," said he, "I'm going down there to make an ass of myself. Don't you come. I won't have it."

So the three stayed at home, and sat up for him and he told them, when he came in, at a little after ten, that there had been five Italians present and one of them had slept. Two ladies, deputed by the Woman's Club, had also come, and he wished to thunder women would mind their business and stay at home. But there was the fighting glint in his eye. His father remembered it, and Lydia was learning to know it now. He would give his next lecture, he said, unless nobody was there but the Woman's Club. He drew the line. And next day Lydia slipped away to Madame Beattie and told her the second lecture would be on the following Wednesday night.

That night Jeff stood up before his audience of three, no ladies this time. But Andrea was not there. Jeff thought a minute and decided there was no need of him.

"Will you tell me," said he, looking down from the shallow platform at his three men, "why I'm not talking in English anyway? You vote, don't you? You read English. Well, then, listen to it."

But he was not permitted to begin at once. There was a stir without and the sound of feet. The door opened and men tramped in, men and men, more than the little hall would hold, and packed themselves in the aisles and at the back. And with the foremost, one who carried himself proudly as if he were extremely honored, came Madame Beattie in a long-tailed velvet gown with a shining gold circlet across her forehead, and a plethora of jewels on her ungloved hands. She kept straight on, and mounted the platform beside Jeff, and there she bowed to her audience and was cheered. When she spoke to Jeff, it was with a perfect self-possession, an implied mastery of him and the event.

"I'll interpret."

After all, why not fall in with her, old mistress of guile? He began quite robustly and thought he was doing very well. In twenty minutes he was, he thought, speaking excellently. The men were warmly pleased. They sat up and smiled and glistened at him. Once he stopped short and threw Madame Beattie a quick aside.

"What are they laughing at?"

"I have to put it picturesquely," said Madame Beattie, in a stately calm. "That's the only way they'll understand. Go on."

It is said in Addington that those lectures lasted even until eleven o'clock at night, and there were petitions that The Prisoner should go to the old hall and talk every evening, instead of twice a week. The Woman's Club said Madame Beattie was a dear to interpret for him, and some of the members who had not studied any language since the seventies, when they learned the rudiments of German, to read Faust, judged it would be a good idea to hear her for practice. But somebody told her that, and she discouraged it. She was obliged, she said, to skip hastily from one dialect to another and they would only be confused; therefore they thought it better, after all, to remain undisturbed in their respective calm. Jeff sailed securely on through Lincoln's administration to the present day, and took up the tariff even, in an elementary fashion. There he was obliged to be drily technical at points, and he wondered how Madame Beattie could accurately reproduce him, much less to a response of eager faces. But then Jeff knew she was an old witch. He knew she had hypnotised wives that hated her and husbands sworn to cast her off. He knew she had sung after she had no voice, and bamboozled even the critics, all but one who wrote for an evening paper and so didn't do his notice until next day. And he saw no reason why she should not make even the tariff a primrose path.

Madame Beattie loved it all. Also, there was the exquisite pleasure, when she got home late, of making Sophy let her in and mix her a refreshing drink, and of meeting Esther the next day at dinner and telling her what a good house they had. Business, Madame Beattie called it, splendid business, and Esther hated her for that, too. It sounded like shoes or hosiery. But Ether didn't dare gainsay her, for fear she would put out a palmist's sign, or a notice of séances at twenty-five cents a head. Esther knew she could get no help from grandmother. When she sought it, with tears in her eyes, begging grandmother to turn the unprincipled old witch out for good, grandmother only pulled the sheet up to her ears and breathed stertorously.

But Madame Beattie was tired, though this was the flowering of her later life.

"My God!" she said to Lydia one night, before getting up to dress for a lecture, "I'm pretty nearly—what is it they call it—all in? I may drop dead. I shouldn't wonder if I did. If I do, you take Jeff into the joke. Nobody'd appreciate it more than Jeff."

"You don't think the men like him the less for it?" said Lydia.

"Oh, God bless me, no. They adore him. They think he's a god because he tells their folk tales and their stories. I give you my word, Lydia, I'd no idea I knew so many things."

"What did you tell last night?" said Lydia.

"Oh, stories, stories, stories. To-night I may spice it up a little with modern middle-Europe scandal. Dear souls! they love it."

"What does Jeff think they're listening to?" asked Lydia.

"The trusts, last time," said Madame Beattie. "My Holy Father! that's what he thinks. The trusts!"

XXV

The colonel thrived, about this time, on that fallacious feeling, born of hope eternal, that he was growing young. It is one of the precautionary lies of nature, to keep us going, that, the instant we are tinkered in any part, we ignore its merely being fitted up for shortened use. Hope eternal tells us how much stronger it is than it was before. If you rub unguent into your scanty hair you can feel it grow, as a poet hears the grass. A nostrum on your toil-hardened hands brings back, to keen anticipation, the skin of youth. All mankind is prepared to a perfect degree of sensitiveness for response to the quack doctor's art. We believe so fast that he need hardly do more than open his mouth to cry his wares. The colonel, doing a good day's work and getting tired enough to sleep at night, felt, on waking, as if life were to last the measure of his extremest appetite. The household went on wings, so clever and silent was Anne in administration and so efficient Mary Nellen. Only Anne was troubled in her soul because Lydia would go slipping away for these secret sessions with Madame Beattie. She even proposed going with her once or twice, but Lydia said she had put it off for that night; and next time she slipped away more cleverly. Once in these calls Lydia met Esther at the head of the stairs, and they said "How do you do?" in an uncomfortable way, Esther with reproving dignity and Lydia in a bravado that looked like insolence. And then Esther sent for Alston Choate, and in the evening he came.

Esther was a pathetic pale creature, as she met him in the dusk of the candle-lighted room, little more than a child, he thought, as he noted her round arms and neck within the film of her white dress. Esther did not need to assume a pathos for the moment's needs. She was very sorry for herself. They sat there by the windows, looking out under the shade of the elms, and for a little neither spoke. Esther had some primitive feminine impulses to put down. Alston had an extreme of pity that gave him fervencies of his own. To Esther it was as natural as breathing to ask a man to fight her battles for her, and to cling to him while she told him what battles were to be fought. Alston had the chafed feeling of one who cannot follow with an unmixed ardency the lines his heart would lead him. He was always angry, chiefly because she had to suffer so, after the hideousness of her undeserved destiny, and yet he saw no way to help that might not make a greater hardship for her. At last she spoke, using his name, and his heart leaped to it.

"Alston, what am I going to do?"

"Things going badly?" he asked her, in a voice moved enough to hearten her. "What is it that's different?"

"Everything. Aunt Patricia has those horrible men come here and talk with her—"

"It's ridiculous of her," said Alston, "but there's no harm in it. They're not a bad lot, and she's an old lady, and she won't stay here forever."

"Oh, yes, she will. She gets her food, at least, and I don't believe she could pay for even that abroad. And this sort of thing amuses her. It's like gipsies or circus people or something. It's horrible."

"What does your grandmother say?"

"Nothing."

"She must stand for it, in a way, or Madame Beattie couldn't do it."

"I don't believe grandmother understands fully. She's so old."

"She isn't tremendously old."

"Oh, but she looks so. When you see her in her nightcap—it's horrible, the whole thing, grandmother and all, and here I am shut up with it."

"I'm sorry," said Alston, in a low tone. "I'm devilish sorry."

"And I want to go away," said Esther, her voice rising hysterically, so that Alston nervously hoped she wouldn't cry. "But I can't do that. I haven't enough to live on, away from here, and I'm afraid."

"Esther," said he, daring at last to bring out the doubt that assailed him when he mused over her by himself, "just what do you mean by saying you are afraid?"

"You know," said Esther, almost in a whisper. She had herself in hand now.

"Yes. But tell me again. Tell me explicitly."

"I'm afraid," said Esther, "of him."

"Of your husband? If that's it, say it."

"I'm afraid of Jeff. He's been in here. I told you so. He took hold of me. He dragged me by my wrists. Alston, how can you make me tell you!"

The appeal sickened him. He got up and walked away to the mantel where the candles were, and stood there leaning against the shelf. He heard her catch her breath, and knew she was near sobs. He came back to his chair, and his voice had resumed so much of its judicial tone that her breath grew stiller in accord.

"Esther," said he, "you'd better tell me everything."

"I can't," said she, "everything. You are—" the rest came in a startling gush of words—"you are the last man I could tell."

It was a confession, a surrender, and he felt the tremendous weight of it. Was he the last man she could tell? Was she then, poor child, withholding herself from him as he, in decency, was aloof from her? He pulled himself together.

"Perhaps I can't do anything for you," he said, "in my own person. But I can see that other people do. I can see that you have counsel."

"Alston," said she, in what seemed to him a beautiful simplicity, "why can't you do anything for me?"

This was so divinely childlike and direct that he had to tell her.

"Esther, don't you see? If you have grounds for action against your husband, could I be the man to try your case? Could I? When you have just said I am the last man you could tell? I can't get you a divorce——" he stopped there. He couldn't possibly add, "and then marry you afterward."

"I see," said Esther, yet raging against him inwardly. "You can't help me."

"I can help you," said Alston. "But you must be frank with me. I must know whether you have any case at all. Now answer me quite simply and plainly. Does Jeff support you?"

"Oh, no," said Esther.

"He gives you no money whatever?"

"None."

"Then he's a bigger rascal than I've been able to think him."

"I believe——" said Esther, and stopped.

"What do you believe?"

"I think the money must come from his father. He sends it to me."

"Then there is money?"

"Why, yes," said Esther irritably, "there's some money, or how could I live?"

"But you told me there was none."

"How do you think I could live here with grandmother and expect her to dress me? Grandmother's very old. She doesn't see the need of things."

"It isn't a question of what you can live on," said Alston. "It's a question of Jeff's allowing you money, or not allowing you money. Does he, or does he not?"

"His father sends me some," said Esther, in a voice almost inaudible. It sounded sulky.

"Regularly?"

"Yes, I suppose so."

"Don't you know?"

"Yes. He sends it regularly."

"How often?"

"Four times a year."

"Haven't you every reason to believe that money is from Jeff?"

"No," said Esther. "I haven't any reason to think so at all. His father signs the cheques."

"Isn't it probable that his father would do that when Jeff was in prison, and that he should continue doing it now?"

Esther did not answer. There was something in the silence of the room, something in the peculiar feel of the atmosphere that made Alston certain she had balked. He recognised that pause in the human animal under inquisition, and for a wonder, since he had never been wound up to breaking point himself, knew how it felt. The machinery in the brain had suddenly stopped. He was not surprised that Esther could not go on. It was not obstinacy that deterred her. It was panic. He had put her, he knew, to too harsh a test. Now he had to soothe her affrighted mind and bring it back to its clear uses; and since he could honestly do it, as the lawyer exercising professional medicine, he gave himself gladly to the task.

"Esther," he said, "it is infernal to ask you these personal questions. But you will have to bring yourself to answer them if we are to decide whether you have any case and whether I can send you to another man. But if you do engage counsel, you'll have to talk to him freely. You'll have to answer all sorts of questions. It's a pretty comprehensive thing to admit the law into your private life, because you've got to give it every right there. You'll be questioned. And you'll have to answer."

Esther sat looking at him steadily. As she looked, her pale cheek seemed to fill and flush and a light ran into her eyes, until the glow spilled over and dazzled him, like something wavering between him and her. He had never seen that light in her eyes, nor indeed the eyes of any woman, nor would he have said that he could bear to see it there unsummoned. Yet had he not summoned it unconsciously, hard as he was trying to play the honest game between an unattached woman and a man who sees her fetters where she has ceased to see them, but can only feel them gall her? Had not the inner spirit of him been speaking through all this interview to the inner spirit of her, and was she not willing now to let it cry out and say to him, "I am here"? Esther was willing to cry out. In the bewilderment of it, he did not know whether it was superb of her, though he would have felt it in another woman to be shameless. The lustrous lights of her eyes dwelt upon him, unwavering. Then her lips confirmed them.

"Well," said Esther, "isn't it worth it?"

Alston got up and rather blindly went out of the room. In the street, after the summer breeze had been touching his forehead and yet not cooling it, he realised he was carrying his hat in his hand, and put it on hastily. He was Addington to the backbone, when he was not roaming the fields of fiction, and one of the rules of Addington was against looking queer. He walked to his office and let himself in. The windows were closed and the room had the crude odour of public life: dust, stale tobacco and books. He threw up the windows and hesitated an instant by the gas jet. It was his habit, when the outer world pressed him too heavily, to plunge instantly into a book. But books were no anodyne for the turmoil of this night. Nor was the light upon these familiar furnishings. He sat down by the window, laid his arms on the sill and looked out over the meadows, unseen now but throwing their damp exhalations up to him through the dark. His heart beat hard, and in the physical vigour of its revolt he felt a fierce pleasure; but he was shamed all through in some way he felt he could not meet. Had he seen a new Esther to-night, an Esther that had not seemed to exist under the soft lashes of the woman he thought he knew so well? He had a stiffly drawn picture of what a woman ought to be. She really conformed to Addington ideals. He believed firmly that the austere and noble dwelt within woman as Addington had framed her. It would have given him no pleasure to find a savage hidden under pretty wiles. But Alston believed so sincerely in the control of man over the forces of life, of which woman was one, that, if Esther had stepped backward from her bright estate into a barbarous challenge, it was his fault, he owned, not hers. He should have guided her so that she stayed within hallowed precincts. He should have upheld her so that she did not stumble over these pitfalls of the earth. It is a pity those ideals of old Addington that made Alston Choate believe in women as little lower than the angels and, if they proved themselves lower, not really culpable because they are children and not rightly guided—it is a pity that garden cannot keep on blooming even out of the midden of the earth. But he had kept the garden blooming. Addington had a tremendous grip on him. It was not that he had never seen other customs, other manners. He had travelled a reasonable amount for an Addington man, but always he had been able to believe that Eden is what it was when there was but one man in it and one woman. There was, of course, too, the serpent. But Alston was fastidious, and he kept his mind as far away from the serpent as possible. He thought of his mother and sister, and instantly ceased thinking of them, because to them Esther was probably a sweet person, and he knew they would not have recognised the Esther he saw to-night. Perhaps, though he did not know this, his mother might.

Mrs. Choate was a large, almost masculine looking woman, very plain indeed, Addington owned, but with beautiful manners. She was not like Alston, not like his sister, who had a highbred charm, something in the way of Alston's own. Mother was different. She was of the Griswolds who had land in Cuba and other islands, and were said to have kept slaves there while the Choates were pouring blood into the abolitionist cause. There was a something about mother quite different from anybody in Addington. She conformed beautifully, but you would have felt she understood your not conforming. She never came to grief over the neutralities of the place, and you realised it was because she expressed so few opinions. You might have said she had taken Addington for what it was and exhausted it long ago. Her gaze was an absent, yet, of late years, a placid one. She might have been dwelling upon far-off islands which excited in her no desire to be there. She was too cognisant of the infinite riches of time that may be supposed to make up eternity. If she was becalmed here in Addington, some far-off day a wind would fill her sails and she might seek the farther seas. And, like her son, she read novels.

Alston, going home at midnight, saw the pale glimmer in her room and knew she was at it there. He went directly upstairs and stopped at her door, open into the hall. He was not conscious of having anything to say. Only he did feel a curious hesitation for the moment. Here in Addington was an Esther whom he had just met for the first time. Here was another woman who had not one of Esther's graces, but whom he adored because she was the most beautiful of mothers. Would she be horrified at the little strange animal that had looked at him out of Esther's eyes? He had never seen his mother shocked at anything. But that, he told himself, was because she was so calm. The Woman's Club of Addington could have told him it was because she had poise. She looked up, as he stood in the doorway, and laid her book face downward on the bed. Usually when he came in like this she moved the reading candle round, so that the hood should shield his eyes. But to-night she gently turned it toward him, and Alston did not realise that was because his fagged face and disordered hair had made her anxious to understand the quicker what had happened to him.

I "Sit down," she said.

And then, having fairly seen him, she did turn the hood. Alston dropped into the chair by the bedside and looked at her. She was a plain woman, it is true, but of heroic lines. Her iron-grey hair was brushed smoothly back into its two braids, and her nightgown, with its tiny edge, was of the most pronouncedly sensible cut, of high neck and long sleeves. Yet there was nothing uncouth about her in her elderly ease of dress and manner. She was a wholesome woman, and the heart of her son turned pathetically to her.

"Mary gone to bed?" he asked.

"Yes," said Mrs. Choate. "She was tired. She's been rehearsing a dance with those French girls and their class."

Alston lay back in his chair, regarding her with hot, tired eyes. He wanted to know what she thought of a great many things: chiefly whether a woman who had married Jeff Blake need be afraid of him. But there was a well-defined code between his mother and himself. He was not willing to trap her into honest answers where he couldn't put honest questions.

"Mother," said he, and didn't know why he began or indeed that he was going to say just that at all, "do you ever wish you could run away?"

She gave the corner of the book a pat with one beautiful hand.

"I do run away," she said. "I was a good many miles from here when you came in. And I shall be again when you are gone. Among the rogues, such as we don't see."

"What is it?"

"Mysteries of Paris."

"That's our vice, isn't it," said Alston, "yours and mine, novel reading?"

"You're marked with it," said she.

There was something in the quiet tone that arrested him and made him look at her more sharply. The tone seemed to say she had not only read novels for a long time, but she had had to read them from a grave design. "It does very well for me," she said, "but it easily mightn't for you. Alston, why don't you run away?"

Alston stared at her.

"Would you like to go abroad?" he asked her then, "with Mary? Would you like me to take you?"

"Oh, no," said Mrs. Choate. "Mary wouldn't want to. She's bewitched with those French girls. And I don't want to. I couldn't go the only way I'd like."

"You could go any way you chose," said Alston, touched. He knew there was a war chest, and it irked him to think his mother wouldn't have it tapped for her.

"Oh, no," said she. "I should need to be slim and light, and put on short petticoats and ride horses and get away from tigers. I don't want to shoot them, but I'd rather like to get away from them."

"Mother," said Alston, "what's come over you? Is it this book?"

She laughed, in an easy good-humour.

"Books don't come over me," said she. "I believe it's that old Madame Beattie."

"What's Madame Beattie done that any—" he paused; Esther's wrongs at Madame Beattie's hands were too red before him—"that any lady would be willing to do?"

"I really don't know, Alston," said his mother frankly. "It's only that when I think of that old party going out every night—"

"Not every night."

"Well, when she likes, and getting up on a platform and telling goodness knows what to the descendants of the oldest civilisations, and their bringing her home on their shoulders—"

"No, no, mother, they don't do that."

"I tell you what it makes me feel, Alston: it makes me feel *fat*."

"Madame Beattie weighs twenty pounds more than you do, and she's not so tall by three inches."

"And then I realise that when women say they want to vote, it isn't because they're all piously set on saving the country. It's because they've peeped over the fence and got an idea of the game, and they're crazy to be in it."

"But, mother, there's no game, except a dirty one of graft and politics. There's nothing in it."

"No," said Mrs. Choate. "There isn't in most games. But people play them."

"You don't think Amabel is in it for the game?"

"Oh, no! Amabel's a saint. It wouldn't take more than a basket of wood and a bunch of matches to make her a martyr."

"But, mother," said Alston, "you belong to the antis."

"Do I?" asked his mother. "Yes, I believe I do."

"Do you mean to say you're not sincere?"

"Why, yes, of course I'm sincere. So are they. Only, doesn't it occur to you they're having just as much fun organising and stirring the pot as if it was the other pot they were stirring? Besides they attitudinise while they stir, and say they're womanly. And they like that, too."

"Do you think they're in it for the game?"

"No, no, Alston, not consciously. Nobody's in it for the game except your Weedon Moores. Any more than a nice girl puts on a ribbon to trap her lover. Only nature's behind the girl, and nature's behind the game. She's behind all games. But as to the antis—" said Mrs. Choate impatiently, "they've gone on putting down cards since the rules were changed."

Alston rose and stood looking down at her. She glanced up brightly, met his eyes and laughed.

"All is," said she, in a current phrase even cultured Addington had caught from its "help" from the rural radius outside, "I just happened to feel like telling you if you want to run away, you go. And if I weighed a hundred and ten and were forty-five, I'd go with you. Actually, I should advise you, if you're going to stay here, to stir the pot a little now it's begun to boil so hard."

"Get into politics?" he asked, remembering Jeff.

"Maybe."

She smiled at him, pleasantly, not as a mother smiles, but an implacable mistress of destiny. In spite of her large tolerance, there were moments when she did speak. So she had looked when he said, as a boy, that he shouldn't go to gymnasium, and she had told him he would. And he went. Again, when he was in college and had fallen in with a set of ultra-moderns and swamped himself in decoration and the beguilements of a spurious art, he had seen that look; then she had told him the classics were not to be neglected. Now here was the look again. Alston began to have an uncomfortable sense that he might have to run for office in spite of every predilection he ventured to cherish. He could have thrown himself on the floor and bellowed to be let alone.

"But keep your head, dear," she was saying. "Keep your head. Don't let any man—or woman either—lose it for you. That's the game, Alston, really."

It was such a warm impetuous tone it brought them almost too suddenly and too close together. Alston meant to kiss her, as he did almost every night, but he awkwardly could not. He went out of the room in a shy haste, and when he dropped off to sleep he was thinking, not of Esther, but of his mother. Even so he did not suspect that his mother knew he had come from Esther and how fast his blood was running.

XXVI

Jeff, writing hard on his book to tell men they were prisoners and had to get free, was tremendously happy. He thought he saw the whole game now, the big game these tiny issues reflected in a million mirrors. You were given life and incalculable opportunity. But you were allowed to go it blind. They never really interfered with you, the terrible They up there: for he could not help believing there was an Umpire of the game, though nobody, it seemed, was permitted to see the score until long afterward, when the trumpery rewards had been distributed. (Some of them were not trumpery; they were as big as the heavens and the sea.) He found a great many things to laugh over, sane, kind laughter, in the way the game was played there in Addington. Religion especially seemed to him the big absurd paradox. Here were ingenuous worshippers preserving a form of observance as primitive as the burnt-offerings before a god of bronze or wood. They went to church and placated their god, and swore they believed certain things the acts of their lives repudiated. They made a festival at Christmas time and worshipped at the manger and declared God had come to dwell among men. They honored Joseph who was the spouse of Mary, and who was a carpenter, and on the twenty-sixth of December they nodded with condescension to their own carpenter, if they met him in the street, or they failed to see him at all. And their carpenter, who was doing his level best to prevent them from grinding the face of labour, himself ground the face of his brother carpenter if his brother did not heartily co-operate in keeping hours down and prices up. And everybody was behaving from the prettiest of motives; that was the joke of it. They not only said their prayers before going out to trip up the competitor who was lying in wait to trip up them; they actually believed in the efficacy of the prayer. They glorified an arch apostle of impudence who pricked bubbles for them—a modern literary light—but they went on blowing their bubbles just the same, and when the apostle of impudence pricked them again they only said: "Oh, it's so amusing!" and blew more. And even the apostle of impudence wasn't so busy pricking bubbles that he didn't have time to blow bubbles of his own, and even he didn't know how thin and hollow his own bubbles were, which was the reason they could float so high. He saw the sun on them and thought they were the lanterns that lighted up the show. Jeff believed he had discovered the clever little trick at the bottom of the game, the trick that should give over to your grasp the right handle at last. This was that every man, once knowing he was a prisoner, should laugh at his fetters and break them by his own muscle.

"The trouble is," he said, at breakfast, when Mary Nellen was bringing in the waffles, "we're all such liars."

The colonel sat there in a mild peaceableness, quite another man under the tan of his honest intimacy with the sun. He had been up hoeing an hour before breakfast, and helped himself to waffles liberally, while Mary Nellen looked, with all her intellectual aspirations in her eyes, at Jeff.

"No, no," said the colonel. He was conscious of very kindly feelings within himself, and believed in nearly everybody but Esther. She, he thought, might have a chance of salvation if she could be reborn, physically hideous, into a world obtuse to her.

"Liars!" said Jeff mildly. "We're doing the things we're expected to do, righteous or not. And we're saying the things we don't believe."

"That's nothing but kindness," said the colonel. Mary Nellen made a pretence of business at the side table, and listened greedily. She would take what she had gathered to the kitchen and discuss it to rags. She found the atmosphere very stimulating. "If I asked Lydia here whether she found my hair thin, Lydia would say she thought it beautiful hair, wouldn't you, Lyddy? She couldn't in decency tell me I'm as bald as a rat."

"It is beautiful," said Lydia. "It doesn't need to be thick."

Jeff had refused waffles. He thrust his hands in his pockets and leaned back, regarding his father with a smile. The lines in his face, Lydia thought, fascinated, were smoothed out, all but the channels in the forehead and the cleft between his brows. That last would never go.

"I am simply," said Jeff, "so tickled I can hardly contain myself. I have discovered something."

"What?" said Lydia.

"The world," said Jeff. "Here it is. It's mine. I can have it to play with. It's yours. You can play, too. So can that black-eyed army Madame Beattie has mobilised. So can she."

Anne was looking at him in a serious anxiety.

"With conditions as they are—" said she, and Jeff interrupted her without scruple.

"That's the point. With conditions as they are, we've got to dig into things and mine out pleasures, and shake them in the faces of the mob and the mob will follow us."

The colonel had ceased eating waffles. His thin hand, not so delicate now that it had learned the touch of toil, trembled a little as it held his fork.

"Jeff," said he, "what do you want to do?"

"I want," said Jeff, "to keep this town out of the clutch of Weedie Moore."

"You can't do it. Not so long as Amabel is backing him. She's got unlimited cash, and she thinks he's God Almighty and she wants him to be mayor."

"It's a far cry," said Jeff, "from God Almighty to mayor. But Alston Choate is going to be nominated for mayor, and he's going to get it."

"He won't take it," said Anne impulsively, and bit her lip.

"How do you know?" asked Jeff.

"He hates politics."

"He hates Addington more as it is."

They got up and moved to the library, standing about for a moment, while Farvie held the morning paper for a cursory glance, before separating for their different deeds. When Farvie and Anne had gone Jeff took up the paper and Lydia lingered. Jeff felt the force of her silent waiting. It seemed to bore a hole through the paper itself and knock at his brain to be let in. He threw the paper down.

"Well?" said he.

Lydia was all alive. Her small face seemed drawn to a point of eagerness. She spoke.

"Alston Choate isn't the man for mayor."

"Who is?"

"You."

Jeff slowly smiled at her.

"I?" he said. "How many votes do you think I'd get?"

"All the foreign vote. And the best streets wouldn't vote at all."

"Why?"

She bit her lip. She had not meant to say it.

"No," said Jeff, interpreting for her, "maybe they wouldn't. That's like Addington. It wouldn't stand for me, but it would be too well-bred to stand against me. No, Lyddy, I shouldn't get a show. And I don't want a show. All I want is to bust Weedon Moore."

Lydia looked the unmovable obstinacy she felt stiffening every fibre of her.

"You're all wrong," she said. "You could have anything you wanted."

"Who says so?"

"Madame Beattie."

"I wish," said Jeff, "that old harpy would go to Elba or Siberia or the devil. I'm not going to run for office."

"What are you going to do?" asked Lydia, in a small voice. She was resting a hand on the table, and the hand trembled.

"It's a question of what I won't do, at present. I won't go down there to the hall and make an ass of myself talking history and be dished by that old marplot. But if I can get hold of the same men—having previously gagged Madame Beattie or deported her—I'll make them act some plays."

"What kind of plays?"

"Shakespeare, maybe."

"They can't do that. They don't know enough."

"They know enough to understand that old rascal's game, whatever it is, and hoot with her when she's done me. And she's given me the tip, with her dramatics up there on the platform, and the way they answered. They're children, and they want to play. She had the cleverness to see it. And they shall play with me."

"But they won't act Shakespeare," said Lydia. "They only care about their own countries. That's why they love Madame Beattie."

"What are their countries, Lydia?"

"Greece, Italy, Poland, Russia—oh, a lot more."

"Aren't they voting here in this country?"

"Why, yes, ever so many of them."

"Then," said Jeff, "this is their country, and this is their language, and they've got to learn some English plays and act them as God pleases. But act them they shall. Or their children shall. And you may give my compliments to Madame Beattie and tell her if she blocks my game I'll block hers. She'll understand. And they've got to learn what England was and what America meant to be till she got on the rocks."

"Jeff," said Lydia, venturing, "aren't you going into business?"

"I am in business," said Jeff. "It's my business to bail out the scuppers here in Addington and bust Weedie Moore."

"If you went into business," said Lydia, "and made money you could—"

"I could pay off my creditors? No, I couldn't, Lydia. I could as easily lift this house."

"But you could pay something—"

"Something on a dollar? Lydia, I've been a thief, a plain common thief. I stole a chicken, say. Well, the chicken got snatched away somehow and scrambled for, and eaten. Anyway, the chicken isn't. And you want me to steal another—"

"No, no."

"Yes, you do. I should have to steal it. I haven't time enough in my whole life to get another chicken as big and as fat, unless I steal it. No, Lydia, I can't do it. If you make me try, I shall blow my nut off, that's all."

Lydia was terrified and he reassured her.

"No. Don't worry. I sha'n't let go my grip on the earth. When I walk now I'm actually sticking my claws into her. I've found out what she is."

But Lydia still looked at him, hungry for his happiness, and he despairingly tried to show her his true mind.

"You mustn't think for a minute I can wipe out my old score and show you a perfectly clean slate with a nice scrollwork round it. Can't do it, Lydia. I sha'n't come in for any of the prizes. I've got to be a very ordinary, insignificant person from now on."

That hurt her and it did no good. She didn't believe him.

Not many days from this Jeff started out talking to men. He frankly wanted something and asked for it. Addington, he told them, if they built more factories and put in big industries, as they were trying to do, was going to call in more and more foreign workmen. It was going to be a melting-pot of small size. That was a current catchword. Jeff used it as glibly as the women of the clubs. The pot was going to seethe and bubble over and some demagogue—he did not mention Weedie—was going to stir it, and the Addington of our fathers would be lost. The business men looked at him with the slow smile of the sane for the fanatic and answered from the fatuous optimism of the man who expects the world to last at least his time. Some of them said something about "this great country", as if it were chartered by the Almighty to stand the assaults of other races, and when he reminded them that Addington was not trying to amalgamate its aliens with its own ideals, and was giving them over instead to Weedon Moore, they laughed at him.

"What's Weedon Moore?" one man said. "A dirty little shyster. Let him talk. He can't do any harm."

"Do you know what he's telling them?" Jeff inquired.

They supposed they did. He was probably asking them to vote for him.

"Not a bit of it," said Jeff. "He'll do that later. He's telling them they hold the key of the treasury and they've only to turn it to be inside. He's giving no credit to brains and leadership and tradition and law and punishment for keeping the world moving. He's telling the man with the hod and the man with the pickaxe that simply by virtue of the hod and the pickaxe the world is his: not a fraction of it, mind you, but the earth. To kick into space, if he likes. And kick Addington with it."

They smoothed him down after one fashion or another, and put their feet up and offered him a cigar and wanted to hear all about his prison experiences, but hardly liked to ask, and so he went away in a queer coma of disappointment. They had not turned him out, but they didn't know what he was talking about. Every man of them was trying either to save the dollar he had or to make another dollar to keep it warm. Jeff went home sore at heart; but when he had plucked up hope again out of his sense of the ironies of things, he went back and saw the same men and hammered at them. He explained, with a categorical clearness, that he knew the West couldn't throw over the East now she'd taken it aboard. Perhaps we'd got to learn our lesson from it. Just as it might be it could learn something from us; and since it was here in our precincts, it had got to learn. We couldn't do our new citizens the deadly wrong of allowing the seeds of anarchy to be planted in them before they even got over the effects of the voyage. If there were any virtue left in the republic, the fair ideal of it should be stamped upon them as they came, before they were taught to riot over the rights no man on earth could have unless men are going to fight out the old brute battle for bare supremacy.

Then one day a man said to him, "Oh, you're an idealist!" and all his antagonists breathed more freely because they had a catchword. They looked at him, illuminated, and repeated it.

One man, a big coal dealer down by the wharves, did more or less agree with him.

"It's this damned immigration," he said. "They make stump speeches and talk about the open door, but they don't know enough to shut the door when the shebang's full."

It was the first pat retort of any sort Jeff had got.

"I'm not going back so far as that," he leaped at the chance of answering. "I don't want to wait for legislation to crawl along and shut the stable door. I only say, we've invited in a lot of foreigners. We've got to teach 'em to be citizens. They've got to take the country on our plan, and be one of us."

But the coal man had tipped back in his chair against the coal shed and was scraping his nails with his pocket knife. He did it with exquisite care, and his half-closed eyes had a look of sleepy contentment; he might have been shaping a peaceful destiny. His glimmer of responsiveness had died.

"I don't know what you're goin' to do about it," he said.

"We're going to put in a decent man for mayor," said Jeff. "And we're going to keep Weedon Moore out."

"Moore ain't no good," said the coal man. "But I dunno's he'd do any harm."

The eyes of them all were holden, Jeff thought. They were prisoners to their own greed and their own stupidity. So he sat down and ran them into his book, as blind custodians of the public weal. His book was being written fast. He hardly knew what kind of book it was, whether it wasn't a queer story of a wandering type, because he had to put what he thought into the mouths of people. He had no doubt of being able to sell it. When he first came out of prison three publishing firms of the greatest enterprise had asked him to write his prison experiences. To one of these he wrote now that the book was three-quarters done, and asked what the firm wanted to do about it. The next day came an up-to-date young man, and smoked cigarettes incessantly on the veranda while he asked questions. What kind of a book was it? Jeff brought out three or four chapters, and the young man whirled over the leaves with a practised and lightning-like faculty, his spectacled eyes probing as he turned.

"Sorry," said he. "Not a word about your own experiences."

"It isn't my prison experience," said Jeff. "It's my life here. It's everybody's life on the planet."

"Couldn't sell a hundred copies," said the young man. Jeff looked at him in admiration, he was so cocky and so sure. "People don't want to be told they're prisoners. They want you to say you were a prisoner, and tell how innocent you were and how the innocent never get a show and the guilty go scot free."

"How do you think it's written?" Jeff ventured to ask.

"Admirably. But this isn't an age when a man can sit down and write what he likes and tell the publisher he can take it and be damned. The publisher knows mighty well what the public wants. He's going to give it to 'em, too."

"You'd say it won't sell."

"My dear fellow, I know. I'm feeling the pulse of the public all the time. It's my business."

Jeff put out his hands for the sheets and the censor gave them up willingly.

"I'm frightfully disappointed," he said, taking off his eyeglasses to wipe them on his handkerchief and looking so babyishly ingenuous that Jeff broke into a laugh. "I thought we should get something 'live out of you, something we could push with conviction, you know. But we can't this; we simply can't." He had on his glasses now, and the all-knowingness had come mysteriously back. His eyes seemed to shoot arrows, and clutch and hold you so that you wanted to be shot by them again. "Tell you what, though. We might do this. It's a crazy book, you know."

"Is it?" Jeff inquired.

"Oh, absolutely. Daffy. They'd put it in the eccentric section of a library, with books on perpetual motion and the fourth dimension. But if you'd let us publish your name—"

"Decidedly."

"And do a little preliminary advertising. How prison life had undermined your health and even touched your reason, so you weren't absolutely—you understand? *Then* we'd publish it as an eccentric book by an eccentric fellow, a victim of prison regulations."

Jeff laid his papers down on the table beside him and set a glass on them to keep them from blowing away.

"No," said he. "I never was saner in my life. I'm about the only sane man in this town, because I've discovered we're all mad and the rest of 'em don't know it."

"That very remark!" said the young man, in unmixed approval. "Don't you see what that would do in an ad? My dear chap, they all think the other man's daffy."

Jeff carried the manuscript into the house, and asked the wise young judge to come out and see his late corn, and offered him a platter of it if he'd stay to supper. And he actually did, and proved to be a very good fellow indeed, born in the country, and knowing all its ways, only gifted with a diabolical talent for adapting himself to all sorts of places and getting on. He was quite shy in the face of Anne and Lydia. All his cockiness left him before their sober graces, and when Jeff took him to the station he had lost, for the moment, his rapier-like action of intellect for an almost maudlin gratitude over the family he had been privileged to meet.

Anne and Lydia had paid him only an absent-minded courtesy. They were on the point of giving an evening of folk-dancing, under Miss Amabel's patronage, and young foreigners were dropping in all the time now to ask questions and make plans. And whoever they were, these soft-eyed aliens, they looked at Jeff with the look he knew. To them also he was The Prisoner.

XXVII

With these folk dances began what has been known ever since as the Dramatic Movement in Addington. On this first night the proudly despairing ticket-seller began to repeat by seven o'clock: "Every seat taken." Many stood and more were turned away. But the families of the sons and daughters who were dancing were clever enough to come early, and filled the body of the hall. Jeff was among them. He, too, had gone early, with Anne and Lydia, to carry properties and help them with the stage. And when he wasn't needed behind the scenes, he went out and sat among the gay contingent from Mill End, magnificent creatures by physical inheritance, the men still rough round the edges from the day's work, but the women gay in shawls and beads and shiny combs. Andrea was there and bent forward until Jeff should recognise him, and again Jeff realised that smiles lit up the place for him. Even the murmured name ran round among the rows. They were telling one another, here was The Prisoner. Whatever virtue there was in being a prisoner, it had earned him adoring friends.

He sat there wondering over it, and conventional Addington came in behind and took the vacant places. Jeff was glad not to be among them. He didn't want their sophisticated views. This wasn't a pageant for critical comment. It was Miss Amabel's pathetic scheme for bringing the East and the West together and, in an exquisite hospitality, making the East at home.

But when the curtain went up, he opened his eyes to the scene and ceased thinking of philanthropy and Miss Amabel. Here was beauty, the beauty of grace and traditionary form. They were dancing the tarantella. Jeff had seen it in Italy, more than one night after the gay little dinners Esther had loved to arrange when they were abroad. She had refused all the innocent bohemianisms of foreign travel; she had taken her own atmosphere of expensive conventionalities with her, and they had seen Europe through that medium. In all their travelling they had never touched racial intimacies. They were like a prince and princess convoyed along in a royal progress, seeing only what is fitting for royal eyes to see. The tarantella then was no more than an interlude in a play. To-night it was no such spectacle. Jeff, who had a pretty imagination of his own, felt hot waves of homesickness for the beauties of foreign lands, and yet not those lands as he had seen them unrolled for the perusal of the traveller. He sat in a dream of the heaven of beauty that lies across the sea, and he felt toward the men who had left it to come here to better themselves a compassion in the measure of his compassion for himself. How bare his own life had been, even when the world opened before him her illuminated page! He had not really enjoyed these exquisite delights of hers; he had not even prepared himself for enjoying. He had kept his eyes fixed on the game that ensures mere luxury, and he had let Esther go out into the market and buy for them both the only sort of happiness her eyes could see. He loved this dancing rout. He envied these boys and girls their passion and facility. They were, the most ignorant of them, of another stripe from arid New Englanders encased in their temperamental calm, the women, in a laughable self-satisfaction, leading the intellectual life and their men set on "making good". The poorest child of the East and South had an inheritance that made him responsive, fluent, even while it left him hot-headed and even froward. There was something, he saw, in this idea of the melting-pot, if only the mingling could be managed by gods that saw the future. You couldn't make a wonder of a bell if you poured your metal into an imperfect mould. The mould must be flawless and the metal cunningly mixed; and then how clear the tone, how resonant! It wasn't the tarantella only that led him this long wandering. It was the quality of the dancers; and through all the changing steps and measures Anne and Lydia, too, were moving, Lydia a joyous leader in the temperamental rush and swing.

Mrs. Choate, stately in dark silk and lace and quite unlike the revolutionary matron who had lain in bed and let her soul loose with the "Mysteries of Paris," sat between her son and daughter and was silent though she grew bright-eyed. Mary whispered to her:

"Anne looks very sweet, doesn't she? but not at all like a dancer."

"Sweet," said the mother.

"Anne doesn't belong there, does she?" said Alston.

"No," said the mother. "Lydia does."

"Yes."

Alston, too, was moved by the spectacle, but he thought dove-like Anne far finer in the rout than gipsy Lydia. His mother followed his thoughts exactly, but while she placidly agreed, it was Lydia she inwardly envied, Lydia who had youth and a hot heart and not too much scruple to keep her from giving each their way.

When it was over, Jeff waited for Anne and Lydia, to carry home their parcels. He stood for a moment beside Andrea, and Andrea regarded him with that absurd devotion he exuded for The Prisoner. Jeff smiled at him even affectionately, though quizzically. He wished he knew what picture of him was under Andrea's skull. A sudden impulse seized him to make the man his confidant.

"Andrea," said he, "I want you fellows to act plays with me."

Andrea looked enchanted.

"What play?" he asked.

"Shakespeare," said Jeff. "In English. That's your language, Andrea, if you're going to live here."

Andrea's face died into a dull denial. A sort of glaze even seemed to settle over the surface of his eyes. He gave a perfunctory grunt, and Jeff caught him up on it.

"Won't she allow it?" he hazarded. "Madame Beattie?"

Andrea was really caught and quite evidently relieved, too, if Jeff understood so well. He smiled again. His eyes took on their wonted shining. Jeff, relying on Anne's and Lydia's delay, stayed not an instant, but ran out of the side door and along to the front where Madame Beattie, he knew, was making a stately progress, accepting greetings in a magnificent calm. He got to the door as she did, and she gave him the same royal recognition. She was dressed in black, her head draped with lace, and she really did look a distinguished personage. But Jeff was not to be put off with a mere greeting. He called her name.

"You may take me home," she said.

"I can't," said Jeff ruthlessly, when he had got her out of earshot. "I'm going to carry things for Anne."

"No, you're not." She put her hand through his arm and leaned heavily and luxuriously. "Good Lord, Jeff, why can't New Englanders dance like those shoemakers' daughters? What is it in this climate that dries up the blood?"

"Madame Beattie," said Jeff, "you've got to give away the game. You've got to tell me how you've hypnotised every man Jack of those people there to-night so they won't do a reasonable thing I ask 'em unless they've had your permission."

"What do you want to do?" But she was pleased. There was somebody under her foot.

"I want to rehearse some plays in English. And I gather from the leader of the clan—"

"Andrea?"

"Yes, Andrea. They won't do it unless you tell them to."

"Of course they won't," said Madame Beattie.

"Then why won't they? What's your infernal spell?"

"It's the spell of the East. And you can't tempt them with anything that comes out of the West."

"Their food comes out of the West," said Jeff, smarting.

"Oh, that! Well, that's about all you can give them. That's what they come for."

"All of them? Good God!"

"Not good God at all. Don't you know what a man is led by? His belly. But they don't all come for that. Some come for—" She laughed, a rather cackling laugh.

"What?" Jeff asked her sternly. He shook her arm involuntarily.

"Freedom. That's talked about still. And a lot of demagogues like your Weedon Moore get hold of 'em and debauch 'em and make 'em drunk."

"Drunk?"

"No, no. Not on liquor. Better if they did. But they tell 'em they're gods and all they've got to do is to climb up on a throne and crown themselves."

"Then why won't you," said Jeff, in wrath, "let me knock something else into their heads. You can't do it by facts. There aren't many facts just now that aren't shameful. Why can't you let me do it by poetry?"

Madame Beattie stopped in the street and gazed up at the bright heaven. She was remembering how the stars looked in Italy when she was young and sure her voice would sound quite over the world. She seldom challenged the stars now, they moved her so, in an almost terrible way. What had she made of life, they austerely asked her, she who had been driven by them to love and all the excellencies of youth? But then, in answer, she would ask them what they had done for her.

"Jeff," said she, "you couldn't do it in a million years. They'll do anything for me, because I bring their own homes to them, but they couldn't make themselves over, even for me."

"They like me," said Jeff, "for some mysterious reason."

"They like you because I've told them to."

"I don't believe it." But in his heart he did.

"Jeff," said she, "life isn't a matter of fact, it's a matter of feeling. You can't persuade men and women born in Italy and Greece and Syria and Russia that they're happy in this little bare town. It doesn't smell right to them.

Their hearts are somewhere else. And they want nothing so much in the world as to get a breath from there or hear a story or see somebody that's lived there. Lived—not stayed in a *pension*."

"Do they feel so when they've seen their sisters and cousins and aunts carved up into little pieces there?" Jeff asked scoffingly. But she was hypnotising him, too. He could believe they did.

"What have you to offer 'em, Jeff, besides wages and a prospect of not being assassinated? That's something, but by God! it isn't everything." She swore quite simply because out in the night even in the straight street of a New England town she felt like it and was carelessly willing to abide by the chance of God's objecting.

"But I don't see," said Jeff, "why you won't let me have my try at it." He was waiting for her to signify her readiness to go on, and now she did.

"Because now, Jeff, they do think you're a god. If they saw you trying to produce the Merchant of Venice they'd be bored and they wouldn't think so any more."

"Have you any objection," said Jeff, "to my trying to produce the Merchant of Venice with English-speaking children of foreigners?"

"Not a grain," said Madame Beattie cordially. "There's your chance. Or you can get up a pageant, if you like-, another summer. But you'll have to let these people act their own historic events in their own way. And, Jeff, don't be a fool." They were standing before her door and Esther at the darkened window above was looking down on them. Esther had not gone to the dances because she knew who would be there. She told herself she was afraid of seeing Jeff and because she had said it often enough she believed it. "Tell Lydia to come to see me to-morrow," said Madame Beattie. Sophy had opened the door. It came open quite easily now since the night Madame Beattie had called Esther's name aloud in the street. Jeff took off his hat and turned away. He did not mean to tell Lydia. She saw enough of Madame Beattie, without instigation.

XXVIII

Lydia needed no reminder to go to Madame Beattie. The next day, in the early afternoon, she was taking her unabashed course by the back stairs to Madame Beattie's bedchamber. She would not allow herself to be embarrassed or ashamed. If Esther treated Madame Beattie with a proper hospitality, she reasoned when her mind misgave her, it would not be necessary to enter by a furtive way. Madame Beattie was dressed and in a high state of exhilaration. She beckoned Lydia to her where she sat by a window commanding the street, and laid a hand upon her wrist.

"I've actually done it," said she. "I've got on her nerves. She's going away."

The clouds over Lydia seemed to lift. Yet it was incredible that Esther, this charming sinister figure always in the background or else blocking everybody's natural movements, should really take herself elsewhere.

"It's only to New York," said Madame Beattie. "She tells me that much. But she's going because I've ransacked her room till she sees I'm bound to find the necklace."

Lydia was tired from the night before; her vitality was low enough to waken in her the involuntary rebuttal, "I don't believe there is any necklace." But she only passed a hand over her forehead and pushed up her hair and then drew a little chair to Madame Beattie's side.

"So you think she'll come back?" she asked drearily.

"Of course. She's only going for a couple of days. You don't suppose she'd leave me here to conspire with Susan? She'll put the necklace into a safe. That's all."

"But you mustn't let her, must you?"

"Oh, I sha'n't let her. Of course I sha'n't."

"What shall you do?"

"She's not going till night. She takes Sophy, of course."

"But what can you do?"

"I shall consult that dirty little man. He's a lawyer and he's not in love with her."

"Mr. Moore? You haven't much time, Madame Beattie. She'll be going."

"That's why I'm dressed," said Madame Beattie. "I shall go in a minute. He can give me a warrant or something to search her things."

Lydia went at once, with a noiseless foot. She felt a sudden distaste for the accomplished fact of Esther face to face with justice. Yet she did not flinch in her certainty that nemesis must be obeyed and even aided. Only the secrecy of it led her to a hatred of her own silent ways in the house, and as she often did, she turned to her right instead of to her left and walked to the front stairs. There at her hand was Esther's room, the door wide open. Downstairs she could hear her voice in colloquy with Sophy. Rhoda's voice, on this floor, made some curt remark. Everybody was accounted for. Lydia's heart was choking her, but she stepped softly into Esther's room. It seemed to her, in her quickened feeling, that she could see clairvoyantly through the matter that kept her from her quest. A travelling bag, open, stood on the floor. There was a hand-bag on the bed, and Lydia, as if taking a predestined step, went to it, slipped the clasp and looked. A purse was there, a tiny mirror, a book that might have been an address book, and in the bottom a roll of tissue paper. Nothing could have stopped her now. She had to know what was in the roll. It was a lumpy parcel, thrown together in haste as if, perhaps, Esther had thought of making it look as if it were of no account. She tore it open and found, with no surprise, as if this were an old dream, the hard brightness of the jewels.

"There it is," she whispered to herself, with the scant breath her choking heart would lend her. "Oh, there it is!"

She rolled the necklace in its paper and closed the bag. With no precaution she walked out of the room and down the stairs. The voices still went on, Esther's and Sophy's from the library, and she did not know whether Madame Beattie had already left the house. But opening the front door, still with no precaution, she closed it sharply behind her and walked along the street in sunshine that hurt her eyes.

Lydia went straight home, not thinking at all about what she had done, but wondering what she should do now. Suddenly she felt the unfriendliness of the world. Madame Beattie, her ally up to this moment, was now a foe. For whether justly or not, Madame Beattie would claim the necklace, and how could Lydia know Jeff had not already paid her for it? And Anne, soft, sweet Anne, what would she do if Lydia threw it in her lap and said, "Look! I took it out of Esther's bag." She was thinking very clearly, it seemed to her, and the solution that looked most like a high business sagacity made it likely that she ought to carry it to Alston Choate. He was her lawyer. And yet indeed he was not, for he did nothing for her. He was only playing with her, to please Anne. But all the while she was debating her feet carried her to the only person she had known they would inevitably seek. She went directly upstairs to Jeffrey's room where he might be writing at that hour.

He was there. His day's work had gone well. He was beginning to have the sense the writer sometimes has, in a fortunate hour, of divine intention in his task. Jeff was enjoying an egoistic interlude of feeling that the things which had happened to him had been personally intended to bring him to a certain deed. The richness of the world was crowding on him, the bigness of it, the dangers. He could scarcely choose, among such diversities, what to say. And dominating everything he had to say in the compass of this one book was the sense of life, life at its full, and the stupidity of calling such a world bare of wonders. And to him in his half creative, half exulting dream came Lydia, her face drawn to an extremity of what looked like apprehension. Or was it triumph? She might have been under the influence of a drug that had induced in her a wild excitement and at the same time strung her nerves to highest pitch. Jeff, looking up at her, pushed his papers back.

"What is it?" he asked.

Lydia, for answer, moved up to his table and placed the parcel there before him. It was the more shapeless and disordered from the warm clutch of her despairing hand. He took it up and carelessly unrolled it. The paper lay open in his palm; he saw and dropped the necklace to the table. There it lay, glittering up at him. Lydia might have expected some wondering or tragic exclamation; but she did not get it. He was astonished. He said quite simply:

"Aunt Patricia's necklace." Then he looked up at her, and their eyes met, hers with desperate expectation and his holding her gaze in an unmoved questioning. "Did she give it to you?" he asked, and she shook her head with a negation almost imperceptible. "No," said Jeffrey to himself. "She didn't have it. Who did have it?"

He let it lie on the table before him and gazed at the bauble in a strong distaste. Here it was again, a nothingness coming between him and his vision of the real things of the earth. It seemed singularly trivial to him, and yet powerful, too, because he knew how it had moved men's minds.

"Where did you get it?" he asked, looking up at Lydia.

Something inside her throat had swollen. She swallowed over it with difficulty before she spoke. But she did speak.

"I took it."

"Took it?"

He got up, and, with a belated courtesy, pulled forward a chair. But Lydia did not see it. Her eyes were fixed on his face, as if in its changes would lie her destiny.

"You mean you found it."

"No. I didn't find it. I took it."

"You must have found it first."

"I looked for it," said Lydia.

"Where?"

"In Esther's bag."

Jeffrey stood staring at her, and Lydia unwinkingly stared at him. She was conscious of but one desire: that he would not scowl so. And yet she knew it was the effort of attention and no hostile sign. He spoke now, and gently because he saw how great a strain she was under.

"You'll have to tell me about it, Lydia. Where was the bag?"

"It was on her bed," said Lydia. "I went into the room and saw it there. Madame Beattie told me she was going to New York—"

"That Madame Beattie was?"

"No. Esther. To hide the necklace. So Madame Beattie shouldn't get it. And I saw the bag. And I knew the necklace must be in it. So I took it."

By this time her hands were shaking and her lips chattered piteously. Jeffrey was wholly perplexed, but bitterly sorry for her.

"What made you bring it here, dear?" said he.

Lydia caught at the endearing word, and something like a spasm moved her face.

"I had to," said she. "It has made all the trouble."

"But I don't want it," said Jeffrey. "Whatever trouble it made is over and done with. However this came into Esther's hands—"

"Oh, I know how that was," said Lydia. "She stole it. Madame Beattie says so."

"And whatever she is going to do with it now—that isn't a matter for me to meddle with."

"Don't you care?" said Lydia, in a passionate outcry. "Now you've got it in your hand, don't you care?"

"Why," said Jeff, "what could I do with it?"

"If you know it's Madame Beattie's, you can take it to her and tell her she can go back to Europe and stop hounding you for money."

"How do you know she's hounded me?"

"She says so. She wants you to get into politics and into business and pay her back."

"But that's what you've wanted me to do yourself."

"Oh," said Lydia, in a great breath of despairing love, "I want you to do what you want to. I want you to sit here at this table and write. Because then you look happy. And you don't look so any other time."

Jeff stood gazing at her in a compassion that brought a smart to his eyes. This, a sad certainty told him, was love, the love that is unthinking. She was suffocated by the pure desire to give the earth to him and herself with it. What disaster might come from it to her or to the earth, her lulled brain did not consider. The self-immolation of passion had benumbed her. And now she looked at him beseechingly, as if to beg him only not to scorn her gift. Her emotion transferred itself to him. He must be the one to act; but disappointingly, he knew, with the mind coming in to school disastrous feeling and warn it not again to scale such heights or drop into such depths.

"Lydia," said he, "you must leave this thing here with me."

His hand indicated by a motion the hateful bauble that lay there glittering at them.

"Why, yes," said she. "I've left it with you."

"I mean you must leave it altogether, the decision what to do with it, even the fact of your having had anything whatever to do with it yourself."

Lydia nodded, watching him. It had not occurred to her that there need be any concealment. She had meant to indicate that to herself when she walked so boldly down the front stairs and clanged the door and went along the street with the parcel plainly in her hand. If there was a slight drop in her expectation now, she did not show it. What she had indeed believed was that Jeff would greet the necklace with an incredulous joy and flaunt it in the face of Esther who had stolen it, while he gave it back to Madame Beattie, who had preyed on him.

"Do you understand?" said he. "You mustn't speak of it."

"I shall have to tell," said Lydia, "if anybody asks me. If I didn't it would be—queer."

"It's a great deal more than queer," said Jeff.

He smiled now, and she drew a happy breath. And he was amused, in a grim way. He had been, for a long time, calling himself plain thief, and taking no credit because his theft was what might have seemed a crime of passion of a sort. He had put himself "outside ", and now this child had committed a crime of passion and she was outside, too. Her ignorant daring frightened him. At any instant she might declare her guilt. She needed to be brought face to face, for her own safety, with the names of things.

"Lydia," said he, "you know what it would be called—this taking something out of another woman's bag?"

"No," said Lydia.

"Theft," said he. He meant to have no mercy on her until he had roused her dormant caution. "If you take what is not yours you are a thief."

"But," said Lydia, "I took it from Esther and it wasn't hers, either." She was unshaken in her candour, but he noted the trembling of her lip and he could go no further.

"Leave it with me," he said. "And promise me one thing. Don't speak to anybody about it."

"Unless they ask me," said Lydia.

"Not even if they ask you. Go to your room and shut yourself in. And don't talk to anybody till I see you again."

She turned obediently, and her slender back moved him with a compassion it would have been madness to recognise. The plain man in him was in physical rebellion against the rules of life that made it criminal to take a sweet creature like this into your arms to comfort her when she most needed it and pour out upon her your gratitude and adoration.

Jeff took the necklace and its bed of crumpled paper with it, wrapped it up and, holding it in his hand as Lydia had done, walked downstairs, got his hat and went off to Esther's. What he could do there he did not fully know, save to fulfil the immediate need of putting the jewels into some hand more ready for them than his own. He had no slightest wish to settle the rights of the case in any way whatever. "Then," his mind was saying in spite of him, "Esther did have the necklace." But even that he was horribly unwilling to face. There was no Esther now; but he hated, from a species of decency, to drag out the bright dream that had been Esther and smear it over with these blackening certainties. "Let be," his young self cried to him. "She was at least a part of youth, and youth was dear." Why should she be pilloried since youth must stand fettered with her for the old wrongs that were a part of the old imagined sweetness? The sweetnesses and the wrongs had grown together like roots inextricably mingled. To tear out the weeds you would rend also the roots they twined among.

In a stern musing he was at Esther's door before he had decided what to say, had knocked and Sophy, large-eyed and shaken out of her specious calm, had admitted him. She did not question him nor did Jeffrey even ask for Esther. With the opening of the door he heard voices, and now the sound of an angry crying, and Sophy herself had the air of an unwilling servitor at a strange occasion. Jeffrey, standing in the doorway of the library, faced the group there. Esther was seated on a low chair, her face crumpled and red, as if she had just wiped it free of tears. The handkerchief, clutched into a ball in her angry fist, gave further evidence. Madame Beattie, enormously amused, sat in the handsome straight-backed chair that became her most, and unaffectedly and broadly smiled. And Alston Choate, rather pale in a sternness of judicial consideration, stood, hands in his pockets, and regarded them. At Jeffrey's entrance they looked up at him and Esther instantly sprang to her feet and retreated to a position at the right of Choate, where he might be conceived of as standing in the position of tacitly protecting her. Jeff, the little parcel in his hand, advanced upon them.

"Here is the necklace," said he, in a perfectly commonplace tone. "I suppose that's what you are talking about."

Esther's eyes, by the burning force he felt in them, seemed to draw his, and he looked at her, as if to inquire what was to be done with it now it was here. Esther did not wait for any one to put that question. She spoke sharply, as if the words leaped to utterance.

"The necklace was stolen. It was taken out of this house. Who took it?"

Jeffrey had not for a moment wondered whether he might be asked. But now he saw Lydia as he had left her, in her childish misery, and answered instantly: "I took it."

Alston Choate gave a little exclamation, of amazement, of disgust. Then he drew the matter into his own judicial hands. "Where did you take it from?" he asked.

Jeffrey looked at him in a grave consideration. Alston Choate seemed to him a negligible quantity; so did Esther and so did Madame Beattie. All he wanted was to clear the slender shoulders of poor savage, wretched Lydia at home.

"Do you mind telling me, Jeffrey?" Alston was asking, in quite a human way considering that he embodied the majesty of the law. "You couldn't have walked into this house and taken a thing which didn't belong to you and carried it away."

His tone was rather a chaffing one, a recall to the intercourse of everyday life. "Be advised," it said. "Don't carry a dull joke too far."

"Certainly I took it," said Jeffrey, smiling at Alston broadly. He was amused now, little more. He saw how his background of wholesale thievery would serve him in the general eye. Not old Alston's. He did not think for a moment Alston would believe him, but it seemed more or less of a grim joke to ask him to. "Don't you know," he said, "I'm an ex-convict? Once a jailbird, always a jailbird. Remember your novels, Choate. You know more about 'em than you do about law anyway."

Then he saw, with a shock, that Alston really did believe him. He also knew at the same instant why. Esther was pouring the unspoken flood of her persuasion upon him. Jeff could almost feel the whiff and wind of the temperamental rush. He knew how Esther's belief set upon you like an army with banners when she wanted you also to believe. And still he held the little crumpled packet in his hand.

"Will you open it?" Alston asked him, with a gentleness of courtesy that indicated he was sorry indeed, and Jeffrey laid it on the table, unrolled the paper and let the bauble lie there drinking in the light and throwing it off again a million times enhanced. Alston advanced to it and gravely looked down upon it without touching it. Madame Beattie turned upon it a cursory gaze, and gave a nod that seemed to accept its identity. But Esther did not look at all. She put her hand on the table to sustain herself, and her burning eyes never once left Alston's face. He looked round at her.

"Is this it?" he asked.

She nodded.

"Are you sure?"

"Of course I'm sure," said Esther.

She seemed to ask how a woman could doubt the identity of a trinket she had clasped about her neck a thousand times, and pored over while it lay in some hidden nest.

"Ask her," said Madame Beattie, in her tiniest lisp, "if the necklace is hers."

There flashed into Alston Choate's mind the picture of Lydia, as she came to his office that day in the early summer, to bring her childish accusation against Esther. The incident had been neatly pigeonholed, but only as it affected Anne. It could not affect Esther, he had known then, with a leap at certainty measured by his belief in her. The belief had been big enough to offset all possible evidence.

"Ask her," said Madame Beattie, with relish, "where she got it."

When Esther had cried a little at the beginning of the interview, the low lamenting had moved him beyond hope of endurance, and he had wondered what he could do if she kept on crying. But now she drew herself up and looked, not at him, but at Madame Beattie.

"How dare you?" she said, in a low tone, not convincingly to the ears of those who had heard it said better on the stage, yet with a reproving passion adequate to the case.

But Alston asked no further questions. Madame Beattie went amicably on.

"Mr. Choate, this matter of the necklace is a family affair. Why don't you run away and let Jeffrey and his wife—and me, you know—let us settle it?"

Alston, dismissed, forgot he had been summoned and that Esther might be still depending on him. He turned about to the door, but she recalled him.

"Don't go," she said. The words were all in one breath. "Don't go far. I am afraid."

He hesitated, and Jeffrey said equably but still with a grim amusement:

"I think you'd better go."

So he went out of the room and Esther was left between her two inquisitors.

XXIX

That she did look upon Jeff as her tormentor he could see. She took a darting step to the door, but he was closing it.

"Wait a minute," he said. "There are one or two things we've got to get at. Where did you find the necklace?"

She met his look immovably, in the softest obstinacy. It smote him like a blow. There was something implacable in it, too, an aversion almost as fierce as hate.

"This is the necklace," he went on. "It was lost, you know. Where did you find it, Esther?"

But suddenly Esther remembered she had a counter charge to make.

"You have broken into this house," she said, "and taken it. If it is Aunt Patricia's, you have taken it from her."

"No," said Aunt Patricia easily, "it isn't altogether mine. Jeff made me a payment on it a good many years ago."

Esther turned upon her.

"He paid you for it? When?"

"He paid me something," said Madame Beattie. "Not the value of the necklace. That was when you stole it, Esther. He meant to pay me the full value. He will, in time. But he paid me what he could to keep you from being found out. Hush money, Esther."

Queer things were going on in Jeff's mind. The necklace, no matter what its market price, seemed to him of no value whatever in itself. There it lay, a glittering gaud; but he had seen a piece of glass that threw out colours as divinely. Certainly the dew was brighter. But as evidence, it was very important indeed. The world was a place, he realised, where we play with counters such as this. They enable us to speak a language. When Esther had stolen it, the loss had not been so much the loss of the gems as of his large trust in her. When Madame Beattie had threatened him with exposing her he had not paid her what he could because the gems were priceless, but that Esther's reputation was. And so he had learned that Madame Beattie was unscrupulous. What was he learning now? Nothing new about Madame Beattie, but something astounding about Esther. The first upheaval of his faith had merely caused him to adjust himself to a new sort of Esther, though only to the old idea of women as most other men had had the sense to take them: children, destitute of moral sense and its practical applications, immature mammals desperately in love with enhancing baubles. He had not believed then that Esther lied to him. She had, he was too sure for questioning, actually lost the thing. But she had not lost it. She had hidden it, with an inexplicable purpose, for all these years.

"Esther!" he said. She lifted her head slightly, but gave no other sign of hearing. "We'll give this back to Madame Beattie."

"No, you won't, Jeff," said Madame Beattie. "I'd rather have the money for it. Just as soon as you get into the swing again, you'll pay me a little on the transaction."

"Sell the damned thing then, if you don't want it and do want money," said Jeff. "You've got it back."

"I can't sell it." She had half closed her eyes, and her lips gave an unctious little relish to the words.

"Why can't you?"

"My dear Jeffrey, because, when the Royal Personage who gave it to me was married, I signed certain papers in connection with this necklace and I can't sell it, either as a whole or piecemeal. I assure you I can't."

"Very well," said Jeff. "That's probably poppycock, invented for the occasion. But you've got your necklace. There it is. Make the most of it. I never shall pay you another cent."

"Oh, yes, you will," said Madame Beattie. She was unclasping and clasping a bracelet on her small wrist, and she looked up at him idly and in a perfect enjoyment of the scene. "Don't you want to pay me for not continuing my reminiscences in that horrid little man's paper? Here's the second chapter of the necklace. It was stolen. You come walking in here and say you've stolen it again. But where from? Out of Esther's hand-bag. Do you want the dirty little man to print that? Necklace found in Mrs. Jeffrey Blake's hand-bag?"

Jeff was looking at her sharply.

"I never said I took it from a hand-bag," he rejoined.

Madame Beattie broke down and laughed. She gave the bracelet a final snap.

"You're quite a clever boy," said she. "Alston Choate wouldn't have seen that if he'd hammered at it a week. Yes, it was in Esther's bag. I don't care much how it got out. The question is, how did it get in? How are you going to shield Esther?"

He was aware that Esther was looking at him in a breathless waiting. The hatred, he knew, must have gone out of her face. She was the abject human animal beseeching mercy from the stronger. That she could ask him whom she had repudiated to stand by her in her distress, hurt him like a personal degradation. But he was sorry for her, and he would fight. He answered roughly, at a venture, and he felt her start. Yet the roughness was not for her.

"No. I shall do nothing whatever," he said, and heard her little cry and Madame Beattie's assured tone following it, with an uncertainty whether he had done well.

"You're quite decided?" Madame Beattie was giving him one more chance. "You're going to let Esther serve her time in the dirty little man's paper? It'll be something more than publicity here. My word! Her name will fly over the globe."

He heard Esther's quick breathing nearer and nearer, and then he felt her hand on his arm. She had crept closer, involuntarily, he could believe, but drawn by the instinct to be saved. He felt his own heart beating thickly, with sorrow for her, an agonising ruth that she should have to sue to him. But he spoke sharply, not looking at her, his eyes on Madame Beattie's.

"I shall not assume the slightest responsibility in the matter. I have told you I took the necklace. You can say that in Weedon Moore's paper till you are both of you—" he paused.

The hand was resting on his arm, and Esther's breathing presence choked him with a sense of the strangeness of things and the poignant suffering in mere life.

"I sha'n't mention you," said Madame Beattie. "I know who took the necklace."

"What?"

His movement must have shaken the touch on his arm, for Esther's hand fell.

"You don't suppose I'm a fool, do you?" inquired Madame Beattie. "I knew it was going to happen. I saw the whole thing."

"Then," said Esther, slipping away from him a pace, "you didn't do it after all."

If he had not been so shaken by Madame Beattie's words he could have laughed with the grim humour of it. Esther was sorry he had not done it.

"So," said Madame Beattie, "you'd better think twice about it. I'll give you time. But I shall assuredly publish the name of the person who took the necklace out of Esther's bag, as well as the fact that it had to be in Esther's bag or it couldn't have been taken out. Two thieves, Jeff. You'd better think twice."

"Yes," said Jeff. "I will think. Is it understood?" He walked over to her and stood there looking down at her.

She glanced pleasantly up at him.

"Of course, my dear boy," she said. "I shouldn't dream of saying a word— till you've thought twice. But you must think quick, Jeff. I can't wait forever."

"I swear," said Jeff, "you are—" Neither words nor breath failed him, but he was afraid of his own passion.

Madame Beattie laughed.

"Jeff," said she, "I've no visible means of support. If I had I should be as mild—you can't think!"

He turned and, without a look at Esther, strode out of the room. Esther hardly waited for the door to close behind him before she fell upon Madame Beattie.

"Who did it?" she cried. "That woman?"

Madame Beattie was exploring a little box for a tablet, which she took composedly.

"What woman?" she asked.

"That woman upstairs."

"Rhoda Knox? God bless me, no! Rhoda Knox wouldn't steal a button. She's New England to the bone."

"Sophy?"

"Esther, you're a fool. Why don't you let me manage Jeff in my own way? You won't manage him yourself." She got up with a clashing of little chains and yawned broadly. "Don't forget Alston Choate sitting in the dining-room waiting like a messenger boy."

"In the dining-room?"

"Yes. Did you think he'd go? He's waiting there to hear Jeff assault you, and come to the rescue. You told him you were afraid." She was on her way to the door, but she turned. "I may as well take this," she said idly, and swept the necklace into her hand. She held it up and shook it in the light, and Esther's eyes, as she knew they would, dwelt on it with a hungry passion.

"You are taking it away," said Esther. "You've no right to. He said he had paid you money on it when it was lost. If he did, it belongs to him. And I'm his wife."

"I might as well take it with me," said Madame Beattie. "You don't act as if you were his wife."

A quick madness shot into Esther's brain and overwhelmed it, anger, or fright, she could not tell what. She did not cry out because she knew Alston Choate was in the next room, but she spoke sobbingly:

"He did take it out of my bag. You have planned it between you to get it back into your hands."

Madame Beattie laughed pleasantly and went upstairs. And Esther crossed the little hall and stood in the dining-room door looking at Alston Choate. As she looked, her heart rose, for she saw conquest easy, in his bowed head, his frowning glance. He had not wanted to stay, his attitude told her; he was even yet raging against staying. But he could not leave her. Passion in him was fighting side by side with feminine implacability in her against the better part of him. She went forward and stood before him droopingly, a most engaging picture of the purely feminine. But he did not look at her, and she had to throw what argument she might into her voice.

"You were so good to stay," she said, with a little tired sigh. "They've gone. Come back into the other room."

He rose heavily and followed her, but in the library he did not sit down. Esther sank into a low chair, leaned back in it and closed her eyes. She really needed to give way a little. Her nerves were trembling from the shock of more than one attack on them; fear, anger, these were what her husband and Madame Beattie had roused in her. Jeffrey was refusing to help her, and she hated him. But here was another man deftly moved to her proximity by the ever careful hand of providence that had made the creatures for her.

Alston stood by the mantel, leaning one elbow on it, with a strange implication of wanting to put his head down and hide his face.

"Esther!" said he. There was no pretence now of being on terms too distant to let him use her name.

She looked up at him, softly and appealingly, though he was not looking at her. But Esther, if she had played Othello, would have blacked herself all over. Alston began again in a voice of what sounded like an extreme of irritation.

"For God's sake, tell me about this thing."

"You know all I do," she said brokenly.

"I don't know anything," said Choate. "You tell me your husband———"

"Don't call him that," she entreated.

"Your husband entered this house and took the necklace. I want to know where he took it from."

"She told you," said Esther scornfully.

He gained a little courage now and ventured to look at her. If she could repel Madame Beattie's insinuation, it must mean she had something on her side. And when he looked he wondered, in a rush of pity, how he could have felt anything for that crushed figure but ruth and love. So when he spoke again his voice was gentler, and Esther's courage leaped to meet it.

"I am told the necklace was in your bag. How did it get there?"

"I don't know," said Esther, in a perfect clarity.

His new formed hope crumbled. He could hear inexorably, like a counter cry, Lydia's voice, saying, "She stole it." Had Esther stolen it? But Esther did not know Lydia had said it, or that it had ever been said to him at all, and she was daring more than she would have dared if she had known of that antagonist.

"It is a plot between them," she said boldly.

"Between whom?"

"Aunt Patricia and him."

"What is the plot?"

"I don't know."

"If you think there was a plot, you must have made up your mind what the plot was and what they were to gain by it. What do you believe the plot to have been?"

This was all very stupid, Esther felt, when he might be assuring her of his unchanged and practical devotion.

"Oh, I don't know," she said irritably. "How should I know?"

"You wouldn't think there was a plot without having some idea of what it was," he was insisting, in what she thought his stupid way. "What is your idea it was?"

This was really, she saw, the same question over again, which was another instance of his heavy literalness. She had to answer, she knew now, unless she was to dismiss him, disaffected.

"She put the necklace in my bag," she ventured, with uncertainty as to the value of the statement and yet no diminution of boldness in making it.

"What for?"

"To have him steal it, I suppose."

"To have him steal her own necklace? Couldn't she have given it to him?"

"Oh, I don't know," said Esther. "She is half crazy. Don't you see she is? She might have had a hundred reasons. She might have thought if he tried to steal it he'd get caught, and she could blackmail him."

"But how was he to know she had put it in the bag?"

"I don't know." Esther was settling into the stolidity of the obstinate when they are crowded too far; yet she still remembered she must not cease to be engaging.

"Why was it better to have him find it in your bag than anywhere else in the house?" he was hammering on.

"I don't know," said Esther again, and now she gave a little sigh.

That, she thought, should have recalled him to his male responsibility not to trap and torture. But she had begun to wonder how she could escape when the door opened and Jeff came in. Alston turned to meet him, and, with Esther, was amazed at his altered look. Jeff was like a man who had had a rage and got over it, who had even heard good news, or had in some way been recalled. And he had. On the way home, when he had nearly reached there, in haste to find Lydia and tell her the necklace was back in Madame Beattie's hands, he had suddenly remembered that he was a prisoner and that all men were prisoners until they knew they were, and it became at once imperative to get back to Esther and see if he could let her out. And the effect of this was to make his face to shine as that of one who was already released from bondage. To Esther he looked young, like the Jeff she used to know.

"Don't go, Choate," he said, when Alston picked himself up from the mantel and straightened, as if his next move might be to walk away. "I wanted to see Esther, but I'd rather see you both. I've been thinking about this infernal necklace, and I realise it's of no value at all."

Choate's mind leaped at once to the jewels in Maupassant's story, and Madame Beattie's quick disclaimer when he ventured to hint the necklace might be paste. Did Jeff know it was actually of no value?

Jeff began to walk about the room, expressing himself eagerly as if it were difficult to do it at all and it certainly could not be done if he sat.

"I mean," said he, "the only value of anything tangible is to help you get at something that isn't tangible. The necklace, in itself, isn't worth anything. It glitters. But if we were blind we shouldn't see it glitter."

"We could sell it," said Choate drily, "or its owner could, to help us live and support being blind."

Esther looked from one to the other. Jeffrey seemed to her quite mad. She had known him to talk in erratic ways before he went into business and had no time to talk, but that had been a wildness incident to youth. But Choate was meeting him in some sort of understanding, and she decided she could only listen attentively and see what Choate might find in him.

"It's almost impossible to say what I want to," said Jeff. The sweat broke out on his forehead and he plunged his hands in his pockets and stood in an obstinate wrestling with his thought. "I mean, this necklace, as an object, is of no more importance, really, than that doorstone out there. But the infernal thing has captured us. It's made us prisoner. And we've got to free ourselves."

Now Esther was entirely certain he was mad. Being mad, she did not see that he could say anything she need combat. But her own name arrested her and sent the blood up into her face.

"Esther," said he, "you're a prisoner to it because you've fallen in love with its glitter, and you think if you wore it you'd be lovelier. So it's made you a prisoner to the female instinct for adornment."

Alston was watching him sharply now. He was wondering whether Jeff was going to accuse her of appropriating it in the beginning.

"Choate is a prisoner," said Jeff earnestly and with such simplicity that even Choate, with his fastidious hatred of familiarity, could not resent it. "He's a prisoner to your charm. But here's where the necklace comes in again. If he could find out you'd done unworthy things to get it your charm would be broken and he'd be free."

This was so true that Choate could only stare at him and wish he would either give over or brutally tell him whether he was to be free.

"Madame Beattie uses the necklace as a means of livelihood," said Jeff. He was growing quite happy in the way his mind was leading him, because it did seem to be getting him somewhere, where all the links would hold. "Because she can get more out of it, in some mysterious way I haven't fathomed, than by selling it. And so she's prisoner to it, too."

"I shall be able to tell what the reason is," said Choate, "before long, I fancy. I've sent for the history of the Beattie necklace. I know a man in Paris who is getting it for me."

"Good!" said Jeff. "Now I propose we all escape from the necklace. We're prisoners, and let's be free."

"How are you a prisoner?" Alston asked him.

Jeff smiled at him.

"Why," said he, "if, as I told you, I took the necklace from this house, I'm a criminal, and the necklace has laid me by the heels. Who's got it now?"

This he asked of Esther and she returned bitterly:

"Aunt Patricia's got it. She walked out of the room with it, shaking it in the sun."

"Good!" said Jeff again. "Let her have it. Let her shake it in the sun. But we three can escape. Have we escaped? Choate, have you?"

He looked at Choate so seriously that Choate had to take it with an equal gravity. He knew how ridiculous the situation could be made by a word or two. But Jeff was making it entirely sane and even epic.

"We know perfectly well," said Jeff, "that the law wouldn't have much to do if all offenders and all witnesses told the truth. They don't, because they're prisoners—prisoners to fear and prisoners to selfishness and hunger. But if we three told each other the truth—and ourselves, too—we could be free this instant. You, Esther, if you would tell Choate here how you've loved that necklace and what you've done for it, why, you'd free him."

Esther cried out here, a little sharp cry of rage against him.

"I see," said she, "it's only an attack on me. That's where all your talk is leading."

"No, no," said Jeff earnestly. "I assure you it isn't. But if you owned that, Esther, you'd be ashamed to want glittering things. And Choate would get over wanting you. And that's what he'd better do."

The impudence of it, Choate knew, was only equalled by its coolness. Jeff was at this moment believing so intently in himself that he could have made anybody—but an angry woman—believe also. Jeff was telling him that he mustn't love Esther, and virtually also that this was because Esther was not worthy to be loved. But if Choate's only armor was silence, Esther had gathered herself to snatch at something more effectual.

"You say we're all prisoners to something," she said to Jeffrey. Her face was livid now with anger and her eyes glowed upon him. "How about you? You came into this house and took the necklace. Was that being a prisoner to it? How about your being free?"

Choate turned his eyes away from her face as if it hurt him. The taunt hurt him, too, like unclean words from lips beloved. But he looked involuntarily at Jeff to see how he had taken them. Jeff stood in silence looking gravely at Esther, but yet as if he did not see her. He appeared to be thinking deeply. But presently he spoke, and as if still from deep reflection.

"It's true, Esther. I'm a prisoner, too. I'm trying to see how I can get out."

Choate spoke here, adopting the terms of Jeff's own fancy.

"If you want us all to understand each other, you could tell Esther why you took the necklace. You could tell us both. We seem to be thrown together over this."

"Yes," said Jeff. "I could. I must. And yet I can't." He looked up at Alston with a smile so whimsical that involuntarily Alston met it with a glimmer of a smile. "Choate, it looks as if I should have to be a prisoner a little longer—perhaps for life."

He went toward the door like a man bound on an urgent errand, and involuntarily Alston turned to follow him. The sight hurt Esther like an indignity. They had forgotten her. Their man's country called them to settle man's deeds, and the accordance of their going lashed her brain to quick revolt. It had been working, that shrewd, small brain, through all their talk, ever since Madame Beattie had denied Jeff's having taken the necklace, and now it offered its result.

"You didn't take it at all," she called after them. "It was that girl that's had the entry to this house. It's Lydia French."

XXX

At the words Alston turned to Jeff in an involuntary questioning. Jeff was inscrutable. His face, as Alston saw it, the lines of the mouth, the down-dropped gaze, was sad, tender even, as if he were merely sorry. They walked along the street together and it was Choate who began awkwardly.

"Miss Lydia came to me, some weeks ago, about these jewels."

Here Jeff stopped him, breaking in upon him indeed when he had got thus far.

"Alston, let's go down under the old willow and smoke a pipe."

Alston was rather dashed at having the tentative introduction of Lydia at once cut off, and yet the proposition seemed to him natural. Indeed, as they turned into Mill Street it occurred to him that Jeff might be providing solitude and a fitting place to talk. As they went down the old street, unchanged even to the hollows worn under foot in the course of the years, something stole over them and softened imperceptibly the harsh moment. There was Ma'am Fowler's where they used to come to buy doughnuts. There was the house where the crippled boy lived, and sat at the window waving signals to the other boys as they went past. At the same window a man sat now. Jeff was pretty sure it was the boy grown up, and yet was too absorbed in his thought of Lydia to ask. He didn't really care. But it was soothing to find the atmosphere of the place enveloped him like a charm. It wasn't possible they were so old, or that they had been mightily excited a minute before over a foolish thing. Presently after leaving the houses they turned off the road and crossed the shelving sward to the old willow, and there on a bench hacked by their own jackknives they sat down to smoke. Jeff remembered it was he who had thought to give the bench a back. He had nailed the board from tree to tree. It was here now or its fellow—he liked to think it was his own board—and he leaned against it and lighted up. The day's perturbation had taken Choate in another way. He didn't want to smoke. But he rolled a cigarette with care and pretended to take much interest in it. He felt it was for Jeff to begin. Jeff sat silent a while, his eyes upon the field across the flats where the boys were playing ball. Yet in the end he did begin.

"That necklace, Choate," said he, "is a regular little devil of a necklace. Do you realise how much mischief it's already done?"

Between Esther's asseverations and Lydia's theories Choate's mind was in a good deal of a fog. He thought it best to give a perfunctory grunt and hope Jeff would go on.

"And after all," said Jeff, "as I said, the devilish thing isn't of the slightest real value in itself. It can, in an indirect way, send a fellow to prison. It can excite an amount of longing in a woman's mind colossal enough to make one of the biggest motives possible for any sort of crime. Because it glitters, simply because it glitters. It can cause another woman who has done caring for glitter, to depend on it for a living."

"You mean Madame Beattie," said Alston. "If it's her necklace and she can sell it, why doesn't she do it? Royal personages don't account for that."

But Jeff went on with his ruminating.

"Alston," said he, "did it ever occur to you that, with the secrets of nature laid open before us as they are now—even though the page isn't even half turned—does it occur to you we needn't be at the mercy of sex? Any of us, I mean, men and women both. Have we got to get drunk when it assaults us? Have we got to be the cave man and carry off the woman? And lie to ourselves throughout? Have we got to say, 'I covet this woman because she is all beauty'? Can't we keep the lookout up in the cockloft and let him judge, and if he says, 'That isn't beauty, old man'—believe him?"

"But sometimes," said Alston, "it is beauty."

He knew what road Jeff was on. Jeff was speaking out his plain thought and at the same time assuring them both that they needn't, either of them, be submerged by Esther, because real beauty wasn't in her. If they ate the fruit of her witchery it would be to their own damnation, and they would deserve what they got.

"Yes," said Jeff, "sometimes it is real beauty. But even then the thing that grows out of sex madness is better than the madness itself. Sometimes I think the only time some fellows feel alive is when they're in love. That's what's given us such an idea of it. But when I think of a man and woman planking along together through the dust and mud—good comrades, you know—that's the best of it."

"Of course," said Alston stiffly, "that's the point. That's what it leads to."

"Ah, but with some of them, you'd never get there; they're not made for wives—or sisters—or mothers. And no man, if he saw what he was going into, would dance their dance. He wouldn't choose it, that is, when he thinks back to it."

Alston took out his match-box, and felt his fingers quiver on it. He was enraged with himself for minding. This was the warning then. He was told, almost in exact words, not to covet his neighbour's wife, cautioned like a boy not to snatch at forbidden fruit, and even, unthinkably, that the fruit was, besides not being his, rotten. And at his heart he knew the warning was fair and true. Esther had dealt a blow to his fastidious idealities. Her deceit had slain something. She had not so much betrayed it to him by facts, for facts he could, if passion were strong enough, put aside. But his inner heart searching for her heart, like a hand seeking a beloved hand, had found an emptiness. He was so bruised now that he wanted to hit out and hurt Jeff, perhaps, at least force him to naked warfare.

"You want me to believe," he said, "that—Esther—" he stumbled over the word, but at such a pass he would not speak of her more decorously—"years ago took Madame Beattie's necklace."

Jeff was watching the boys across the flats, critically and with a real interest.

"She did," he said.

Alston bolstered himself with a fictitious anger.

"And you can tell me of it," he blustered.

"You asked me."

"You believe she did?"

"It's true," said Jeff, with the utmost quietness. "I never have said it before. Not to my father even. But he knows. He did naturally, in the flurry of that time."

"Yet you tell me because I ask you."

Alston seemed to be bitterly defending Esther.

"Not precisely," said Jeff. "Because you're bewitched by her. You must get over that."

The distance wavered before Choate's eyes, He hated Jeffrey childishly because he could be so calm.

"You needn't worry," he said. "She is as completely separated from me as if—as if you had never been away from her."

"That's it," said Jeff. "You can't marry her unless she's divorced from me. She's welcome to that—the divorce, I mean. But you can't go drivelling on having frenzies over her. Good God, Choate, don't you see what you're doing? You're wasting yourself. Shake it off. You don't want Esther. She's shocked you out of your boots already. And she doesn't know there's anything to be shocked at. You're Addington to the bone, and Esther's a primitive squaw. You've nothing whatever to do with one another, you two. It's absurd."

Choate sat looking at the landscape which no longer wavered. The boys ran fairly straight now. Suddenly he began to laugh. He laughed gaspingly, hysterically, and Jeff regarded him from time to time tolerantly and smoked.

"I know what you're thinking," he said, when Alston stopped, with a last splutter, and wiped his eyes. "You're thinking, between us we've broken all the codes. I have vilified my wife. I've warned you against her and you haven't resented it. It shows the value of extreme common-sense in affairs of the heart. It shows also that I haven't an illusion left about Esther, and that you haven't either. And if we say another word about it we shall have to get up and fight, to save our self-respect."

So Alston did now light his cigarette and they went on smoking. They talked about the boys at their game and only when the players came down to the scow, presumably to push over and buy doughnuts of Ma'am Fowler, did they get up to go. As they turned away from the scene of boyish intimacies, involuntarily they stiffened into another manner; there was even some implication of mutual dislike in it, of guardedness, one against the other. But when they parted at the corner of the street Alston, out of his perplexity, ventured a question.

"I should be very glad to be told if, as you say, you took the necklace out of Esther's bag, why you took it."

"Sorry," said Jeff. "You deserve to be told the whole business. But you can't be."

So he went home, knowing he was going to an inquiring Lydia. And how would an exalted common-sense work if presented to Lydia? He thought of it all the way. How would it do if, in these big crises of the heart, men and women actually told each other what they thought? It was not the way of nature as she stood by their side prompting them to their most picturesque attitude, that her work might be accomplished, saying to the man, "Prove yourself a devil of a fellow because the girl desires a hero," and to the girl, "Be modesty and gentleness ineffable because that is the complexion a hero loves." And the man actually believes he is a hero and the girl doesn't know she is hiding herself behind a veil too dazzling to let him see her as she is. How would it be if they outwitted nature at her little game and gave each other the fealty of blood brothers, the interchange of the true word?

Lydia came to the supper table with the rest. She was rather quiet and absorbed and not especially alive to Jeff's coming in. No quick glance questioned him about the state of things as he had left them. But after supper she lingered behind the others and asked him directly:

"Couldn't we go out somewhere and talk?"

"Yes," said he. "We could walk down to the river."

They started at once, and Anne, seeing them go, sighed deeply. Lydia was shut away from her lately. Anne missed her.

Lydia and Jeff went down the narrow path at the back of the house, a path that had never, so persistent was it, got quite grown over in the years when the maiden ladies lived here. Perhaps boys had kept it alive, running that way. At the foot and on the river bank were bushes, alder and a wilderness of small trees bound by wild grape-vines into a wall. Through these Lydia led the way to the fallen birch by the waterside. She turned and faced Jeffrey in the gathering dusk. He fancied her face looked paler than it should.

"Does she know it?" asked Lydia.

"Who?"

"Esther. Does she know I stole it out of the bag?"

"Yes," said Jeff. Suddenly he determined to tell the truth to Lydia. She looked worthy of it. He wouldn't save her pain that belonged to the tangle where they groped. He and she would share the pain together. "She guessed it. Nobody told her she was right."

"Then," said Lydia, "I must go away."

"Go away?"

"To save Farvie and Anne. They mustn't know it. I wanted to go this afternoon, just as soon as you took the necklace away from me and I realised what people would say. But I knew that would be silly. People can't run away and leave notes behind. But I can tell Anne I want to go to New York and get pupils. And I could get them. I can do housework, too."

She was an absolutely composed Lydia. She had forestalled him in her colossal common-sense.

"But, Lydia," said he, "you don't need to. Madame Beattie has her necklace. I gave it back into her hand. I daresay the old harpy will want hush money, but that's not your business. It's mine. I can't give her any if I would, and she knows it. She'll simply light here like a bird of prey for a while and harry me for money to shield Esther, to shield you, and when she finds she can't get it she'll sail peacefully off."

"Madame Beattie wouldn't do anything hateful to me," said Lydia.

"Oh, yes, she would, if she could get an income out of it. She wouldn't mean to be hateful. That night-hawk isn't hateful when it spears a mole."

"Do you mean," said Lydia, "that just because Madame Beattie has her necklace back, they couldn't arrest me? Because if they could I've certainly got to go away. I can't kill Farvie and Anne."

"Nobody will arrest anybody," said Jeff. "You are absolutely out of it. And you must keep your mouth tight and stay out."

"But you said Esther knew I did it."

"She guessed. Let her keep on guessing. Let Madame Beattie keep on. I have told them I did it and I shall keep on telling them so."

Lydia turned upon him.

"You told them that? Oh, I can't have it. I won't. I shall go to them at once."

She had even turned to fly to them.

"No," said Jeff. "Stay here, Lydia. That damnable necklace has made trouble enough. It goes slipping through our lives like a detestable snake, and now it's stopped with its original owner, I propose it shall stay stopped. It's like a property in a play. It goes about from hand to hand to hand, to bring out something in the play. And after all the play isn't about the necklace. It's about us—us—you and Esther and Choate and Madame Beattie and me. It's betraying us to ourselves. If it hadn't been for the necklace in the first place and Esther's coveting it, I might have been a greasy citizen of Addington instead of a queer half labourer and half loafer; my father wouldn't have lost his nerve, Choate wouldn't have been in love with Esther, and you wouldn't have been doing divine childish things to bail me out of my destiny."

Lydia selected from this the fact that hit her hardest.

"Is Alston Choate in love with Esther?"

"He thinks he is."

"Then I must tell Anne."

"For God's sake, no! Lydia, I'm talking to you down here in the dusk as if you were the sky or that star up there. The star doesn't tell."

"But Anne worships him."

"Do you mean she's in love with Choate?"

"No," said Lydia, "I don't mean that. I mean she thinks he's the most beautiful person she ever saw."

"Then let her keep on thinking so," said Jeff. "And sometime he'll think that of her."

Lydia was indignant.

"If you think Anne——" she began, and he stopped her.

"No, no. Anne is a young angel. Only a feeling of that kind—Lydia, I am furious because I can't talk to you as I want to."

"Why can't you?" asked Lydia.

"Because it isn't possible, between men and women. Unless they've got a right to. Unless they can throw even their shams and vanities away, and live in each other's minds. I am married to Esther. If I tell you I won't ask you into my mind because I am married to her you'll think I am a hero. And if I do ask you in, you'll come—for you are very brave—and you'll see things I don't want you to see."

"You mean," said Lydia, "see that you know I am in love with you. Well, I'm not, Jeff, not in the way people talk about. Not that way."

His quick sense of her meanings supplied what she did not say: not Esther's way. She scorned that, with a youthful scorn, the feline domination of Esther. If that was being in love she would have none of it. But Jeff was not actually thinking of her. He was listening to some voice inside himself, an interrogatory voice, an irresponsible one, not warning him but telling him:

"You do care. You care about Lydia. That's what you're facing—love—love of Lydia."

It was disconcerting. It was the last thing for a man held by the leg in several ways to contemplate. And yet there it was. He had entered again into youth and was rushing along on the river that buoys up even a leaf for a time and feels so strong against the leaf's frail texture that every voyaging fibre trusts it joyously. The summer air felt sweet to him. There were wild perfumes in it and the smell of water and of earth.

"Lydia!" he said, and again he spoke her name.

"Yes," said Lydia. "What is it?"

She stood there apart from him, a slim thing, her white scarf held tight, actually, to his quickened sense, as if she kept the veil of her virginity wrapped about her sternly. For the moment he did not feel the despair of his greater age, of his tawdry past or his fettered present. He was young and the night air was as innocently sweet to him as if he had never loved a woman and been repulsed by her and dwelt for years in the anguish of his own recoil.

"Lydia," he said, "what if you and I should tell each other the truth?"

"We do," said Lydia simply. "I tell you the truth anyway. And you could me. But you don't understand me quite. You think I'd die for you. Yes, I would. But I shouldn't think twice about wanting to be happier with you. I'm happy enough now."

A thousand thoughts rushed to his lips, to tell her she did not know how happy they could be. But he held them back. All the sweet intimacies of life ran before him, life here in Addington, secure, based on old traditions, if she were his wife and they had so much happiness they could afford to be careless about it as other married folk were careless. There might not be daily banquets of delight, but cool fruits, the morning and the evening, the still course of being that seemed to him now, after his seething first youth, the actual paradise. But Lydia was going on, an erect slim figure in her enfolding scarf.

"And you mustn't be sorry I stole the necklace—except for Anne and Farvie, if she does anything to me." "She" was always Esther, he had learned. "I'm glad, because it makes us both alike."

"You and me?"

"Yes. You took something that makes you call yourself a thief. Now I'm a thief. We're just alike. You said, when you first came home, doing a thing like that, breaking law, makes you feel outside."

"It isn't only feeling outside," he made haste to tell her. "You are outside. You're outside the social covenant men have made. It's a good righteous covenant, Lydia. It was come to through blood and misery. It's pretty bad to be outside."

"Well," said Lydia, "I'm outside anyway. With you. And I'm glad of it. You won't feel so lonesome now."

Jeff's eyes began to brim.

"You little hateful thing," he said. "You've made me cry."

"Got a hanky?" Lydia inquired solicitously.

"Yes. Besides, it isn't a hanky cry, unless you make it worse. Lydia, I wish you and Anne would go away and let father and me muddle along alone."

"Do you," said Lydia joyously. "Then you do like me. You like me awfully. You think you'll tell me so if I stay round."

"Do I, you little prying thing?" He thought he could establish some ground of understanding between them if he abused her. "You're a good little sister, Lydia, but you're a terrifying one."

"No," said Lydia. "I'm not a sister." She let the enfolding scarf go and the breeze took its ends and made them ripple. "Anne's a sister. She likes you almost as well as she does Farvie. But she does like Farvie best. I don't like Farvie best. I like you best of all the world. And I love to. I'm determined to. You ought to be liked over and over, because you've had so much taken away from you. Why, that's what I'm for, Jeff. That's what I was born for. Just to like you."

He took a step toward her, and the rippling scarf seemed to beckon him on. Lydia stepped back. "But if you touched me, Jeff," she said, "if you kissed me, I'd kill you. I'm glad you did it once when you didn't think. But if we did it once more——"

She stopped and he heard her breath and then the click of her teeth as if she broke the words in two.

"Don't be afraid, Lydia," he said. "I won't."

"I'm not afraid," she flashed.

"And don't talk of killing."

"You thought I'd kill myself. No. What would it matter about me? If I could make you a little happier—not so lonesome—why, you might kiss me. All day long. But you'd care afterward. You'd say you were outside." There was an exquisite pity in the words. She was older than he in her passion for him, stronger in her mastery of it, and she loved him overwhelmingly and knew she loved him. "Now you see," said Lydia quietly. "You know the whole. You can call me your sister, if you want to. I don't care what you call me. I suppose some sisters like their brothers more than anybody else in the world. But not as I like you. Nobody ever liked anybody as I like you. And when you put your arms down on the table and lay your head on them, you can think of that."

"How do you know I put my head on the table?" said Jeff. It was wholesome to him to sound rough to her.

"Why, of course you do," she said. "You did, one of those first days. I wish you didn't. It makes me want to run out doors and scream because I can't come in and 'poor' your hair."

"I won't do it again," said Jeff. "Lydia, I can't say one of the things I want to. Not one of them."

"I don't expect you to," said Lydia. "I understand you and me too. All I wanted was for you to understand me."

"I do," said Jeff. "And I'll stand up to it. Shake hands, Lydia."

"No," said Lydia, "I don't want to shake hands." She folded the scarf again about her, tighter, it seemed, than it was before. "You and I don't need signs and ceremonies. Now I'm going back and read to Farvie. You go to walk, Jeff. Walk a mile. Walk a dozen miles. If we had horses we'd get on 'em bareback and ride and ride."

Jeff stood and watched her while he could see the white scarf through the dusk. Then he turned to go along the river path, but he stopped. He, too, thought of galloping horses, devouring distance with her beside him through the night. He began to strip off his clothes and Lydia, on the rise, heard his splash in the river. She laughed, a wild little laugh. She was glad he was conquering space in some way, his muscles taut and rejoicing. Lydia had attained woman's lot at a bound. All she wanted was for him to have the full glories of a man.

XXXI

Alston Choate went home much later consciously to his mother, and she comforted him though he could not tell her why he needed it. She and Mary were sitting on the back veranda, looking across the slope of the river, doing nothing, because it was dusk, and dropping a word here and there about the summer air and the night. Alston put down his hat and, as he sat, pushed up his hair with the worried gesture both women knew. Mary at once went in to get him a cool drink, her never-failing service, and his mother turned an instant toward him expectantly and then away again. He caught the movement. He knew she was leaving him alone.

"Mother," he said, "you never were disgusted through and through. With yourself."

"Oh, yes," said she. "It's more or less my normal state. I'm disgusted because I haven't courage. If I'd had courage, I should have escaped all the things that make me bad company for myself now."

Alston, in his quickened mood, wondered what it was she had wanted to escape. Was it Addington? Was it his father even, a courteous Addington man much like what Alston was afraid he might be in the end, when he was elderly and pottered down town with a cane? He hated to be what he was afraid he inevitably must. It came upon him with renewed impetus, now that he had left Esther with a faint disgust at her, and only a wearied acquiescence in the memory that she had once charmed him. He wished he were less fastidious even. How much more of a man he should have felt if he had clung to his passion for her and answered Jeffrey with the oath or blow that more elemental men found fitting in their rivalry.

"Mother," said he, "does civilisation rot us after all? Have we got to be savages to find out what's in us?"

"Something seems to rot us round the edges," said the mother. "But that's because there don't appear to be any big calls while we're so comfortable. You can't get up in the midst of dinner and give a war-cry to prove you're a big chief. It would be silly. You'd be surprised, dear, to know how I go seething along and can't find anything to burn up—anything that ought to be burned. Sometimes when Mary and I sit crocheting together I wonder whether she won't smell a scorch."

He thought of the night when she had lain in bed and told how she was travelling miles from Addington in her novel.

"You never owned these things before, mother," he said. "What makes you now?"

"That I'm a buccaneer? Maybe because you've got to the same point yourself. You half hate our little piffling customs, and yet they've bound you hand and foot because they're what you're used to. And they're the very devil, Alston, unless you're strong enough to fight against 'em and live laborious days."

"What's the matter with us? Is it Addington?"

"Good old Addington! Not Addington, any more than the world. It's grown too fat and selfish. Pretty soon somebody's going to upset the balance and then we shall fight and the stern virtues will come back."

"You old Tartar," said Alston, "have we really got to fight?"

"We've got to be punished anyhow," said his mother. "And I suppose the only punishment we should feel is the punishment of money and blood."

"Let's run away, mother," said Alston. "Let's pick up Mary and run away to Europe."

"Oh, no," said she. "They're going to fight harder than we are. Don't you see there's an ogre over there grinning at them and sharpening his claws? They've got to fight Germany."

"England can manage Germany," said Alston, "through the pocket. Industrial wars are the only ones we shall ever see."

"If you can bank on that you're not so clever as I am," said his mother. "I see the cloud rising. Every morning it lies there thick along the east. There's going to be war, and whether we're righteous enough to stand up against the ogre, God knows."

Alston was impressed, in spite of himself. His mother was not given to prophecy or passionate asseveration.

"But anyhow," said she, "you can't run away, for they're going to ask you to stand for mayor."

"The dickens they are! Who said so?"

"Amabel. She was in here this afternoon, as guileless as a child. Weedon Moore told her they were going to ask you to stand and she hoped you wouldn't."

"Why?"

"Because Moore's the rival candidate, and she thinks he has an influence with the working-man. She thinks the general cause of humanity would be better served by Moore. That's Amabel."

"She needn't worry," said Alston, getting up. "I shouldn't take it."

"Alston," said his mother, "there's your chance. Go out into the rough-and-tumble. Get on a soap box. Tell the working-man something that will make him think you haven't lived in a library all your life. It may not do him any good, but it'll save your soul alive."

She had at last surprised him. He was used to her well-bred acquiescence in his well-bred actions. She knew he invited only the choice between two equally irreproachable goods: not between the good and evil. Alston had a vague uncomfortable besetment that his mother would have had a warmer hope for him if he had been tempted of demons, tortured by doubts. Then she would have bade him take refuge on heights, even have dragged him there. But she knew he was living serenely on a plain. Alston thought there ought to be some sympathy accorded men who liked living on a plain.

"Good Lord!" said he, looking down at her and liking her better with every word she said. "You scare me out of my boots. You're a firebrand on a mountain."

"No," said his mother. "I'm a decent Addington matron with not a hundredth part of a chance of jolting the earth unless you do it for me. I can't jolt for myself because I'm an anti. There's Mary. Hear the ice clink. I'll draw in my horns. Mary'd take my temperature."

Alston stayed soberly at home and read a book that evening, his nerves on edge, listening for a telephone call. It did not come, but still he knew Esther was willing him to her.

Esther sat by the window downstairs, in the dusk, in a fever of desire to know what, since the afternoon, he was thinking of her, and for the first time there was a little fleeting doubt in her heart whether she could make him think something else. As to Alston, she had the hesitations of an imperfect understanding. There were chambers where he habitually dwelt, and these she never entered at all. His senses were keenly yet fastidiously alive. They could never be approached save through shaded avenues she found it dull to traverse, and where she never really kept her way without great circumspection. The passion of men was, in her eyes, something practically valuable. She did not go out to meet it through an overwhelming impetus of her own. It was a way of controlling them, of buying what they had to give: comforts and pretty luxuries. She would have liked to live like an adored child, all her whims supplied, all her vanities fed. And here in this little circle of Addington Alston Choate was the one creature who could lift her out of her barren life and give her ease at every point with the recognition of the most captious world.

And she was willing him. As the evening wore on, she found she was breathing hard and her wrists were beating with loathing of her own situation and hatred of those who had made it for her, if she could allow herself to think she hated. For Esther had still to preserve the certainty that she was good. Madame Beattie, up there with her night-light and her book, she knew she hated. Of Jeff she did not dare to think, he made her wrists beat so, and of Alston Choate she knew it was deliberately cruel of him not to come. And then as if her need of something kind and unquestioning had summoned him, a step fell on the walk, and she saw Reardon, and went herself to let him in. There he was, florid, large, and a little anxious.

"I felt," said he, "as if something had happened to you."

She stood there under the dim hall-light, a girlish creature in her white dress, but with wonderful colour blooming in her cheeks. He could not know that hate had brought it there. She seemed to him the flower of her own beauty, rich, overpowering. She held the door open for him, and when he had followed her into the library, she turned and put both her hands upon his arm, her soft nearness like a perfume and a breath. To Reardon, she was immeasurably beautiful and as far as that above him. His heart beating terribly in his ears, he drew her to him sure that, in her aloofness, she would reprove him. But Esther, to his infinite joy and amazement, melted into his arms and clung there.

"God!" said Reardon. She heard him saying it more than once as if entirely to himself and no smaller word would do. "You don't—" he said to her then, "you don't—care about me? It ain't possible." Reardon had reverted to oldest associations and forgotten his verb.

She did not tell him whether she cared about him. She did not need to. The constraining of her touch was enough, and presently they were sitting face to face, he holding her hands and leaning to hear her whispered words. For she had immediately her question ready:

"Do you think I ought to live like this—afraid?"

"Afraid?" asked Reardon. "Of him?"

"Yes. He came this afternoon. There is nobody to stand between us. I am afraid."

Reardon made the only answer possible, and felt the thrill of his own adequacy.

"I'll stand between you."

"But you can't," she said. "You've no right."

"There's but one thing for you to do," said Reardon. "Tell what you're telling me to a lawyer. And I'll—" he hesitated. He hardly knew how to put it so that her sense of fitness should not be offended. "I'll find the money," he ended lamely.

The small hands stayed willingly in his. Reardon was a happy man, but at the same time he was curiously ashamed. He was a clean man who ate moderately and slept well and had the proper amount of exercise, and this excess of emotion jarred him in a way that irritated him. He did blame Jeff, who was at the bottom of this beautiful creature's misery. Still, if Jeff had not left her, she would not be sitting here now with the white hands in his. But he was conscious of a disturbing element of the unlawful, like eating a hurtful dish at dinner. Reardon had lived too long in a cultivating of the middle way to embark with joyousness on illicit possessing. As the traditions of Addington were wafting Alston Choate away from this primitive little Circe on her isle, so his acquired habits of safe and healthful living were wafting him. If his inner refusals could have been spoken crudely out they would have amounted to a miserable plea:

"Look here. It ain't because I don't want you. But there's Jeff."

For Reardon was not only a good fellow, but he had gazed with a wistful awe on the traditions of Addington's upper class. He had tried honestly to look like the men born to it; he never owned even to himself that he felt ill at ease in it. Yet he did regard it with a reverence the men that made it were far from feeling, and he knew something was due it. He drew back, releasing gently the white hands that lay in his. He wanted to kiss them, but he was not even yet sure they were enough his to justify it. He cleared his throat.

"The man for you to go to," said he, "is Alston Choate. I don't like him, but he's square as a die. And if you can get yourself where it'll be possible to speak to you without knowing there's another man stepping between—" he hesitated, his own heart beating for her and the decencies of Addington holding him back. "Hang it, Esther," he burst forth, "you know where I stand."

"Do I?" said Esther.

She rose, and, looking wan, gave him her hand. And Reardon got out of the room, feeling rather more of a sneak than Alston had when he went away. Esther stood still until she heard the door close behind him. Then she ran out of the room and upstairs, to hide herself, if she could, from the exasperated thought of the men who had failed her. She hated them all. They owed her something, protection, or cherishing tenderness. She could not know it was Addington that had got hold of them in one way or another and kept them doggedly faithful to its own ideals. As she was stepping along the hall, Madame Beattie called her.

"Esther, stop a minute. I want you."

Esther paused, and then came slowly to the door and stood there. She looked like a sulky child, with the beauty of the child and the charm. She hated Madame Beattie too much to gaze directly at her, but she knew what she should see if she did look: an old woman absolutely brazen in her defiance of the softening arts of dress, divested of every bewildering subterfuge, sitting in a circle of candlelight in the adequate company of her book.

"Esther," said Madame Beattie, "you may have the necklace."

Then Esther did glance quickly at her. She wondered what Madame Beattie thought she could get out of giving up the adored gewgaw into other hands.

"I don't want it," said Madame Beattie. "I'd much rather have the money for it. Get the money and bring it to me."

Esther curled her lip a little in the scorn she really felt. She could not conceive of any woman's being so lost to woman's perquisites as to confess baldly her need of money above trinkets.

"But you'd better go to the right man for it," said Madame Beattie. "It isn't Alston Choate. Jeff's the man, my dear. He's cleverer than the devil if you once get him started. Not that I think you could. He's done with you, I fancy."

Esther, still speechless, wondered if she could. It was a challenge of precisely the force Madame Beattie meant it to be.

XXXII

The next morning, a sweet one of warmth and gently drifting leaves, Esther went to call on Lydia, and Madame Beattie, with a satirical grin, looked after her from the window. Madame Beattie's understanding of the human mind had given her a dramatic hold on the world when the world loved her, and it was mechanically serving her now in these little deeds that were only of a mean importance, though, from the force of habit, she played the game so hard. Esther was very fresh and pretty in her white dress with an artful parasol that cast a freshening glow. She had the right expression, too, the calmness of one who makes a commonplace morning call.

And it was not Lydia who saw her coming. It was Jeff, in his working blouse and shabby trousers, standing on a cool corner of the veranda and finishing his morning smoke before he went out to picking early apples. Esther knew at precisely what instant he caught sight of her, and saw him knock out his pipe into the garden bed below the veranda and lay it on the rail. Then he waited for her, and she was almost amusedly prepared for his large-eyed wonder and the set of the jaw which betrayed his certainty of having something difficult to meet. It was not thus he had been used to greet her on sweet October mornings in those other days. Suddenly he turned with a quick gesture of the hand as if he were warning some one back, and Esther, almost at the steps, understood that he had heard Lydia coming and had tried to stop her. Lydia evidently had not understood and ran innocently out on some errand of her own. Seeing Esther, she halted an appreciable instant. Then something as quickly settled itself in her mind, and she advanced and stood at the side of Jeff. Esther furled her parasol and came up the steps, and her face did not for an instant change in its sweet seriousness. She looked at Lydia with a faint, almost, it might seem, a pitying smile.

"I thought," said she, "after what I said, I ought to come, to reassure you."

Neither Jeff nor Lydia seemed likely to move, and Esther stood there looking from one to the other with her concerned air of having something to do for them. It was only a moment, yet it seemed to Lydia as if they had been communing a long time, in some hidden fashion, and learning amazingly to understand each other. That is, she was understanding Esther, and the outcome terrified her. Esther seemed more dangerous than ever, bearing gifts. But Lydia could almost always do the sensible thing in an emergency and keep emotion to be quelled in solitude.

"Come in," said she, "and sit down. Jeff, won't you move the chairs into the shady corner? We'd better not go into the library. Farvie's there."

Jeff awoke from his tranced surprise and the two women followed him to the seclusion of the vines. There Esther took the chair he set for her, and looked gravely at Lydia, as she said:

"I was very hasty. I told him—" She indicated Jeff with a little gesture. It seemed she found some significance in the informality of the pronoun—"I told him I had found out who took the necklace. I knew of course he would tell you. And I came to keep you from being troubled."

"Lydia," said Jeff, with the effect of stepping quickly in between them, "go into the house. This is something that doesn't concern you in the least."

Lydia, very pale now, was looking at Esther, in a fixed antagonism. Her hands were tightly clasped. She looked like a creature braced against a blow. But Esther seemed of all imaginable persons the least likely to deliver a blow of any sort. She was gracefully relaxed in her chair, one delicate hand holding the parasol and the other resting, with the fingers upcurled like lily petals, on her knee.

"No," said Lydia, not looking at Jeff, though she answered him, "I sha'n't go in. It does concern me. That's what she came for. She's told you so. To accuse me of taking it."

With the last words, a little scorn ran into her voice. It was a scorn of what Esther might do, and it warmed her and made her suddenly feel equal to the moment.

"No," said Esther, in her softest tone, a sympathetic tone, full of a grave concern. "It was only to confess I ought not to have said it. Whatever I knew, I ought to have kept it to myself. For there was the necklace. You had sent it back. You had done wrong, but what better could you do than send it back? And I understand—" she glowed a little now, turning to Jeff—"I understand how wonderful it was of you to take it on yourself."

Jeff was frowning, and though facing her, looking no further than the lily-petalled hand. Esther was quite sure he was dwelling on the hand with inevitable appreciation. She had a feeling that he was frowning because it distracted him from his task of pleasing Lydia and at the same time meeting her own sympathetic tribute. But he was not. Esther knew a great many things about men, but she was naïvely unconscious of their complete detachment from feminine allurements when they are summoned to affairs.

"Esther," said Jeff, before Lydia could speak, "just why are you here?"

"I told you," said Esther, with a pretty air of pained surprise. "To tell Lydia she mustn't be unhappy."

Then Lydia found her tongue.

"I'm not unhappy," she said, with a brutality of incisiveness which offers the bare fact with no concern for its effect. "I took the necklace. But I don't know," said Lydia, with one of her happy convictions that she really had a legal mind and might well follow its inspirations, "I don't know whether it is stealing to take a thing away from a person who has stolen it herself."

"Lydia!" said Jeff warningly.

He hardly knew why he was stopping her. Certainly not in compassion for Esther; she, at this moment, was merely an irritating cause of a spoiled morning. But Lydia, he felt, like a careering force that had slipped control, must be checked before she did serious harm.

"You know," said Lydia, now looking Esther calmly in the eye, "you know you were the first to steal the necklace. You stole it years ago, from Madame Beattie. No, I don't know whether it's stealing to take it from you when you'd no business to have it anyway. I must ask some one."

Lydia was no longer pale with apprehension. The rose was on her cheek. Her eyes glowed with mischief and the lust of battle. Once she darted a little smiling look at Jeff. "Come on," it seemed to say. "I can't be worse off than I am. Let's put her through her paces and get something out of it—fun, at least."

Esther looked back at her in that pained forbearance which clothed her like a transfiguring atmosphere. Then she drew a sharp breath.

"Jeff!" she said, turning to him.

The red had mounted to his forehead. He admired Lydia, and with some wild impulse of his own, loved her bravado.

"Oh, come, Lydia," he said. "We can't talk like that. If Esther means to be civil—"

Yet he did not think Esther meant to be civil. Only he was hard pushed between the two, and said the thing that came to him. But it came empty and went empty to them, and he knew it.

"She doesn't mean to be civil," said Lydia, still in her wicked enjoyment. "I don't know what she does mean, but it's not to be nice to me. And I don't know what she's come for—" here her old vision of Jeff languishing unvisited in the dungeon of her fancy rose suddenly before her and she ended hotly—"after all this time."

Again Esther turned to Jeff and spoke his name, as if summoning him in a situation she could not, however courageous, meet alone. But Lydia had thought of something else.

"I don't know what you can do to me," she said, "and I don't much care. Except for Farvie and Anne. But I know this. If you can arrest me for stealing from you something you'd stolen before, why then I shall say right off I did it. And when I do it, I shall tell all I know about the necklace and how you took it from Madame Beattie—and oh, my soul!" said Lydia, rising from her chair and putting her finger tips together in an unconsidered gesture, "there's Madame Beattie now."

Esther too rose, murder in her heart but still a solicitous sadness in her eyes, and turned, following Lydia's gaze, to the steps where Denny had drawn up and Madame Beattie was alighting from the victoria. Jeff, going forward to meet her, took courage since Denny was not driving away. Whatever Madame Beattie had come to do, she meant to make quick work of it.

"Jeff," said Esther, at his elbow, "Jeff, I must go. This is too painful for everybody. I can't bear it."

"That's right," said Jeff in the kindness of sudden relief. "Run along."

Madame Beattie had decided otherwise. At the top of the steps in her panoply of black chiffon, velvet, ostrich feathers—clothes so rich in the beginning and so well made that they seemed always too unchanged to be thrown away and so went on in a squalid perpetuity—she laid a hand on Esther's wrist.

"Come, come, Esther," said she, "don't run away. I came to see you as much as anybody."

Esther longed to shake off the masterful old hand, but she would not. A sad passivity became her best unless she relinquished every possible result of the last ten minutes. And it must have had some result. Jeff had, at least, been partly won. Surely there was an implied intimacy in his quick undertone when he had bade her run along. So Madame Beattie went on cheerfully leading her captive and yet, with an art Esther hated her for, seeming to keep the wrist to lean on, and Lydia, who had brought another chair, greeted the new visitor with an unaffected pleasure. She still liked her so much that it was not probable anything Madame Beattie could say or do would break the tie. And Madame Beattie liked her: only less than the assurance of her own daily comfort. The pure stream of affection had got itself sadly sullied in these later years. She hardly thought now of the way it started among green hills under a morning sun.

She seated herself, still not releasing Esther until she also had sunk into a chair by her side, and refreshed herself from a little viniagrette. Then she winked her eyes open in a way she had, as if returning from distant considerations and said cheerfully:

"I suppose you're talking about that stupid necklace."

Lydia broke into a little laugh, she did not in the least know why, except that Madame Beattie was always so amusing to her. Madame Beattie gave her a nod as if in acknowledgment of the tribute of applause, continuing:

"Now I've come to be disagreeable. Esther has been agreeable, I've no doubt. Jeff, I hope you're being nice to her."

A startled look came into Lydia's eyes. Why should Madame Beattie want Jeff to be nice to her when she knew how false Esther had been and would always be?

"Esther," continued Madame Beattie, "has been a silly child. She took my necklace, years ago, and Jeff very chivalrously engaged to pay me for it and—"

"That will do," said Jeff harshly. "We all know what happened years ago. Anyhow Esther does. And I do. We'll leave Lydia out of this. I don't know what you've come here to say, Madame Beattie, but whatever it is, I prefer it should be said to me. I'm the only one it concerns."

"No, you're not," said Lydia, swelling with rage at everybody who would keep her from him. "I'm concerned. I'm concerned more than anybody."

Esther glanced up at her quickly and Madame Beattie shook her head.

"You've been a silly child, too," she said. "You took the necklace to give it back to me. Through Jeff, I understand."

"No, I didn't," said Lydia, in a passion to tell the truth at a moment when it seemed to her they were all willing, for one result or another, to turn and twist it. "I gave it back to Jeff so he could carry it to you and say, 'Here it is. I've paid you a lot of money on it—'"

"Who told you that?" flashed Esther. She had forgotten her patient calm.

"I told her," said Madame Beattie. "Don't be jealous, Esther. Jeff never would have told her in the world. He's as dumb as a fish."

"And so he could say to you," Lydia went on breathlessly, "'Here's the horrid thing. And now you've got it I don't owe you money but'"—here one of her legal inspirations came to her and she added triumphantly—"'if anything, you owe me.'"

"You're a good imp," said Madame Beattie, in careless commendation, "but if everybody told the truth as you do there wouldn't be any drama. Now I'm going to tell the truth. This is just what I propose doing, and what I mean somebody else shall do. I've got the necklace. Good! But I don't want it. I want money."

"I have told you," said Jeff, "to sell it. If it's worth what you say—"

"I have told you," said Madame Beattie, "that I can't. It is a question of honour," she ended somewhat pompously. Yet it was only a dramatic pomposity. Jeff saw that. "When it was given me by a certain Royal Personage," she continued and Jeff swore under his breath. He was tired of the Royal Personage—"I signed an agreement that the necklace should be preserved intact and that I would never let it go into other hands. We've been all over that."

Jeff moved uneasily in his chair. He thought there were things he might say to Madame Beattie if the others were not present.

"But," said Madame Beattie dramatically, "Esther stole it. Lydia here, from the sweetest and most ridiculous of motives, stole it from Esther. Nobody knows that but us three and that cold-blooded fish, Alston Choate. He won't tell. But unless Jeff—you, Jeff dear—unless Jeff makes himself responsible for my future, I propose to tell the whole story of the necklace in print and make these two young women wish I hadn't. Better protect them, Jeff. Better make yourself responsible for Aunt Patricia."

"You propose telling it in print," said Jeff slowly. "You said so yesterday. But I ought to have warned you then that Weedon Moore won't print it—not after I've seen him. He knows I'd wring his neck."

"There are plenty of channels," said Madame Beattie, with an unmoved authority. "Journals here, journals abroad. Why, Jeff!" suddenly her voice rose in a shrill note and startled them. Her face convulsed and a deeper hue ran into it. "I'm a personage, Jeff. The world is my friend. You seem to think because I've lost my voice I'm not Patricia Beattie. But I am. I am Patricia Beattie. And I have power."

Lydia made a movement toward her and laid her hands together, impetuously, in applause. Whether Madame Beattie were willing, as it had seemed a second ago, to sacrifice her for the sake of squeezing money out of Jeff, she did not care. Something dramatic in her discerned its like in the other woman and responded. But Jeff, startled for an instant, felt only the brutal impulse to tell Madame Beattie if the world were so much her friend, it might support her. And here appeared the last person any of them desired to see if they were to fight matters to a finish: the colonel in his morning calm, his finger, even so early, between the leaves of a book. As the year had waned and there was not so much outside work to do he had betaken himself to his gentler pursuits, and in the renewed health of his muscles felt himself a better man. He had his turn of being startled, there was no doubt of that. Esther here! his eyes were all for her. It meant something significant, they seemed to say. Why, except for an emphatic reason, should she, after this absence, have come to Jeff? He even seemed to be ignoring Madame Beattie as he stepped forward to Esther, with outstretched hand. There was a welcome in his manner, a pleasure it smote Lydia's heart to see. She knew what the scene meant to him: some shadowy renewal of the old certainties that had made Jeff's life like other men's. For an instant under the spell of the colonel's belief, she saw Jeff going back and loving Esther as if the break had never been. It seemed incredible that any one could look at her as the colonel was looking now, with warmth, even with gratitude, after she had been so hateful. And Esther was receiving it all with the prettiest grace. She might even have been pinning the olive leaf into her dress.

"Well," said he. "Well!"

Lydia was maliciously glad that even he could find nothing more to say.

"What a pleasant morning," he ended lamely yet safely, and conceived the brilliant addition, "You'll stay to dinner." As he said it he was conscious, too late, that dinner was several hours away. And meantime Esther stood and looked up in his eyes with an expression for which Lydia at once mentally found a name: soulful, that was what it was, she viciously decided.

Madame Beattie gave a little ironic crow of laughter.

"Sit down, Esther," she said, "and let Mr. Blake shake hands with me. No, I can't stay to dinner. Esther may, if she likes, but I've business on my hands. It's with that dirty little man Jeff's got such a prejudice against."

"Not Weedon Moore," conjectured the colonel. "If you've any law business, Madame Beattie, you'd far better go to Alston Choate. Moore's no kind of a man."

"He's the right kind for me," said Madame Beattie. "No manners, no traditions, no scruples. It's a dirty job I've got for him, and it takes a dirty man to do it."

She had risen now, and was smiling placidly up at the colonel. He frowned at her, involuntarily. He was ready to accept Madame Beattie's knowing neither good nor evil, but she seemed to him singularly unpleasant in flaunting that lack of bias. She was quite conscious of his distaste, but it didn't trouble her. Unproductive opinions were nothing to her now, especially in Addington.

"You're not going, too," said the colonel, as Esther rose and followed her. "I hoped—" But what he hoped he kept himself from saying.

"I must," said Esther, with a little deprecatory look and another significant one at Madame Beattie's back. "Good-bye."

She threw Lydia, in her scornful silence there in the background, a smile and nod.

"But—" the colonel began. Again he had to stop. How could he ask her to come again when he was in the dark about her reason for coming at all?

"I have to go," she said. "I really have to, this time."

Meantime Jeff, handing Madame Beattie into the carriage, had had his word with her.

"You'll do nothing until I see you."

"If you see me moderately soon," said Madame Beattie pleasantly. "Esther, are you coming?"

"No," said Esther, with a scrupulous politeness. "No, thank you. I shall walk."

But before she went, and well in the rear of the carriage, so that even Denny should not see, she gave Jeff one look, a suffused, appealing look that bade him remember how unhappy she was, how unprotected and, most of all, how feminine. She and the carriage also had in the next instant gone, and Jeff went stolidly back up the steps. There was sweat on his forehead and he drew his breath like a man dead-tired.

"My son," began the colonel.

"Don't," said Jeff shortly. He knew what his father would like to do: ask, in the sincerest sympathy, why Esther had come, discuss it and decide with him whether she was to come again and stay, whether it would be ill or well for him. The red mounted to the colonel's forehead, and Jeff put a hand on his shoulder. He couldn't help remembering that his father had called him "son" in a poignancy of sympathy all through the trials of the past, and it hurt to hear it now. It linked that time with this, as Madame Beattie, in her unabashed self-seeking, linked it. Perhaps he was never to escape. A prisoner, that was what he was. They were all prisoners, Madame Beattie to her squalid love of gain, Esther to her elementary love of herself, Lydia— he looked at her as she stood still in the background like a handmaid waiting. Why, Lydia was a prisoner, as he had thought before, only not, as he had believed then, to the glamour of love, but love, actual love for him, the kind that stands the stress of all the homely services and disillusioning. A smile broke over his face, and Lydia, incredulously accepting it, gave a little sob that couldn't be prevented in time, and took one dancing step. She ran up to the colonel, and pulled him away from Jeff. It seemed as if she were about to make him dance, too.

"Don't bother him, Farvie," said she. "He's out of prison! he's out of prison!"

She had said it, the cruel word, and Jeff knew she could not possibly have ventured it if she did not see in him something fortunate and free.

XXXIII

"Jeff!" said the colonel. Esther's coming seemed so portentous that he could not brook imperfect knowledge of it. "Jeff, did Esther come to—" He paused there. What could Esther, in the circumstances, do? Make advances? Ask to be forgiven?

But Jeff was meeting the half question comprehensively.

"I don't quite know what she came for."

"Couldn't you have persuaded her," said the colonel, hesitating, "to stay?"

"No," said Jeff. "Esther doesn't want to stay. We mustn't think of that."

"I am sorry," said the colonel, and Lydia understood him perfectly. He was not sorry Esther had gone. But he was sorry the whole business had been so muddled from the start, and that Jeff's life could not have moved on like Addington lives in general: placid, all of a piece. Lydia thought this yearning of his for the complete and perfect was because he was old. She felt quite capable of taking Jeff's life as it was, and fitting it together in a striking pattern.

"Come in, Farvie," she said. "You haven't corrected Mary Nellen's translation."

Jeff was being left alone for his own good, and he smiled after the kind little schemer, before he took his hat and went down town to find Weedon Moore. As he went, withdrawn into a solitariness of his own, so that he only absently answered the bows of those he met, he thought curiously about his own life. And he was thinking as his father had: his life was not of a pattern. It was a succession of disjointed happenings. There was the first wild frothing of the yeast of youth. There was the nemesis who didn't like youth to make such a fool of itself. She had to throw him into prison. While he was there he had actually seemed to do things that affected prison discipline. He was mentioned outside. He was even, because he could write, absurdly pardoned. It had seemed to him then desirable to write the life of a gentleman criminal, but in that he had quite lost interest. Then he had had his great idea of liberty: the freedom of the will that saved men from being prisoners. But the squalid tasks remained to him even while he bragged of being free: to warn Moore away from meddling with women's names, no matter how Madame Beattie might invite him to do her malicious will, to warn Madame Beattie even, in some fashion, and to protect Lydia. Of Esther he could not think, save in a tiring, bewildered way. She seemed, from the old habit of possession justified by a social tie, somehow a part of him, a burden of which he could never rid himself and therefore to be borne patiently, since he could not know whether the burden were actually his or not. And he began to be conscious after that morning when Esther had looked at him with primitive woman's summons to the protecting male that Esther was calling him. Sometimes it actually tired him as if he were running in answer to the call, whether toward it or away from it he could not tell. All the paths were mazes and the lines of them bewildering to his eyes. He would wake in the night and wish there were one straight path. If he could have known that at this time Reardon and Alston Choate had also, in differing ways, this same consciousness of Esther's calling it could not have surprised him. He would not have known, in his own turmoil, whether to urge them to go or not to go. Esther did not seem to him a disturbing force, only a disconcerting one. You might have to meet it to have done with it.

But now at Weedon's office door he paused a moment, hearing a voice, the little man's own, slightly declamatory, even in private, and went in. And he wished he had not gone, for Miss Amabel sat at the table, signing papers, and he instantly guessed the signatures were not in the pursuance of her business but to the advantage of Weedon Moore. Whatever she might be doing, she was not confused at seeing him. Her designs could be shouted on the housetops. But Moore gave him a foolishly cordial greeting mingled with a confused blotting of signatures and a hasty shuffling of the papers.

"Sit down, sit down," he said. "You haven't looked me up before, not since—"

"No," said Jeff. "Not since I came back. I don't think I ever did. I've come now in reference to a rather scandalous business."

Miss Amabel moved her chair back. She was about to rise.

"No, please," said Jeff. "Don't go. I'd rather like you to know that I'm making certain threats to Moore here, in case I have to carry them out. I'd rather you'd know I have some grounds. I never want you to think the worst of me."

"I always think the best of you," said Miss Amabel, with dignity yet helplessly. She sat there in an attitude of waiting, her grave glance going from one to the other, as she tried to understand.

"Madame Beattie," said Jeff curtly to Moore, "is likely to give you some personal details of her life. If you print them you'll settle with me afterward."

"O Jeffrey!" said Miss Amabel. "Why put it so unpleasantly? Mr. Moore would never print anything which could annoy you or any one. We mustn't assume he would."

Moore, standing, one fat and not overclean hand on the table, looked a passionate gratitude to her. He seemed about to gush into protest. Of course he wouldn't. Of course he would publish only what was of the highest character and also what everybody wanted him to.

"That's all," said Jeff. He, too, was standing and he now turned to go.

"I wish—" said Miss Amabel impulsively. She got on her feet and stood there a minute, a stately figure in spite of her blurred lines. "I wish we could have your cooperation, Jeff. Mr. Moore is going to run for mayor."

"So I hear," said Jeff, and his mind added, "And you are financing his campaign, you old dear, and only a minute ago you were signing over securities."

"It means so much," said Miss Amabel, "to have a man who is a friend of labour. We ought to combine on that. It's enough to heal our differences."

"Pardon me," said Jeff. "I have to go. But mayn't I take you home?"

"No," said Amabel; "I've another bit of business to settle. But think it over, Jeff. We can't afford to let personal issues influence us when the interest of the town is at stake."

"Surely not," said Jeff. "Addington forever!"

As he went down the stairs he smiled a little, remembering Weedie had not spoken a word after his first greeting. But Jeff didn't waste much thought on Weedie. He believed, at the crisis, Weedie could be managed. Miss Amabel had startled his mind broad awake to what she called the great issues and what he felt were vital ones. He went on over the bridge, and up the stairs of the old Choate Building to Alston's office, and, from some sudden hesitancy, tapped on the door.

"Come in," called Alston, and he went.

Alston sat at the table, not reading a novel as Lydia and too many of his clients had found him, but idle, with not even a book at hand. There were packets of papers, in a methodical sequence, but everything on the table bore the aspect of an order not akin to work. Choate looked pale and harassed. "You?" said his upward glance. "You, of all the people I've been thinking of? What are you here for?"

There was though, in the look, a faint relief. Perhaps he thought something connected with the harassing appeal of Esther, the brutalising stir of her in the air, could be cleared up. Jeff was to surprise him.

"Choate," said he, "have you been asked to run for mayor?"

Choate frowned. He wasn't thinking of public office.

"I've been—approached," he said, as if the word made it the more remote.

"What did you say?"

"Said I wouldn't. Jeff, I believe you started the confounded thing."

"I've talked a lot," said Jeff. "But any fool knows you've got to do it. Choate, you're about the only hope of tradition and decency here in Addington. Don't you know that?"

"I'm a weak man," said Alston, looking up at him unhappily. "I don't half care for these things. I like the decent thing done, but, Jeff, I don't want to pitch into the dirty business and call names and be called names and uncover smells. I'd rather quit the whole business and go to Europe."

"And let Addington go to pot? Why, we'd all rather go to Europe, if Addington could be kept on her pins without us. But she can't. We've got to see the old girl through."

"She's gone to pot anyway," said Choate. "So's the country. There aren't any Americans now. They're blasted aliens."

"Ain't you an American?" asked Jeff, forgetting his grammar. "I am. And I'm going to die in my tracks before I'm downed."

"You will be downed."

"I don't care. I don't care whether in a hundred years' time it's stated in the history books that there was once a little tribe called New Englanders and if you want to learn about 'em the philologists send you to the inscriptions of Mary Wilkins and Robert Frost."

(This was before Robert Frost had come into his fame, but New England had printed a verse or two and then forgotten them.)

"I didn't know you were such a fellow," said Choate, really interested, in an impersonal way. "You go to my head."

"Sometimes I think," said Jeff, not half noticing him, "that what really was doing in me in jail was country—country—patriotism, a kind of irrational thing—sort of mother love applied to the soil—the thing men die for. Call it liberty, if you want to, but it's all boiled down now to Addington. Choate, don't you see Addington took hold on eternal things? Don't you know how deep her roots go? She was settled by English. You and I are English. We aren't going to let east of Europe or south of Europe or middle Europe come over here and turn old Addington into something that's not Anglo-Saxon. O Choate, wake up. Come alive. Stop being temperate. Run for mayor and beat Weedie out of his skin."

"Dear fellow," said Choate, looking at him as if for an instant he too were willing to speak out, "you live in a country where the majority rules. And the majority has a perfect right to the government it wants. And you will be voted down by ten aliens this year and a hundred next, and so on, because the beastly capitalist wants more and more aliens imported to do his work and the beastly politician wants them all thrown into citizenship neck and heels, so he can have more votes. You're defeated, Jeff, before you begin. You're defeated by sheer numbers."

"Then, for God's sake," said Jeff, "take your alien and make an American of him."

"You can't. Could I take you to Italy and make an Italian of you, or to Germany and make a German? You might do something with their children."

"They talk about the melting-pot," said Jeff rather helplessly.

"They do. It's a part of our rank sentimentalism. You can pour your nationalities in but they'll no more combine than Tarquin's and Lucretia's blood. No, Jeff. America's gone, the vision, as she was in the beginning. They've throttled her among them."

Jeff stood looking at him, flushed, dogged, defiant. He had a vivid beauty at the moment, and Alston woke to a startled sense of what the young Jeff used to be. But this was better. There was something beaten into this face finer far than youth.

Jeff seemed to be meeting him as if their minds were at grapples.

"The handful of us, old New England, the sprinkling of us that's left, we've got to repel invasion. The aliens are upon us."

"They've even brought their insect pests," put in Alston.

"Folks," said Jeff, "that know no more about the passions and faithfulnesses this government was founded on than a Hottentot going into his neighbour's territory."

"Oh, come," said Alston, "give 'em a fair show. They've come for liberty. You've got to take their word for it."

"Some of 'em have come to avoid being skinned alive, by Islam, some to get money enough to go back with and be *rentiers*. The Germans have come to show us the beatitude of their specially anointed way of life."

"Well," said Alston curtly, "we've got 'em. And they've got us. You can't leaven the whole lump."

"I can't look much beyond Addington," said Jeff. "I believe I'm dotty over the old girl. I don't want her to go back to being Victorian, but I want her to be right—honest, you know, and standing for decent things. That's why you're going to be mayor."

Alston made no answer, but when, in a few weeks' time, some citizens of weight came to ask him again if he would accept the nomination, he said, without parley, that he would. And it was not Jeff that had constrained him; it was the look in his mother's eyes.

XXXIV

The late autumn had a profusion of exhilarating days. The crops kept Jeff in the garden and brought his father out for his quota of pottering care. When the land was cleared for ploughing and even the pile of rubbish burned, Jeff got to feeling detached again, discontented even, and went for long tramps, sometimes with Alston Choate. Esther, seeing them go by, looked after them in a consternation real enough to blanch her damask cheek. What was the bond between them? Whatever bond they had formed must be to the exclusion of her and her dear wishes, and their amity enraged her.

Once, in walking, she saw Jeff turn in at Miss Amabel's gate, and she did not swerve but actually finished her walk and came back that way praying, with the concentration of thought which is an assault of will, that he might be coming out and meet her. And it happened according to her desire. There, at the gate was Jeff, handsomer, according to a woman's jealous eye, than she had ever seen him, fresh-coloured, his face set in a determination that was not feigned, hard, fit for any muscular task more than the average man might do. Esther was looking her prettiest. She continued to look her prettiest now, so far as woman's art could serve her, for she could not know what moment might summon her to bring her own special strength to bear. Jeff, at sight of her, took off his hat, but stopped short standing inside the gate. Esther understood. He wasn't going to commit her to walk with him where Addington might see. She, too, stopped, her heart beating as fast as she could have desired and giving her a bright accession of colour. Esther greatly prized her damask cheek.

Jeff, feeling himself summoned, then came forward. He looked at her gravely, and he was at a loss. How to address her! But Esther, with a beguiling accent of gentleness, began.

"Isn't it strange?" she said, wistfully and even humbly, as if it were not a question but a reflection of her own, not necessarily to be answered.

"What is strange?" asked Jeff, with a kindly note she found reassuring.

"You and me," said Esther, "standing here, when—I don't believe you were going to speak."

Her poor little smile looked piteous to him and the lift of her brows. Jeff was sorry for her, sorry for them both. At that moment he was not summoning energy to distrust her, and this was as she hoped.

"I'm sorry, Esther," he said impulsively. "I did mean to speak. It wasn't that. I only don't mean to make you—in other folks' eyes, you know—seem to be having anything to do with me when—when you don't want to."

"When I don't want to!" Esther repeated. There was musing in the soft voice, a kind of wonder.

"It's an infernal shame," said Jeff. He was glad to tell her he hated the privation she had to bear of having cast him off and yet facing her broken life without him. "I know what kind of time you have as well as you could tell me. You've got Madame Beattie quartered on you. There's grandmother upstairs. No comfort in her. No companionship. I've often thought you don't go out as much as you might for fear of meeting me. You needn't feel that. If I see it's going to happen I can save you that, at least."

Esther stood looking up at him, her lips parted, as if she drank what he had to say through them, and drank it thirstily.

"How good you are!" she said. "O Jeff, how good! When I've—" There she paused, still watching him. But Esther had the woman's instinctive trick of being able to watch accurately while she did it passionately.

Jeff flushed to his hair, but her cleverness did not lead her to the springs of his emotion. He was ashamed, not of her, but of himself.

"You're off," he said, "all wrong. I do want to save you from this horrible mix-up I've made for you. But I'm not good, Esther. I'm not the faithful chap it makes me seem. I'm different. You wouldn't know me. I don't believe we ever knew each other very well."

Something like terror came into her beautiful eyes. Was he, that inner terror asked her, trying to explain that she had lost him? Although she might not want him, she had always thought he would be there.

"You mean—" she began, and strove to keep a grip on herself and decide temperately whether this would be best to say. But some galled feeling got the better of her. The smart was too much. Hurt vanity made her wince and cry out with the passion of a normal jealousy. "You mean," she continued, "you are in love with another woman."

It was a hit. He had deserved it, he knew, and he straightened under it. Let him not, his alarmed senses told him, even think of Lydia, lest these cruelly clever eyes see Lydia in his, Lydia in his hurried breath, even if he could keep Lydia from his tongue.

"Esther," he said, "don't say such a thing. Don't think it. What right have I to look at another woman while you are alive? How could I insult a woman—" He stopped, his own honest heart knocking against his words. He had dared. He had swept his house of life and let Lydia in.

"Yes," said Esther thoughtfully, and, it seemed, hurt to the soul, "you love somebody else. O Jeff, I didn't think—" She lifted widened eyes to his. Afterward he could have sworn they were wet with tears. "I stand in your way, don't I? What can I do, not to stand in your way?"

"Do?" said Jeff, in a rage at all the passions between men and women. "Do? You can stop talking sentiment about me and putting words into my mouth. You can make over your life, if you know how, and I'll help you do it, if I can. I thought you were trying to free yourself. You can do that. I won't lift a hand. You can say you're afraid of me, as you have before. God knows whether you are. If you are, you're out of your mind. But you can say it, and I won't deny you've just cause. You mustn't be a prisoner to me."

"Jeff!" said Esther.

"What is it?" he asked.

She spoke tremblingly, weakly really as if she had not the strength to speak, and he came a step nearer and laid his hand on the granite gatepost. It was so hard it gave him courage. There were blood-red vines on it, and when he disturbed their stems they loosened leaves and let them drift over his hand.

"Now I see," said Esther, "how really alone I am. I thought I was when you were away, but it was nothing to this."

She walked on, listlessly, aimlessly even though she kept the path and she was going on her way as she had elected to before she saw him. But to Jeff she seemed to be a drifting thing. A delicate butterfly floated past him, weakened by the coldness of last night and fluttering on into a night as cold.

"Esther," he called, and hurried after her. "You don't want me to walk with you?" he asked impatiently. "You don't want Addington to say we've made it up?"

"I don't care about Addington," said Esther. "It can say what it pleases—if you're kind to me."

"Kind!" said Jeff. "I could have you trounced. You don't play fair. What do you mean by mixing me all up with pity and things—" Esther's lids were not allowed to lift, but her heart gave a little responsive bound. So she had mixed him up!—"Getting the facts all wrong," Jeff went on irritably. "You ignore everything you've felt before to-day. And you begin to-day and say I've not been kind to you."

Now Esther looked at him. She smiled.

"Scold away," she said. "I've wanted you to scold me. I haven't been so happy for months."

"Of course I scold you," said Jeff. "I want to see you happy. I want to see you rid of me and beginning your life all over, so far as you can. You're not the sort to live alone. It's an outrage against nature. A woman like you—"

But Esther never discovered what he meant by "a woman like you." He had gone a little further than her brain would take her. Did he mean a woman altogether charming, like her—or? She dropped the inquiry very soon, because it seemed to lead nowhere and it was pleasanter to think the things that do not worry one.

Jeff remembered afterward that he had known from the beginning of the walk with her that they should meet all Addington. But it was not the Addington he had irritably dreaded. It was Lydia. His heart died as he saw her coming, and his brain called on every reserve within him to keep Esther from knowing that here was his heart's lady, this brave creature whose honour was untainted, who had a woman's daring and a man's endurance. He even, after that first alarm of a glance, held his eyes from seeing her and he kept on scolding Esther.

"What's the use," he said, "talking like that?" And then his mind told him there must be no confusion in what he said. He was defending Lydia. He was pulling over her the green leaves of secrecy. "I advise you," he said, "to get away from here. Get away from Madame Beattie—get away from grandmother—" Lydia was very near now. He felt he could afford to see her. "Ah, Lydia!" he said casually, and took off his hat.

They were past her, but not before Esther had asked, in answer:

"Where shall we go? I mean—" she caught herself up from her wilful stumbling—"where could I go—alone?"

They were at her own gate, and Jeff stopped with her. Since they left Lydia he had held his hat in his hand, and Esther, looking up at him saw that he had paled under his tan. The merciless woman in her took stock of that, rejoicing. Jeff smiled at her faintly, he was so infinitely glad to leave her.

"We must think," he said. "You must think. Esther, about money, I'll try—I don't know yet what I can earn—but we'll see. Oh, hang it! these things can't be said."

He turned upon the words and strode off and Esther, without looking after him, went in and at once upstairs.

"Good girl!" Madame Beattie called to her, from her room. "Well begun is half done."

Esther did not answer. Neither did she take the trouble to hate Aunt Patricia for saying it. She went instantly to her glass, and smiled into it. The person who smiled back at her was young and very engaging. Esther liked her. She thought she could trust her to do the best thing possible.

Jeff went home and stood just inside his gateway to wait for Lydia. He judged that she had been going to Amabel's, and now, her thoughts thrown out of focus by meeting him with Esther, she would give up her visit and come home to be sad a little by herself. He was right. She came soon, walking fast, after her habit, a determined figure. He had had time to read her face before she drew its veil of proud composure, and he found in it what he had expected: young sorrow, the anguish of the heart stricken and with no acquired power of staunching its own wounds. When she saw him her face hardly changed, except that the mournful eyes sought his. Had Esther got power over him? the eyes asked, and not out of jealousy, he believed. The little creature was like a cherishing mother. If Esther had gained power she would fight it to the uttermost, not to possess him but to save his intimate self. Esther might pursue it into fastnesses, but it should be saved. To Jeff, in that instant of meeting the questioning eyes, she seemed an amazing person, capable of exacting a tremendous loyalty. He didn't feel like explaining to her that Esther hadn't got him in the least. The clarity of understanding between them was inexpressibly precious to him. He wouldn't break it by muddling assertions.

"I've been to Amabel's," he said. "You were going there, too, weren't you?"

Lydia's face relaxed and cleared a little. She looked relieved, perhaps from the mere kindness of his voice.

"I didn't go," she said. "I didn't feel like it."

"No," said Jeff. "But now we're home again, both of us, and we're glad. Couldn't we cut round this way and sit under the wall a little before Anne sees us and makes us eat things?"

He took her hand, this time of intention to make her feel befriended in the intimacy of their common home, and they skirted the fence and went across the orchard to the bench by the brick wall. As they sat there and Jeff gave back her little hand he suddenly heard quick breaths from her and then a sob or two.

"Lydia," said he. "Lydia."

"I know it," said Lydia.

She sought out her handkerchief and seemed to attack her face with it, she was so angry at the tears.

"You're not hurt," said Jeff. "Truly you're not hurt, Lydia. There's been nothing to hurt you."

Soon her breath stopped catching, and she gave her eyes a final desperate scrub. By that time Jeff had begun to talk about the land and what he hoped to do with it next year. He meant at least to prune the orchard and maybe set out dwarfs. At first Lydia did not half listen, knowing his purpose in distracting her. Then she began to answer. Once she laughed when he told her the colonel, in learning to dig potatoes, had sliced them with the hoe. Father, he told her, was what might be called a library agriculturist. He was reading agricultural papers now. He could answer almost any question you asked. As for bugs and their natural antidotes, he knew them like a book. He even called himself an agronomist. But when it came to potatoes! By and by they were talking together and he had succeeded in giving her that homely sense of intimacy he had been striving for. She forgot the pang that pierced her when she saw him walking beside the woman who owned him through the law. He was theirs, hers and her father's and Anne's, because they knew him as he was and were desperately seeking to succour his maimed life.

But as she was going to sleep a curious question asked itself of Lydia. Didn't she want him to go back to his wife and be happy with her, if that could be? Lydia had no secrets from herself, no emotional veilings. She told herself at once that she didn't want it at all. No Esther made good as she was fair, by some apt miracle, could be trusted with the man she had hurt. According to Lydia, Esther had not in her even the seeds of such compassion as Jeff deserved.

XXXV

When the cold weather came and Alston Choate and Weedon Moore became rival candidates for the mayoralty of Addington, strange things began to happen. Choate, cursing his lot inwardly, but outwardly deferential to his mother who had really brought it on him, began to fulfil every last requirement of the zealous candidate. He even learned to make speeches, not the lucid exponents of the law that belonged to his court career, but prompt addresses, apparently unconsidered, at short notice. The one innovation he drew the line at was the flattering recognition of men he had never, in the beaten way of life, recognised before. He could not, he said, kiss babies. But he would tell the town what he thought it needed, coached, he ironically added when he spoke the expansive truth at home, by his mother and Jeff. They were ready to bring kindling to boil the pot, Mrs. Choate in her grand manner of beckoning the ancient virtues back, Jeff, as Alston told, him, hammer and tongs. Jeff also began to make speeches, because, at one juncture when Alston gave out from hoarseness—his mother said it was a psychological hoarseness at a moment when he realised overwhelmingly how he hated it all—Jeff had taken his place and "got" the men, labourers all of them, as Alston never had.

"It's a mistake," said Mrs. Choate afterward when he came to the house to report, and ask how Alston was, and the three sat eating one of Mary's quick suppers. "You're really the candidate. Those men know it. They know it's you behind Alston, and they're going to take him patiently because you tell them to. But they don't half want him."

Jeff was very fine now in his robustness, fit and strong, no fat on him and good blood racing well. He was eating bread and butter heartily, while he waited for Mary to serve him savoury things, and Mrs. Choate looked discontentedly at Mary bending over his plate, all hospitality, with the greater solicitude because he was helping Alston out. Mrs. Choate wished the nugatory Esther were out of the way, and she could marry Mary off to Jeff. Mary, pale, yet wholesome, fair-haired, with the definite Choate profile, and dressed in her favourite smoke colour and pale violet, her mother loved conscientiously, if impatiently. But she wished Mary, who had not one errant inclination, might come to her some day and say, "Mother, I am desperately enamoured of an Italian fruit-seller with Italy in his eyes." Mrs. Choate would have explained to her, with a masterly common-sense, that such vagrom impulses meant, followed to conclusions, shipwreck on the rocks of class misunderstanding; but it would have warmed her heart to Mary to have so to explain. But here was Mary to whom no eccentricity ever had to be elucidated. She could not even have imagined a fruit-seller outside his heaven-decreed occupation of selling fruit. Mrs. Choate smiled a little to herself, wondering what Mary would say if she could know her mother was willing to consign the inconvenient Esther to perpetual limbo and marry her to handsome Jeff. "Mother!" she could imagine her horrified cry. It would all be in that.

Jeff was more interested in his eating than in answering Mrs. Choate with more than an encouraging:

"We've got 'em, I think. But I wish," he said, "we had more time to follow up Weedie. What's he saying to 'em?"

"Ask Madame Beattie," said Alston, with more distaste than he could keep out of his voice. "I saw her last night on the outskirts of his crowd, sitting in Denny's hack."

"Speaking?" asked Jeff. "She'd have spoken, if she got half a chance."

Alston laughed quietly.

"Moore got the better of her. He was in his car. All he had to do was to make off. She made after him, but he's got the whip-hand, with a car."

The next night, doubtless taught the advisability of vying with her enemy, Madame Beattie, to the disgust of Esther, came down cloaked and muffled to the chin and took the one automobile to be had for hire in Addington. She was whirled away, where Esther had no idea. She was whirled back again at something after ten, hoarse yet immensely tickled. But Reardon knew what she had done and he telephoned it to Esther. She was making speeches of her own, stopping at street corners wherever she could gather a group, but especially running down to the little streets by the water where the foreign labourers came swarming out and cheered her.

"It's disgraceful," said Esther, almost crying into the telephone. "What is she saying to them?"

"Nobody knows, except it's political. We assume that," said Reardon. "All kinds of lingo. They tell me she knows more languages than a college professor."

"Find out," Esther besought him. "Ask her. Ask whom you shall vote for. It'll get her started."

That seemed to Reardon a valuable idea, and he actually did ask her, lingering before the door one night when she came out to take her car. He put her into it with a florid courtesy she accepted as her due—it was the best, she thought, the man had to offer—and then said to her jocosely:

"Well, Madame Beattie, who shall I vote for?"

Madame Beattie looked at him an instant with a quizzical comprehension it was too dark for him to see.

"I can tell whom you'd better not vote for," she said. "Don't vote for Esther. Tell him to go on."

Reardon did tell the man and then stood there on the pavement a moment, struck by the certainty that he had been warned. She seemed to him to know everything. She must know he was somehow likely to get into trouble over Esther. Reardon was bewitched with Esther, but he did so want to be safe. Nevertheless, led by man's destiny, he walked up to the door and Esther, as before, let him in. He thought it only fair to tell her he had found out nothing, and he meant, in a confused way, to let her see that things must be "all right" between them. By this he meant that they must both be safe. But once within beside her perfumed presence—yet Esther used no vulgar helps to provoke the senses—he forgot that he must be safe, and took her into his arms. He had been so certain of his stability, after his recoil from Madame Beattie, that he neglected to resist himself. And Esther did not help him. She clung to him and the perfume mounted to his brain. What was it? Not, even he knew, a cunning of the toilet; only the whole warm breath of her.

"Look here," said Reardon, shaken, "what we going to do?"

"You must tell me," she whispered. "How could I tell you?"

Reardon afterward had an idea that he broke into rough beseeching of her to get free, to take his money, everything he had, and buy her freedom somehow. Then, he said, in an awkwardness he cursed himself for, they could begin to talk. And as she withdrew from him at sound of Rhoda Knox above, he opened the door and ran away from her, to the ordered seclusion of his own house. Once there he wiped his flustered brow and cursed a little, and then telephoned her. But Sophy answered that Mrs. Blake was not well. She had gone to her room.

Reardon had a confused multitude of things to say to her. He wanted to beg her to understand, to assure her he was thinking of her and not himself, as indeed he was. But meantime as he rehearsed the arguments he had at hand, he was going about the room getting things together. His papers were fairly in order. He could always shake them into perfect system at an hour's notice. And then muttering to himself that, after all, he shouldn't use it, he telephoned New York to have a state-room reservation made for Liverpool. The office was closed, and he knew it would be, yet it somehow gave him a dull satisfaction to have tried; and next day he telephoned again.

Within a week Jeff turned his eyes toward a place he had never thought of, never desired for a moment, and yet now longed for exceedingly. A master in a night school founded by Miss Amabel had dropped out, and Jeff went, hot foot, to Amabel and begged to take his place. How could she refuse him? Yet she did warn him against propaganda.

"Jeff, dear," she said, moving a little from the open fire where he sat with her, bolt upright, eager, forceful, exactly like a suppliant for a job he desperately needs, "you won't use it to set the men against Weedon Moore?"

Jeff looked at her with a perfectly open candour and such a force of persuasion in his asking eyes that she believed he was bringing his personal charm to influence her, and shook her head at him despairingly.

"I won't in that building or the school session," he said. "Outside I'll knife him if I can."

"Jeff," said Miss Amabel, "if you'd only work together."

"We can't," said Jeff, "any more than oil and water. Or alkali and acid. We'd make a mighty fizz. I'm in it for all I'm worth, Amabel. To bust Weedie and save Addington."

"Weedon Moore is saving Addington," said she.

"Do you honestly believe that? Think how Addington began. Do you suppose a town that old boy up there helped to build—" he glanced at his friend, the judge—"do you think that little rat can do much for it? I don't."

"Perhaps Addington doesn't need his kind of help now, or yours. Addington is perfectly comfortable, except its working class. And it's the working man Weedon Moore is striving for."

"Addington is comfortable on a red-hot crater," said Jeff. "She's like all the rest of America. She's sat here sentimentalising and letting the crater get hotter and hotter under her, and unless we look out, Amabel, there isn't going to be any America, one of these days. Mrs. Choate says it's going to be the spoil of damned German efficiency. She thinks the Huns are waking up and civilisations going under. But I don't. I believe we're going to be a great unwieldy, industrial monster, no cohesion in us and no patriotism, no citizenship."

"No patriotism!" Miss Amabel rose involuntarily and stood there trembling. Her troubled eyes sought the pictured eyes of the old Judge. "Jeff, you don't know what you're saying."

"I do," said Jeff, "mighty well. Sit down, dear, or I shall have to salute the flag, too, and I'm too lazy."

She sat down, but she was trembling.

"And I'm going to save Addington, if I can," said Jeff. "I haven't the tongue of men and angels or I'd go out and try to salvage the whole business. But I can't. Addington's more my size. If there were invasion, you know, a crippled man couldn't do more than try to defend his own dooryard. Dear old girl, we've got to save Addington."

"I'm trying," said she. "Jeff, dear, I'm trying. And I've a lot of money. I don't know how it rolled up so."

"Don't give it to Weedon Moore, that's all," he ventured, and then, in the stiffening of her whole body, he saw it was a mistake even to mention Moore. Her large charity made her fiercely partisan. He ventured the audacious personal appeal. "Give me some, Amabel, if you've really got so much. Let me put on some plays, in a simple way, and try to make your workmen see what we're at, when we talk about home and country. They despise us, Amabel, except on pay day. Let's hypnotise 'em, please 'em in some other way besides shorter hours and easier strikes. Let's make 'em fall over themselves to be Americans."

Miss Amabel flushed all over her soft face, up to the line of her grey hair.

"Jeff," she said.

"What'm?"

"I have always meant when you were at liberty again—" that seemed to her a tolerable euphemism—"to turn in something toward your debt."

"To the creditors?" Jeff supplied cheerfully. "Amabel, dear, I don't believe there are any little people suffering from my thievery. It's only the big people that wanted to be as rich as I did. Anne and Lydia are suffering in a way. But that's my business. I'm going to confess to you. Dear sister superior, I'm going to confess."

She did not move, hardly by an eyelash. She was afraid of choking his confidence, and she wanted it to come abundantly. Jeff sat for a minute or two frowning and staring into the fire. He had to catch himself back from what threatened to become silent reverie.

"I've thought a good deal about this," he said, "when I've had time to think, these last weeks. I'd give a lot to stand clear with the world. I'd like to do a spectacular refunding of what I stole and lost. But I'd far rather pitch in and save Addington. Maybe it means I'm warped somehow about money, standards lowered, you know, perceptions blunted, that sort of thing. Well, if it's so I shall find it out sometime and be punished. We can't escape anything, in spite of their doctrine of vicarious atonement."

She moved slightly at this, and Jeff smiled at her.

"Yes," said he, "we have to be punished. Sometimes I suppose the full knowledge of what we've done is punishment enough. Now about me. If anybody came to me to-day and said, 'I'll make you square with the world,' I should say, 'Don't you do it. Save Addington. I'd rather throw my good name into the hopper and let it grind out grist for Addington.'"

Miss Amabel put out the motherly hand and he grasped it.

"And I assure you," he said again, "I don't know whether that's common-sense—tossing the rotten past into the abyss and making a new deal—or whether it's because I've deteriorated too much to see I've deteriorated. You tell, Amabel."

She took out her large handkerchief—Amabel had a convenient pocket—and openly wiped her eyes.

"I'll give you money, Jeff," she said, "and you can put it into plays. I'd like to pay you something definite for doing it, because I don't see how you're going to live."

"Lydia'll help me do it," said Jeff, "she and Anne. They're curiously wise about plays and dances. No, Amabel, I sha'n't eat your money, except what you pay me for evening school. And I have an idea I'm going to get on. I always had the devil's own luck about things, you know. Look at the luck of getting you to fork out for plays you've never heard the mention of. And I feel terrible loquacious. I think I shall write things. I think folks'll take 'em. They've got to. I want to hand over a little more to Esther."

Even to her he had never mentioned the practical side of Esther's life. Miss Amabel looked at him sympathetically, inquiringly.

"Yes," he said, "she's having a devil of a time. I want to ease it up somehow—send her abroad or let her get a divorce or something."

"You couldn't—" said Amabel. She stopped.

His brows were black as thunder.

"No," said he, "no. Esther and I are as far apart as—" he paused for a simile. Then he smiled at her. "No," he said. "It wouldn't do."

As he went out he stopped a moment more and smiled at her with the deprecating air of asking for indulgence that was his charm when he was good. His eyes were the soft bright blue of happy seas.

"Amabel," said he, "I don't want to cry for mercy, though I'd rather have mercy from you than 'most anybody. Blame me if you've got to, but don't make any mistake about me. I'm not good and I'm not all bad. I'm nothing but a confusion inside. I've got to pitch in and do the best thing I know. I'm an undiscovered country."

"You're no mystery to me," she said. "You're a good boy, Jeff."

He went straight home and called Lydia and Anne to council, the colonel sitting by, looking over his glasses in a benevolent way.

"I've been trying to undermine Weedie," said Jeff, "with Amabel. I can't quite do it, but I've got her to promise me some of her money. For plays, Lydia, played by Mill End. What do you say?"

"She hasn't money enough for real plays," said Lydia. "All she's got wouldn't last a minute."

"Not in a hall?" asked Jeff. "Not with scenery just sketched in, as it were? But all of it patriotic. Teach them something. Ram it down their throats. English language."

Lydia made a few remarks, and Jeff sat up and stared at her. The colonel and Anne, endorsing her, were not surprised. They had heard it all before. It seems Lydia had a theory that the province of art is simply not to be dull. If you could charm people, you could make them do anything. The kite of your aspirations might fly among the stars. But you couldn't fly it if it didn't look well flying. The reason nobody really learns anything by plays intended to teach them something, Lydia said, is because the plays are generally dull. Nobody is going to listen to "argufying" if he can help it. If you tell people what it is beneficial for them to believe they are going home and to bed, unchanged. But they'll yawn in your faces first. Lydia had a theory that you might teach the most extraordinary lessons if you only made them bewitching enough. Look at the Blue Bird. How many people who loved to see Bread cut a slice off his stomach and to follow the charming pageant of the glorified common things of life, thought anything save that this was a "show" with no appeal beyond the visual one? Yet there it was, the big symbolism beating in its heart and keeping it alive. The Children of Light could see the symbolism quick as a wink. Still the Children of Darkness who never saw any symbolism at all and who were the ones to yawn and go home to bed, helped pay for tickets and keep the thing running. We must bewitch them also. Jeff inquired humbly if she would advise taking up Shakespeare with the Mill Enders and found she still wouldn't venture on it at once. She'd do some fairy plays, quite easy to write on new lines. Everything was easy if you had "go" enough, Lydia said. Jeff ventured to inquire about scenic effects, and discovered, to his enlightenment, that Lydia had the greatest faith in the imagination of any kind of audience. Do a thing well enough, she said, and the audience would forget whether it was looking at a painted scene or not. It could provide its own illusion. Think of the players, she reminded him, who, when they gave the Trojan Women on the road, and sought for a little Astyanax, were forbidden by an asinine city government to bring on a real child. Think how the actors crouched protectingly over an imaginary Astyanax, and how plainly every eye saw the child who was not there. Perhaps every woman's heart supplied the vision of her dream-child, of the child she loved. Think of the other play where the kettle is said to be hissing hot and everybody shuns it with such care that onlookers wince too. Lydia thought she could write the fairy plays and the symbolic plays, all American, if Jeff liked, and he might correct the grammar.

Just then Mary Nellen, passionately but silently grieved to have lost such an intellectual feast, came in on the tail of these remarks. She brought Jeff a letter. It was a publisher's letter, and the publisher would print his book about prisoners. It said nothing whatever of trying to advertise him as a prisoner. Jeff concluded the man was a decent fellow. He swaggered a little over the letter and told the family he had to, it was such luck.

They were immensely proud and excited at once. The colonel called him "son" with emphasis, and Lydia got up and danced a little by herself. She invited Anne to join her, but Anne sat, soft-eyed and still, and was glad that way. Jeff thought it an excellent moment to tell them he was going to teach in the evening school, upon which Lydia stopped dancing.

"But I want to," he said to her, with a smile for her alone. "Won't you let me if I want to?"

"I want you to write," said Lydia obstinately.

"I shall. I shall write. And talk. It's a talking age. Everybody's chattering, except the ones that are shrieking. I'm going to see if I can't down some of the rest."

XXXVI

A carnival of motor cars kept on whirling to all parts of the town where Madame Beattie was likely to speak. She spoke in strange places: at street corners, in a freight station, at the passenger station when the incoming train had brought a squad of workmen from the bridge repairing up the track. It was always to workmen, and always they knew, by some effective communication, where to assemble. The leisure class, too, old Addingtonians, followed her, as if it were all the best of jokes, and protested they sometimes understood what she said. But nobody did, except the foreigners and not one of them would own to knowing. Weedon Moore made little clipped bits of speeches, sliced off whenever her car appeared and his audience turned to her in a perfect obedience and glowing interest. Jeff, speaking for Alston, now got a lukewarm attention, the courtesy born out of affectionate regard. None of the roars and wild handclappings were for him. Madame Beattie was eating up all the enthusiasm in town. Once Jeff, walking along the street, came on her standing in her car, haranguing a group of workmen, all intent, eager, warm to her with a perfect sympathy and even a species of adoration.

He stepped up in the car beside her. He had an irritated sense that, if he got near enough, he might find himself inside the mystic ring. She turned to him with a gracious and dramatic courtesy. She even put a hand on his arm, and he realised, with more exasperation, that he was supporting her while she talked. The crowd cheered, and, it appeared, they were cheering him.

"What are you saying?" he asked her, in an irascible undertone. "Talk English for ten minutes. Play fair."

But she only smiled on him the more sympathetically, and the crowd cheered them both anew. Jeff stuck by, that night. He stayed with her until, earlier than usual because she had tired her voice, she told the man to drive home.

"I am taking you with me to see Esther," she mentioned unconcernedly, as they went.

"No, you're not," said Jeff. "I'm not going into that house."

"Very well," said Madame Beattie. "Then tell him to stop here a minute, while we talk."

Jeff hesitated, having no desire to talk, and she herself gave the order.

"Poor Esther!" said Jeff, when the chauffeur had absented himself to a sufficient distance, and, according to Madame Beattie's direction, was walking up and down. "Isn't it enough for you to pester her without bringing me into it? Why are you so hard on her?"

"I've been quite patient," said Madame Beattie, "with both of you. I've sat down and waited for you to make up your minds what is going to be done about my necklace. You're doing nothing. Esther's doing nothing. The little imp that took it out of Esther's bag is doing nothing. I've got to be paid, among you. If I am not paid, the little dirty man is going to have the whole story to publish: how Esther took the necklace, years ago, how the little imp took it, and how you said you took it, to save her."

"I have told Weedon Moore," said Jeff succinctly, "in one form or another that I'll break his neck if he touches the dirty job."

"You have?" said Madame Beattie. She breathed a dramatic breath, whether of outraged pride or for calculated effect he could not tell. "Jeff, I can assure you if the little man refuses to do it—and I doubt whether he will—I'll have it set up myself in leaflets, and I'll go through the town distributing them from this car. Jeff, I must have money. I must have it."

He sat back immovable, arms folded, eyes on the distance, and frowningly thought. What use to blame her who acted after her kind and was no more to be stirred by appeals than a wild creature red-clawed upon its prey?

"Madame Beattie," said he, "if I had money you should have it. Right or wrong you should have it if it would buy you out of here. But I haven't got it."

"It's there you are a fool," she said, moved actually now by his numbness to his own endowment. "I could beat my head and scream, when I think how you're throwing things away, your time, in that beastly night school, your power, your personal charm. Jeff, you've the devil's own luck. You were born with it. And you simply won't use it."

He had said that himself in a moment of hope not long before: that he had the devil's own luck. But he wasn't going to accept it from her.

"You talk of luck," he said, "to a man just out of jail."

"You needn't have been in jail," she was hurling at him in an unpleasant intensity of tone, as if she would have liked to scream it and the quiet street denied her. "If you hadn't pleaded guilty, if you hadn't handed over every scrap of evidence, if you had been willing to take advantage of what that clerk was ready to swear—why, you might have got off and kept on in business and be a millionaire to-day."

How she managed to know some of the things she did he never fathomed. He had never seen anybody of the direct and shameless methods of Madame Beattie, willing to ask the most intimate questions, make the most unscrupulous demands. He remembered the young clerk who had wanted to perjure himself for his sake.

"That would have made a difference, I suppose," he said, "young Williams' testimony. I wonder how he happened to think of it."

"He thought of it because I went to him," said Madame Beattie. "I said, 'Isn't there anything you could swear to that would help him?' He knew at once. He turned white as a sheet. 'Yes,' he said, 'and I'll swear to it.' I told him we'd make it worth his while."

"You did?" said Jeff. "Well, there's another illusion gone. I took a little comfort in young Williams. I thought he was willing to perjure himself because he had an affection for me. So you were to make it worth his while."

She laughed a little, indifferently, with no bitterness, but in retrospect of a scene where she had been worsted.

"You needn't mourn that lost ideal," she said. "Young Williams showed me the door. It was in your office, and he actually did show me the door. He was glad to perjure himself, he said, for you. Not for money. Not for me."

Jeff laughed out.

"Well," he said, "that's something to the good anyway. We haven't lost young Williams. He wrote to me, not long ago. When I answer it, I'll tell him he's something to the good."

But Madame Beattie was not going to waste time on young Williams.

"It ought to be a criminal offence," she said rapidly, "to be such a fool. You had the world in your hand. You've got it still. You and Esther could run such a race! think what you've got, both of you, youth, beauty, charm. You could make your way just by persuasion, persuading this man to one thing and that man to another. How Esther could help you! Don't you see she's an asset? What if you don't love her? Love! I know it from the first letter to the last, and there's nothing in it, Jeff, nothing. But if you make money you can buy the whole world."

Her eager old face was close to his, the eyes, greedy, ravenous, glittered into his and struck their base messages deeper and deeper into his soul. The red of nature had come into her cheeks and fought there with the overlying hue of art. Jeff, from an instinct of blind courage, met her gaze and tried to think he was defying it bravely. But he was overwhelmed with shame for her because she was avowedly what she was. Often he could laugh at her good-tempered cynicism. Over her now, for he actually did have a kind of affection for her, he could have cried.

"Don't!" he said involuntarily, and she misunderstood him. His shame for her disgrace she had taken for yielding and she redoubled the hot torrent of temperamental persuasion.

"I will," she said fiercely, "until you get on your legs and act like a man. Go to Esther. Go to her now, this night. Come with me. Make love to her. She's a pretty woman. Sweep her off her feet. Tell her you're going to make good and she's going to help you."

Jeff rose and stepped out of the car. The ravenous old hand still dragged at his arm, but he lifted it quietly and gave it back to her. He stood there a moment, his hat off, and signalled the chauffeur. Madame Beattie leaned over to him until her eyes were again glittering into his.

"Is that it?" she asked. "Are you going to run away?"

"Yes," said Jeff, quietly. "I'm going to run away."

The man came and Jeff stood there, hat still in hand, until the car had started. He felt like showing her an exaggerated courtesy. Jeff thought he had never been so sorry for anybody in his life as for Madame Beattie.

Madame Beattie drew her cloak the closer, sunk her chin in it and concluded Jeff was done with her. She was briefly sorry though not from shame. It scarcely disconcerted her to find he liked her even less than she had thought. Where was his large tolerance, she might have asked, the moral neutrality of the man of the world?

He had made it incumbent on her merely to take other measures, and next day, seeing Lydia walk past the house, she went to call on Anne. Her way was smooth. Anne herself came to the door in the neighbourly Addington fashion when help was busy, and took her into the library, expressing regret that her father was not there. The family had gone out on various errands. This she offered in her gentle way, even with a humorous ruefulness, Madame Beattie would find her so inadequate. To Anne, Madame Beattie was exotic as some strange eastern flower, not less impressive because it was a little wilted and showed the results of brutal usage.

Madame Beattie composedly took off her cloak and put her feet up on the fender, an attitude which perilously tipped her chair. On this Anne solicitously volunteered to move the fender and did it, bringing the high-heeled shoes comfortably near the coals. Then Madame Beattie, wasting no time in preliminaries, began, with great circumspection and her lisp, and told Anne the later story of the necklace. To her calm statement of Esther's thievery Anne paid a polite attention though no credence. She had not believed it when Lydia told her. Why should she be the more convinced from these withered lisping lips? But Madame Beattie went on explicitly, through the picturesque tale of Lydia and the necklace and the bag. Then Anne looked at her in unaffected horror. She sat bolt upright, her slender figure tense with expectation, her hands clasped rigidly. Madame Beattie enjoyed this picture of a sympathetic attention, a nature played upon by her dramatic mastery. Anne had no backwardness in believing now, the deed was so exactly Lydia's. She could see the fierce impulse of its doing, the reckless haste, no pause for considering whether it were well to do. She could appreciate Lydia's silence afterward. "Poor darling" she murmured, and though Madame Beattie interrogated sharply, "What?" she was not to hear. All the mother in Anne, faithfully and constantly brooding over Lydia, grew into passion. She could hardly wait to get the little sinner into her arms and tell her she was eternally befriended by Anne's love. Madame Beattie was coming to conclusions.

"The amount of the matter is," she said, "I must be paid for the necklace."

"But," Anne said, with the utmost courtesy, "I understand you have the necklace."

"That isn't the point," said Madame Beattie. "I have been given a great deal of annoyance, and I must be compensated for that. What use is a necklace that I can neither sell nor even pawn? I am in honour bound "—and then she went on with her story of the Royal Personage, to which Anne listened humbly enough now, since it seemed to touch Lydia. Madame Beattie came to her alternative: if nobody paid her money to ensure her silence, she would go to Weedon Moore and give him the story of Esther's thievery and of Lydia's. Anne rose from her chair.

"You have come to me," she said, "to ask a thing like that? To ask for money—"

"You are to influence Jeff," Madame Beattie lisped. "Jeff can do almost anything he likes if he doesn't waste himself muddling round with turnips and evening schools. You are to tell him his wife and the imp are going to be shown up. He wouldn't believe me. He thinks he can thrash Moore and there'll be an end of it. But it won't be an end of it, my dear, for there are plenty of channels besides Weedon Moore. You tell him. If he doesn't care for Esther he may for the little imp. He thinks she's very nice."

Madame Beattie here, in establishing an understanding, leered a little in the way of indicating a man's pliability when he thought a woman "very nice", and this finished the utter revolt of Anne, who stood, her hand on a chair back, gazing at her.

"I never," said Anne, in a choked way, "I never heard such horrible things in my life." Then, to her own amazement, for she hardly knew the sensation and never with such intensity as overwhelmed her now, Anne felt very angry. "Why," she said, in a tone that sounded like wonder, "you are a dreadful woman. Do you know what a dreadful woman you are? Oh, you must go away, Madame Beattie. You must go out of this house at once. I can't have you here."

Madame Beattie looked up at her in a pleasant indifference, as if it rather amused her to see the grey dove bristling for its young. Anne even shook the chair she held, as if she were shaking Madame Beattie.

"I mean it," she said. "I can't have you stay here. My father might come in and be civil to you, and I won't have anybody civil to you in this house. Lydia might come in, and Lydia likes you. Why, Madame Beattie, can you bear to think Lydia likes you, when you're willing to say the things you do?"

Madame Beattie was still not moved except by mild amusement. Anne left the chair and took a step nearer.

"Madame Beattie," she said, "you don't believe a word I say. But I mean it. You've got to go out of this house, or I shall put you out of it with my hands. With my hands, Madame Beattie—and I'm very strong."

Madame Beattie was no coward, but she was not young and she had a sense of physical inadequacy. About Anne there was playing the very spirit of tragic anger, none of it for effect, not in the least gauged by any idea of its efficiency. Those slender hands, gripping each other until the knuckles blanched, were ready for their act. The girl's white face was lighted with eyes of fire. Madame Beattie rose and slowly assumed her cloak.

"You're a silly child," she said. "When you're as old as I am you'll have more common-sense. You'd rather risk a scandal than tell Jeff he has a debt to pay. By to-morrow you'll see it as I do. Come to me in the morning, and we'll talk it over. I won't act before then."

She walked composedly to the door and Anne scrupulously held it for her. They went through the hall, Anne following and ready to open the last door also. But she closed it without saying good-bye, in answer to Madame Beattie's oblique nod over her shoulder and the farewell wave of her hand. For an instant Anne felt like slipping the bolt lest her adversary should return, but she reflected, with a grimness new to her gentle nature, that if Madame Beattie did return her own two hands were ready. She stood a moment, listening, and when the carriage wheels rolled away down the drive, she went to the big closet under the stairs and caught at her own coat and hat. She was going, as fast as her feet would carry her, to see Alston Choate.

XXXVII

Alston Choate was working, and he was alone. Anne, bright-eyed and anxious, came in upon him and brought him to his feet. Anne had learned this year that you should not knock at the door of business offices, but she still half believed you ought, and it gave her entrance something of deprecation and a pretty grace.

"I am so troubled," she said, without preliminary. "Madame Beattie has just been to see me."

Alston, smiling away her agitation, if he might, by a kind assumption that there was no conceivable matter that could not be at once put right, gave her a chair and himself went back to his judicial seat. Anne, not loosening her jacket, looked at him, her face pure and appealing above the fur about her throat, as if to beg him to be as kind as he possibly could, since it all involved Lydia.

"I've no doubt it's Madame Beattie," said Alston carelessly, even it might have been a little amused at the possibilities. "If there's a ferment anywhere north of Central America she's pretty certain to have set it brewing."

Anne told him her tale succinctly, and his unconcern crumbled. He frowned over the foolishness of it, and considered, while she talked, whether he had better be quite open with her, or whether it was sufficient to take the responsibility of the thing and settle it like a swaggering god warranted to rule. That was better, he concluded.

"I'll go to see Madame Beattie," he said. "Then I'll report to you. But you'd better not speak to Lydia about it. Or Jeff. Promise me."

"Oh, I'll promise," said Anne, a lovely rose flush on her face. "Only, if Lydia is in danger you must tell me in time to do something. I don't know what, but you know for Lydia I'd do anything."

"I will, too," said Alston. "Only it won't be for Lydia wholly. It'll be for you."

Then for an instant, though so alive to her, he seemed to withdraw into remote cogitation, and she wondered whether he was really thinking of the case at all. Because she was in a lawyer's office she called it a case, timorously; that made it much more serious. But Alston, in that instant, was thinking how strange it was that the shabby old office, witness of his unwilling drudgery and his life-saving excursions into the gardens of fiction, should be looking now on her, seated there in her earnestness and purity, and that he should at last be recognising her. She was a part of him, Alston thought, beloved, not because she was so different but so like. There was no assault of the alien nature upon his own, irresistible because so piquing. There were no unexplored tracts he couldn't at least fancy, green swards and clear waters where a man might be refreshed. Everything he found there would be, he knew, of the nature of the approaches to that gentle paradise. What a thing, remote, extraordinary to think of in his office while she brought him the details of a tawdry scandal. Yet the office bore, to his eyes, invisible traces of past occupancy: men and women out of books were there, absolutely vivid to his eyes, more alive than half the Addingtonians. The walls were hung with garlands of fancy, the windows his dreaming eyes had looked from were windows into space beyond Addington. No, these were no common walls, yet unfitting to gaze on while you told a client you loved her. After all, on rapid second thought, it might not seem so inapt seen through his mother's eyes, as she was betraying herself now in more than middle age. "Ask her wherever you find yourselves," he fancied his mother saying. "That is part of the adventure."

Alston looked at Anne and smiled upon her and involuntarily she smiled back, though she saw no cause for cheerfulness in the dismal errand she had come on. She started a little, too, for Alston, in the most matter of fact way, began with her first name.

"Anne," said he, "I have for a long time been—" he paused for a word. The ones he found were all too dignified, too likely to be wanted in a higher cause—"bewitched," he continued, "over Esther Blake."

The colour ran deeper into Anne's face.

"You don't want," she said, "to do anything that might hurt her? I shouldn't want to, either. But it isn't Esther we're talking about. It's Madame Beattie."

"I know," said Alston, "but I want you to know I have been very much— I've made a good deal of a fool of myself over Mrs. Blake."

Still he obstinately would not say he had been in love. Anne, looking at him with the colour rising higher and higher, hardly seemed to understand. But suddenly she did.

"You don't mean—" she stammered. "Mr. Choate, she's married, you know, even if she and Jeff aren't together any more. Esther is married."

"I know it," said Alston drily. "I've wished they weren't married. I've wished I could ask her to marry me. But I don't any longer. You won't understand at all why I say it now. Sometime I'll tell you when you've noticed how I have to stand up against my cut and dried ways. Anne, I'm talking to you."

She had got on her feet and was fumbling with the upper button of her coat which had not been unloosed. But that she didn't remember now. She was in a mechanical haste of making ready to go. Alston rose, too, and was glad to find he was the taller. It gave him a mute advantage and he needed all he could get.

"I'm telling you something quite important," he said, in a tone that set her momentarily and fallaciously at ease. "It's going to be very important to both of us. Dear Anne! darling Anne!" He broke down and laughed, her eyes were so big with the surprise of it, almost, it might be, with fright. "That's because I'm in love with you," said Alston. "I've forgotten every other thing that ever happened to me, all except this miserable thing I've just told you. I had to tell you, so you'd know the worst of me. Darling Anne!" He liked the sound of it.

"I must go," said Anne.

"You'd better," said Alston. "It'll be much nicer to ask you the rest of it in a proper place. Anne, I've had so much to do with proper places I'm sick of 'em. That's why I've begun to say it here. Nothing could be more improper in all Addington. Think about it. Be ready to tell me when I come, though that won't be for a long time. I'm going to write you things, for fear, if I said them, you'd say no. And don't really think. Just remember you're darling Anne."

She gave him a grave look—Alston wondered afterward if it could possibly be a reproving one—and, with a fine dignity, walked to the door. Since he had begun to belie his nature, mischief possessed him. He wanted to go as far as he audaciously could and taste the sweet and bitter of her possible kindness, her almost certain blame.

"Good-bye," he said, "darling Anne."

This was as the handle of the door was in his grasp ready to be turned for her. Anne, still inexplicably grave, was looking at him.

"Good-bye," she said, "Mr. Choate."

He watched her to the head of the stairs, and then shut the door on her with a click. Alston was conscious of having, for the joy of the moment, really made a fool of himself. But he didn't let it depress him. He needed his present cleverness too much to spend a grain of it on self-reproach. He went to his safe and took out a paper that had been lying there ready to be used, slipped it into his pocket and went, before his spirit had time to cool, to see Madame Beattie.

Sophy admitted him and left him in the library, while she went to summon her. And Madame Beattie came, finding him at the window, his back turned on the warm breathing presences of Esther's home. If he had penetrated, for good cause, to Circe's bower, he didn't mean to drink in its subtle intimacies. At the sound of a step he turned, and Madame Beattie met him peaceably, with outstretched hand. Alston dropped the hand as soon as possible. Lydia might swear she was clean and that her peculiarily second-hand look was the effect of overworn black, but Alston she had always impressed as much-damaged goods that had lost every conceivable inviting freshness. She indicated a chair conveniently opposite her own and he sat down and at once began.

"Madame Beattie, I have come to talk over this unfortunate matter of the necklace."

"Oh," said Madame Beattie, with a perfect affability and no apparent emotion, "Anne French has been chattering to you."

"Naturally," said Choate. "I am their counsel, hers and her sister's."

"These aren't matters of law," said Madame Beattie. "They are very interesting personal questions, and I advise you to let them alone. You won't find any precedent for them in your books."

"I have been unpardonably slow in coming to you," said Alston. "And my coming now hasn't so very much to do with Lydia and Anne. I might have come just the same if you hadn't begun to annoy them."

"Well," said Madame Beattie impatiently. She wanted her nap, for she was due that evening at street corners in Mill End. "Get to the point, if you please."

"The point is," said Alston, "that some months ago when you began to make things unpleasant for a number of persons—"

"Nonsense!" said Madame Beattie briskly. "I haven't made things unpleasant. I've only waked this town out of its hundred years' sleep. You'd better be thankful to me, all of you. Trade is better, politics are most exciting, everything's different since I came."

"I sent at once to Paris," said Alston, with an impartial air of conveying information they were equally interested in, "for the history of the Beattie necklace. And I've got it. I've had it a week or more, waiting to be used." He looked her full in the face to see how she took it. He would have said she turned a shade more unhealthy, in a yellow way, but not a nerve in her seemed to blench.

"Well," said she, "have you come to tell me the history of the Beattie necklace?"

"Briefly," said Alston, "it was given the famous singer, as she states, by a certain Royal Personage. We are not concerned with his identity, his nationality even. But it was a historic necklace, and he'd no business to give it to her at all. There were some rather shady transactions before he could get his hands on it. And the Royal Family never ceased trying to get it back. The Royal Personage was a young man when he gave it to her, but by the time the family'd begun to exert pressure he wasn't so impetuous, and he, too, wanted it back. His marriage gave the right romantic reason, which he used. He actually asked the famous singer to return it to him, and at the same time she was approached by some sort of agent from the family who offered her a fat compensation."

"It was a matter of sentiment," said Madame Beattie loftily. "You've no right to say it was a question of money. It is extremely bad taste."

"She had ceased singing," said Alston. "Money meant more to her than the jewels it would have been inexpedient to display. For by that time, she didn't want to offend any royal families whatever. So she was bought off, and she gave up the necklace."

"It is not true," said she. "If it was money I wanted, I could have sold it."

"Oh, no, I beg your pardon. There would have been difficulties in the way of selling historic stones; besides there were so many royal personages concerned in keeping them intact. It might have been very different when the certain Royal Personage was young enough and impetuous enough to swear he stood behind you. He'd got to the point where he might even have sworn he never gave them to you."

She uttered a little hoarse exclamation, a curse, Alston could believe, in whatever tongue.

"Besides," he continued, "as I just said, Madame Beattie wasn't willing, on the whole, to offend her royal patrons, though she wasn't singing any longer. She had a good many favours to ask of the world, and she didn't want Europe made too hot to hold her."

He paused to rest a moment from his thankless task, and they looked at each other calmly, yet quite recognising they were at grips.

"You forget," said she, "that I have the necklace at this moment in my possession. You have seen it and handled it."

"No," said Alston, "I have never seen the necklace. Nobody has seen it on this side the water. When you came here years ago and got Jeff into difficulties you brought another necklace, a spurious one, paste, stage jewels, I daresay, and none of us were clever enough to know the difference. You said it was the Beattie necklace, and Esther was hypnotised and—"

"And stole it," Madame Beattie put in, with a real enjoyment now.

"And Jeff was paralysed by loving Esther so much that he didn't look into it. And as soon as he was out of prison you came here and hypnotised us all over again. But it's not the necklace."

Madame Beattie put back her head and burst into hoarse and perfectly spontaneous laughter.

"And it was for you to find it out," she said. "I didn't think you were so clever, Alston Choate. I didn't know you were clever at all. You refresh me. God bless us! to think not one of them had the sense, from first to last, to guess the thing was paste."

Alston enjoyed his brief triumph, a little surprised at it himself. He had no idea she would back down instantly, nor indeed, though it were hammered into her, that she would own the game was up. The same recoil struck her and she ludicrously cocked an eye.

"I shall give you a lot of trouble yet though. The necklace may be a dead issue, but I'm a living dog, Alston Choate. Don't they say a living dog is better than a dead lion? Well, I'm living and I'm here."

He saw her here indefinitely, rolling about in hacks, in phaetons, in victorias, in motors, perpetually stirring two houses at least to nervous misery. There would be no running away from her. They would have her absurdly tied about their necks forever.

"Madame Beattie!" said he. This was Alston's great day, he reflected, with a grimace all to himself. He had never put so much impetuosity, so much daring to the square inch, into any day before. He lounged back a little in his chair, put his hands in his pockets and tried to feel swaggering and at ease. Madame Beattie, he knew, wouldn't object to swagger. And if it would help him dramatically, so much the better. "Madame Beattie," he repeated, "I've a proposition to make to you. I thought of it within the last minute."

Her eyes gleamed out at him expectantly, avariciously, with some suspicion, too. She hoped it concerned money, but it seemed unlikely, so chill a habit of life had men of Addington.

"It is absolutely my own idea," said Alston. "Nobody has suggested it, nobody has anything whatever to do with it. If I give myself time to think it over I sha'n't make it at all. What would you take to leave Addington, lock, stock and barrel, cut stick to Europe and sign a paper never to come back?

There'd be other things in the paper. I should make it as tight as I knew how."

Madame Beattie set her lips and looked him over, from his well-bred face and his exceedingly correct clothes to his feet. She would never have suspected an Addington man of such impetus, no one except perhaps Jeff in the old days. What was the utmost an Addington man would do? She had been used to consider them a meagre set.

"Well?" said Alston.

Madame Beattie blinked a little, and her mind came back.

"Ten thousand," she tossed him at a venture, in a violence of haste.

Alston shook his head.

"Too much," said he.

Madame Beattie, who had not known a tear for twenty years at least, could have cried then, the money had seemed so unreasonably, so incredibly near.

"You've got oceans of money," said she, in a passion of eagerness, "all you Addington bigwigs. You put it away and let it keep ticking on while you eat noon dinners and walk down town. What is two thousand pounds to you? In another year you wouldn't know it."

"I sha'n't haggle," said Alston. "I'll tell you precisely what I'll put into your hand—with conditions—if you agree to make this your farewell appearance. I'll give you five thousand dollars. And as a thrifty Addingtonian—you know what we are—I advise you to take it. I might repent."

She leaned toward him and put a shaking hand on his knee.

"I'll take it," she said. "I'll sign whatever you say. Give me the money now. You wouldn't ask me to wait, Alston Choate. You wouldn't play a trick on me."

Alston drew himself up from his lounging ease, and as he lifted the trembling old hand from his knee, gave it a friendly pressure before he let it fall.

"I can't give it to you now," he said. "Not this minute. Would you mind coming to my office to-morrow, say at ten? We shall be less open to interruption."

"Of course I'll come," she said, almost passionately.

He had never seen her so shaken or indeed actually moved from her cynical calm. She was making her way out of the room without waiting for his good-bye. At the door she turned upon him, her blurred old face a sad sight below the disordered wig. Esther, coming downstairs, met her in the hall and stopped an instant to stare at her, she looked so terrible. Then Esther came on to Alston Choate.

"What is it?" she began.

"I was going to ask for you," said Alston. "I want to tell you what I have just been telling Madame Beattie. Then I must see Jeff and his sisters." This sounded like an afterthought and yet he was conscious that Anne was in his mind like a radiance, a glow, a warm sweet wind. "Everybody connected with Madame Beattie ought to understand clearly what she can do and what she can't. She seems to have such an extraordinary facility for getting people into mischief."

He placed a chair for her and when she sank into it, her eyes inquiringly on his face, he began, still standing, to tell her briefly the history of the necklace. Esther's face, as he went on, froze into dismay. He was telling her that the thing which alone had brought out passionate emotion in her had never existed at all. Not until then had he realised how she loved the necklace, the glitter of it, the reputed value, the extraordinary story connected with it. Esther's life had been built on it. And when Alston had finished and found she could not speak, he was sorry for her and told her so.

"I'm sorry," he said simply.

Esther looked at him a moment dumbly. Then her face convulsed. She was crying.

"Don't," said Choate helplessly. "Don't do that. The thing isn't worth it. It isn't worth anything to speak of. And it's made you a lot of trouble, all of you, and now she's going back to Europe and she'll take it with her."

"Going back?" Esther echoed, through her tears. "Who says she's going back?"

"She says so," Alston rejoined weakly. He thought his hush money might fairly be considered his own secret. It was like a candle burned in gratitude for having found out he had dared to say, "darling Anne".

"If she would go back!" said Esther. "But she won't. She'll stay here and talk to mill hands and drag dirty people up those stairs. And I shall live here forever with her and grandmother, and nobody will help me. Nobody will ever help me, Alston Choate. Do you realise that? Nobody."

Her melting eyes were on his and she herself was out of her chair and tremulously near. But Esther made no mistake of a too prodigal largess a man like Reardon was bewitched by, even if he ran from it. She stood there in sorrowful dignity and let her eyes plead for her. And Alston, though he had accomplished something for her as well as for Anne, felt only a sense of shame and the misery of falling short. He had thought he loved her (he had got so far now as to say to himself he thought so) and he loved her no more. He wished only to escape, and his wish took every shred of the hero out of him.

"We'll all help you," he said with the cheerfulness exasperatingly ready to be pumped up when things are bad and there is no adequate remedy. "I'd like to. And so will Jeff."

With that he put out his hand to her, and when she unseeingly accorded him hers gave it what he thought an awkward, cowardly pressure and left her. There are no graceful ways for leaving Circe's isle, Alston thought, as he hurried away, unless you have at least worn the hog's skin briefly and given her a showing of legitimate triumph. And that night, because he had a distaste for talking about it further, he wrote the story to Jeff, still omitting mention of his candle-burning honorarium. To Anne, he sent a little note, the first of a long series, wondering at himself as he wrote it, but sticking madly to his audacity, for that queerly seemed the way to win her.

> "Darling Anne," the note said. "It's all right. I'll tell you sometime. Meanwhile you're not to worry.

"Your lover,

XXXVIII

While the motor cars were whirling about Addington and observers were in an ecstasy over Madame Beattie's electioneering, Reardon was the more explicitly settling his affairs and changing his sailing from week to week as it intermittently seemed possible to stay. He was in an irritation of unrest when Esther did not summon him, and a panic of fear at the prospect of her doing it. He was beginning dimly to understand that Esther, even if the bills were to be paid, proposed to do nothing herself about getting decently free. Reardon thought he could interpret that, in a way that enhanced her divinity. She was too womanly, he determined. How could a creature like her give even the necessary evidence? If any one at that time believed sincerely in Esther's clarity of soul, it was Reardon who had not thought much about souls until he met her. Esther had been a wonderful influence in his life, transmuting everyday motives until he actually stopped now to think a little over the high emotions he was not by nature accustomed even to imagine. There was something pathetic in his desire to better himself even in spiritual ways. No man in Addington had attained a higher proficiency in the practical arts of correct and comfortable living, and it was owing to the power of Esther's fastidious reserves that he had begun to think all women were not alike, after all. There must be something in class, something real and uncomprehended, or such a creature as she could not be born with a difference. When she came nearer him, when she of her own act surrendered and he had drawn the exquisite sum of her into his arms, he still believed in her moral perfection to an extent that made her act most terribly moving to him. The act grew colossal, for it meant so matchless a creature must love him unquestioningly or she could not step outside her fine decorum. Every thought of her drew him toward her. Every manly and also every ambitious impulse of his entire life—the ambition that bade him tread as near as possible to Addington's upper class—forbade his seeking her until he had a right to. And if she would not free herself, the right would never be his.

One day, standing by his window at dusk moodily looking out while the invisible filaments that drew him to her tightened unbearably, he saw Jeff go past. At once Reardon knew Jeff was going to her, and he found it monstrous that the husband whose existence meant everything to him should be seeking her unhindered. He got his hat and coat and hurried out into the street in time to see Jeff turn in at her gate. He strode along that way, and then halted and walked back again. It seemed to him he must know at least when Jeff came out.

Jeff had been summoned, and Esther met him with no pretence at an artifice of coolness. She did not ask him to sit down. They stood there together in the library looking at each other like two people who have urgent things to say and limited time to say them in.

"Jeff," she began, "you're all I've got in the world. Aunt Patrica's going away."

Jeff clutched upon his reason and hoped it would serve him while something more merciful kept him kind.

"Good!" said he. "That's a relief for you."

"In a way," said Esther. "But it leaves me alone, with grandmother. It's like being with a dead woman. I'm afraid of her. Jeff, if you'd only thought of it yourself! but I have to say it. Won't you come here to live?"

"If he had only thought of it himself!" his heart ironically repeated. Had he not in the first years of absence from her dreamed what it would be to come back to a hearth she was keeping warm?

"Esther," he said, "only a little while ago you said you were afraid of me."

Esther had no answer to make. Yet she could take refuge in a perfect humility, and this she did.

"I ask you, Jeff," she said. "I ask you to come back."

The world itself seemed to close about him, straiter than the walls of the room. Had he, in taking vows on him when he truly loved her, built a prison he must dwell in to the end of his life or hers? Did moral law demand it of him? did the decencies of Addington?

"I ask you to forgive me," said Esther. "Are you going to punish me for what I did?"

"No," said Jeff, in a dull disclaimer. "I don't want to punish you."

But he did not want to come back. This her heart told her, while it cautioned her not to own she knew.

"I shouldn't be a burden on you," she said. "I should be of use, social use, Jeff. You need all the pull you can get, and I could help you there, tremendously."

The same bribe Madame Beattie had held out to him, he remembered, with a sorry smile. Esther, Madame Beattie had cheerfully determined, was to help him placate the little gods. Now Esther herself was offering her own abetment in almost the same terms. He saw no way even vaguely to resolve upon what he felt able to do, except by indirection. They must consider it together.

"Esther," he said, "sit down. Let me, too, so we can get hold of ourselves, find out what we really think."

They sat, and she clasped her hands in a way prayerfully suggestive and looked at him as if she hung on the known value of his words. Jeff groped about in his mind for their common language. What had it been?—laughter, kisses, the feverish commendation of the pageant of life. He sat there frowning, and when his brow cleared it was because he decided the only way possible was to open the door of his own mind and let her in. If she found herself lonesome, afraid even in its furnishings as they inevitably were now, that would tell them something. She need never come again.

"Esther," he said, "the only thing I've found out about myself is that I haven't found out anything. I don't know whether I'm a decent fellow, just because I want to be decent, or whether I'm stunted, calloused, all the things they say happen to criminals."

"Don't," said Esther sharply. "Don't talk of criminals."

"I've got to. You let me wander on a minute. Maybe it'll get us somewhere." He debated whether he should tell her he wanted to save Addington. No, she wouldn't understand. Could he tell her that at that minute he loved Addington better than anything but Lydia? and Lydia he must still keep hidden in the back of his mind under the green leaves of secrecy. "Esther," said he, "Esther, poor child, I don't want you to be a prisoner to me. And I don't want to be a prisoner to you. It would be a shocking wrong to you to be condemned to live with me all your life just because an old woman has scared you. What a penalty to pay for being afraid of Madame Beattie—to live with a husband you had stopped thinking about at all."

Esther gave a patient sigh.

"I don't understand," she said, "what you are talking about. And this isn't the way, dear, for us to understand each other. If we love each other, oughtn't we to forgive?"

"We do," said Jeff. "I haven't a hostile thought toward you. I should be mighty sorry if you had for me. But, Esther, whatever we feel for each other, will the thing stand the test of the plain truth? If it's going to have any working basis, it's got to. Now, do you love me? No, you don't. We both know we've changed beyond—" he paused for a merciful simile—"beyond recognition. Now because we promised to live together until death parted us, are we going to? Was that a righteous promise in view of what might happen? The thing, you see, has happened. If we had children it might be righteous to hang together, for their sakes. Is it righteous now? I don't believe it."

Esther lifted her clasped hands and struck them down upon her knee. The rose of her cheek had paled, and all expression save a protesting incredulity had frozen out of her face.

"I have never," she said, "been so insulted in my life."

"That's it," said Jeff. "I tried to tell the truth and you can't stand it. You tell it to me now, and I'll see if I can stand your side of it."

She was out of her chair and on her feet.

"You must go," she said. "You must go at once."

"I'm sorry," said Jeff. He was looking at her with what Miss Annabel called his beautiful smile. "You can't possibly believe I want things to be right for you. But it's true. I mean to make them righter than they are, too. But I don't believe we can shackle ourselves together. I don't believe that's right."

He went away, leaving her trembling. There was nothing for it but to go. On the sidewalk not far from her door he met Reardon with a casual nod, and Reardon blazed out at him, "Damn you!" At least that was what Jeff for the instant thought he said and turned to look at him. But Reardon was striding on and the back of his excellent great-coat looked so handsomely conventional that Jeff concluded he had been mistaken. He went on trying to sift his distastes and revulsions from what he wanted to do for Esther. Something must be done. Esther must no more be bound than he.

Reardon did not knock at her door. He opened it and went in and Esther even passionately received him. They greeted each other like acknowledged lovers, and he stood holding her to him while she sobbed bitterly against his arm.

"What business had he?" he kept repeating. "What business had he?"

"I can't talk about it," said Esther. "But I can never go through it again. You must take me away."

"I'm going myself," said Reardon. "I'm booked for Liverpool."

Esther was spent with the weariness of the years that had brought her no compensating joys for her meagre life with grandmother upstairs and her most uneasy one since Madame Beattie came. How could she, even if Reardon furnished money for it, be sure to free herself from Jeff in time to taste some of the pleasures she craved while she was at her prime of beauty? After all, there were other lands to wander in; it wasn't necessary to sit down here and do what Addingtonians had done since they settled the wretched place on the date they seemed to find so sacred. So she told him, in a poor sad little whisper:

"I shall die if you leave me."

"I won't go," said Reardon, at once. "I'll stand by."

"You will go," said Esther fiercely, half in anger because he had to be cajoled and prompted, "and take me with you."

Reardon, standing there feeling her beating heart against his hand, thought that was how he had known it would be. He had always had a fear, the three-o'clock-waking-in-the-morning fear, that sometime his conventions would fall from him like a garment he had forgotten, and he should do some act that showed him to Addington as he was born. He had too, sometimes, a nightmare, pitifully casual, yet causing him an anguish of shame: murdering his grammar or smoking an old black pipe such as his father smoked and being caught with it, going to the club in overalls. But now he realised what the malicious envy of fortune had in store for him. He was to run off with his neighbour's wife. For an instant he weakly meant to recall her to herself, to remind her that she didn't want to do it. But it seemed shockingly indecorous to assume a higher standard than her own, and all he could do was to assure her, as he had been assuring her while he was swept along that dark underground river of disconcerted thought: "I'll take care of you."

"What do you mean?" she returned, like a wild thing leaping at him. "Do you mean really take care of me? over there?"

"Yes," said Reardon, without a last clutch at his lost vision, "over there. We'll leave here Friday, for New York."

"I shall send my trunks in advance," said Esther. "By express. I shall say I am going for dressmaking and the theatre."

Reardon settled down to bare details. It would be unwise to be seen leaving on the same train, and he would precede her to New York. It would be better also to stay at different hotels. Once landed they would become—he said this in the threadbare pathetic old phrase—man and wife "in the sight of God". He was trying honestly to spare her exquisite sensibilities, and Esther understood that she was to be saved at all points while she reaped the full harvest of her desires. Reardon kissed her solemnly and went away, at the door meeting Madame Beattie, who gave him what he thought an alarming look, at the least a satirical one. Had she listened? had she seen their parting? But if she had, she made no comment. Madame Beattie had her own affairs to manage.

"I have told Sophy to do some pressing for me," she said to Esther. "After that, she will pack."

"Sophy isn't very fond of packing," said Esther weakly. She was quite sure Sophy would refuse and was immediately sorry she had given Madame Beattie even so slight a warning. What did Sophy's tempers matter now? She would be left behind with grandmother and Rhoda Knox. What difference would it make whether in the sulks or out of them?

"Oh, yes," said Madame Beattie quietly. "She'll do it."

Esther plucked up spirit. For weeks she had hardly addressed Madame Beattie at all. She dared not openly show scorn of her, but she could at least live apart from her. Yet it seemed to her now that she might, as a sort of deputy hostess under grandmother, be told whether Madame Beattie actually did mean to go away.

"Are you—" she hesitated.

"Yes," said Madame Beattie, "I am sailing. I leave for New York Friday morning."

Esther had a rudimentary sense of humour, and it did occur to her that it would be rather a dire joke if she and Madame Beattie, inexorably linked by destiny, were to go on the same boat. But Madame Beattie drily if innocently reassured her. And yet was it innocently? Esther could not be sure. She was sailing, she explained, for Naples. She should never think of venturing the northern crossing at this season.

And that afternoon while Madame Beattie took her drive, Esther had her own trunks brought to her room and she and Sophy packed. Sophy was enchanted. Mrs. Blake was going to New York, so Mrs. Blake told her, and as soon as she got settled Sophy would be sent for. She was not to say anything, however, for Mrs. Blake's going depended on its being carried out quietly, for fear Madame Beattie should object. Sophy understood. She had been quiet about many things connected with the tranquillity dependent on Madame Beattie, and she even undertook to have the express come at a certain hour and move the trunks down carefully. Sophy held many reins of influence.

When Madame Beattie came back from driving, Andrea was with her. She had called at the shop and taken him away from his fruity barricades, and they had jogged about the streets, Madame Beattie talking and Andrea listening with a profound concentration, his smile in abeyance, his black eyes fiery. When they stopped at the house Esther, watching from the window, contemptuously noted how familiar they were. Madame Beattie, she thought, was as intimate with a foreign fruit-seller as with one of her own class. Madame Beattie seemed impressing upon him some command or at least instructions. Andrea listened, obsequiously attentive, and when it was over he took his hat off, in a grand manner, and bending, kissed her hand. He ran up the steps and rang for her, and after she had gone in, Esther saw him, dramatic despondency in every drooping muscle, walk sorrowfully away.

Madame Beattie, as if she meant to accomplish all her farewells betimes, had the hardihood, this being the hour when Rhoda Knox took an airing, to walk upstairs to her step-sister's room and seat herself by the bedside before grandmother had time to turn to the wall. There she sat, pulling off her gloves and talking casually as if they had been in the habit of daily converse, while grandmother lay and pierced her with unyielding eyes. There was not emotion in the glance, no aversion or remonstrance. It was the glance she had for Esther, for Rhoda Knox. "Here I am," it said, "flat, but not at your mercy. You can't make me do anything I don't want to do. I am in the last citadel of apparent helplessness. You can't any of you drag me out of my bed. You can't even make me speak." And she would not speak. Esther, creeping out on the landing to listen, was confident grandmother never said a word. What spirit it was, what indomitable pluck, thought Esther, to lie there at the mercy of Madame Beattie, and deny herself even the satisfaction of a reply. All that Madame Beattie said Esther could not hear, but evidently she was assuring her sister that she was an arch fool to lie there and leave Esther in supreme possession of the house.

"Get up," Madame Beattie said, at one point. "There's nothing the matter with you. One day of liberty'd be better than lying here and dying by inches and having that Knox woman stare at you. With your constitution, Susan, you've got ten good years before you. Get up and rule your house. I shall be gone and you won't have me to worry you, and in a few days she'll be gone, too."

So she knew it, Esther realised, with a quickened heart. She slipped back into her room and stood there silent until Madame Beattie, calling Sophy to do some extra service for her, went away to her own room. And still grandmother did not speak.

XXXIX

On the morning Madame Beattie went, a strange intermittent procession trickled by the house, workmen, on their way to different activities, diverted from their usual road, and halting an instant to salute the windows with a mournful gaze. Some of them took their hats off, and the few who happened to catch a glimpse of Madame Beattie gave eager salutation. At one time a group of them had collected, and these Esther looked down on with a calm face but rage in her heart, wondering why she must be disgraced to the last. But when Madame Beattie really went there was no one in the street, and Esther, a cloak about her, stood by the carriage in a scrupulous courtesy, stamping a little, ostensibly to keep her feet warm but more than half because she was in a fever of impatience lest the unwelcome guest should be detained. Madame Beattie was irritatingly slow. She arranged herself in the hack as if for a drive long enough to demand every precaution. Esther knew perfectly well she was being exasperating to the last, and in that she was right. But she could hardly know Madame Beattie had not a malevolent impulse toward her: only a careless understanding of her, an amused acceptance. When she had tucked herself about with the robe, undoing Denny's kind offices and doing them over with a tedious moderation, she put out her arms to draw Esther into a belated embrace. But Esther could not bear everything. She dodged it, and Madame Beattie, not at all rebuffed, gave her hoarse little crow of laughter.

"Well," said she, "I leave you. But not for long, I daresay."

"You'll be coming back by spring," said Esther, willing to turn off the encounter neatly.

"I might," said Madame Beattie, "if Susan dies and leaves me everything. But I sha'n't depend on seeing you. We shall meet, of course, but it'll be over there." Again she laughed a little at a disconcerted stare from Esther. "Tell him to go along," she said. "You'd better make up your mind to Italy. Everything seems right, there, even to New Englanders—pretty nearly everything. *Au revoir.*"

She drove away chuckling to herself, and Esther stood a moment staring blankly. It had actually happened, the incredible of which she had dreamed. Madame Beattie was going, and now she herself was following too soon to get the benefit of it.

Lydia was out that morning and Denny, who saw her first, drew up of his own accord. It was not to be imagined by Denny that Madame Beattie and

Lydia should have spent long hours jogging together and not be grateful for a last word. Madame Beattie, deep in probing of her little hand-bag, looked up at the stopping of the hack, and smiled most cordially.

"Come along, imp," said she. "Get in here and go to the station with me."

Lydia stepped in at once, very glad indeed of a word with her unpopular friend.

"Are you truly going, Madame Beattie?" she asked, adding tumultuously, since there was so little time to be friendly, "I'm sorry. I like you, you know, Madame Beattie."

"Well, my dear," said Madame Beattie good-naturedly, "I fancy you're the only soul in town that does, except perhaps those nice workmen I've played the devil with. I only hope they'll succeed in playing the devil themselves a little, even if I'm not here to coach them. I've explained it all very carefully, just as I got the dirty little man to explain it to me, and I think they'll be able to manage. When it all comes out you can tell Jeff I did it. I began it when I thought it might be of some advantage to me, but I've told Andrea to go on with it. It'll be more amusing, on the whole."

"Go on with what?" inquired Lydia.

"Never mind. But you must write me and tell me how the election went. I won't bother you with my address, but Alston Choate'll give it to you. He intends to keep his eye on me, the stupid person. I wouldn't come over here again if I were paid for it."

At the station Lydia, a little sick and sorry, because she hated changes and also Madame Beattie kept some glamour for her, stepped out and gave her old friend a firm hand to help her and then an arm to lean on. Madame Beattie bade Denny a carelessly affectionate farewell and left him her staunch ally. She knew how to bind her humbler adherents to her, and indeed with honesty, because she usually liked them better than the people who criticised her and combated and admired her from her own plane. After the trunks were checked and she still had a margin of time, she walked up and down the platform leaning on Lydia's arm, and talked about the greyness of New England and the lovely immortalities of Italy. When they saw the smoke far down the track, she stopped, still leaning on Lydia.

"You've been a droll imp," she said. "If I had money I'd take you with me and amuse myself seeing you in Italy. Your imp's eyes would be rounder than they are now, and you'd fall in love with some handsome scamp and find him out and grow up and leave him and we'd take an apartment and sit there and laugh at everything. You can tell Jeff—" the train was really nearing now and she bent and spoke at Lydia's ear—"tell him he's going to be a free man, and if he doesn't make use of his freedom he's a fool. She's going to run away. With Reardon."

"Who's going to run away?" Lydia shrilled up into her face. "Not Esther?"

"Esther, to be sure. I gather they're off to-night. That's why I'm going this morning. I don't want to be concerned in the silly business, though when they're over there I shall make a point of looking them up. He'd pay me anything to get rid of me."

The train was in, and her foot was on the step. But Lydia was holding her back, her little face one sharp interrogation.

"Not to Europe?" she said. "You don't mean they're going to Europe?"

"Of course I do," said Madame Beattie, extricating herself. "Where else is there to go? No, I sha'n't say another word. I waited till you wouldn't have a chance to question me. Tell Jeff, but not till to-morrow morning. Then they'll be gone and it won't be his responsibility. Good-bye, imp."

She did not threaten Lydia with envelopment in her richness of velvet and fur. Instead, to Lydia's confusion and wonder, ever-growing when she thought about it afterward, she caught up her hand and gave it a light kiss. Then she stepped up into the car and was borne away.

"I don't believe it," said Lydia aloud, and she walked off, glancing down once at the hand that had been kissed and feeling gravely moved by what seemed to her an honour from one of Madame Beattie's standing. Lydia was never to forget that Madame Beattie had been a great lady, in a different sense from inherited power and place. She was of those who are endowed and to whom the world must give something because they have given it so much. Should she obey her, and tell Jeff after the danger of his stopping Esther was quite past? Lydia thought she would. And she owned to herself the full truth about it. She did not for an instant think she ought to keep her knowledge in obedience to Madame Beattie, but she meant at least to give Jeff his chance. And as she thought, she was walking home fast, and when she got there she hurried into the library without taking off her hat, and asked the colonel:

"Where's Jeff?"

The colonel was sitting by the fire, a book in his hand in the most correct position for reading. He had been deep in one of his friendly little naps and had picked the book up when he heard her step and held it with a convincing rigour.

"He's gone off for a tramp," said he, looking at her sleepily. "He'd been writing and didn't feel very fit. I advised him to go and make a day of it."

Anne came in then, and Lydia stared at her, wondering if Anne could help. And yet, whatever Anne said, she was determined not to tell Jeff until the morning. So she slowly took off her things and made brisk tasks to do about the house. Only when the two o'clock train was nearly due she seized her hat and pinned it on, slipped into her coat and walked breathlessly to the station. She was there just before the train came in and there also, a fine figure in his excellently fitting clothes, was Reardon. He was walking the platform, nervously Lydia thought, but he seemed not to be waiting for any one. Seeing her he looked, though she might have fancied it, momentarily disconcerted, but took off his hat to her and turned immediately to resume his march. Suppose Esther came, Lydia wondered. What should she do? Should she stop her, block her way, bid her remember Jeff? Or should she watch her to the last flutter of her hatefully pretty clothes as she entered the car with Reardon and, in the noise of the departing train, give one loud hurrah because Jeff was going to be free? But the train came, and Reardon, without a glance behind, though in a curious haste as if he wanted at least to escape Lydia's eyes, entered and was taken away.

Again Lydia went home, and now she sat by the fire and could not talk, her elbows on her knee, her chin supported in her hands.

"What is it?" Anne asked her. "You look mumpy."

Yes, Lydia, said, she was mumpy. She thought she had a cold. But though Anne wanted to minister to her she was not allowed, and Lydia sat there and watched the clock. At the early dark she grew restless.

"Farvie," said she, "shouldn't you think Jeff would come?"

"Why, no," said he, looking at her over his glasses, doing the benevolent act, Lydia called it. "There's a moon, and he'll probably get something to eat somewhere or even come back by train. It isn't his night at the school."

At six o'clock Lydia began to realise that if Esther were going that day she would take the next train. It would not be at all likely that she took the "midnight" and got into New York jaded in the early morning. She put on her hat and coat, and was going softly out when Anne called to her:

"Lyd, if you've got a cold you stay in the house."

Lydia shut the door behind her and sped down the path. She thought she should die—Lydia had frequent crises of dying when the consummations of life eluded her—if she did not know whether Esther was going. Yet she would not tell Jeff until it was too late, even if he were there on the spot and if he blamed her forever for not telling him. This time she stayed in a sheltering corner of the station, and not many minutes before the train a dark figure passed her, Esther, veiled, carrying her hand-bag, and walking fast. Lydia could have touched her arm, but Esther, in her desire of secrecy, was trying to see no one. She, too, stopped, in a deeper shadow at the end of the building. Either she had her ticket or she was depending on the last minute for getting it. Lydia, with a leap of conjecture concluded, and rightly, that she had sent Sophy for it in advance. The local train came in, bringing the workmen from the bridge, still being repaired up the track, and Lydia shrank back a little as they passed her. And among them, finishing a talk he had taken up on the train, was, incredibly, Jeff. Lydia did not parley with her dubieties. She slipped after them in the shadow, came up to him and touched him on the arm.

"Jeff!" she said.

He turned, dropped away from the men and stood there an instant looking at her. Lydia's heart was racing. She had never felt such excitement in her life. It seemed to her she should never get her breath again.

"What's the matter?" said Jeff. "Father all right?"

"She's going to run away with Reardon," said Lydia, her teeth clicking on the words and biting some of them in two. "He went this afternoon. They're going to meet."

"How do you know?"

Neither of them, in the course of their quick sentences, mentioned Esther's name.

"Madame Beattie told me. Look over by that truck. Don't let her see you."

Jeff turned slightly and saw the figure by the truck.

"She's going to take this train," said Lydia. "She's going to Reardon. O Jeff, it's wicked."

Lydia had never thought much about things that were wicked. Either they were brave things to do and you did them if you wanted to, or they were underhand, hideous things and then you didn't want to do them. But suddenly Esther seemed to her something floating, tossed and driven to be caught up and saved from being swamped by what seas she knew not. Jeff walked over to the dark figure by the truck. Whether he had expected it to be Esther he could not have said, but even as it shrank from him he knew.

"Come," said he. "Come home with me."

Esther stood perfectly silent like a shrinking wild thing endowed with a protective catalepsy.

"Esther," said he, "I know where you're going. You mustn't go. You sha'n't. Come home with me."

And as she did not move or answer he put his arm through hers and guided her away. Just beyond the corner of the station in a back eddy of solitude, she flung him off and darted three or four steps obliquely before he caught her up and held her. Lydia, standing in the shadow, her heart beating hard, heard his unmoved voice.

"Esther, you're not afraid of me? Come home with me. I won't touch you if you'll promise to come. I can't let you go. I can't. It would be the worst thing that ever happened to you."

"How do you know," she called, in a high hysterical voice, "where I'm going?"

"You were going with somebody you mustn't go with," said Jeff. "We won't talk about him. If he were here I shouldn't touch him. He's only a fool. And it's your fault if you're going. But you mustn't go."

"I am going," said Esther, "to New York, and I have a perfect right to. I shall spend a few days and get rested. Anybody that tells you anything else tells lies."

"The train is coming," said Jeff. "Stand here, if you won't walk away with me, and we'll let it go."

She tried again to wrench herself free, but she could not. Lydia, standing in the shadow, felt a passionate sympathy. He was kind, Lydia saw, he was compelling, but if he could have told the distracted creature he had something to offer her beyond the bare protection of an honourable intent, then she might have seen another gate open besides the one that led nowhere. Almost, at that moment, Lydia would have had him sorry enough to put his arms about her and offer the semblance of love that is divinest sympathy. The train stopped for its appointed minutes and went on.

"Come," said Jeff, "now we'll go home."

She turned and walked with him to the corner. There she swerved.

"No," said Jeff, "you're coming with me. That's the place for you. They'll be good to you, all of them. They're awfully decent. I'll be decent, too. You sha'n't feel you've been jailed. Only you can't walk off and be a prisoner to—him. Things sha'n't be hard for you. They shall be easier."

Lydia, behind, could believe he was going on in this broken flow of words to soothe her, reassure her. "Oh," Lydia wanted to call to him, "make love to her if you can. I don't care. Anything you want to do I'll stand by, if it kills me. Haven't I said I'd die for you?"

But at that moment of high excitement Lydia didn't believe anything would kill her, even seeing Jeff walk away from her with this little wisp of wrong desires to hold and cherish.

Jeff took Esther up the winding path, opened the door and led her into the library where his father sat yawning. Lydia slipped round the back way to the kitchen and took off her hat and coat.

"Cold!" she said to Mary Nellen, to explain her coming, and warmed her hands a moment before she went into the front hall and put her things away.

"Father," said Jeff, with a loud cheerfulness that sounded fatuous in his own ears, "here's Esther. She's come to stay."

The colonel got on his feet and advanced with his genial courtesy and outstretched hand. But Esther stood like a stone and did not touch the hand. Anne came in, at that moment, Lydia following. Anne had caught Jeff's introduction and looked frankly disconcerted. But Lydia marched straight up to Esther.

"I've always been hateful to you," she said, "whenever I've seen you. I'm not so hateful now. And Anne's a dear. Farvie's lovely. We'll all do everything we can to make it nice for you."

Jeff had been fumbling at the back of Esther's veil and Anne now, seeing some strange significance in the moment, put her quick fingers to work. The veil came off, and Esther stood there, white, stark, more tragic than she had ever looked in all the troubles of her life. The colonel gave a little exclamation of sorrow over her and drew up the best chair to the fire, and Anne pushed back the lamp on the table so that its light should not fall directly on her face. Then there were commonplace questions and answers. Where had Jeff been? How many miles did he think he had walked? And in the midst of the talk, while Lydia was upstairs patting pillows and lighting the fire in the spare-chamber, Esther suddenly began to cry in a low, dispirited way, no passion in it but only discouragement and physical overthrow. These were real enough tears and they hurt Jeff to the last point of nervous irritation.

"Don't," he said, and then stopped while Anne knelt beside her and, in a rhythmic way, began to rub one of her hands, and the colonel stared into the fire.

"Perhaps if you went upstairs!" Anne said to her gently. "I could really rub you if you were in bed and Lydia'll bring up something nice and hot."

"No, no," moaned Esther. "You're keeping me a prisoner. You must let me go." Then, as Jeff, walking back and forth, came within range of her glance, she flashed at him, "You've no right to keep me prisoner."

"No," said Jeff miserably, "maybe not. But I've got to make sure you're safe. Stay to-night, Esther, and to-morrow, when you're rested, we'll talk it over."

"To-morrow," she muttered, "it will be too late."

"That's it," said Jeff, understanding that it would be too late for her to meet Reardon. "That's what I mean it shall be."

Anne got on her feet and held out a hand to her.

"Come," she said. "Let's go upstairs."

Esther shrank all over her body and gave a glance at Jeff. It was a cruel glance, full of a definite repudiation.

"No, no," she said again, in a voice where fear was intentionally dominant.

It stung him to a miserable sorrow for her and a hurt pride of his own.

"For God's sake, no!" he said. "You're going to be by yourself, poor child! Run away with Anne."

So Esther rose unwillingly, and Anne took her up to the spacious chamber where firelight was dancing on the wall and Lydia had completed all sorts of hospitable offices. Lydia was there still, shrinking shyly into the background, as having no means of communication with an Esther to whom she had been hostile. But Esther turned them both out firmly, if with courtesy.

"Please go," she said to Anne. "Please let me be."

This seemed to Anne quite natural. She knew she herself, if she were troubled, could get over it best alone.

"Mayn't I come back?" she asked. "When you're in bed?"

"No," Esther said. "I am so tired I shall sleep. You're very kind. Good night."

She saw them to the door with determination even, and they went downstairs and sat in the dining-room in an excited silence, because it seemed to them Jeff might want to see his father and talk over things. But Jeff and his father were sitting on opposite sides of the table, the colonel pretending to read and Jeff with his elbows on the table, his head resting on his hands. How was he to finish what he had begun? For she hated him, he believed, with a childish hatred of the discomfort he had brought her. If there were some hot betrayal of the blood that had driven her to Reardon he almost thought, despite Addington and its honesties and honours, he would not lift his hand to keep her. Addington was very strong in him that night, the old decent loyalties to the edifice men and women have built up to protect themselves from the beast in them. Yet how would it have stood the assault of honest passion, sheer human longing knocking at its walls? If she could but love a man at last! but this was no more love than the puerile effort of a meagre discontent to make itself more safe, more closely cherished, more luxuriously served.

"Father," said he at last, breaking the silence where the clock ticked and the fire stirred.

"Yes," said the colonel. He did not put down his book or move his finger on it. He meant, to the last line of precaution, to invite Jeff's confidence.

"Whatever she does," said Jeff, "I'm to blame for it."

"Don't blame yourself any more," the colonel said. "We won't blame anybody."

He did not even venture to ask what Esther would be likely to do.

"I don't understand—" said Jeff, and then paused and the sentence was never finished. But what he did not understand was the old problem: how accountability could be exacted from the irresponsible, how an ascetic loyalty to law could be demanded of a woman who was nothing but a sweet bouquet of primitive impulses, flowered out of youth and natural appetites. He saw what she was giving up with Reardon: luxury, a kindly and absolutely honest devotion. If she went to him it would be to what she called happiness. If he kept her out of the radius of disapproval, she might never feel a shadow of regret. But Reardon would feel the shadow. Jeff knew him well enough to believe that. It would be the old question of revolt against the edifice men have built. You thought you could storm it, and it would capitulate; but when the winter rigours came, when passion died and self got shrunken to a meagre thing, you would seek the shelter of even that cold courtyard.

"Yes," he said aloud, "I've got to do it."

All that evening they sat silent, the four of them, as if waiting for an arrival, an event. At eleven Anne came in.

"I've been up and listened," she said. "She's perfectly quiet. She must be asleep."

Jeff rose.

"Come, father," he said. "You'll be drowsy as an owl to-morrow. We'd better get up early, all of us."

"Yes," said Anne. She knew what he meant. They had, somehow, a distasteful, puzzling piece of work cut out for them. They must be up to cope with this strange Esther.

Lydia fell asleep almost, as the cosy saying goes, as soon as her head touched the pillow. She was dead tired. But in what seemed to her the middle of the night, she heard a little noise, and flew out of bed, still dazed and blinking. She thought it was the click of a door. But Esther's door was shut, the front door, too, for she crept into the hall and peered over the railing. She went to the hall window and looked out on the dark shrubbery above the snow, and the night was still and the scene so kind it calmed her. But she could not see, beyond the shrubbery, the black figure running softly down the walk. Lydia went back to bed, and when the "midnight" hooted she drew the clothes closer about her ears and thought how glad she was to be so comfortable. It was not until the next morning that she knew the "midnight" had carried Esther with it.

XL

It was strangely neutral, the hue of the moment when they discovered she had gone. They had not called her in the morning, but Anne had listened many times at the door, and Lydia had prepared a choice tray for her, and Mary Nellen tried to keep the coals at the right ardour for toasting. Jeff had stayed in the house, walking uneasily about, and at a little after ten he came out of his chair as if he suddenly recognised the folly of staying in it so apathetically.

"Go up," he said to Lydia. "Knock. Then try the door."

Lydia got no answer to her knock, and the door yielded to her. There was the bed untouched, on the hearth the cold ashes of last night's fire. She stood stupidly looking until Jeff, listening at the foot of the stairs, called to her and then himself ran up. He read the chill order of the room and his eyes came back to Lydia's face.

"Oh," said Lydia, "will he be good to her?"

"Yes," said Jeff, "he'll be good enough. That isn't it. What a fool I am! I ought to have watched her. But Esther wasn't daring. She never did anything by herself. I couldn't get to New York now—" He paused to calculate.

He ran downstairs, and without speaking to his father, on an irrational impulse, over to Madam Bell's. There he came unprepared upon the strangest sight he had ever seen in Addington. Sophy, her cynical, pert face actually tied up into alarm, red, creased and angry, was standing in the library, and Madam Bell, in a wadded wrapper and her nightcap, was counting out money into her trembling hand. To Sophy, it was as terrifying as receiving money from the dead. She had always looked upon Madam Bell as virtually dead, and here she was ordering her to quit the house and giving her a month's wages, with all the practicality of a shrewd accountant. Madam Bell was an amazing person to look at in her wadded gown and felt slippers, with the light of life once more flickering over her parchment face.

"Rhoda Knox is gone," she announced to Jeff, the moment he walked in. "I sent her yesterday. This girl is going as soon as she can pack."

Jeff gave Sophy a directing nod and she slipped out of the room. She was as afraid of him as of the masterful dead woman in the quilted wrapper. Anything might happen since the resurrection of Madam Bell.

"Where is she?" asked Jeff, when he had closed the door.

"Esther?" said Madam Bell. "Gone. She's taken every stitch she had that was worth anything. Martha told me she was going for good."

"Who's Martha? Oh, yes, yes—Madame Beattie."

The light faded for an instant from the parchment face.

"Don't tell me," she sharply bade him, "Esther's coming back?"

"No," said Jeff. "If she does, she shall come to me."

He went away without another word, and Madam Bell called after him:

"Tell Amabel to look round and get me some help. I won't have one of these creatures that have been ruling here—except the cook. Tell Amabel to come and see me."

Jeff did remember to do that, but not until he had telephoned New York, and got his meagre fact. One of the boats sailing that morning had, among its passengers, J. L. Reardon and Mrs. Reardon. He did not inquire further. All that day he stayed at home, foolishly, he knew, lest some message come for him, not speaking of his anxiety even to Lydia, and very much let alone. That Lydia must have given his father some palliating explanation he guessed, for when Jeff said to him:

"Father, Esther's gone abroad," the colonel answered soothingly:

"Yes, my son, I know. It is in every way best."

The next week came the election, and Jeff had not got into the last grip of contest. He had meant to do some persuasive speaking for Alston. He thought he could rake in all Madame Beattie's contingent, now that she was away, still leaving them so friendly. But he was dull and absent-minded. Esther's going had been a defeat another braver, cleverer man, he believed, need not have suffered. At Lydia he had hardly looked since the day of Esther's going. To them all he was a closed book, tight-lipped, a mask of brooding care. Lydia thought she understood. He was raging over what he might have done. Nothing was going to make Lydia rage, she determined. She had settled down into the even swing of her one task: to help him out, to watch him, above all, whatever the emergency, to be ready.

Once, when Jeff was trying to drag his flagging energies into election work again, he met Andrea, and stopped to say he would be down at Mill End that night. But Andrea seemed, while keeping his old fealty, betokened by shining eyes and the most open smiles, to care very little about him in a political capacity. He even soothingly suggested that he should not come.

Better not, Andrea said. Too much work for nothing. They knew already what to do. They understood.

"Understand what?" Jeff asked him.

They had been told before the signora went, said Andrea. She had explained it all. They would vote, every man of them. They knew how.

"It's easy enough to learn how," said Jeff impatiently. "The thing is to vote for the right man. That's what I'm coming down for."

Andrea backed away, deferentially implying that Jeff would be most welcome always, but that it was a pity he should be put to so much pains. And he did go, and found only a few scattering listeners. The others, he learned afterward, were peaceably at a singing club of their own. They had not, Jeff thought, with mortification, considered him of enough importance to listen to.

Weedon Moore, in these last days, seemed to be scoring; at least circumstance gave him his own head and he was much in evidence. He spoke a great deal, flamboyantly, on the wrongs suffered by labour, and his own consecration to the holy joy of righting them. He spoke in English wholly, because Andrea, with picturesque misery, had regretted his own inability to interpret. Andrea's throat hurt him now, he said. He had been forbidden to interpret any more. Weedie mourned the defection of Andrea. It had, he felt, made a difference, not only in the size but the responsiveness of his audiences. Sometimes he even felt they came to be amused, or to lull his possible suspicion of having lost their old allegiance. But they came.

That year every man capable of moving on two legs or of being supported into a carriage, turned out to vote. Something had been done by infection. Jeff had done it through his fervour, and Madame Beattie a thousand times more by pure dramatic eccentricity. People were at least amusedly anxious to see how it was going, and old Addingtonians felt it a cheerful duty to stand by Alston Choate. The Mill Enders voted late, all of them, so late that Weedon Moore, who kept track of their activities, wondered if they meant to vote at all. But they did vote, they also to the last man, and a rumour crept about that some irregularity was connected with the ballot. But whatever they did, it was by concerted action, after a definite design. Weedon Moore, an agitated figure, meeting Jeff, was so worried and excited by it that he had to cackle his anxiety.

"What are they doing?" he said, stopping before Jeff on the pavement. "They've got up some damned thing or other. It's illegal, Blake. I give you my word it's illegal."

"What is it?" Jeff inquired, looking down on Weedie with something of the feeling once popularly supposed to be the desert of toads before that warty personality had been advertised as beneficent to gardens.

"I don't know what it is," said Moore, almost weeping. "But it's some damned trick, and I'll be even with them."

"If they elect you—" Jeff began coldly.

"They won't elect me," said Moore, from his general overthrow. "Six months ago every man Jack of 'em was promised to me. Somebody's tampered with 'em. I don't know whether it's you or Madame Beattie. She led me on, a couple of weeks ago, into telling her what I knew about trickery at the polls—"

"All you knew?" Jeff could not resist saying. "All you know about trickery, Weedie?"

"As a lawyer," said Weedie, "I told her about writing in names. I told her about stickers—"

"What did she want to know for?" Jeff asked. He, too, was roused to sudden startled interest.

"You know as much as I do. She was interested in my election, said she was speaking for me, wanted to know how we managed to crowd in an extra name not on the ballot. Had heard of that. It worried her, she said. Blake, that old woman is as clever as the devil."

Jeff made his way past the fuming candidate and walked on, speculating. Madame Beattie had assuredly done something. She had left the inheritance of her unleashed energy, in some form, behind her.

He did not go home that late afternoon and in the early evening strolled about the streets, once meeting Choate and passing on Weedie's agonised forecast. Alston was mildly interested. He thought she couldn't have done anything effective. Her line seemed to be the wildly dramatic. Stage tricks wouldn't tip the scales, when it came to balloting. Whatever she had done, Alston, in his heart, hoped it would defeat him, and leave him to the rich enjoyment of his play-day office and his books. His mother could realise then that he had done his best, and leave him to a serene progress toward middle age. But when he got as far as that he remembered that his defeat would magnify Weedon Moore and miserably concluded he ought rather to suffer the martyrdom of office. Would Anne like him if he were defeated? He, too, was wandering about the town, and the bravado of his suit to her came back to him. It was easy to seek her out, it seemed so natural to be with her, so strange to live without her. Laughing a little, though nervously, at himself, he walked up the winding pathway to her house and asked for her. No, he would not come in, if she would be so good as to come to him. Anne came, the warmth of the firelight on her cheeks and hands. She had been sitting by the hearth reading to the colonel. Alston took her hands and drew her out to him.

"It's not very cold," he said. "One minute, Anne. Won't you love me if I am not a mayor?"

Anne didn't answer. She stood there, her hands in his, and Alston thought she was the stillest thing he had ever seen.

"You might be a snow maiden," he said. "Or an ice maiden. Or marble. Anne, I've got to melt you if you're snow and ice. Are you?" Then all he could think of was the old foolishness, "Darling Anne."

When he kissed her, immediately upon this, it was in quite a commonplace way, as if they were parting for an hour or so and had the habit of easy kissing.

"Why don't you speak," said Alston, in a rage of delight in her, "you little dumb person, you?"

Anne did better. She got her hands out of his and lifted them to draw his face again to hers.

"How silly we are," said Anne. "And the door is swinging open, and it'll let all the cold in on Farvie's feet."

Alston said a few more things of his own, wild things he was surprised at and forgot immediately and that she was always to remember, and they really parted now with the ceremonial of easy kissing. But both of them had forgotten about mayors.

Jeff, with the returns to take her, that night before going home ran in to Amabel. He believed he ought to be the first to tell her. She would be disappointed, for after all Weedon Moore was her candidate. As he got to the top of the steps Moore came scuttling out at the front door and Jeff stood aside to let him pass. He walked in, calling to her as he went. She did not answer, but he found her in the library, standing, a figure of quivering dignity, of majesty hurt and humbled. When she saw him Amabel's composure broke, and she gave a sob or two, and then twice said his name.

"What is it?" said Jeff.

He went to her and she faced him, the colour running over her face.

"That man—" she said, and stopped.

"Moore?"

"Yes. He has insulted me."

"Moore?" he repeated.

"He has asked me—Jeff, I am a woman of sixty and over—he has asked me to marry him."

"Wait a minute," said Jeff. "I've forgotten something."

He wheeled away from her and ran out and down the path after Weedie Moore. Weedie's legs, being short, had not covered ground very fast. Jeff had no trouble in overtaking him.

In less than ten minutes, he walked into Miss Amabel's library again, a little breathless, with eyes shining somewhat and his nostrils big, it might be thought, from haste. She had composed herself, and he knew her confidence was neither to be repeated nor enlarged upon. There she sat awaiting him, dignity embodied, a little more tense than usual and her head held high. All her ancestors might have been assembled about her, invisible but exacting, and she accounting to them for the indignity that had befallen her, and assuring them it was to her, as it would have been to them, incredible. She was even a little stiff with Jeff at first, because she had told him what she would naturally have hidden, like a disgraceful secret. Jeff understood her perfectly. She had met Weedon Moore on philanthropic grounds, an equal so long as they were both avowed philanthropists. But when the little man aspired unduly and ventured to pull at the hem of her maiden gown, Christian tolerance went by the board and she was Addington and he was Weedon Moore. She would never be able to summon Christian virtues to the point of a community of interests with him again. Jeff understood Moore, too, Moore who was probably on his way home at the moment getting himself together after a disconcerting bodily shock such as he had not encountered since their old school days when he had done "everything—and told of it ". He had counted on her sympathy over his defeat, and chosen that moment to make his incredible plea.

"Did you do what you had forgotten?" Amabel asked.

"Yes," said Jeff glibly. "I did it quite easily. I've come to tell you the news. Perhaps you know it already. Alston Choate's elected."

"Yes," said Miss Amabel, in a stately manner. "I had just heard it."

"I'm going round there," said Jeff, "to congratulate his mother. It's her campaign, you know. He never'd have run if it hadn't been for her."

"I didn't know Mrs. Choate had any such interest in local affairs," said Amabel.

She was aware Jeff was smoothing her down, ruffled feather after feather, and she was pathetically grateful. If she hadn't kept a strong grip on herself, her lip would have been quivering still.

"In a way she's not. She doesn't care about Addington as we do, but she hates to see old traditions go to the dogs. I've an idea she'll stand behind Alston and really run the show. Put on your bonnet and come with me. It's a shame to stay in the house a night like this."

She still knew his purpose and acquiesced in it. He hated to leave her to solitary thoughts of the indignity Moore had offered her, and also she hated to be left. She put on her thick cloak and her bonnet—there were no assumptions with Miss Amabel that she wasn't over sixty—and they went forth. But Mrs. Choate was not at home, nor was Mary. The maid thought they had gone down town for the return. Jeff told her Mr. Choate was to be mayor—no one in Addington seemed to pay much attention to the rest of the ticket that year—and she returned quite prosaically, "God save us!"

"Save us from Alston?" asked Jeff, as they went away, and Miss Amabel forgot Moore and laughed.

They went on down town with the purpose of seeing life, as Jeff said, and got into a surge of shiny-eyed Mill Enders who looked to Jeff as if they were commiserating him although it was his candidate that won. Andrea, indeed, in the moment of their meeting and parting almost wept over him. And face to face they met Lydia.

"I've lost Farvie," she said, "and Anne. Can't I come with you?"

So they went on together, Lydia much excited and Miss Amabel puzzled, in her wistful way, at finding social Addington and working Addington shoulder to shoulder in their extraordinary interest in the election though never in the common roads of life.

"But why the deuce," said Jeff, "Andrea and his gang look so mournful I can't see."

"Why," said Lydia, "don't you know? They voted for you, and their votes were thrown out."

"For me?"

"Yes, Madame Beattie told them to. She'd planned it before she went away, but somehow it fell through. They were to put stickers on the ballot, but at the last the stickers scared them, and they just wrote in your name."

"Lydia," said Jeff, "you're making this up."

"Oh, no, I'm not," said Lydia. "Mr. Choate told me. I knew it was going to happen, but he's just told me how it was. They wrote 'Prisoner Blake' in all kinds of scrawls and skriggles. They didn't know they'd got to write your real name. I call it a joke on Madame Beattie."

To Lydia it looked like a joke on herself also, though a sorry one. She thought it very benevolent of Madame Beattie to have prepared such a dramatic surprise, and that it was definite ill-fortune for Jeff to have missed the full effect of it. But the earth to Lydia was a flare of dazzling roads all leading from Jeff; he might take any one of them.

To Amabel the confusion of voting was a matter of no interest, and Jeff said nothing. Lydia was not sure whether he had even really heard. Then Amabel said if there were going to be speeches she hardly thought she cared for them, and they walked home with her and left her at the door, though not before she had put a kind hand on Jeff's shoulder and told him in that way how grateful she was to him. After she had gone in Jeff, so curious he had to say it before they started to walk away, turned upon Lydia.

"How do you know so much about her?" he began.

"Madame Beattie? We used to talk together," said Lydia demurely.

"You knew her confounded plans?"

"Some of them."

"And never told?"

"They were secrets," said Lydia. "Come, let's walk along."

"No, no. I want you where I can look at you, so you won't do any romancing about that old enchantress. If you know so much, tell me one thing more. She's gone. She can't hurt you."

"What is it?" asked Lydia.

"What did she tell those fellows about me?"

"Andrea?"

"Andrea and his gang. To make them treat me like a Hindoo god. No, I'll tell you how they treated me. As savages treat the first white man they've ever seen till they find he's a rotten trader."

"Oh," said Lydia, "it can't do any harm to tell you that."

"Any harm? I ought to have known it from the first. Out with it."

"Well, she told them you had been in prison, and you were sent there by Weedon Moore and his party—"

"His party? What was that?"

"Oh, I don't know. Anybody can have a party. Something like Tammany, maybe. You'd been sent to prison because it was you that had got them their decent wages, and had the nice little houses built down at Mill End. And there was a conspiracy against you, and she heard of it and came over to tell them how it was. But you were in prison because you stood up for labour."

"My word!" said Jeff. "And they believed her."

"Anybody'd believe anything from Madame Beattie," Lydia said positively. "She told them lots of stories about you, lovely stories. Sometimes she'd tell them to me afterward. She made you into a hero."

"Moses," said Jeff, "leading them out of bondage."

"Yes. Come, we can't stand here. If Miss Amabel sees us she'll think we're crazy."

They walked down the path and out between the stone pillars where he had met Esther. Jeff remembered it, and out of his wish to let Lydia into his mind said, as they passed into the street:

"I have heard from her."

Lydia's sudden happiness in the night and in his company—in knowing, too, she was well aware, that there was no Esther near—saw the cup dashed from her lips. Jeff didn't wait for her to answer.

"From the boat," he said. "It was very short. She was with him. We weren't to send her any more money. She said she had taken his name."

"How can she?" said Lydia stupidly. "She couldn't marry him."

"Maybe she thinks she can," said Jeff. He was willing to keep alive her unthinking innocence. It was not the outcome of ignorance that cramps and stultifies. He meant Lydia should be a child for a long time. "Now, see. Her going makes it possible for me to be free—legally, I mean. When I can marry, Lydia—" He stopped there. They were walking on the narrow pavement, but not even their hands touched. "Do you love me," Jeff asked, "as much as you thought? That way, I mean?"

"Yes," said Lydia. "But I know what you'd like. Not to talk about it, not to think about it much, but take care of Farvie—and you write—and both of us work on plays—and sometime—"

"Yes," said Jeff, "sometime—"

One tremendous desire, of all the desires tumultuous in him, was strongest. If Lydia was to be his—though already she seemed supremely his in all the shy fealties of the moment—not a petal of the flower of love should be lost to her. She should find them all dewy and unwithered in her bridal crown. There should not be a kiss, a hot protestation, the tawdry path of love half tasted yet long deferred. Lydia should, for the present, stay a child. His one dear thought, the thought that made him feel unimaginably free, came winging to him like a bird with messages.

"We aren't," he said, "going to be prisoners, either of us."

"No," said Lydia soberly. She knew by her talk with him and reading what he had imperfectly written, that he meant to be eternally free through fulfilling the incomprehensible paradox of binding himself to the law.

"We aren't going to be downed by loving each other so we can't stand up to it and say we'll wait."

"I can stand up to it," said Lydia. "I can stand up to anything—for you."

"I don't know," he said, "just how we're coming out. I mean, I don't know whether I'm coming out something you'll like or not like. How can a man be sure what's in him? Shall I wake up some time and know, because I've been a thief, I ought never to think of anything now but money—paying back, cent for cent, or cents for dollars, what I lost? I don't know. Or shall I think I'm right in not doing anything spectacular and plodding along here and working for the town? I don't know that. One thing I know—you. If I said I loved you it wouldn't be a millionth part of what I do. I'm founded on you. I'm rooted in you. There! that's enough. Stop me. That's the thing I wasn't going to do."

They were at their own gate. They halted there.

"You'd better go down and find Anne and Farvie," said Lydia.

She stood in the light from the lamp and he looked full at her. This was a Lydia he meant never to call out from her maiden veiling after to-night until the day when he could summon her for open vows and unstinted cherishing. He wanted to learn her face by heart. How was her brave soul answering him? The child face, sweet in every tint and line of it, turned to him in an unhesitating response. It was the garden of love, and, too, a pure unhindered happiness.

"I'm going in," said Lydia, "to get something ready for them to eat—Farvie and Anne. For us, too."

She took a little run away from him, and he watched her light figure until the shrubbery hid her. At the door, it must have been, she gave a clear call. Jeff answered the call, and then went on to find his father and Anne. He knew he should not see just the Lydia that had run away from him until the day she came back again, into his arms.

THE END

Milton Keynes UK
Ingram Content Group UK Ltd.
UKHW030622061024
449204UK00004B/409